MITHDRAWN

Nixon in the World

Nixon in the World

American Foreign Relations, 1969–1977

Edited by Fredrik Logevall and Andrew Preston

OXFORD
UNIVERSITY PRESS
2008

OXFORD
UNIVERSITY PRESS

Oxford University Press, Inc., publishes works that further
Oxford University's objective of excellence
in research, scholarship, and education.

Oxford New York
Auckland   Cape Town   Dar es Salaam   Hong Kong   Karachi
Kuala Lumpur   Madrid   Melbourne   Mexico City   Nairobi
New Delhi   Shanghai   Taipei   Toronto

With offices in
Argentina   Austria   Brazil   Chile   Czech Republic   France   Greece
Guatemala   Hungary   Italy   Japan   Poland   Portugal   Singapore
South Korea   Switzerland   Thailand   Turkey   Ukraine   Vietnam

Copyright © 2008 by Oxford University Press, Inc.

Published by Oxford University Press, Inc.
198 Madison Avenue, New York, New York 10016

www.oup.com

Oxford is a registered trademark of Oxford University Press

Library of Congress Cataloging-in-Publication Data
Nixon in the world: American foreign relations, 1969–1977 / edited by
Fredrik Logevall and Andrew Preston.
p.   cm.
Includes bibliographical references and index.
ISBN 978-0-19-531535-6; 978-0-19-531536-3 (pbk.) 1. United States—
Foreign relations—1969–1974. 2. United States—Foreign relations—
1974–1977. 3. Nixon, Richard M. (Richard Milhous), 1913–1994—
Political and social views. 4. Kissinger, Henry, 1923– Political and social
views. 5. Ford, Gerald R., 1913–2006—Political and social views.
I. Logevall, Fredrik, 1963– II. Preston, Andrew 1973–
E855.N46 2008
973.924—dc22   2007048019

9 8 7 6 5 4 3 2 1
Printed in the United States of America
on acid-free paper

Acknowledgments

Inverting the traditional progression of most edited volumes, *Nixon in the World* began life as a book long before it was the subject of a conference. But against all expectations, we were able to hold a conference around the book's chapters. It would be terribly remiss of us, then, not to thank Bob McMahon, the generous inspiration—not to mention the source of planning and funding—behind the conference. We will never forget Bob's offer, which came totally out of the blue, to host a workshop on the chapters of this book at his home institution, Ohio State University. In December 2006, in a seminar room at Ohio State's Mershon Center for International Security Studies, each of our contributors presented a draft of their chapter; each chapter was then commented upon by an outside participant, usually from Ohio State but in some cases from farther away. Richard Herrmann, the Director of the Mershon Center, not only graciously provided space and amenities, but was also an enthusiastic participant. Ann Powers organized everything—from travel and hotel arrangements to a steady supply of coffee—with such efficiency that the workshop participants were free to focus on the task at hand. We were exceptionally fortunate to have an all-star roster of commentators and are grateful for their valuable and stimulating participation. In every case, they have enabled us to write better chapters and thus to put together a much better book. And so, for participating as commentators, we would like to thank the following: from Ohio State, Carole Fink, Peter Hahn, Ted Hopf, John Mueller, Jason Parker (now at Texas A&M), Randall Schweller, and Alexander Wendt; from Ohio University, Alonzo Hamby and Chester Pach; from Bowling Green, Gary Hess; from Miami University, Jeffrey Kimball; and from the University of Akron, Walter Hixson. We are also grateful to many others from Ohio State, and beyond, for participating in the workshop on a more informal basis by attending the sessions and providing excellent commentary during the discussions. Our deepest thanks again to Bob and everyone at Ohio State for putting on such a memorable and valuable event.

We are also, of course, indebted to the excellent staff at Oxford University Press. Mary Kelly did an outstanding job to streamline the text of several chapters on disparate subjects written by a wide range of people. Most of all, we're grateful to our editor, the talented and indefatigable Susan Ferber, who had the faith in us to embrace our project and the expertise to improve it in innumerable ways.

Abbreviations in the Notes

DNSA   Digital National Security Archive

FRUS   *Foreign Relations of the United States* (Washington: Government Printing Office)

GRFL   Gerald R. Ford Library, Ann Arbor, Michigan

NARA   National Archives II, College Park, Maryland

NPMP   Nixon Presidential Materials Project, National Archives II, College Park, Maryland

NSA   National Security Archive, George Washington University, Washington, D.C.

PPP   *Public Papers of the Presidents of the United States: Richard Nixon* (Washington: Government Printing Office)

Contents

Contributors

ROBERT BOTHWELL is professor of history and director of the International Relations Program at the University of Toronto, where he has worked since 1970. From 1972 to 1980, he was coeditor of the *Canadian Historical Review*. He is the author of numerous books, including *Canada and the United States* (1992), *The Big Chill: Canada and the Cold War* (1998), *The Penguin History of Canada* (2006), and, most recently, *Alliance and Illusion: Canadian Foreign Relations, 1945–1984* (2007). He also coauthored *C. D. Howe* (1979), *Canada Since 1945* (two editions, 1982 and 1989), *Canada, 1900–1945* (1987), and *Pirouette: Pierre Trudeau and Canadian Foreign Policy* (1990).

FRANCIS J. GAVIN is the Tom Slick professor of international affairs at the LBJ School of Public Affairs, and the founding director of studies for the Robert S. Strauss Center for International Security and Law, at the University of Texas at Austin. He also directs "The Next Generation Project—U.S. Global Policy and the Future of International Institutions," a multiyear national initiative sponsored by The American Assembly at Columbia University. He previously was an Olin National Security fellow at Harvard University and a research fellow at the University of Virginia. His book, *Gold, Dollars, and Power: The Politics of International Monetary Relations, 1958–1971*, was published in 2004. He is also a member of the Council on Foreign Relations.

DAVID GREENBERG is assistant professor of history and of journalism & media studies at Rutgers University, specializing in American political and cultural history. His first book, *Nixon's Shadow: The History of an Image* (2004) won the Washington Monthly Political Book Award, the American Journalism

History Book Award, and Columbia University's Bancroft Dissertation Award. In 2006, he published *Calvin Coolidge* for the American Presidents Series and *Presidential Doodles*. A columnist for *Slate* and a contributing editor at *The New Republic*, Greenberg has also written for the *New York Times*, *The New Yorker*, *The Atlantic Monthly*, *Foreign Affairs*, the *Journal of American History*, and numerous other scholarly and popular publications.

JUSSI M. HANHIMÄKI is professor of international history and politics at the Graduate Institute of International Studies (Institut universitaire de hautes études internationales) in Geneva, Switzerland. His most recent publications include *The Flawed Architect: Henry Kissinger and American Foreign Policy* (2004) and, with Odd Arne Westad, *The Cold War: A History in Documents and Eyewitness Accounts* (2003). A recipient of the Bernath Prize from the Society for Historians of American Foreign Relations, he is also one of the founding editors of the journal *Cold War History* and a member of the editorial board of *Diplomatic History*. Currently at work on refugees and the Cold War, his next book will be *United Nations: A Very Short Introduction*.

MARK ATWOOD LAWRENCE is associate professor of history at the University of Texas at Austin. He is the author of *Assuming the Burden: Europe and the American Commitment to War in Vietnam* (2005) and *The Vietnam War: A Concise International History* (2008). He has also published several chapters and articles on U.S. foreign relations and coedited (with Fredrik Logevall) *The First Vietnam War: Colonial Conflict and Cold War Crisis* (2007).

FREDRIK LOGEVALL is professor of history at Cornell University. He has published numerous books and articles on U.S. foreign policy in the Cold War era, and is currently at work on a study of the French Indochina War of 1945–1954 and its aftermath, as well as (with Campbell Craig) an interpretive history of America's Cold War. He is also coauthor of *A People and A Nation: A History of the United States* (2008).

MARGARET MacMILLAN is the warden of St. Antony's College and a professor of international history at Oxford University; she is also a professor of history at the University of Toronto. She was editor of the *International Journal* from 1995 to 2003. Her publications include *Women of the Raj* (1988) and *Peacemakers: The Paris Conference of 1919 and Its Attempt to Make Peace* (2001), which was published in North America as *Paris 1919: Six Months* *that Changed the World* (2002). Her most recent book is *Nixon and Mao: The Week that Changed the World* (2006).

ROBERT J. McMAHON is the Ralph D. Mershon professor of history at Ohio State University. He previously taught at the University of Florida and has held visiting appointments at University College Dublin and the University of the Virginia. He is the author, among other works, of *Colonialism and Cold War: The United States and the Struggle for Indonesian Independence, 1945–49* (1981); *Cold War on the Periphery: The United States, India, and Pakistan* (1994); and *Limits of Empire: The United States and Southeast Asia since World War II* (1999). His latest book, *Dean Acheson: Romantic Realist*, is due to be published in 2008. McMahon also served as president of the Society for Historians of American Foreign Relations in 2001.

MICHAEL COTEY MORGAN is completing his Ph.D. in international history at Yale University, where he is writing a dissertation on the international origins of the Helsinki Final Act. He received his B.A. from the University of Toronto and his M.Phil. from the University of Cambridge. He is currently book review editor of the *International Journal* and a doctoral fellow at the Miller Center of Public Affairs at the University of Virginia. His work has appeared in the *Wall Street Journal* and the *Globe and Mail*, among other publications.

LIEN-HANG T. NGUYEN is assistant professor of history at the University of Kentucky. She is currently writing a book, entitled "Between the Storms: An International History of the Vietnam War, 1954–1973," which uses materials from Vietnamese, American, and European archives. She has published articles in the *Journal of Vietnamese Studies* and *Orbis* and has contributed essays in *The Third Indochina War* (2006), *The First Vietnam War* (2007), and *Making Sense of the Vietnam Wars* (2008). She has been a fellow in the Social Sciences at the Center for International Security and Cooperation (CISAC) at Stanford University and at the John M. Olin Institute for National Security at Harvard University.

ANDREW PRESTON is university lecturer in history and a fellow of Clare College at the University of Cambridge. He is also a fellow at the Cold War Studies Centre at the London School of Economics and features editor at the *International Journal*. He is the author of *The War Council: McGeorge Bundy, the NSC, and Vietnam* (2006).

DOMINIC SANDBROOK is a member of the history faculty at the University of Oxford and a weekly columnist for the London *Evening Standard*. He is the author of *Eugene McCarthy and The Rise and Fall of Postwar American Liberalism* (2004), and his recent publications *Never Had It So Good: A History of Britain from Suez to the Beatles* (2005) and *White Heat: A History of Britain in the Swinging Sixties* (2006) were both named as books of the year in major British newspapers. A former Senior Fellow at the Rothermere American Institute, Oxford, he writes regularly for the London newspapers *The Observer*, *The Sunday Times*, and *The Daily Telegraph*. He is currently working on *Spirit of '76*, a history of American politics and society in the 1970s.

MARY ELISE SAROTTE is a tenured associate professor at the University of Southern California, where she teaches international relations in both historical and contemporary perspectives. She has held fellowships from the Alexander von Humboldt Foundation in Bonn, the Kennedy School of Government at Harvard, the International Institute for Strategic Studies (IISS) in London, and the Institute for Advanced Study in Princeton. Her publications include *Dealing with the Devil: East Germany, Détente, and Ostpolitik, 1969–1973* (2001) and *German Military Reform and European Security* (2001). She is also a book reviewer for *The Economist* and has appeared as a commentator on the BBC, CNN, and Sky News.

ROBERT D. SCHULZINGER is College Professor of Distinction of history and international affairs at the University of Colorado, Boulder, where he has taught since 1977. He is the author or coauthor of twelve books on the history of U.S. foreign relations and recent U.S. history. Among them are: *Henry Kissinger: Doctor of Diplomacy* (1989); *A Time for War: The United States and Vietnam, 1941–1976* (1997); *A Time for Peace: The Legacy of the Vietnam War* (2006); *U.S. Diplomacy Since 1900*, sixth edition (2008); and, as coauthor with Michael Schaller and Karen Anderson, *Present Tense: The United States Since 1945* (2004). He is also the editor-in-chief of *Diplomatic History: The Journal of the Society for Historians of American Foreign Relations*.

JEREMI SURI is professor of history at the University of Wisconsin-Madison. He is the author of three books: *Henry Kissinger and the American Century* (2007); *The Global Revolutions of 1968* (2007); and *Power and Protest: Global Revolution and the Rise of Detente* (2003). He has also published widely in scholarly journals, newspapers, and magazines. Suri has been recognized by the Smithsonian Institution as one of America's "Top Young Innovators."

SALIM YAQUB is associate professor of history at the University of California, Santa Barbara, where he specializes in the history of U.S. foreign relations, with a particular focus on U.S. involvement in the Middle East since 1945. He is the author of *Containing Arab Nationalism: The Eisenhower Doctrine and the Middle East* (2004). He is currently writing a book on U.S.-Arab relations in the 1970s.

THOMAS W. ZEILER is professor of history, and former department chair, at the University of Colorado, Boulder. He serves as the executive editor of *Diplomatic History* and as the editor-in-chief of *American Foreign Relations Since 1600: A Guide to the Literature*. A member of the State Department's Historical Advisory Committee, he also directs a program to bring the secretaries of defense to Boulder for teaching, lectures, and oral histories. He gave the Bernath Lecture in 2001 and has lived in Buenos Aires and Tokyo as a Senior Fulbright Scholar. The most recent of his six books is *Ambassadors in Pinstripes: The Spalding World Baseball Tour and the Birth of the American Empire* (2006).

Nixon in the World

Introduction

The Adventurous Journey of Nixon in the World

Fredrik Logevall and Andrew Preston

In the grand trajectory of "the American Century," the 1970s stand out as a curious anomaly. For most of this era, especially the periods following World War II and the end of the Cold War, the United States was far more powerful than any other country—more powerful, even, than its only superpower rival, the Soviet Union. The strength and endurance of American power lay not only in its military might, important though it was; in addition to arms, America had few real challengers in terms of economic, political, diplomatic, and cultural power. But in the late 1960s, and for a variety of reasons that all peaked around the same time, America's dominance began to wane.

How American foreign policy fared under such pressures is the principal concern of this book, which focuses on the period from the start of Richard Nixon's administration in 1969 to the end of Gerald Ford's brief term in January 1977. It was, it could be said, the Kissinger Era. Among senior officials, only Henry Kissinger served the entire eight years. Moreover, at all times he was at the very center of decision making, first as national security adviser and then as secretary of state (indeed, for more than two years he held both jobs, a feat unprecedented at the time and unmatched since). With his conspicuous brilliance, penchant for drama, glamorous girlfriends, and diplomatic achievements, Kissinger's profile often eclipsed those of the presidents he served. "Super K," as the media nicknamed him, became a national celebrity and an international icon. Thus the delicate, unwanted chore of coping with the nation's decline fell largely to Kissinger.

It is something of a paradox that Kissinger, whose hard-headed worldview is based on strength, built and enhanced his reputation in a time of American weakness and declining power on the world stage. This is but one facet to his complex personality. But Kissinger's innate, enigmatic contradictions pale next to those that characterized the worldview of his boss, President Richard Nixon. Shy and awkward in person but deftly sure-footed on the world stage, Nixon was a hawkish, staunchly anti-communist politician whose signature achievement was the frequency with which he negotiated with communists.

While Kissinger acted as Nixon's chief diplomatic architect and Gerald Ford inherited Nixon's international problems and solutions, it was still very much the Age of Nixon, in which his willingness to navigate flexibly within the new contours of world politics and his use of the diplomatic "big play" dominated the scene and largely regained the international initiative for America. And of course any national security adviser or secretary of state, no matter how powerful or renowned, conducts foreign policy at the president's pleasure. Ultimately, the president is the responsible party. Metaphorically speaking, then, the reshaping of U.S. foreign policy, from its traditional poles of liberal interventionism and conservative isolationism into a policy of active but conservative engagement, was very much a journey of "Nixon in the world."

Given the waning of America's global influence, Nixon's odyssey was more an adventure than a mission or a crusade. It was certainly not a journey postwar Americans were accustomed to. The erosion of American power, the simultaneous ascent of rivals, the truculence of normally loyal allies, and the outbreak of severe international crises made the 1960s and 1970s perhaps the most challenging era for the makers of U.S. foreign policy. Inheriting a disastrous and unpopular war in Southeast Asia, facing myriad crises elsewhere, challenged by a resurgent Soviet Union and a recalcitrant People's Republic of China, burdened with mounting economic difficulties, and finding little help from traditional allies in Europe, Japan, and Canada, it was Nixon who found himself in the eye of this geopolitical hurricane. Following the economic miracles in western Europe and Japan, and the long, painful process of decolonization in Africa and Asia, the Vietnam era brought forth an increasingly complex world in which power, both economic and military, was diffusing beyond its traditional centers in Europe and the United States. Even without the "purgatory" of Vietnam, Kissinger later observed, "a major reassessment of American foreign policy would have been in order, for the age of America's nearly total dominance of the world stage was drawing to a close."[1]

But power, of course, is relative. In absolute terms, Britain after World War II was in many ways stronger militarily, certainly in terms of sheer firepower, than it had been a century before. What had changed in the intervening years was not so much the decline of British power itself but the decline of its status in relation to that of other powers, such as the United States and the Soviet Union.[2] In the late 1960s and early 1970s, a similar process affected America's global position. In absolute terms, the raw power of the United States had not diminished—it still produced the world's most advanced technology and possessed its largest economy, and it could project a broad range of military power further and more deeply than any other nation, including the Soviet Union, could possibly dream. Yet the United States was no longer able to carry the burden of the Cold War by itself. Faced with the vigor of emerging political, economic, and military rivals, and above all crippled by the continuing war in Vietnam, American leaders could not simply rely on their nation's sheer economic, political, and military might to overcome all international obstacles. In between the peaks of American power in the post–World War II and post–Cold War eras, the United States of the Vietnam era strangely found itself in the unfamiliar position of the weary titan. The certainties of the early Cold War no longer applied. "We no longer live in so simple a world," Kissinger declared in 1975. "Our margin of safety has shrunk."[3]

As Nixon and Kissinger saw it, exceptional times called for exceptional measures in terms of process as well as policy. Distrusting the professional diplomats of the State Department and determined to control foreign policy from the White House, they restructured the machinery of government to place the National Security Council in charge of decision making and put Kissinger in charge of the NSC. Secretary of State William Rogers, chosen for his post precisely because he knew little about diplomacy and could be counted on to keep a low profile, was routinely cut out of policymaking, as was Secretary of Defense Melvin Laird. Their respective departments, meanwhile, were kept busy producing gargantuan studies that seldom saw the light of day. To further cement White House control, Kissinger conducted secret "back channel" diplomacy with leaders of other countries, notably the Soviets. He also doubled the size of the NSC staff, further enlarging the "little State Department," which the NSC staff had in effect become.[4] To keep tabs on this enlarged bureaucracy under him, he wire-tapped the telephones of his own subordinates. "The impression I get," one former secretary of state, Dean Rusk, wrote to another, Dean Acheson, in 1971, "is that … Henry Kissinger is gutting the role and responsibilities of Bill Rogers."[5] What was a painful reality for Rogers had become painfully obvious to all.

But Nixon and Kissinger put such extraordinary measures into effect because their many challenges were tremendously difficult and their ambitions extremely high. To meet the disparate challenges confronting the nation internationally, Nixon and Kissinger devised a grand strategy that aimed to halt the erosion of American power and maintain America's position as one of the world's indisputable superpowers. Unlike the British in 1945, Nixon and Kissinger did not expect the position of the United States to be eclipsed, either in absolute or relative terms, by any other nation. They perceived American power as enduring and were confident that the nation's political, economic, and military problems would fade after they had ended the Vietnam War. Their approach, then, was a holding action rather than an effort in managing decline. Eventually, America's wounded power would recover and reassume its rightful position of global leadership. "As we enter this last third of the twentieth century the hopes of the world rest with America," Nixon declared in a 1967 speech that he delivered in the twin shadows of war in Indochina and violent unrest in America's cities. "Whether peace and freedom survive in the world depends on American leadership." Most important, he argued, "it happens that we are on the right side—the side of freedom and peace and progress against the forces of totalitarianism, reaction and war."[6] America was still the indispensable nation.

To compensate for the war in Vietnam and the tremendous systemic economic and political pressures that were bedeviling U.S. foreign policy, Nixon sought to transform America's relations with friend and foe alike. His first and most important task was to begin extricating American soldiers from Vietnam. He justified doing so with the Nixon Doctrine, which committed the United States to extend political, economic, and diplomatic support, but not military intervention, on behalf of America's allies. "We should assist, but we should not dictate," Nixon told reporters at a stopover on Guam during his 1969 tour of Asia. America "must avoid that kind of policy that will make countries in Asia so dependent upon us that we are dragged into conflicts such as the one that we have in Vietnam."[7] Applied to the war, the Nixon Doctrine was known as Vietnamization: as American troops withdrew from the battlefield, South Vietnamese troops would take their place.

As with all presidential foreign policy doctrines, Nixon's declaration at Guam enshrined a general principle that had arisen from a particular circumstance. But unlike most other presidents Nixon, with a great deal of input from Kissinger, devised an intricate conceptual apparatus that would guide his administration's foreign policy. Ever since Woodrow Wilson, Americans were accustomed to their leaders pursuing an idealistic foreign policy, but under Nixon realism—an international relations theory that values the protection of power, security, and stability over the promotion of ideals, values, and progress—became the guiding philosophy. Most radically, when it came to negotiations, Nixon and Kissinger refused to distinguish between ideological friends and foes. They were willing to talk to anyone; no state or social system was beyond the pale.[8] With realism dominant in the White House, all nations were judged primarily by the traditional standards of the national interest. For the first time in decades, American leaders flattened out their relations with the world's nations, devaluing past friendships and relaxing old animosities. Allies and adversaries were now valued for their utility, not their ideology or domestic political system; they even, most notably in the case of China, switched roles. Europe and Japan, the pillars of American foreign policy since World War II, became less central to American policy, while relations with the Soviet Union and China, existential adversaries since the early Cold War, became increasingly normalized and, occasionally should the situation warrant, allied.

At once revolutionary in its methods and conservative in its aims, the inherent tensions and contradictions in Nixon's foreign policy led to success and failure, triumph and tragedy in equal measure. Under Nixon and Kissinger, foreign policy was characterized by internal inconsistencies that stemmed in large part from its flexibility. Often the flexibility worked to America's advantage; sometimes it did not. But it betrayed the fact that Nixon and his foreign policy team often found themselves reacting to a turbulent international system they could not control. And above all, as the chapters in this book illustrate, Nixon's foreign policy was complex: flexible yet inconsistent, realistic but also ideological, strong as well as weak. Everything was linked to everything else, from nuclear weapons to European communism, from relations with China to domestic politics, and from the Vietnam War to Latin America and the Middle East.

The emphasis on linkage, Nixon believed, did not simply reflect a goal—it represented reality. Economic, military, and political revolutions had changed the world irrevocably, resuming the integrating process of globalization that the two world wars had violently interrupted. By the late 1960s, then, the world was becoming much more interconnected, and if Nixon and Kissinger sought to link together solutions to crises it was largely because they felt they had little choice. In urging Nixon to reform the federal bureaucracy by forcing it to deal with integrated problems in an integrated fashion, Kissinger noted that "because of the sensational development of communications and transportation, the globe has shrunk with distances between formerly faraway countries having been reduced to mere hours of flight time." As a result, "the hallmark, today, of relations among States, even among continents, is *inter*dependence rather than independence."[9] Nixon, who viewed the world in similar terms, needed little prodding. "I am convinced that the great issues are fundamentally interrelated," he wrote to Secretary of Defense Melvin Laird in February 1969, a few weeks after they had assumed office. "I do believe that crisis or confrontation in one place and real cooperation in another cannot long be sustained simultaneously."[10]

If flexibility and complexity, and linkage and integration, were key themes to U.S. foreign policy under Nixon and Kissinger, so too was morality. Most variants of realist theory posit that the national interest is, and should be, the state's primary goal, and that its pursuit is fundamentally incompatible with ethics and morality. States are not individuals, realists argue, and should therefore not be bound by the same ethical and moral concerns that otherwise govern human behavior.[11] This *amoral* view of world politics, which repudiates idealism as prone to dangerous excess, in many ways framed the American worldview under Nixon and Kissinger. Rather than unrealistically demonizing its adversaries, America had to recognize its own limitations and realize that in an increasingly globalized world it could no longer seal off its rivals. America and its allies "must find ways of living in the real world," Nixon declared to a summit meeting of the North Atlantic Treaty Organization. "Those who think simply in terms of 'good' nations and 'bad' nations—of a world of staunch allies and sworn enemies—live in a world of their own. Imprisoned by stereotypes, they do not live in the real world."[12]

Yet many of their critics on both the right and the left charged that an amoral worldview was effectively *immoral*. Those on the right charged that the central achievements of Nixon's foreign policy—détente with the Soviet Union and rapprochement with the People's Republic of China—were tantamount to recognizing the legitimacy of communist dictatorships. It was morally wrong for the United States, the world's champion of freedom and democracy, to sully its hands in negotiations with such tyrants and effectively abandon the idealistic crusade to rid the world of their influence. The conservative activist Phyllis Schlafly bemoaned the death of "our once-sacred honor" and referred to Kissinger as "a demiurge of exquisite craftsmanship and imagination." Kissinger "lacks the courage to stand up to the Soviet Union with its massive nuclear power [and] has repeatedly refused to criticize Soviet police-state methods and totalitarianism" because he was "a man obsessed with nuclear holocaust" instead of human rights. His greatest crime, Schlafly charged, was his "total inability to understand or appreciate what might be called typical American values."[13] Détente, the hard-charging Ronald Reagan declared during his campaign for the Republican presidential nomination in 1976, was simply "putting our stamp of approval on Russia's enslavement of the captive nations" of Eastern Europe.[14]

Critics on the left, on the other hand, argued that it was Nixon and Kissinger's means, not their ends, that were immoral. If conservatives viewed diplomacy with Moscow and Beijing as immoral, liberals and radicals believed passionately that the application of military power, especially in Indochina, and support for authoritarian, right-wing dictatorships, in Latin America and elsewhere, were unjust bases for U.S. foreign policy. The invasion of Cambodia in 1970 led the *Christian Century*, a prominent liberal religious newspaper, to conclude that "the presidency is out of control."[15] During the 1972 Christmas bombings of North Vietnam, the antiwar campaigner Norma Becker recalled that she "was just overwhelmed with this horror, and was feeling powerless—this utter, total, unbelievable horror that human beings could do this … It was such barbarity, and such dehumanization that was taking place. The whole thing was a horror show."[16]

Of course, neither Nixon nor Kissinger believed that their foreign policy was immoral. They claimed the pursuit of peace as their primary goal and that their balance-of-power realism and use of military force were unavoidable, realist means to achieve an idealistic end. Circumstances—especially Vietnam and nuclear parity—rather than ideology led them to follow a realist path to world politics. What could be a greater moral objective than the avoidance of a "nuclear holocaust" that would inevitably accompany a superpower war? "In such conditions," Kissinger argued before a somewhat skeptical "heartland" audience in Minneapolis, "the necessity of peace is itself a moral imperative."[17] Justice for those oppressed by communism was important, but not at the expense of international order. In this sense, creating order was moral while tolerating chaos, even in the name of justice, was not. "The greatest honor history can bestow is the title of peacemaker," Nixon declared in his first inaugural address, in 1969. "This honor now beckons America—the chance to help lead the world at last out of the valley of turmoil and onto that high ground of peace that man has dreamed of since the dawn of civilization. … This is our summons to greatness."[18]

Peace, however, would come on American terms. Critics on the right who charged Nixon, Kissinger, and Ford with "defeatism" by relinquishing the initiative in the Cold War underestimated their ultimate confidence and ambition.[19] Yet although Nixon, Kissinger, and Ford recognized the limits of American power and warned of the renewed vigor of America's rivals, they did not intend their foreign policy to be weak or defensive. If détente was a holding action, its ultimate purpose was to retain as much of America's strength as possible until the nation, and the international system, had digested the ramifications of the Vietnam War. Détente and the opening to China were not forms of surrender, but tactical withdrawals designed to preserve American power and provide it the opportunity to grow again in a less demanding international environment. Similarly, Nixon's strategy for Vietnam aimed to secure the same objective—the long-term survival of an independent, non-communist South Vietnam—albeit with different means, as its predecessors. If that was not possible, Kissinger was determined to create at least a "decent interval" between the departure of American forces and the fall of Saigon. Negotiations, then, were the continuation of the Cold War by other means.[20]

This is but one source of the paradox of a grand strategy that was at once revolutionary and conservative. Its revolutionary aspects—it was the first time since World War II an American president had dealt with the Soviet Union or China more or less as equals, and Nixon did so simultaneously—buttressed the same adherence to containment that had guided the foreign policy of every president since Harry Truman. Multilateralism was but a tool; the objective was still American primacy and eventual victory in the Cold War. Underneath the apparently modest approach was therefore an enormous reservoir of confidence and ambition, best illustrated by the continuing belief in the political and diplomatic uses of military power. Nixon, for example, believed that the drastic escalation of the air war in Vietnam, knowingly launched with the risk of antagonizing the Soviets and thus undermining détente, "demonstrated not only that we had the power but also that we had the will to use it when our interests were threatened, and that fact made us worth talking to."[21] Recognizing America's limits, then, was not pessimistic, but realistic, unavoidable, and, when buttressed by the willingness to use military power, prudent. "Any statesman is in part the prisoner of necessity," Kissinger later reflected. Conducting foreign policy "is a continual struggle to rescue an element of choice from the pressure of circumstance."[22] This was particularly true of American statesmen of the Vietnam era. And it was Kissinger's uncanny ability to turn the diplomatic trick of transforming apparent weakness into strength and setbacks into advantages that sealed his fame.

Of course, it was not all about grand strategy, about making intricate moves on the geopolitical chessboard. Another game board mattered too, this one at home. Loath though Nixon and Kissinger were to admit that crass partisan concerns ever influenced foreign policy—in 1974, as the Watergate affair closed in on the White House and speculation was rife about the scandal's impact on diplomacy, Kissinger proclaimed that American foreign policy had always been, and continued to be, made on a bipartisan basis in the national interest—the internal record proves otherwise. Domestic politics always entered the equation, from January 1969 to the end. To listen to even a few of the Nixon tapes is to be struck by the degree to which foreign policy options were evaluated in terms of their likely effect on the administration's standing at home, especially with key interest groups, and how they would help or hurt Nixon's reelection chances in 1972. Or consider the extraordinary diary kept by Chief of Staff H. R Haldeman, which shows Nixon expressing ambivalence in mid 1972 about whether a deal with Hanoi to end the Vietnam War should come before or after the election that fall. On August 30, for example, Haldeman recorded that the president "wants to be sure [Army Vice-Chief of Staff Alexander] Haig doesn't let Henry's desire for a settlement prevail; that's the one way we can lose the election. We have to stand firm on Vietnam and not get soft."[23] As Nixon and Kissinger well understood, domestic politics, if they could not be avoided in the pursuit of foreign policy, often required awkward compromises.

The main accomplishments of the Nixon-Kissinger grand strategy were the summits with the Soviets and Chinese in 1972 and the Paris Peace Accords to end the Vietnam War a year later. But what did these diplomatic initiatives in fact achieve? Détente was perhaps the least adventurous of these initiatives because it simply formalized a process that President John F. Kennedy began, somewhat haphazardly, in the twelve months following the Cuban Missile Crisis in 1962.[24] Although Lyndon Johnson, Kennedy's successor, found himself preoccupied with Vietnam and allowed détente to languish, he also believed in the endeavor and quite purposefully kept alive the framework for Soviet-American cooperation and negotiation and did his best not to aggravate relations with Moscow.[25] For their part, while they too sought smoother relations with the United States, the Soviets used their humiliation in Cuba and America's in Vietnam as a spur to equal the U.S. nuclear arsenal. The combination of superpower nuclear parity and Vietnam forced Nixon—just as it would have forced any president—to deal with the Soviet Union in a less confrontational manner than in the past. But Nixon and Kissinger intended détente to be something more than a tactical, defensive maneuver; they hoped that negotiating with Moscow would allow them to set the international agenda, and even influence Soviet behavior in a more positive direction. As Kissinger explained to members of the Senate Foreign Relations Committee in 1974, "Détente encourages an environment in which competitors can regulate and restrain their differences and ultimately move from competition to cooperation."[26]

In creating such an international system, Nixon and Kissinger sought to manage the Cold War in a way that would ensure American primacy, and in order to do so they relied on three related concepts rooted deeply in the realist mindset: the balance of power, triangulation, and linkage. The emergence of China, and especially the eruption of a deep rift in Sino-Soviet relations, meant it was unlikely that a single state could dominate the international system, and even if one of the powers had the potential to dominate, in its weakened condition the United States did not seem to be a likely candidate. Nixon and Kissinger recognized and took advantage of an international balance of power of the kind not seen since before World War II. This, in turn, gave them the opportunity to improve relations with both Moscow and Beijing and thereby enable the United States to play one communist power against the other. Thus while the Sino-Soviet split had made the world tripolar instead of bipolar, the United States could place itself at the top of a pyramid in which China and the Soviet Union stood at the other two points. The simple, timeless political art of triangulation, then, would enable America to regain the upper hand. But triangulation would not simply happen on its own. Nixon and Kissinger realized that the United States would need to negotiate with Moscow and Beijing. Ostensibly, negotiations would occur on a basis of equality, but Nixon and Kissinger believed, correctly, that two realities gave them the upper hand: first, that China and the Soviet Union now feared each other more than they feared the United States; and second, that both communist powers desperately wanted the benefits of American technological and economic assistance. Holding the ultimate advantage, the United States hoped to induce changes in the foreign policy of both communist powers, naturally conducive to American interests, by explicitly linking such changes to the granting of American aid and diplomatic support. Nixon and Kissinger believed, incorrectly as it turned out, that linkage would allow them to dictate important aspects of Chinese and Soviet foreign policy.

This included their policies toward Vietnam, which from the start stood out as the most important test for the Nixon and Kissinger grand strategy. The need to extricate America from Vietnam was indeed what made such a grand strategy necessary in the first place. At first, Nixon implemented those components of a plan for extrication that the United States could control on its own. These included the promulgation of the Nixon Doctrine; the withdrawal of American military forces from South Vietnam; the expansion of the war, on the ground and in the air, to Cambodia and Laos in order to curtail the rate of North Vietnamese infiltration into the South; and the process of Vietnamization, in which the U.S. military transferred the task of fighting the war to the South Vietnamese military largely by vastly increasing amounts of military aid. But if America was to bring about a "peace with honor" in Indochina, Nixon was going to need help from his new negotiating partners in Moscow and Beijing. In return for U.S. trade, credit, and technology, and in the Chinese case in exchange for U.S. intelligence data on Soviet military maneuvers and intentions, Nixon and Kissinger expected both Moscow and Beijing to apply pressure on Hanoi to settle the war at least partly along the lines of "peace with honor."[27] In fact, by Nixon's calculations peace with honor in Vietnam and détente with the Soviet Union could only work in tandem; without both in place, neither would succeed. As he confided to a delegation at the Republican National Convention in 1968, he intended to "sit down with the Soviet leadership quite directly, not only about Vietnam, [because] you have got to broaden the canvas—because in Vietnam they have no reason to end the war." How would Nixon make this work if ending the war was not a Soviet priority? The answer, which he provided once the 1968 election was safely behind him, was quite simple: American inducements, combined with the threat of renewed escalation in Vietnam, would pressure Moscow to "use what influence it could appropriately to help to being the war to a conclusion."[28] Beijing was expected to respond in a similarly helpful way. But it was here, where it counted most, that linkage failed to achieve its goal. It turned out that the Soviets and Chinese were not particularly willing to apply pressure to the North Vietnamese; and when they did, it is equally clear that the North Vietnamese were unwilling to bow to such pressures. The Soviets and Chinese, Nixon and Kissinger were startled to learn, actually had quite limited influence in Hanoi.[29]

Dealing with adversaries as equals led to widespread expectations that a relaxation of tensions, rather than the management of tensions, would lead to peace and harmony between the superpowers. Many Americans, in other words, believed that détente would enable Nixon to end the Cold War. Détente, of course, achieved nothing of the kind, and both sides eventually came to believe that the other was taking advantage of détente and using it for its own purposes. From the Soviet perspective, détente merely enabled the United States to assert its dominance in the Middle East, especially after the 1973 Arab-Israeli war. And from the American perspective, détente quite possibly stimulated the opposite effect by encouraging a more assertive Soviet foreign policy in the developing world, especially Africa. "Détente does not in the slightest abolish, nor can it abolish or alter, the laws of the class struggle," Soviet Premier Leonid Brezhnev declared in 1976. "We make no secret of the fact that we see détente as the way to create

more favorable conditions for peaceful socialist and communist construction."[30] As Kissinger almost certainly realized, neither the United States nor
the Soviet Union believed détente would in fact lead to superpower cooperation. Both sides pursued détente as a way to further their own interests
within an overall framework of managed competition. Neither side sought
an end to the Cold War; rather, détente would enable each side to withstand
the uncertainties of a new era and eventually prevail in the Cold War. There
was simply no room for both sides to realize this mutually exclusive goal.

Still, there was likely no escaping détente. Given a similar set of international circumstances, in which America was reeling and competitors were
gaining strength, any other president almost certainly would have pursued
something quite like détente. For all of Reagan's anti-communist bluster
during the 1976 primaries and throughout his first term as president, there
was little Nixon and Kissinger could do to prosecute the Cold War more
aggressively. After 1981, as Kissinger later observed, Reagan "led a nation
that had largely recovered from the Vietnam trauma and had grown dis-
gusted with the humiliations of the Iran hostage crisis … [and] inherited a
psychologically recovered American people ready for a stronger course as
well as a Soviet Union weakened by overextension."[31] Reagan, then, was fortunate in his historical timing, and the assertive triumphalism of the 1980s
had never really been an option for Nixon and Kissinger a decade before.

Nor was it an option for Gerald Ford, who assumed the presidency in
August 1974 when Nixon, facing impeachment because of the Watergate
scandal, resigned from office. A long-time congressman before replacing
Spiro Agnew as vice president, the likable and unpretentious Ford understood well the workings of the federal government, but he had little background in world affairs. Few were surprised that he emphasized continuity
in foreign policy, or that he retained Kissinger as national security adviser
and secretary of state. As the two men worked to maintain established
policies, however, they found themselves battling an increasingly aggressive Congress. This legislative assertiveness began under Nixon with various
efforts to end the war in Vietnam or at least limit its expansion in Cambodia
and Laos, but it gained more force in 1974–1975. Lawmakers refused to
back initiatives the White House considered vital and enacted measures of
their own that undermined existing policies, most notably détente. Kissinger,
disdainful of this Capitol Hill rebellion, later commented on the "irony that
the Congress [Ford] genuinely loved and respected had harassed his foreign
policy unmercifully from the beginning and encumbered it with unprecedented restrictions."[32]

By the start of the 1976 presidential campaign, the Nixon-Kissinger grand strategy was reeling under the blows. The Vietnam War had ended ingloriously the previous year, as North Vietnamese forces conquered Saigon. Détente had become a millstone around the administration's neck, so much so that Ford outlawed the use of the word by his campaign staff and Kissinger acknowledged that it "is a word I would like to forget."[33] Even the 1975 Helsinki Accords, which would have enormous long-term results, became a liability for the administration. On election day, Jimmy Carter, promising a new era in American foreign policy, claimed victory with 297 electoral votes to Ford's 240.

The chapters in *Nixon in the World* reflect upon and make sense of the tumultuous, contradictory, and often perplexing nature of the Nixon era. The first section, "Parameters," establishes the intellectual and political framework of both the era and the book's principal figures. Jussi Hanhimäki explores the grand strategy devised by Nixon and Kissinger and concludes that U.S. foreign policy was in fact driven more by spontaneous reaction to unfolding events than by an overall, consistent pursuit of a particular strategic vision. Because they were so personally integral to the conduct of foreign policy, the next two chapters in the section examine the background and personalities of the book's two main figures. In his essay on Nixon, David Greenberg argues that the Watergate burglary, which ultimately cost Nixon his presidency, was not an aberration but a true reflection of the way the Nixon White House operated. Nixon's secrecy, deception, and paranoia pervaded foreign relations, too, and drove it to unnecessary excesses that often ran counter to the national interest and America's reputation abroad. Jeremi Suri, in an examination of Kissinger's upbringing in Weimar and Nazi Germany, and later as a teenage immigrant to the United States, emphasizes the forces that shaped Kissinger's realism, especially the distrust, even fear, of unchecked majority rule. Finally, Dominic Sandbrook illustrates the many ways in which domestic politics informed, and often actually determined, Nixon's approach to foreign policy. The perceptions—or "salesmanship," as Sandbrook puts it—generated by foreign policy were often as important as its substantive benefits. Nixon and Kissinger's great failing, he concludes, was not their excessive pursuit of salesmanship but an inability to do it well.

The four chapters in the book's second section, "Openings," examine the bold new initiatives of the Nixon and Ford administrations—and the ways in which the United States reacted to equally bold moves by other powers. In her essay on the opening to China, Margaret MacMillan observes that some sort of rapprochement between Washington and Beijing was probable,

but highlights the pivotal role played by Nixon himself in actually bringing it about. Francis J. Gavin focuses on the other signature achievement
of Nixon's foreign policy, détente with the Soviet Union, by concentrating
especially upon détente's central concern, arms control. Gavin argues that
because neither Nixon nor Kissinger believed that nuclear arms had fundamentally changed the principles of great power politics, they did not think
that arms control efforts, by themselves, could ease the Cold War. Arms
control thus had political purposes that could transcend disarmament and
further America's geopolitical interests. Mary Elise Sarotte turns the tables
on Nixon and Kissinger by analyzing their reaction to another startling initiative of the era, West Germany's policy of Ostpolitik, a warming of relations with communist Europe and especially East Germany. Détente and
Ostpolitik, she demonstrates, should have been complementary, but instead
American and West German priorities often clashed and the two initiatives
often ended up competing with one another. Michael Cotey Morgan's essay
on East-West negotiations for a final settlement of the problems caused by
the postwar division of Europe rounds out the section and highlights the
unintended, long-term consequences of U.S. diplomacy. Doubting their rele-
vance and potential importance, Ford and Kissinger mostly ignored the talks,
held over several years in Helsinki, and participated only due to pressure
from West European allies. But by enshrining human rights as a fundamental
principle of great-power politics, the Helsinki Final Act ultimately laid the
foundations for the erosion of communist control in Eastern Europe—an
ironic result considering the Ford administration's emphasis on realism.
Combined, these four "openings" had a tremendous impact on U.S. foreign
relations—indeed, on the very structure of international relations—and
helped lay the foundations for world politics in the post-Cold War era.

The third section, "Closings," deals with the intractable problem of
Vietnam. Why did the war drag on for so long when both candidates for
president in 1968 had pledged to end the war? With their aim of achieving
"peace with honor," did Nixon and Kissinger simply seek the victory that
had eluded officials before them? What role did Congress play in ending the
war? How did domestic politics influence the delicate diplomacy between
Kissinger and the North Vietnamese? These are some of the thorny questions
this section's two chapters seek to answer. Lien-Hang Nguyen delves into
Nixon and Kissinger's attempts to follow through on a campaign promise to
end the war. Robert D. Schulzinger picks up the story in 1973 and looks at
the ways in which Vietnam continued to plague American society and foreign policy. Nguyen and Schulzinger both pay great attention to Kissinger's

role in prolonging U.S. involvement in the name of its international credibility, and to Nixon's tendency always to refract events in Vietnam through the prism of domestic partisan politics. Essentially, Nguyen and Schulzinger both conclude, the war dragged on simply because the White House thought it should.

The fourth and final section, "Flashpoints, Hotspots, and Allies," contains five chapters that examine how Nixon, Kissinger, and Ford dealt with some of the disparate crises and problems that emerged beyond the Vietnam War and the spheres of American-Soviet and American-Chinese relations. However, two common threads connect these chapters. The first is Washington's determination to fit, however awkwardly or inappropriately, regional crises into a framework of great power (usually Soviet-American) relations. The second is the adverse long-term consequences that followed the pursuit of short-term, mostly ephemeral gains. Thus Salim Yaqub's essay on the Middle East deals with the American response to Arab-Israeli tensions and Kissinger's largely successful efforts to block the Soviets from increasing their influence in the region. Robert J. McMahon tells a similar story regarding South Asia, particularly the 1971 Indo-Pakistani war that saw the United States isolated in its support for Pakistan, mainly for reasons that actually had little to do with events in South Asia. Mark Atwood Lawrence continues this theme in his chapter on U.S. policy toward Latin America, which focuses mainly on Nixon and Kissinger's response to crises in Cuba and Chile. But allies, too, caused headaches for the United States by posing economic and political challenges to American leadership from within. Thomas W. Zeiler analyzes the Japanese-American alliance to show how the burdens of Cold War leadership brought about tremendous economic strains that resulted in significant political problems. Finally, Robert Bothwell's discussion of Canada's role as a loyal but unappreciated ally underscores the malign neglect suffered by some of America's closest and most reliable allies while Nixon and Kissinger focused obsessively on great power relations.

If power is relative, it is also cyclical. By the 1980s, America was fast regaining its primacy in world politics. A decade later, with the Cold War won, the economy booming, and no serious geopolitical rival in sight, an "America unrivaled" was enjoying its "unipolar moment" of unquestioned supremacy and unprecedented latitude in international relations.[34] As Reagan's political career illustrates, the national mood had shifted dramatically. After the Nixon and Kissinger era of balance and constraint, Americans wanted their leaders to be optimists, not realists. After leaving the White House in 1974, Nixon complained bitterly that his Republican successors all but ignored him; although Kissinger was easily the Republican Party's most experienced and influential foreign policy analyst no subsequent Republican president would offer him a position of influence.[35] In the optimistic, head-strong decades that followed the malaise of the 1970s, the Nixon-Kissinger brand of realism had become deeply unfashionable.

Until, that is, the Iraq War. Having once campaigned as something of a realist, following the attacks of September 11, 2001, President George W. Bush emphatically rejected the notion that American power and purpose have limits.[36] A successful and unexpectedly brief war in Afghanistan resulted from 9/11 and raised the tantalizing prospect that Saddam Hussein could be overthrown in similarly quick fashion. But contrary to expectations, the war in Iraq, launched in March 2003, tied the United States down in a quagmire not dissimilar to that of the Vietnam War. And so, at a time of American vulnerability unseen since the early 1970s, Kissinger reentered the foreign policy arena as a frequent, if informal, adviser to Bush, Vice President Dick Cheney, and Secretary of State Condoleezza Rice. Thanks to the ebbing of American power, Kissinger's inimitable brand of *realpolitik* was once again in style.[37] Indeed, as Bush, Cheney, and Rice would come to appreciate, the delicate and difficult art of "rescuing choice from circumstance" was something of a specialty for those who had been through the most trying of foreign policy circumstances.[38]

Notes

1. Henry Kissinger, *Diplomacy* (New York, 1994), 703.
2. David Reynolds, *Britannia Overruled: British Policy and World Power in the 20th Century*, 2nd ed. (London, 2000), 17–22. See also Paul Kennedy, *The Rise and Fall of the Great Powers: Economic Change and Military Conflict from 1500 to 2000* (New York, 1987); and Aaron L. Friedberg, *The Weary Titan: Britain and the Experience of Relative Decline, 1895–1905* (Princeton, 1988).
3. Henry Kissinger, "The Moral Foundations of Foreign Policy," address to the Upper Midwest Council, Minneapolis, July 15, 1975, *Department of State Bulletin*, August 4, 1975, 163.
4. On the growth of the NSC, see Amy B. Zegart, *Flawed by Design: The Evolution of the CIA, JCS and NSC* (Stanford, 1999); Andrew Preston, "The Little State Department: McGeorge Bundy and the National Security Council Staff, 1961–1965," *Presidential Studies Quarterly* 31 (December 2001): 635–659; and David J. Rothkopf, *Running the World: The Inside Story of the National Security Council and the Architects of American Power* (New York, 2005).

5. Quoted in Jussi Hanhimäki, *The Flawed Architect: Henry Kissinger and American Foreign Policy* (New York, 2004), 115.

6. Address by Richard Nixon to the Bohemian Club, San Francisco, July 29, 1967, *FRUS, 1969–1976*, vol. I, 8–9.

7. Nixon, "Informal Remarks in Guam with Newsmen," July 25, 1969, *PPP, 1969* (Washington, D.C., 1971), 548.

8. On the unwillingness of previous Cold War presidents to engage in diplomacy with communist adversaries, see Fredrik Logevall, "Bernath Lecture: A Critique of Containment," *Diplomatic History* 28 (September 2004): 473–499. As Kissinger would say of this earlier policy, "containment allowed no role for diplomacy until the climactic final scene in which the men in the white hats accepted the conversion of the men in the black hats." Kissinger, *Diplomacy*, 471.

9. Kissinger paper, "The Modern World, a Single 'Strategic Theater,'" September 29, 1969, *FRUS, 1969–1976*, I: 111. Emphasis in original.

10. Nixon to Melvin Laird, February 4, 1969, ibid., 57.

11. Jack Donnelly, *Realism and International Relations* (Cambridge, 2000). Incisive portraits of three leading twentieth-century American realists are found in Campbell Craig, *Glimmer of a New Leviathan: Total War in the Realism of Niebuhr, Morgenthau, and Waltz* (New York, 2003). For an important exception which argues for the necessity of morality in traditional realism, see Richard Ned Lebow, *The Tragic Vision of Politics: Ethics, Interests, and Orders* (Cambridge, 2003).

12. Nixon address at the Commemorative Session of the North Atlantic Council, April 10, 1969, *PPP, 1969*, 272–273.

13. Phyllis Schlafly and Chester Ward, *Kissinger on the Couch* (New Rochelle, N.Y., 1975), 122, 123, 780–781, 783.

14. Quoted in Hanhimäki, *Flawed Architect*, 444.

15. Quoted in Charles DeBenedetti, *An American Ordeal: The Antiwar Movement of the Vietnam Era* (Syracuse, N.Y., 1990), 285.

16. Quoted in Tom Wells, *The War Within: America's Battle over Vietnam* (Berkeley, 1994), 559–560.

17. Kissinger, "The Moral Foundations of Foreign Policy," 164. For the context of this speech, in which Kissinger felt compelled to justify U.S. foreign policy through an educational speaking tour of the American "heartland," see Hanhimäki, *Flawed Architect*, 434–436.

18. Richard Nixon, Inaugural Address, January 20, 1969, *PPP, 1969*, 1.

19. Just as it was for nearly all of critics on the right, Kissinger's "defeatism" and lack of appreciation for the true, limitless potential of American power is one of the major themes in Schlafly and Ward, *Kissinger on the Couch.*

20. On the pursuit of victory in Indochina—that is, the survival of South Vietnam—see Larry Berman, *No Peace, No Honor: Nixon, Kissinger, and Betrayal in Vietnam* (New York, 2001). On the pursuit of a "decent interval," see Jeffrey Kimball, *Nixon's Vietnam War* (Lawrence, Kans.,

1998); Kimball, *The Vietnam War Files: Uncovering the Secret History of Nixon-Era Strategy* (Lawrence, Kans., 2004), 24–28, 121–198; and Jussi Hanhimäki, "Some More 'Smoking Guns?' The Vietnam War and Kissinger's Summitry with Moscow and Beijing, 1971–73," *SHAFR Newsletter* 32 (December 2001).

21. Richard Nixon, *The Real War* (New York, 1980), 112.

22. Henry Kissinger, *White House Years* (Boston, 1979), 54.

23. H. R. Haldeman, *The Haldeman Diaries: Inside the Nixon White House* (New York, 1994), 500.

24. Vladislav Zubok and Constantine Pleshakov, *Inside the Kremlin's Cold War: From Stalin to Khrushchev* (Cambridge, Mass., 1996), 236–274; Aleksandr Fursenko and Timothy Naftali, *"One Hell of a Gamble": Khrushchev, Castro, and Kennedy, 1958–1964* (New York, 1997), 336–338; Marc Trachtenberg, *A Constructed Peace: The Making of the European Settlement, 1945–1963* (Princeton, 1999), 352–402; Jeremi Suri, *Power and Protest: Global Revolution and the Rise of Détente* (Cambridge, Mass., 2003), 41–43.

25. Frank Costigliola, "Lyndon B. Johnson, Germany, and 'the End of the Cold War,'" in *Lyndon Johnson Confronts the World: American Foreign Policy, 1969–1977*, ed. Warren I. Cohen and Nancy Bernkopf Tucker (Cambridge, 1994), 192–208; H. W. Brands, *The Wages of Globalism: Lyndon Johnson and the Limits of American Power* (New York, 1995), 119–120; Thomas Alan Schwartz, *Lyndon Johnson and Europe: In the Shadow of Vietnam* (Cambridge, Mass., 2003). For the argument that Johnson intended war in Vietnam to act as a buffer for détente, see Andrew Preston, *The War Council: McGeorge Bundy, the NSC, and Vietnam* (Cambridge, Mass., 2006), 54–55, 69–74.

26. Quoted in John Lewis Gaddis, *Strategies of Containment: A Critical Appraisal of American National Security Policy during the Cold War*, rev. ed. (New York, 2005), 309.

27. Raymond L. Garthoff, *Détente and Confrontation: American-Soviet Relations from Nixon to Reagan*, rev. ed. (Washington, D.C., 1994), 35–37; Kimball, *Nixon's Vietnam War*, 114–123; Pierre Asselin, *A Bitter Peace: Washington, Hanoi, and the Making of the Paris Agreement* (Chapel Hill, N.C., 2002), 34–37.

28. Quoted in Gareth Porter, *A Peace Denied: The United States, Vietnam, and the Paris Agreement* (Bloomington, Ind., 1975), 80, 86.

29. Ilya Gaiduk, *The Soviet Union and the Vietnam War* (Chicago, 1996), 194–222; Qiang Zhai, *China and the Vietnam Wars, 1950–1975* (Chapel Hill, N.C., 2000), 193–206; Shen Zhihua, "Sino-U.S. Reconciliation and China's Vietnam Policy," in *Behind the Bamboo Curtain: China, Vietnam, and the World Beyond Asia*, ed. Priscilla Roberts (Washington and Stanford, 2006), 349–368.

30. Quoted in Peter W. Rodman, *More Precious than Peace: The Cold War and the Struggle for the Third World* (New York, 1994), 154. See also Garthoff,

Détente and Confrontation, 588; and Odd Arne Westad, *The Global Cold War: Third World Interventions and the Making of Our Times* (Cambridge, 2005), 203–206.

31. Henry Kissinger, *Years of Renewal* (New York, 1999), 110. See also Kissinger, *Diplomacy*, 766–768.

32. Kissinger, *Years of Renewal*, 1064.

33. Quoted in Walter LaFeber, *America Russia and the Cold War, 1945–2006*, 10th ed. (Boston, 2008), 297.

34. On American primacy following the Cold War, see the essays in G. John Ikenberry, ed., *America Unrivaled: The Future of the Balance of Power* (Ithaca, N.Y., 2002).

35. For Nixon's complaints that he was ignored by Ronald Reagan and George H. W. Bush, see Monica Crowley, *Nixon Off the Record* (New York, 1996). For Kissinger's strained relations with Reagan and Bush, see Walter Isaacson, *Kissinger: A Biography* (New York, 1992), 718–729.

36. On this point, see especially Ivo H. Daalder and James. M. Lindsay, *America Unbound: The Bush Revolution in Foreign Policy* (Washington, D.C., 2003).

37. Bob Woodward, *State of Denial* (New York, 2006), 406–410; Joe Hagan, "The Once and Future Kissinger," *New York*, December 4, 2006; "A return to realism? How Rice has learnt to play a weaker US hand," *Financial Times*, April 23, 2007, 9. For Kissinger's own thoughts, see Henry Kissinger, "A political program to exit Iraq," *International Herald Tribune*, July 3, 2007.

38. John Lewis Gaddis, "Rescuing Choice form Circumstance: The Statecraft of Henry Kissinger," in *The Diplomats, 1939–1979*, eds. Gordon A. Craig and Francis L. Loewenheim (Princeton, 1994), 564–592.

Part I

Parameters

1

An Elusive Grand Design

Jussi M. Hanhimäki

In February 1969, *Time* magazine's cover showed a picture of a man who would, in future years, become a central figure in American diplomacy. "Bonn, London, and Paris may disagree on a score of issues, but they are in happy unanimity in their respect for him; even Moscow is not displeased," the article commented. It went on to describe how Richard Nixon's new national security adviser, Henry Kissinger, "knows more foreign leaders than many State Department careerists." The article ended presciently with a quote from the nineteenth-century Austrian statesman, Prince Metternich: "I was born to make history, not to write novels."[1]

Although some of his critics have since hinted that Kissinger's memoirs are best read as novels rather than true historical accounts, *Time* had clearly figured out where the true decisions about foreign policy would be made in years to come. With Kissinger at the helm, there would be "new approaches to friend and foe," *Time* announced. By the end of Nixon's first term, Kissinger would have orchestrated seemingly impossible breakthroughs with China, the Soviet Union, and North Vietnam. By 1972, the edifice of the "structure of peace" that Nixon had promised in his inaugural address was erected. Détente, triangular diplomacy, and the exit from Vietnam highlighted the birth of a new American grand strategy. Within the context of that grand strategy, the role of diplomacy—and Henry Kissinger as America's chief diplomat—was magnified.

What Nixon called "the structure of peace" depended upon a number of key concepts, the most influential of them being détente and the Nixon Doctrine. In different ways both of these concepts were designed to retain as much American influence as possible while simultaneously recognizing the limits of how American power could in practice be applied. Détente and triangular diplomacy were supposed to increase American influence over Soviet policy by engaging them more directly (while simultaneously pressuring them indirectly by deploying the so-called China card), the Nixon Doctrine aimed at creating a network of "special relationships" with key regional powers that would, in turn, project American power indirectly by, say, "policing" the Middle East (for example, Iran and Israel). But did this amount to a new grand strategy? Or were they simply a series of policies and tactical moves that were ingeniously popularized to show that the Nixon administration was reinventing the wheel of American foreign policy?

My argument leans toward the latter assessment. I do not doubt that there was an American grand strategy at work in the early 1970s. But this strategy was not a revolutionary shift from earlier policies; rather, it aimed to accomplish, ultimately, a basic goal that had been central to U.S. foreign policy since the 1940s: the containment of Soviet power and influence. Nor were the tactics employed to accomplish this goal entirely new: the opening to China and détente with the USSR (and most certainly an exit from Vietnam), were policies that the Johnson administration had pursued in the 1960s. Nixon and Kissinger were able to achieve these goals because the circumstances—at home and abroad—were more favorable after 1969 than before. But because they pursued these policies in part with domestic gains in mind—most obviously Nixon's reelection in 1972—Nixon and Kissinger ultimately oversold their grand design. The end result was a severe domestic backlash, exacerbated by Watergate, which made it impossible for Nixon's successor to build upon the undeniable foreign policy accomplishments of the first Nixon administration. Thus, if durability is a measure of achievement, the Nixon-Kissinger grand design that unfolded in the early 1970s was, at best, a mixed success.[2]

There are few equally unlikely relationships in the annals of American foreign policy than the one between Henry Kissinger and Richard Nixon. Their backgrounds were about as different as possible. Nixon was the ultimate American political animal of the postwar era. A congressman and senator from California, Nixon was elected vice president before his 40th birthday. In this post he developed an appetite for foreign policy that was rivaled only by his political ambition. After a bitter loss for the presidency to John F. Kennedy in 1960, Nixon finally triumphed in the 1968 presidential election. Soon after, he chose Henry Kissinger, a Jewish immigrant from Germany who held a professorship at Harvard University's international relations department, as his national security adviser.[3]

The only known meeting between the two men before November 1968 had been a five-minute talk at a Christmas party in 1967 that had apparently not left a lasting impression on either man. And yet, when Henry Cabot Lodge, who had worked with Kissinger while he was ambassador to Vietnam and had been Nixon's running mate in 1960, recommended Kissinger to the president-elect as a potential national security adviser, Nixon indicated that he was already seriously considering such an appointment. Accordingly, on November 22, 1968, Kissinger received a call from David Chapin, Nixon's appointments secretary. A week later, after a successful meeting with Nixon in the interim, Kissinger accepted the job. The public announcement followed on December 2, 1968. Nixon said he wanted a "fresh approach"— which was true enough—but then assured that "Dr. Kissinger is keenly aware of the necessity not to set himself up as a wall between the Secretary State [and the President]."[4] This, later events would bear out, was simply untrue. In the next two years Kissinger clearly emerged as Nixon's key foreign policy aide; if anything, the debate would focus upon whether it was the president or the national security adviser who was running foreign policy. But why had Nixon chosen Kissinger?

Kissinger had many qualities that made him an appealing choice to Nixon. He was a Harvard academic with connections to the eastern establishment that provided links to the parts of American elite that Nixon had grown to hate—but whose approval he seemed to crave—during his political career. There was also Kissinger's connection to Nelson Rockefeller, Nixon's rival for the Republican presidential nomination and a leader of the party's moderate wing; by appointing Kissinger, Nixon may have hoped to heal some of the wounds within the Republican Party that had opened up during the 1968 primaries. Alternatively, as the historian Joan Hoff suspects, Nixon may have wanted to "strike a blow at Rockefeller by 'stealing' someone close to him."[5]

Such petty motivations aside, what about the possibility that Nixon simply considered Kissinger the best man for the job? As Kissinger's aide Peter Rodman told an interviewer, Nixon had made queries about having Kissinger join his staff immediately after securing the Republican nomination. In Rodman's words: "Nixon, I think, largely realized that Kissinger was really the outstanding person on the Republican side."[6] While there was no shortage of supplicants, Kissinger had made a name for himself as Rockefeller's adviser and as one of the few Republican foreign policy intellectuals. Within the Republican field, moreover, there were few other obvious contenders.[7]

In early 1969, few expected that Kissinger would become such a global figure as he eventually did. That he was able to outlive Nixon in office and become, in 1973–1975, the only man to hold the jobs of secretary of state and national security adviser simultaneously probably owed more to the necessity that both saw for centralizing foreign policy decision making. Nixon wanted to be his own secretary of state. Kissinger responded by suggesting that the way around the State Department was to put together a strong National Security Council staff that would be located in the White House. The Departments of State and Defense, the other two agencies that normally played a decisive role in shaping foreign policy, would be kept occupied by the president demanding detailed studies of various foreign policy aspects, the true planning and decision making would take place in the NSC staff and, ultimately, in lengthy meetings between Nixon and Kissinger.

No plans or bureaucratic moves, though, guaranteed the end result. Kissinger did not enter the West Wing Basement of the White House in early 1969 guaranteed to emerge as the foreign policy czar of the new administration. In the end, it depended most of all on Nixon, who had the ultimate power to fashion foreign policy. The emergence of Kissinger as the prime foreign policymaker in the Nixon administration was ultimately, as Rodman later put it, "Nixon's doing." It was hardly possible that a former Harvard professor—even one with extended experience working as a consultant for the two previous administrations—would arrive in Washington with a staff of a few dozen and sweep aside the entire State Department and its thousands of well-connected and experienced personnel. As Kissinger later put it in an interview: "The idea that I went in there to take it away from Nixon's best friend [Secretary of State William Rogers], as a Rockefeller disciple, it's preposterous. I didn't know anybody in the Nixon entourage." That Kissinger managed to establish such a prominent position for himself was ultimately dependent not just on his own bureaucratic skills—although these naturally helped—but on the president's desire to run foreign policy and Kissinger's ability to provide the type of advice that he was seeking.[8]

The challenges facing Nixon and Kissinger on inauguration day were formidable. At the center of American difficulties lay the Vietnam War. The Tet Offensive of February 1968 had exposed the hollow nature of Lyndon Johnson's assurances of late 1967 that the enemy's breaking point was about to be reached and that the war was coming to an end. Instead, the commander of U.S. forces in Vietnam, General William Westmoreland, had asked for another 200,000 troops to top up the half a million already stationed in South Vietnam. Johnson refused the request and announced his decision not to seek a continuation of his presidency. And, although he had ordered a bombing halt in late October, the Vietnam War presented mostly problems and few promising opportunities for the incoming administration in early 1969.

Aside from Vietnam, Kissinger and Nixon faced a host of other challenges and uncertainties. The relationship with the Soviet Union was at a crossroads, as the Soviets approached nuclear parity. While their resources were far from equal with the United States when it came down to other "types" of power, the Kremlin's confidence appeared to have been boosted by the crackdown on Czechoslovakia in August 1968. The measured response of the United States and its West European allies to the arrival of thousands of Warsaw Pact troops in Prague could only have indicated to the Soviets that their "sphere of influence" in East-Central Europe was secure. The inherent right of the USSR and its allies to "defend socialism" in East European countries by force if necessary—often referred to as the Brezhnev Doctrine—had apparently been accepted in Washington. In addition, the Soviets continued to support militarily a number of Arab states, particularly Egypt and Syria, in their quest for retribution after Israeli victories in the 1967 Six Day War. The Soviet Union, in short, was casting its quest for influence far beyond East-Central Europe.

The People's Republic of China (PRC) remained a major question mark, particularly after it had turned increasingly inward with the commencement of Mao's Cultural Revolution in 1966. While Beijing had severed its ties with Moscow, there was no obvious indication in 1969 that the Chinese were looking for rapprochement with Washington. The PRC continued to support North Vietnam and castigate the United States for its support of South Vietnam.

Throughout the 1960s, the Americans also had had trouble with their friends. The European allies were far from happy with America's continued involvement in Vietnam, something French President Charles de Gaulle would take issue with during Nixon's first trip abroad as president. While de Gaulle's furor at the Americans appeared to diminish after France left NATO's integrated military structure in 1966 (it remained formally a member of the alliance), there was also the troublesome nature of West Germany's Ostpolitik. When the Social Democrat leader Willy Brandt became chancellor in September 1969 (after serving as foreign minister in a coalition government), his government moved quickly to improve relations with the Soviet bloc. This, in turn, would threaten to make it impossible to have a unified NATO policy vis-à-vis the USSR, or at least the type of unified policy that left Washington firmly in the driver's seat. Added to these political woes were the economic challenges presented by European integration and the Japanese economic miracle; for the first time in the postwar years, the United States faced a serious economic challenge to its dominance of the international marketplace.

Beyond all that, there existed a volatile "rest of the world." The Arab-Israeli conflict had been left unresolved after the Six Day War. Decolonization in Africa was creating civil wars from which the Soviets (or even the Chinese) could possibly benefit. In Latin America, the Alliance for Progress of the 1960s had not produced more reliable allies but an upsurge in anti-Americanism. In South Asia, old hostilities between India and Pakistan were adding to regional instability already provoked by the Sino-Indian War of 1962 and the Indo-Pakistani War of 1965.

It was, in brief, an unstable world full of challenges. Nixon and Kissinger could hardly have entered high public office at a time when American foreign policy was under greater criticism at home and abroad. In 1968, it seemed that few of the certainties of American Cold War policy remained intact. And yet, even with half a million American forces bogged down in Vietnam, Washington's nuclear superiority in jeopardy, America's influence over its allies in decline, and the impact of decolonization on international relations unresolved, the United States was still the most powerful nation on Earth. Its military might was still unsurpassed, its economic power unequaled, and its human potential enormous. In the end, the real question thus was: how could the United States redeem itself and reestablish trust in American leadership? How could the administration accomplish this in a manner that would be acceptable and respectable to friend and foe at home and abroad?

To Nixon, Kissinger, and others charged with running the foreign policy of the new administration in early 1969 the goal was to find a new global equilibrium that would reflect the changing nature of international relations without jeopardizing the United States' preponderant influence around the globe. It meant creative diplomacy that recognized a simple fact: military intervention as a means of projecting American power abroad was not possible in the near future. Thus there was a need to reinvent the ground rules of American diplomacy in order to restore the United States' role in the world while extricating it from Vietnam.

The basic task facing Nixon and Kissinger in 1969 was clear enough: to sustain American global power. The challenge—to do this without the overt use of military force—defined a set of new tactics that, depending on one's perspective, may have amounted to a grand design. Yet it was clear that, if only for political purposes, Nixon would certainly bill himself as the antithesis of his predecessor. Lyndon Johnson had made war and intervened (in Vietnam and the Dominican Republic); Nixon was going to make peace. Moreover, he promised to build a new structure that would, in effect, make peace a durable condition. The political demand for such a grand design surely was there in the late 1960s. But did Nixon and Kissinger have a realistic plan on how to achieve it?

Of the two, Nixon was the more experienced: having served as Eisenhower's vice president, he had traveled the world, met numerous foreign leaders, participated in the foreign policy process, and then, crucially, had an eight-year hiatus that allowed him to reflect upon the challenges abroad and at home. He was potentially well poised to implement a successful foreign policy: a politician who knew the world and took a long-term view of the issues that faced the United States. He understood, it seems, the great challenges facing his country. In 1967, for example, Nixon had implored:

> We live in a new world.... It is a world of new leaders ... new people ... new ideas. Communism, Marxism, Socialism, anti-colonialism— the great ideas which stirred men to revolution after World War II have lost their pulling power ... Because we live in a new world, many of the old institutions are obsolete and inadequate. The UN, NATO, foreign aid, USIA were set up to deal with the world of twenty years ago. A quick trip around the world will show how different the problems are today.[9]

In this speech Nixon went on to underline, if in a rather vague form, the basic principle that was to characterize his public foreign policy addresses in the future: the United States needed to reassess the way it dealt with its adversaries and friends. In this and other addresses or articles before taking up office, Nixon essentially laid down the trademark of his foreign policy: flexibility of means coupled by an adoption of, in essence, the very same assumptions and goals that had guided his predecessors. For example, there could be détente with the USSR but only if policymakers remembered the fundamental differences between the United States and the Soviet Union. As Nixon put it: "We seek peace as an end in itself. They seek victory with peace being at this time a means toward that end ... [W]e can live in peace with the Soviet Union but until they give up their goal for world conquest it will be for them a peace of necessity and not of choice."[10]

In addition to détente with the USSR, Nixon—before taking office— repeatedly hinted at the possibility that he might change America's policy toward China, understood that the United States needed to rethink the structure of the transatlantic relationship, and, first and foremost, had to exit Vietnam "with honor." Through such speeches and articles, during, before, and after the November 1968 elections, Nixon outlined a relatively straight-forward and necessarily vague grand design for American foreign policy. He would outline it in his inaugural address on January 20, 1969, that empha-sized the new administration's interest in talking to anyone—the Soviets, the Chinese, the Vietnamese apparently included—who wished to do so. As Nixon put it:

> Where peace is unknown, make it welcome; where peace is fragile,
> make it strong; where peace is temporary, make it permanent ...
> After a period of confrontation, we are entering an era of negotiation.
> Let all nations know that during this administration our lines of
> communication will be open ... We cannot expect to make everyone
> our friend, but we can try to make no one our enemy.[11]

Kissinger, who may have winced a bit at the somewhat corny rhetoric, roughly agreed: the United States needed to negotiate with all. Like Nixon, he recognized the need for new approaches. Moreover, perhaps even more than the president, Kissinger saw the world as a whole, as a structure in which different pieces were interrelated. This made the national security adviser ruminate, in a book published at virtually the same time he moved into the West Wing Basement of the White House, that:

> The temptation is great to treat each issue as an immediate
> and isolated problem which once surmounted will permit the
> fundamental stability of the international order to reassert itself.
> But the crises which form the headlines of the day are symptoms
> of deep-seated structural problems ... The current international
> environment is in turmoil because its essential elements are all in flux
> simultaneously.[12]

Kissinger further maintained: "Our deepest challenge will be to evoke the creativity of a pluralistic world, to base order on political multipolarity even though overwhelming military strength will remain with the two superpow-ers." Thus Kissinger further concluded that the "new administration ... must recognize that, in the field of foreign policy, we will never be able to contrib-ute to building a stable and creative world order unless we first form some conception of it."[13]

In short, both Nixon and Kissinger talked about a grand design. Nixon called it a structure of peace; Kissinger wrote about it indirectly yet authoritatively. The trouble, as both Nixon and Kissinger recognized, was that there was ultimately little point in having a clear-cut design because such designs were, almost by some natural law, hostage to fortune and contingency. A year into the administration's tenure, Winston Lord, Kissinger's young aide, wrote that "even if we could construct a master plan, we would not adhere rigidly to it for the sake of consistency if events dictated tactical aberrations." Although Lord was talking mainly about the Nixon Doctrine and its practical application in Asia, the same could easily have been said about the entire foreign policy of the Nixon administration. As Kissinger put it in his memoirs, "once the oath of office has been taken there is no longer time for calm reflection. The policymaker is then like a man on a tightrope; he can avoid a precipitous drop only by moving forward."[14] A brief look at the unfolding of some of the key policies in the first few years of the Nixon administration confirms the limits of even a grand design that had apparently been carefully conceived in advance.

The country that most concerned Nixon and Kissinger was the USSR. Similarly, it is undoubtedly true that the efforts to manage the competitive relationship with Moscow shaped every other aspect of U.S. foreign policy in the early 1970s. The Kremlin's likely reactions and existing policies affected the settlement in Vietnam, the opening to China, and the relationship with America's allies. The USSR was in the foreground when Nixon and Kissinger approached regional conflicts in the Middle East, Africa, and elsewhere.[15]

While the origins of détente may be traced back to the early and mid-1960s, there is no question that its best-known phase was the Nixon-Kissinger era. This was, naturally, the period that included the various agreements on Germany and Berlin, the signing of the Strategic Arms Limitation Treaty (SALT) I and Anti-Ballistic Missile (ABM) agreements at the Moscow Summit of 1972, the summit of 1973 that produced the Prevention of Nuclear War (PNW) agreement, and the 1974 tentative SALT II agreements of Vladivostok (an agreement that Nixon, having bowed out of office in August 1974, could only watch from the sidelines). After 1974, détente began to falter.[16] Under severe domestic attack from both the left and the right, Gerald Ford eventually banned the use of the word in his 1976 presidential campaign.[17]

It would be misleading to argue that the idea of détente was a revolutionary concept as such: relaxing tensions between adversarial powers was and is, after all, the regular fare of the long-term development of any bilateral relationship. Indeed, the question one should probably ask regarding the pursuit of détente is not so much why the relaxation of Soviet-American tensions emerged during the Nixon presidency but what its principal American practitioners thought could be gained by engaging the Kremlin. Was détente meant to launch a structural revolution that would ultimately lead to the end of the Cold War? Or was it simply a way of gaining a "breather" in the Cold War, of making the competition more manageable, perhaps even giving the United States an edge that it seemed to be losing? Did Nixon and Kissinger see détente simply as containment by other means? After all, in a domestic context, where the use of American military power was an extremely risky proposal, diplomacy gained new currency as a policy making tool.

In this regard, Kissinger at the time and for a long time afterward insisted that the real goal of détente was to manage the USSR. As he wrote to Nixon early during the presidency, "Moscow wants to engage us ... [W]e should seek to utilize this Soviet interest, stemming as I think it does from anxiety, to induce them to come to grips with the real sources of tension, notably in the Middle East, but also in Vietnam. This approach also would require continued firmness on our part in Berlin."[18] Indeed, while the sources of détente—as Andreas Wenger and Jeremi Suri have argued[19]—lay much deeper than the specific interests and tactical goals of a few policymakers, the actual practice of détente was, as is well known, a highly centralized matter in the Nixon administration. And at the basis of it lay strategy of linkage: the idea one could create a web of relationships with the USSR and exchange, in effect, favors in one area (for example, the SALT negotiations) to those made in another (say, the Vietnam peace talks).[20]

In February 1969, Nixon and Kissinger established a "back channel" to the Kremlin via the Soviet ambassador to Washington, Anatoly Dobrynin. Although much has been made about the foot dragging either side was guilty of, the real problem at the very beginning was not over the general principle of linkage. Rather, the Soviet ambassador objected to the *type* of linkage that Kissinger and Nixon aimed to pursue. During the meeting in the White House on February 17, 1969, that effectively established the back channel (in addition to Dobrynin and Nixon, it was attended by Kissinger and Malcolm Toon of the State Department), the Soviet ambassador called for serious negotiations "on various subjects and at various levels." When Nixon prodded him, Dobrynin mentioned SALT and the Middle East as the key issues. Nixon responded by stressing that one should separate SALT from "the settlement of larger political issues" but did not foreclose the possibility of holding "parallel" talks. Dobrynin was curious and pressed for clarification on "the linkage between arms talks and negotiations on political issues," and Nixon asserted that "progress in one area is bound to have an influence on progress in all other areas." Further clarifying his central point, Nixon explained that it was his hope that the Soviets would "do what they can to get the Paris talks [on Vietnam] off dead-center." Dobrynin was evasive, maintaining that if a true era of negotiation were to be launched, "it would be wise not to begin with the most difficult issues."[21]

Aside from establishing the Kissinger-Dobrynin back channel, the February 1969 meeting set the tone for Soviet-American negotiations for the next few years. Linkage was real. The bilateral relationship was to be pursued over a number of issues ranging from SALT to Vietnam. But linkage was also a recipe for deadlock. There would be limited progress because both the Americans and the Soviets were, in the end, concerned about the other side gaining some kind of a unilateral advantage. During the months and years to come Kissinger, at Nixon's behest, pressed Dobrynin for help in reaching a settlement on Vietnam, and the Soviet ambassador replied by demanding Americans work toward progress on the Middle East. The end result was that the early talks inevitably focused on areas where both sides did see progress in the offing or the pressure from other countries was insurmountable—such as arms control or the Berlin/German question. No wonder that the early détente process yielded few tangible results until the summer of 1971.[22] Détente was central to the Nixon-Kissinger grand design, to the edifice of the structure of peace. But the contingency had proven unfavorable; the application of linkage had not worked effectively. Something more was needed. Enter China.

The generally accepted view is that at this point Kissinger's secret trip to China suddenly transformed the nature of the Soviet-American relationship. As Kissinger later argued, the "triangular relationship among the United States, the USSR, and China unlocked the door to a series of major breakthroughs: the end of the Vietnam War; an agreement that guaranteed access to divided Berlin; a dramatic reduction of Soviet influence in the Middle East and the beginning of the Arab-Israeli peace process; and the European Security Conference (completed during the Ford Administration). Each of these events contributed to the others. Linkage was operating with a vengeance."[23] In other words, the goals that had not been possible to reach via "mere" bilateral wrangling with the Soviets were transformed into reality as the Soviets, caught unprepared by the Sino-American rapprochement, adjusted their policies in order to stay on America's good side. Dobrynin seems to confirm this view in his memoirs. "No one was more surprised and confused," he writes, "than the Kremlin when it received the news of

Nixon's plan to go to China even before he would meet Brezhnev at the summit in Moscow."[24]

While we do not have a full accounting of the Soviet response to the opening to China nor of the actual shock that it produced, the dramatic reversal implied above calls for some consideration. In particular, one needs to ask whether the shock that the sudden announcement of the "opening" undoubtedly produced could possibly have been matched by a Soviet need to suddenly reverse, or at least review, *all* its policies (as implied by Kissinger). Were the Soviets caught completely off-guard? Even if the preparations for Kissinger's trip remained secret, could the Soviets have missed such obvious signals of an impending rapprochement as Nixon's announcement of relaxation in trade restrictions and the fabled ping-pong diplomacy of the spring of 1971? If so, why did Dobrynin, who should have been in a position to at least *anticipate* a Sino-American rapprochement, not lose his clout inside the Kremlin?[25]

The key point to be made in the context of grand strategy is, simply, that the use of the "China card" did not suddenly surface on July 15, 1971, the day Nixon made a public announcement about Kissinger's secret trip and the president's upcoming visit to China. In fact, Nixon had started hinting at a possible rapprochement with China as early as 1967, Kissinger as early as 1969. While the Soviets may have become more interested in setting a firm date for the Soviet-American summit after July 15, they did not suddenly turn from stubborn stalling to meek accommodation. The Berlin agreement—a result of another series of back channel negotiations—had already been concluded by the time Kissinger traveled to China; that Kissinger had ordered the negotiations to be stalled just prior to his trip did not result in any substantial modifications on the four-power deal announced later in the fall. Nor did the China trip unlock any major problems in the way of the general agreement on SALT. The conceptual agreement of May 1971—the trade-off between limits on offensive and defensive weapons—had already been reached and announced by the time Kissinger feigned a stomachache and disappeared in Pakistan. Perhaps most significantly, the opening to China did not yield positive results on Vietnam: Soviet (as well as Chinese) aid actually increased in the second half of 1971.[26] If anything, the opening to China made it that much easier for the Soviets to maneuver themselves into a closer relationship with Hanoi's leaders.[27]

That is not to argue that the opening to China was an insignificant event. Far from it—if Kissinger and Nixon had a durable impact on the global arena, then surely it is their role in starting the long process of China's transformation from a backward and inward-looking virtual prison for 800 million people to the rapidly rising economic powerhouse we see today. Indeed, explaining the opening to China to a stunned White House staff in July 1971, Nixon put his motivations in simple terms:

> The reason why it was done is that they are one-fourth of the world's population ... They are not a military power now but 25 years from now they will be decisive ... *Where vital interests are involved, great powers consult their vital interests—or else they're played for suckers by those powers that do.*[28]

The Chinese did not quite live up to the prediction regarding their military prowess. Nonetheless, the long-term interests of the United States and the international community at large would hardly have been better served if Kissinger had never feigned a stomach ache in Pakistan before his flight to Beijing or if Nixon had not "seized the hour" and embarked on his dramatic Journey of Peace in February 1972.[29]

In the near and medium term, however, the opening to China hardly yielded as dramatic an end result as often is claimed. The new Sino-American relationship did not translate into a major diplomatic tool. After 1971, there were very few instances when the USSR practiced restraint that could be directly attributed to its concern over a "Washington-Beijing axis." Although the China factor was not inconsequential in determining American policy (usually in favor of the Chinese), it seems to have given little incentive for the USSR to act according to American desires. In some ways, it was almost the diplomatic equivalent of America's short-lived nuclear monopoly in the aftermath of World War II: the fact that the opening had taken place was important but its practical application to other contexts was extremely difficult. In short, the opening to China did change the world in the decades that followed in ways that few imagined in 1971–1972. But it did not yield the short-term strategic gains that those in Washington expected.

Whatever the actual thinking on the Soviet side, Kissinger certainly thought—or wanted everyone else to think—that he was manipulating the Soviets successfully. Indeed, when writing about the decision to embark on a secret trip to Moscow in April 1972, Kissinger remarks that the Soviets "had pressed for months for a clandestine visit, almost certainly for the simple reason that Peking had had a secret trip and they were entitled to equality."[30] In fact, both secret trips put Kissinger in an awkward and disadvantageous position. In China in 1971 he had been completely cut off from communications to the outside world and worked, effectively, under a severe time pressure, which was surely to his Chinese hosts' advantage. In Moscow the following year, with North Vietnamese troops continuing their offensive, Kissinger was caught between a president who wanted him to achieve, yet again, something substantial on Vietnam and his own desire to ensure that a summit in Moscow would take place. The Soviets, undoubtedly, took advantage of this and simply offered to Kissinger during the first day of meetings that they would pass the latest U.S. proposals to Hanoi. In return, Kissinger dropped the issue of Vietnam and focused on the various agreements to be concluded during the Moscow Summit. While the Soviets' willingness to hold the summit despite the subsequent bombing and mining campaign may have indicated that Vietnam was not at the top of Moscow's priorities, Kissinger's eagerness to avoid an extensive discussion over the Spring Offensive probably indicated to Brezhnev and other Soviet leaders that Southeast Asia was no longer such a central issue it had been in 1969. Thus despite later posturing that Nixon's toughness—his decision to go ahead with the Linebacker I mining-bombing campaign on the eve of the Moscow Summit—made it possible for the United States to achieve a double feat (summit plus halting the North Vietnamese offensive), the Brezhnev Politburo was not really presented with such a stark choice. Instead, Kissinger's willingness to engage in detailed discussions over bilateral Soviet-American issues during his visit to Moscow was an indication of the American willingness to "rescue" the summit and minimize the linkage between Vietnam and détente.[31] That, though, was nothing new.

On July 23, 1969, Nixon and his entourage embarked on a trip through a number of Asian countries (including the Philippines, South Vietnam, and Thailand) as well as Romania. The trip's highlight was an unexpected one. In an informal press conference on Guam on the evening of July 25, 1969, Nixon articulated what would soon be dubbed the Nixon Doctrine. In essence, he affirmed three points. First, the United States would keep its treaty commitments to allied nations in the Far East (for example, to those countries that belonged to the Southeast Treaty Organization, SEATO). Second, the president reaffirmed that the United States continued to provide a nuclear shield to its allies as well as to governments that were considered necessary to American national security. Third, Nixon said that in the future, when friendly governments were under a military threat, the United States "is going to encourage and has the right to expect that the responsibility" for these countries defense "be handled by Asian nations themselves."[32]

Although the forum where Nixon announced his doctrine was unexpected, the basic idea—that the United States would not get involved in another Vietnam-like situation—was not new. In many of his writings over the past few years, Kissinger had spoken about the need "to encourage a sense of local responsibility." A week before Nixon's pronouncements, Kissinger had said during his press briefing ("on background," as was customary) that in the future the United States, while keen "to participate" in the defense of its Asian allies, "cannot supply all the conceptions and all the resources." Nixon, for his part, would refer to his doctrine in an address to the United Nations General Assembly in September 1969. Finally, in early November 1969 Nixon would outline the doctrine as "a policy which not only will help end the war in Vietnam, but which is an essential element of our program to prevent future Vietnams." He also further clarified the third point of original formulation as follows: "we shall furnish military and economic assistance when requested in accordance with our treaty commitments. But we shall look to the nation directly threatened to assume the primary responsibility of providing the manpower for its defense." These words would also be found in the administration's first Foreign Policy Report—authored by Kissinger's NSC staff—that was published in February 1970.[33]

The Nixon Doctrine was, at one level, simply the public extension of the policy of Vietnamization. As he planned to do in Vietnam, Nixon would limit direct American involvement in military conflicts and focus American efforts to providing material assistance. Indeed, the announcement coincided with the first troop withdrawals from South Vietnam. Considered more broadly, however, the Nixon Doctrine had a more far-reaching significance. It quickly became considered a global, rather than a purely Asian doctrine. And the flip side of the Nixon Doctrine's affirmation of support for friendly governments that were involved in a war (such as South Vietnam) was the presumption that one could, if acting properly, preempt Vietnam-like situations from arising in the first place. In practice this meant that the Nixon administration would provide strong military assistance to regional powers that would act as the guarantors of stability in their specific corners of the globe. Over the next few years, for example, this would translate to American support to the Shah of Iran. In fact, the Shah himself quickly made the most of the Nixon Doctrine. By 1972, when Nixon visited Iran on his way back home from the Moscow Summit, the Iranian-American special relationship was cemented. Stability, though, remained an elusive quest in the region.[34]

In short, the Nixon Doctrine was both part of the strategy of ending the Vietnam War and a key ingredient in Nixon and Kissinger's global architecture of limiting direct American commitments in disparate regions while retaining Washington's indirect influence. In fact, aside from its obvious application to the third world, the Nixon Doctrine essentially summed up the basic rationale behind an American global strategy that could be seen in, say, the administration's efforts to revamp the transatlantic alliance by emphasizing burden-sharing without seriously contemplating power/decision-sharing.[35]

In the summer of 1969, the Nixon Doctrine was the final opening move in the administration's foreign policy architecture. Along with the Kissinger-Dobrynin back channel, the effort to pressure the North Vietnamese via the bombing of Cambodia and the first halting moves toward China set the stage for the policies that would culminate in 1972–1973. But in a few years' time, certainly by 1976, the edifice of Nixon (already out of office due to Watergate) and Kissinger's structure of peace was under relentless attack at home and abroad. They had built a flimsy cardboard castle that could not be kept standing if a slightest tremor shook the table it rested on. This was not necessarily because of the lack of a grand strategy or a grand design. Rather, the design itself was flawed.

When they came into office, Kissinger and Nixon wanted to assure that, as in previous decades, the United States played a central role in international affairs. However, given that this role was, at the time, being challenged from numerous directions, new strategies were needed. As Kissinger himself later put it, the task facing the new administration was vast indeed: "Simultaneously we had to end a war, manage a global rivalry with the Soviet Union in the shadow of nuclear weapons, reinvigorate our alliance with industrial democracies, and integrate the new nations into a new world equilibrium."[36]

Few could have disagreed with the necessity to acknowledge the limits of American power—so evident in light of the Vietnam War—and to embark on creative new approaches to the United States' main adversary, the Soviet Union. Subsequent breakthroughs with the People's Republic of China and the USSR represented crucially important, not incidental, developments in the history of international relations. Indeed, by 1973, when the October War in the Middle East erupted, the use of American military power was replaced by the use of (at times coercive) American diplomatic power as the key to a peace agreement that managed to enhance U.S. influence in that part of the world. Indeed, Nixon and Kissinger's recognition of the limits of American power was a healthy departure from previous administrations' overextension.

To be sure, there were flaws. The overall emphasis on the "great powers" blinded Nixon and Kissinger to the specific local circumstances that determined the course of the numerous regional conflicts the administration encountered. More specifically, Kissinger's efforts in China, Vietnam, Angola, the Middle East, South Asia, and Europe were all calculated within the context of the U.S. relationship and rivalry with the Soviet Union. His policies—hardly surprisingly—simply reflected the Cold War logic so prevalent in Washington at the time. While the means for pursuing the long twilight struggle were less militaristic and more diplomatic, the end goals of the struggle had hardly changed. In 1969 and the years that followed, many in the United States spoke about a new grand strategy, overseen by Nixon and implemented by Kissinger. In reality, what the two men provided was an elaborate set of new tactics based on well-worn goals and assumptions.

There were several new approaches to friend and foe, as *Time* magazine had predicted in early 1969. But while tactics had changed, the overall strategy and goals of American foreign policy remained much the same as in the two decades preceding Nixon's inauguration.

Notes

1. *Time*, "Presidential Adviser Kissinger: New Approaches to Friend and Foe," February 14, 1969.
2. For historiographical essays, see Robert D. Schulzinger, "Complaints, Self-Justifications, and Analysis: The Historiography of American Foreign Relations Since 1969," in *America in the World: The Historiography of American Foreign Relations since 1941*, ed. Michael J. Hogan (New York, 1995), 395–423; Jussi M. Hanhimäki, "'Dr. Kissinger' or 'Mr. Henry'? Kissingerology, Thirty Years and Counting," *Diplomatic History* 27 (November 2003): 637–676; William Burr, ed., *Kissinger Transcripts: the Top-Secret Talks with Beijing and Moscow* (New York, 1999), 1–26.
3. This well-known history is discussed extensively in Robert Dallek, *Nixon and Kissinger: Partners in Power* (New York, 2007), 60–86.
4. Cited in Jussi Hanhimäki, *The Flawed Architect: Henry Kissinger and American Foreign Policy* (New York, 2004), 22. The most recent treatment of Kissinger's background, focusing particularly on his Jewishness, is Jeremi Suri, *Henry Kissinger and the American Century* (Cambridge, Mass., 2007).
5. Joan Hoff, *Nixon Reconsidered* (New York, 1994), 150.
6. Peter Rodman interview, May 22, 1994, Association for Diplomatic Studies Oral History Collection, Georgetown University.
7. For Kissinger's rise as a public intellectual see Suri, *Kissinger and the American Century*.
8. Rodman interview; Kissinger interview with the author, June 2003.

9. Address by Richard M. Nixon to the Bohemian Club, San Francisco, July 29, 1967, *FRUS, 1969–76*, vol. I: 2–3.

10. Ibid.

11. Nixon's inaugural address, January 20, 1969, in editorial note, ibid., 53–54.

12. Henry A. Kissinger, *American Foreign Policy: Three Essays* (New York, 1969), 52.

13. Ibid.

14. Henry Kissinger, *White House Years* (Boston, 1979), 70.

15. Vojtech Mastny, "The New History of Cold War Alliances," *Journal of Cold War Studies* 4 (Spring 2002): 77.

16. For an interesting set of documents on the Nixon administration's relationship with Afghanistan see the NSA website, http://www.gwu. edu/~nsarchiv/

17. The most exhaustive study dealing with Soviet-American détente remains Raymond Garthoff *Détente and Confrontation: Soviet-American Relations from Nixon to Reagan*, rev. ed. (Washington, D.C., 1994). In addition to the sources cited above, other useful works include Robin Edmonds, *Soviet Foreign Policy: The Brezhnev Years* (Oxford, 1983); Michael B. Froman, *The Development of the Idea of Détente: Coming to Terms* (New York, 1991); Joan Hoff, *Nixon Reconsidered* (New York, 1994); Keith Nelson, *The Making of Détente: Soviet-American Relations in the Shadow of Vietnam* (Baltimore, 1995); Franz Schurman, *The Foreign Politics of Richard Nixon: The Grand Design* (Berkeley, 1986); Richard Thornton, *The Nixon-Kissinger Years: The Reshaping of American Foreign Policy* (New York, 1989); and Adam B. Ulam, *Dangerous Relations: The Soviet Union in World Politics* (Oxford, 1983). See also Jussi M. Hanhimäki, "Ironies and Turning Points: Détente in Perspective," in *Reviewing the Cold War: Approaches, Interpretations, Theory*, ed. Odd Arne Westad (London, 2000), 326–342.

18. Kissinger, *White House Years*, 143–144.

19. Andreas Wenger and Jeremi Suri, "At the Crossroads of Diplomatic and Social History: The Nuclear Revolution, Dissent and Détente," *Cold War History* 1 (April 2001): 1–42; Jeremi Suri, *Power and Protest: Global Revolution and the Rise of Détente* (Cambridge, Mass., 2003).

20. There is no need here to recount the "coup d'etat" that placed much of foreign policy decision making in Kissinger's (and Nixon's) hands. Readers could consult, for example, Dallek, *Nixon and Kissinger*, 60–104; Hanhimäki, *Flawed Architect*, 17–32; Walter Isaacson, *Kissinger: A Biography* (New York, 1992), 151–156; or Robert D. Schulzinger, *Henry Kissinger: Doctor of Diplomacy* (New York, 1989), 23–28.

21. Memcon, Nixon, Kissinger, Toon, and Dobrynin, February 17, 1969, NSC Subject Files, Box 340: "USSR Memcons Dobrynin/President," NPMP.

22. On the various aspects of the German question, see Timothy Garton Ash, *In Europe's Name: Germany and the Divided Continent* (New York, 1993); A. James McAdams, *Germany Divided: From the Wall to Reunification*

(Princeton, 1993); idem, "The New Diplomacy of the West German Ostpolitik," in *The Diplomats, 1939–79*, ed. Gordon A. Craig and Francis L. Loewenheim (Princeton, 1994), 537–563; Mary E. Sarotte, *Dealing with the Devil: East Germany, Detente, and Ostpolitik, 1969–1973* (Chapel Hill, NC, 2001); and Michael Ploetz, *Wie die Sowjetunion den Kalten Krieg verlor: Von der Nachrustung zum Mauerfalt* (Berlin, 2000). For documentation on the SALT talks, see *FRUS, 1969–1976*, vols. XII, XIII, and XIV. These can be accessed at www.state.gov/r/pa/ho/frus/nixon/

23. Henry Kissinger, *Diplomacy* (New York, 1994), 733.

24. Anatoly Dobrynin, *In Confidence* (New York, 1995), 225.

25. This is something that Dobrynin himself fails to address in his memoirs, writing simply that "No one more surprised and confused than the Kremlin when it received the news of Nixon's plan to go to China even before, as it finally turned out, he would meet Brezhnev at the summit in Moscow." Dobrynin, *In Confidence*, 225. On the Pakistani channel, see F. S. Aijazuddin, *From a Head, Through a Head, to a Head: The Secret Channel Between the US and China Through Pakistan* (Karachi, 2000).

26. Hanhimäki, *Flawed Architect*, esp. chapters 10 and 11.

27. One point to note is that in July 1971 the Chinese expressed no particular rush to have Nixon visit Beijing prior to his trip to Moscow. As Zhou put it to Kissinger, it "would be best for President Nixon and the Soviet Union to meet before President Nixon visits China." Kissinger's summary of July 10, 1971 meeting with Zhou, "China visit: Record of previous meetings," Country Files: Far East, Box 90, Kissinger Office Files, NSC Files, NPMP. For the SALT talks, see Garthoff, *Détente and Confrontation*, 146–226.

28. Memorandum for the President's Files, "Briefing of the White House Staff on the July 15 Announcement of the President's Trip to Peking," 19 July, 1971, at http://www.gwu.edu/%7Ensarchiv/NSAEBB/NSAEBB66/ch-41.pdf

29. On Nixon's visit, the best available account is Margaret MacMillan, *Nixon and Mao: The Week that Changed the World* (New York, 2007). See also the essays in Robert Accinelli, ed., *Normalization of U.S.-China Relations: An International History* (Cambridge, Mass., 2006).

30. Kissinger, *White House Years*, 1124.

31. What the Soviets simply agreed to do is pass on the latest American proposals to the Vietnamese and act as a middle-man for a planned Kissinger-Le Duc Tho meeting in Paris prior to the Moscow summit. This meeting, on May 2, achieved nothing and was followed by the escalation of American bombing campaign and the mining of Haiphong harbor. Kissinger's Moscow conversations can be found in "HAK Moscow Trip—April 1972 memcons," Box 72, Country Files: Europe/USSR, HAK Office Files, NSC Files, NPMP.

32. On the Nixon Doctrine, see Jeffrey Kimball, "The Nixon Doctrine: A Saga of Misunderstanding," *Presidential Studies Quarterly* 36 (March 2006): 59–74.

33. Ibid.; Dallek, *Nixon and Kissinger*, 143–144; Isaacson, *Kissinger*, 239–242; Kissinger, *White House Years*, 222–224.

34. See, for example, Kenneth Pollack, *The Persian Puzzle: The Conflict Between Iran and America* (New York, 2005).

35. On this point see, for example, Geir Lundestad, *United States and Western Europe: From "Empire" by Invitation to Transatlantic Drift* (Oxford, 2005), chapter 5.

36. Kissinger, *White House Years*, 69–70.

2

Nixon as Statesman: The Failed Campaign

David Greenberg

It wasn't supposed to turn out this way, at least not as far as Richard Nixon was concerned. From his days as a precocious young California congressman through his terms as Dwight Eisenhower's vice president to his two presidential bids, Nixon had sought to build a legacy for himself based on historic achievements in foreign policy. Over the years he built up an idealized image of himself as a Great Man of History whose command of statecraft would place him among world-straddling giants like Winston Churchill, Charles de Gaulle, and Mao Zedong. His deeds, he imagined, would shape the destiny of nations, bring about peace, and redound to his glory.

It was not to be. To be sure, Nixon earned high marks for his diplomacy as president, particularly with China and the Soviet Union. An influential cohort of Cold War pundits—sober men like Theodore H. White, Hugh Sidey, and Joseph and Stewart Alsop, many of whom had little love for Nixon personally—limned a portrait of him in the popular mind as a master of global affairs. Nixon's friend Clare Boothe Luce predicted that his legacy would be summarized with the single sentence, "He went to China."[1] And by the time of his death in 1994, his foreign policy achievements had earned recognition as a major feature of his presidency, making Luce's prophecy seem plausible, albeit not quite fulfilled.

But in the end Nixon's foreign policy always remained secondary in the accountings of his life and career. The problem was not simply that his national security adviser (and, as of 1973, secretary of state) Henry Kissinger managed to win—unfairly, in many historians' eyes—much of the credit for Nixon's feats. More fundamentally, Nixon's diplomacy was never able to eclipse or mitigate the central element of his presidency, which was Watergate, with all the assorted and sordid meanings that the term implies. Far graver than the "third-rate burglary" that his press secretary Ron Zeigler asserted it to be, Watergate encompassed a welter of constitutional crimes and their cover-ups: burglaries and wiretaps and enemies lists and other abuses of executive power. Watergate was more than the sum of these parts. It was the consummate expression of Nixon's character and view of the world, rooted in his belief that he was entitled to violate established constraints—political, legal, ethical, moral—to promote his own advancement. In policy as in politics, Nixon favored expedience over principle, deviousness over sincerity, secrecy over candor; and the ends that he felt justified these means were, in the final analysis, nothing grander than those of winning—winning elections, winning laurels in the press, and winning a chapter in the history books as a peacemaker and statesman.

In short, the traits within Nixon that culminated in Watergate impressed themselves on everything he did, at home and on the world stage. To understand his foreign policy, one has to understand the man who brought us Watergate.

The fact that Nixon held nothing sacred did violence to his integrity, in the literal sense that his moral functioning never matured. But Nixon's opportunism also vitiated his integrity in another sense of the word: it kept him from becoming a complete, stable human being. Identity for Nixon was, like so much else, disposable, utilitarian. Described as a chameleon and a kaleidoscope, a Rorschach test and a hollow man, an empty vessel and empty shell, an enigma and a shadow, Nixon lacked a firm conception of self. During his half-century in public life he displayed to the public a multiplicity of different faces as the situation demanded. When one persona ceased to sustain his popularity, he adopted another.

As early as the 1950s, observers noted this penchant for reinvention. It gave rise to the curious concept of the "New Nixon." Most often, the term meant a softer Nixon, one who had renounced the below-the-belt campaigning and McCarthyite tactics of his early career. "We have found ourselves," editorialized the Montgomery, Alabama *Advertiser*, in 1953, after having panned his "Checkers" speech a year earlier, "dissolving our previous conception ... the New Nixon rejoices us."[2] The *Advertiser*'s use of the term, apparently the first on record, gave rise to others. Most conveyed doubt that Nixon's professed metamorphoses were genuine. "We keep hearing of a 'new Nixon' and an 'old Nixon'," warned Adlai Stevenson, the Democratic presidential nominee in 1956. "There is no man who can safely say he knows where the vice president stands. This is a man of many masks. Who can say they have seen his real face?"[3]

Stevenson's critique underscored the deeper connotations of the phrase "New Nixon." It captured fears about Nixon's capacity for secrecy and deception—fears, already widespread by the mid-1950s, that he would unhesitatingly mislead the public, even about his core convictions, to serve his private ends. More subtly, the view of Nixon as a man behind a mask implied an inauthenticity, a hollowness at the core. The *Washington Post*'s "Herblock" caught the idea in a 1956 cartoon that showed Nixon choosing from a closetful of political costumes to wear: Nixon donned his garb for the sake of advantage. The phrase "New Nixon" thus came to mean any one of the profusion of his readily donned public identities.[4]

Which of these selves did Nixon believe in? At bottom, he probably saw himself as the scrappy, hard-luck kid who grew up with financial uncertainty and suffered the death of two brothers. Unlike the golden boys who emerged as his foils or rivals—Alger Hiss, Nelson Rockefeller, John F. Kennedy—Nixon felt that he scraped for everything he earned and thus could more faithfully represent the industrious, middle-class families in whose name he spoke. From his first congressional campaign in 1946 through his invocations of the "silent majority" as president, Nixon styled himself the tribune of Middle America.

In moments of self-reflection, however, Nixon could admit that darker impulses moved him. He knew that the portrait of "Tricky Dick," while a caricature proffered by liberal enemies, contained more than a few grains of truth. His White House tapes capture him indulging his basest emotions— saying, for example, that while he could find a staffer to go after an adversary "honorably, I really need a son of a bitch ... who will work his butt off and do it dishonorably."[5] This was not the language of someone led astray by good intentions. Nixon grasped, too, that his bloodthirstiness stemmed from a consuming concern with reputation, from a desperation to gain glory. Indeed, his efforts to craft his public image bordered on self-parody. Once, Nixon told his chief of staff, H. R. Haldeman, that he needed a full-time adviser to coach him on "how I should stand, where the cameras will be," even "whether I should [hold] the phone with my right hand or my left hand." Given "the millions of dollars that go into one lousy thirty-second television spot advertising a deodorant," he wrote in a memo, it was "unbelievable" that his own image didn't receive equal attention.[6]

If Tricky Dick was something like Nixon's id, and the populist paragon of Middle American values was something like his ego, then his superego— the ideal he wished to be—took the form of the world-historic visionary. Believing that men attained greatness not through domestic governance but through leadership in global affairs, Nixon fancied himself a solitary prophet, tapped for leadership, endowed with uncommon skills to engineer world peace. In memos to himself about the image he wished to project, he described himself as a heavyweight who grappled with momentous issues of war and peace, not the filigree of domestic policy-making. The country, Nixon said in 1967 to Theodore H. White, the journalist whose *Making of the President* books had garnered him stature and continued White House access, "could run itself domestically without a president.... All you need is a competent cabinet to run the country at home ... The president makes foreign policy."[7] He scorned Congress, which he described in his memoirs as "cumbersome, undisciplined, isolationist, fiscally irresponsible, overly vulnerable to pressures from organized minorities, and too dominated by the media"—a zoo of narrow-minded Lilliputians who would tie him down and keep him from realizing his grand designs.[8] He made decisions alone, he insisted. "You listen to everybody's argument, but then comes the moment of truth," he told an interviewer in 1970. "I sit alone with my yellow pad," he explained, before making a determination, thinking through the arguments and summoning the judgment born of his experience.[9]

Nixon's view of himself as a high-minded foreign policy adept contained an elitism at odds with both his vindictive side and his everyman persona. Yet the different Nixons complemented one another even as they conflicted. Nixon loathed the Eastern Establishment precisely because he wanted into their club so badly and believed that proving his foreign policy chops would gain him entry. Similarly, his shame about his commonness and his pettiness drove him to distinguish himself from the pack; as often as he hearkened back to his humble roots, he aspired to transcend them. Nixon once said that if he hadn't been a politician, he would have been an Oxford don. The comment made his critics chuckle, but it fit with his favored self-conception. An awkward loner who spent his leisure time sitting in silence with his best friend, Bebe Rebozo, Nixon could imagine himself toiling in the solitude of scholarship, reading and writing weighty tomes. In his post-resignation years, credulous visitors purred over the works of philosophy and history that lined his shelves. Notably, though, the books he flaunted—the works of Tolstoy, biographies of Napoleon and Churchill—weren't the books that intellectuals were reading in the 1980s or 1990s. They were tokens of the stereotype of an intellectual, circa 1955.

Perhaps the most concise way of understanding Nixon's ego ideal is to know that his favorite president was Woodrow Wilson—and not because he was a liberal or a Democrat. Rather, Nixon identified with his predecessor, as

Garry Wills observed long ago, as "a lonely misunderstood leader, ... an intro-spective intellectual somewhat out of place in the glad-handing world of politics."[10] Committed to making diplomacy and peace his signature issues, Nixon went so far as to echo Wilson in promising that Vietnam would be a war to end all wars. (He even used what he believed to have been Wilson's White House desk.) Retaining this Wilsonian self-conception allowed Nixon to flatter and console himself—to hold out hope, even after his disgrace, that history would honor him for his achievements on the world stage.

Nixon's peacemaker self-image was forged in childhood. His mother, Hannah Milhous—quiet, modest, self-possessed—impressed on her son high standards of moral aspiration. Where her short-tempered husband, Frank Nixon, delivered blows of what his fearful son called "the strap,"[11] Richard's mother was a committed Quaker who imparted discipline through a stern, censorious air. Inclined to withhold approval from her son, she administered "silent punishment" that Nixon recalled as worse than his father's physical abuse. She would, he remembered, "just sit you down and she would talk very quietly ... when you got through, you had been through an emotional experience."[12] Yet he always called her a "saint," imputing to her a righteous-ness that he could never match.

Nixon said his biographers didn't recognize the full impact of his mother's Quaker heritage on his personality. Her Quakerism, it is often forgotten, dif-fered from the Eastern, egalitarian variety most Americans know. Imported to Southern California by Indiana Friends who were influenced by itinerant revivalists, the religious style of Southland Quakers was fervent, emotional, and deferent to church authority. Thus, while pacifistic, Hannah's religion was also strict and moralistic. Her admonitions instilled in her son a wish to gain her approval by making his name as a man of peace. As Nixon achieved renown, many commentators found it hard to believe that this polarizing, frequently vicious, and seemingly amoral creature subscribed to any Quaker tenets at all. But rather than hypocrisy, it is more fruitful to regard Nixon's peacemaking instincts as an ideal inherited from his mother about which he was long ambivalent—scorning them when his uglier impulses consumed him (as they often did), elevating them in calmer moments as an ideal. Once in the 1950s, when he physically restrained Senator Joe McCarthy from beat-ing up the journalist Drew Pearson, Nixon was heard to say, "Let a Quaker stop this fight."[13] His mother's religion was the asylum of his nature's better angels.

Soon after Nixon entered Congress, his wish to be a peacemaker joined itself to a serious interest in foreign policy. In 1947, his first year in the

House, he toured Europe with a caravan led by Massachusetts Representative Christian Herter (later Eisenhower's secretary of state), and the experience confirmed him as an internationalist determined to bury the Republican party's isolationist past. When the Old Right, led by Ohio Senator Robert Taft, assailed President Truman's 1950 decision to send American troops to help South Korea fend off the North Korean attack, Nixon defied his partisan instincts to support the Democratic president, though he also charged scurrilously that Truman's equivocal policies toward Soviet communism had invited the North Korean incursion. Such a double game—bashing liberals as soft and unpatriotic while claiming the centrist ground of international-ism—would be a favorite tactic of Nixon's throughout his career.

As vice president, Nixon bolstered his internationalist credentials. He frequently traveled overseas, immersing himself in foreign policy more than all but a few vice presidents before him. In 1958, he faced down crowds of jeering anti-American protesters in Venezuela and Peru, including a mob at the Caracas airport that pelted him with stones, and he returned a conquering hero. He further gained in stature after going toe to toe with Soviet leader Nikita Khrushchev in an exhibition of an American kitchen in Moscow; the performance gave Americans confidence in Nixon's capacity for Cold War brinksmanship. When he ran for president in 1960, he made his international experience the cornerstone of his campaign.

Well before his presidency, then, Nixon had successfully defined himself as a statesman. The cultivation of the image was a political strategy as much as an outgrowth of interest—implemented through public relations and aimed at supplanting his old hatchet-man persona. But because Nixon was never terribly deft at donning his different guises, his junior diplomat pose struck many observers as contrived or disingenuous—another costume from the closet. "Foremost among the roles that Nixon has consciously assumed is that of statesman-companion to the great," wrote Meg Greenfield of *The Reporter* in 1960. She mocked Nixon's "laundry-list approach" of rattling off the countries he visited and his clumsy name-dropping ("As Mr. Castro told me ...").[14] Nixon's jet-setting brought him, on this view, not only wisdom about world affairs, but also frequent-flyer points that he would later redeem for the prize of respect from the Establishment.

After Nixon lost the 1960 presidential race and his 1962 race for governor of California, his career stalled. Yet in these so-called wilderness years, he again journeyed abroad, opined on foreign policy, and persuaded key observers of his expertise in world affairs. Newspapers generously quoted him on international developments, including the escalating war in Vietnam.

(Nixon blasted Lyndon Johnson for not sending more American troops.) By 1968, when he was again seeking the White House, Nixon had woven his emerging statesman identity into the latest "New Nixon" incarnation. As a seasoned veteran, the candidate suggested, he would best be able to superintend the Vietnam War and the coming international crises. He won converts of such skeptics as Teddy White, the longtime columnist Walter Lippmann, and even the radical novelist and convention chronicler Norman Mailer, who discovered in Nixon "the sure, modest moves of an old shortstop ... His modesty was not without real dignity."[15]

As president, Nixon tried to bring his statesman image to fruition. In this effort, public relations and political hardball ranked with diplomacy and statecraft as his chief tools, and understanding his foreign policy in general requires constantly keeping in view Nixon's political machinations. For example, in 1969, to counter a forthcoming Brookings Institute report that he expected to criticize him, Nixon asked for a National Security Study Memorandum that would extol his "approach to major foreign policy issues." A year later, he instructed Kissinger to work up "a plan for the more effective presentation of our accomplishments in Foreign Affairs." As Haldeman summed it up: "The President should become known next year as 'Mr. Peace.'" Even in 1972, when other presidents would have been basking in the glowing coverage Nixon was getting for his initiatives with China and the Soviet Union, he could only complain to Haldeman: "We've had the most brilliant foreign policy in this century, but we've sold it the worst."[16]

The actual merits of Nixon's foreign policy remain in dispute. Yet however one ultimately evaluates the costs and benefits of Nixon's policies—or whether one thinks their costs and benefits can be quantified or tallied at all—it's clear that what runs through them all is a thread of cynicism, expedience, and heedlessness. Indeed, Nixon's foreign policy is characterized above all by an irony: so great was his desire to fulfill an idealized self-image that would endure for posterity that his foreign policy—which was supposed to be the shining expression of that better self—became itself tainted by the very means he used to attain the image.

When Nixon took office in January 1969, ending the Vietnam War was the first order of business. In the preceding year, as turbulent as any since World War II, Nixon had squeaked out an election victory over Vice President Hubert Humphrey on a pledge to achieve "peace with honor" in Indochina, and in his inaugural address the new president gave reason to believe he would deliver. After boasting of having "visited most of the nations of the world" and having "come to know the leaders of the world, and the great forces, the hatreds, the fears that divide the world," Nixon vowed to bind up America's wounds and to "consecrate my office, my energies, and all the wisdom I can summon, to the cause of peace among nations." Peace in Vietnam seemed imminent.[17]

Bringing harmony to Vietnam may have been an impossible task, but ending American involvement in the war need not have been hard. Nixon, however, shuddered at the thought of becoming what he often called "the first American President to lose a war."[18] Concerned also about losing favor among conservatives, Nixon refused to pull out rapidly or even, for the first years of his term, to make concessions that went much beyond those Lyndon Johnson had offered. At the same time, however, he wanted to placate a public that, as the death toll climbed, was growing intolerant of any American presence in Indochina. Faced with this dilemma, Nixon tried to have it both ways: reducing U.S. troop levels to calm the home front while maintaining the commitment to prop up the South Vietnam government.

Nixon focused first on quieting foes of the war. Months into his presidency, after an unexpected but brief honeymoon, he was confronting a surge of the same restiveness that had driven Johnson from office. Starting in June 1969, the moderate Vietnam Moratorium Committee brought into the doves' coalition a cross section of the public far broader than the usual core of students and dedicated activists. In October, the Moratorium staged rallies across the country that added up to the largest protest in American history—and the next month it united with the more radical New Mobilization Committee to End the War in Vietnam to pull off an even bigger set of demonstrations. Nixon now seemed to have no alternative but to end the war.

Instead, however, the president undertook a sweeping campaign to beat back his domestic opposition so that he could continue—and perhaps win—the war. Some moves were rooted in his policy of "Vietnamization," which replaced U.S. troops with South Vietnamese fighters. That policy, along with the decision to end the military draft in favor of a volunteer force, helped appease those who mainly wanted to stop the terrible loss of American life. Beyond these moves, the president also sought to undermine the peace movement directly, with tactics ranging from rhetoric and public relations to outright criminality. Starting with a prime-time address on November 3, 1969, he strove to rally to what he called "the great silent majority of Americans" who supported his course of action, while simultaneously maligning antiwar activists—claiming, for example, that their protests prolonged the war (an argument akin to suggesting that the civil rights movement perpetuated segregation). While the "Silent Majority" speech resonated with much of the public, Nixon took no chances, rigging the reaction to his performance with a secret campaign to drum up supportive letters and telegrams—a classic Nixonian effort of fake grass-roots or "astroturf" support. Nixon also aggressively assailed the news media, whose discouraging reports from Vietnam and increasingly skeptical commentary he held responsible for the flagging public resolve.[19] "The news broadcasters are, of course, trying to kill us," he groused to Kissinger.[20] Seeking to discredit the leading journalistic outlets or browbeat them into rendering more favorable coverage, he obsessively targeted journalists, subjecting them to verbal abuse, wiretaps, IRS audits, and other exertions of presidential power.

Behind the scenes Nixon, Kissinger, and other top administration officials worked to tar antiwar leaders in a similarly nefarious fashion. Under the phony justification of national security, they illegally wiretapped innocent Americans, spied on and disrupted dissenting groups, and hired thugs to violently assault peace protesters. Perhaps most ominously, they created the White House Plumbers Unit—some of whose members were later caught breaking into the Democratic National Headquarters on June 17, 1972—for the purpose of digging up dirt on Nixon's domestic enemies; besides the Watergate burglaries, their most infamous act came in September 1971, when, on Nixon's orders, they ransacked the office of Lewis Fielding, psychiatrist to Daniel Ellsberg, who had leaked to the *New York Times* the Pentagon Papers study of American Vietnam policy.[21] These actions showed Nixon at his most vindictive and petty—Tricky Dick bursting forth from behind the guise of statesman. When the American massacre of Vietnamese civilians at My Lai was made public in 1969, for example, Nixon erupted in rage at unspecified "dirty rotten Jews from New York" and ordered "dirty tricks" against Ron Ridenhour, the soldier who first told of the killings, and Seymour Hersh, the journalist who reported them. In this sense Nixon's Vietnam strategy was the seedbed of Watergate. "Without the Vietnam War," Haldeman later concluded, "there would have been no Watergate."[22]

Coupled with the failure to bring peace, Nixon's abuses of power extended and heightened the domestic strife that he had promised to heal. And while Vietnamization and the end of the draft dampened some antiwar fervor, to others Nixon's changes were merely cosmetic. The most blasé among them charged that Vietnamization was just a way to "change the color of the bodies."[23] Others believed the policy a fig leaf for a U.S. defeat. But many Americans, though they still sat out the rallies, began telling pollsters that they considered the war a mistake and wanted it to end. For them, as Kissinger came to see, Vietnamization was "like salted peanuts ... The more U.S. troops come home, the more will be demanded."[24] For despite Nixon's gestures toward peace, other actions that intensified the American involvement—expanding the war into Cambodia, strafing North Vietnam, mining Haiphong Harbor—revealed the president's determination to pursue military intimidation as his strategy for victory. By the end of his first term, then, Nixon had created a silent majority in reverse: a majority that silently *opposed* his policies.

In January 1973, after he was safely reelected, Nixon finally agreed to a peace deal with both North and South Vietnam, thus ending America's longest war with its first unambiguous defeat. Relief, not celebration, greeted the news—much to irritation of the president, who was hoping, he said, for "the sort of excitement that followed V-J day."[25] The terms of settlement differed little from those Nixon could have reached near the start of his presidency. In the meantime, despite Vietnamization, almost as many Americans died in battle (more than 20,000) as during the previous decade of involvement. Domestic strife festered, deception and secrecy proliferated, and the White House plunged headlong into illegality. Topping it off, Nixon made no provision to prevent North Vietnam from overrunning the South after the American withdrawal. He wanted to ensure only that what Kissinger dubbed "a decent interval" would elapse before the South's collapse. When that collapse came, in April 1975, the frantic American evacuation of Saigon redoubled the painful feeling that all the years of bloodshed had been futile. Concluded Kissinger: "We should never have been there at all."[26]

If dishonesty and vindictiveness marred Nixon's Vietnam policy, frustrating his dreams of greatness, he had little trouble amassing credit in other realms of foreign policy, despite a similar modus operandi. In his own day and afterward, Nixon's China and Russia policies in particular enjoyed continued favor, even though in executing them he was moved by a similar monomania about his public standing and given to the same secretive stratagems that had made his handling of Vietnam such a disaster. But there was a logic to this achievement, too, for successful diplomacy hinges, in no small part, on the successful manipulation of images and perceptions.

The chief exhibit in Nixon's case for his own excellence was his overture to China to reopen diplomatic ties. Those ties had been severed since Mao's Communists took power in 1949. Never an isolationist, Nixon concluded as early as 1961 that a rapprochement with China would serve America's interest. In 1967, with the help of his speechwriter Ray Price, he wrote an article for *Foreign Affairs* entitled "Asia After Viet Nam" that argued for ending China's isolation from "the family of nations," lest it "nurture its fantasies ... and threaten its neighbors." Eyeing the developing rifts between China and the USSR, Nixon also saw a chance to bolster America's global position and, not incidentally, his own.[27]

Once in office, Nixon reached out to the Chinese through intermediaries in Romania and Pakistan. After receiving signals that Mao was ready to talk he secretly sent Kissinger to Beijing in July 1971. To escape scrutiny from the press, the national security adviser feigned stomach pains while in Pakistan, allowing him to hurry off to meet Zhou Enlai. Days later the president dramatically revealed the mission in a televised address from Burbank, California, announcing that he would go to China the next year. The speech, recalled White House reporter Helen Thomas, who covered it, "made the room rock." The nation was stunned and excited. The press corps showered Nixon with praise.[28]

Nixon's China breakthrough touched off an infectious giddiness. Labeling the venture "Nixon's Coup," *Time* endorsed Kissinger's claim that the administration was "turning a new page in history" and lauded the national security adviser. Its account of Nixon's post-speech banquet lingered so adoringly over the minutiae—the dinner at "Perino's, a fashionable Los Angeles restaurant," the "$40 bottle of Château Lafite Rothschild (1961)"—that one might have guessed the magazine's food writer had penned the piece. *Newsweek* likewise judged the move a "masterstroke."[29]

Over the next six months Nixon and Kissinger laid the groundwork for a historic visit. They acceded in the United Nations' decision to admit China (while privately fuming over its expulsion of Taiwan), and meticulously arranged Nixon's pending February visit. Characteristically, the president dwelled on burnishing his statesman veneer for the 1972 campaign. Even in 1971, Nixon and Haldeman had sought to time their various initiatives for maximal benefit. Haldeman noted that Nixon wanted "the Vietnam thing settled this summer, have a [U.S.-Soviet] Summit this fall, and wrap up the first SALT agreement; announce a China visit and have it in March or so of next year."[30] Once the China trip became public, Nixon, exhibiting what Kissinger called Nixon's "monomaniacal obsession ... with public relations," directed his adviser to work with the White House staff in painting the initiative as a triumph of Nixon's personal leadership skills. The president himself pored over the details of the press coverage he hoped to attract, handpicking friendly reporters to accompany him and pointedly black-balling enemies. Kissinger steeled the Chinese for the onslaught of public relations. "I warned Zhou Enlai," he wrote, that while "China had survived barbarian invasions before," it had never faced that more fearsome prospect, "a presidential advance party."[31]

The planning paid off. When Nixon touched down in China in February 1972, he caused a sensation. For several nights running, network news broadcasts showcased a slate of cultural events, ceremonial banquets, and excursions to the Great Wall and the Forbidden City, as American viewers marveled. Nixon's aides could never have scripted a better campaign film—or commandeered so much airtime for its broadcast—but the insecure president, convinced that the media would sell him short, nagged his aides to extract every last drop of good press from the trip. "Success seemed to unsettle Nixon more than failure," Kissinger lamented. "He seemed obsessed by the fear that he was not receiving adequate credit."[32]

Whether out of hostility to Nixon or simply a professional duty to report what they saw, journalists couldn't help noting the trip's public-relations focus. One cartoonist sketched a befuddled Nixon standing amid a sea of reporters, cameras, and lights while his Chinese guide mused: "Just think, all this will have gone to waste if you're not reelected!" The machinations similarly impressed the minimalist composer John Adams, who described his celebrated 1985 work *Nixon in China* as "the first opera ever to use a staged 'media event' as the basis for its dramatic structure." Adams' Nixon, hyperaware of his own image-making, savors his chance to project his peacemaker persona to Middle Americans. His people, he tells Mao, "watch us now; /The three main networks' colors glow/Livid through drapes onto the lawn. /Dishes are washed and homework is done/ … I know America is good/at heart."[33] But in diplomacy, as in opera, image-making created its own reality: whatever technical agreements might result from the trip—and there were disappointments amid the obvious gains—the theatrics themselves established that change was happening.

Yet neither any substantive shortcomings of the summit nor the public awareness of the election-year image-making dampened the excitement. Back in the United States, senators from Democrat George McGovern on the left to Republican Barry Goldwater on the right praised the trip, as did most journalistic opinion leaders. "Mr. Nixon deserves credit for a master stroke both opportune and statesmanlike," offered Howard K. Smith of ABC News in a typical judgment.[34] Nixon's approval rating climbed seven points. Never afraid to nudge history's judgment, the president declared on the last day of his trip, "This was the week that changed the world."[35]

Only slightly less popular with the pundits and the public than Nixon's China opening was his bid to improve U.S.–Soviet relations and halt or slow the nuclear arms race. Détente, as it was called, represented a notable step toward reinforcing a climate of mutual toleration between the superpowers, even if the renewed hostilities in Ronald Reagan's presidency somewhat undid the gains.

Nixon knew that public opinion had shifted markedly from the days when schoolchildren cowered under their desks during air raid drills, learning techniques that, in the event of an attack, would scarcely have spared them contamination or incineration. Indeed, since the Cuban Missile Crisis of 1962, there had been a thaw of sorts in the Cold War. Confrontation had given way to coexistence in the public mind, and popular opinion now fairly demanded a more amicable relationship with the Soviet Union. Nixon also saw potential dividends in friendlier ties: a lessening of pressure to keep building missiles and warheads; economic gains for American exporters; and possibly even diplomatic help in reaching a Vietnam peace deal. Accordingly, in his first few years as president, Nixon not only signed the nuclear nonproliferation treaty that LBJ had struck but also pressed ahead with the Strategic Arms Limitation Talks, or SALT—including an antiballistic missile treaty and an agreement on limiting offensive arms as well.

It was significant that for all the attention that he gave SALT, Nixon never learned the fine points of arms control. What mattered to him, not unreasonably, was the bigger picture: improving U.S.-Soviet communication and trust, and projecting the aura of a peacemaker who would keep America strong. He became especially keen to produce a tangible accomplishment to show the American public as his reelection campaign approached. He understood the value, on the heels of the February 1972 Beijing spectacle, of another splashy, headline-grabbing, camera-pleasing event, and he believed that only a summit in Moscow—the first trip to the Soviet capital by an American president—would do the job.

Ostensibly, the summit would be an occasion to sign the now completed ABM treaty and to nail down an agreement on offensive weapons. But, as Nixon's political aide Chuck Colson noted, the policies themselves were ultimately secondary. "Our task is not to achieve greater public support for SALT," Colson wrote to the president, "but rather to strengthen the president's image as one of the great world leaders of this century."[36] Nixon agreed. "I'm not so sure that the SALT thing is going to be all that important," he told Kissinger. Kissinger too saw the arms pact as a symbolic move, one whose chief virtue would be to "break the back of this generation of Democratic leaders" and give Nixon unrivaled preeminence in foreign affairs.[37]

The White House chose May 1972 as the date for the Moscow summit. As with the China trip, the scheduling was deliberate and artful: "close enough to the fall 1972 election campaign to be effective," Nixon's speechwriter William Safire explained, "far enough away not to be blatantly political."[38] Foreign policy triumphs were emerging as the cornerstone of the case for Nixon's reelection, and despite some fears that the Soviet Union would back out because of new American assaults on North Vietnam, the Moscow summit came off as planned.

From the time of Nixon's arrival in Moscow on May 22, 1972, the summit dominated the news for several nights. Political commentary, dominated by Cold War-era pundits, gushed that it heralded a new age. Notwithstanding some tense negotiating sessions and the usual quota of diplomatic evasions, the nations agreed to both a SALT treaty that capped nuclear and defensive missiles and a sweeping pledge of coexistence. Triumphantly, Nixon returned on June 1, via helicopter from Andrews Air Force Base to a flood-lit U.S. Capitol, where he basked before a joint session of Congress. His speech, if not quite so nakedly the campaign kickoff that the White House had been discussing, underscored the need for Americans to reelect a master of foreign affairs. With lofty words, the president pledged a fulfillment of "man's oldest dream—a world in which all nations can enjoy the blessings of peace."[39] Afterward, the president's men insisted to reporters, *Newsweek* wrote, that come November "the statesmanlike glow left over from Peking and Moscow"—especially if accompanied by an end to the war—would carry Nixon to a second term.[40]

Amid the jubilation, a few critics discerned flaws. The SALT agreements failed to address the issue of piling multiple nuclear warheads onto missiles, allowing both superpowers in the years ahead to exploit an enormous loophole in the treaty. Others complained about the surfeit of symbolic gestures. Since the summit's agreements were completed even before Nixon's departure, John Osborne of *The New Republic* wrote, the event itself was really just "window dressing, ... designed and arranged beforehand to further the impression that Nixon ... [was] accomplishing a lot."[41] A cartoonist drew a stage performance in which Nixon and Soviet leader Leonid Brezhnev locked arms amid rainbows, doves and heavenly clouds; "Turn up the cloud machine, angels enter from the left," Kissinger, the conductor, instructed.[42] Yet, again, awareness of the trip's PR benefits neither dampened the euphoria nor diluted the achievements. *Time* acknowledged that the signing of the accords was "stage-managed," but grasped that the symbolism—"the way in which they were signed and sealed"—nevertheless "gave them special import." It called the summit "the most important since Potsdam," likely to "change world diplomacy."[43] The public concurred. Weary of nuclear anxieties, Cold War adventurism and Vietnam, most Americans welcomed détente. And the SALT treaty, Colson told Haldeman, had an "enormous impact" with swing voters in particular. Nixon's popularity surged again, now far outpacing all Democratic rivals in head-to-head match-ups.[44]

As the election neared, Nixon sought to maximize the benefits of his visit. "It's good to go to China and good to go to Russia, because we're going to have to use everybody in the campaign," he said privately, even as he impugned Democrat George McGovern for politicizing national security.[45] With polls disclosing large leads over McGovern throughout the fall, moreover, Nixon was mostly able to put aside his worries about the slow but sure accumulation of evidence emerging in the *Washington Post* that linked his White House to the Watergate break-in. And when on October 26 Kissinger went on television to declare grandiloquently, "Peace is at hand"—falsely implying that a Vietnam settlement was imminent—the last blot on Nixon's aura of statesmanship was removed, if temporarily. The pundit class, about whom Nixon always complained, fawned. "Foreign policy and national security together are the Number One issue in U.S. Presidential elections," wrote columnist C. L. Sulzberger of the *New York Times* forty-eight hours before election day. "Because of his carefully conceived and executed diplomatic program, which saw establishment of a rapport with China, improved relations with Russia, and elaboration of a peace plan for Vietnam, President Nixon merits victory Tuesday."[46] When Nixon swamped McGovern on November 7 with more than 60 percent of the popular vote, Nixon the statesman and peacemaker seemed to have supplanted Tricky Dick once and for all.

The moment of triumph was, alas, fleeting. Nixon's second term had scarcely begun before the trial of the Watergate burglars and Senate hearings dislodged an avalanche of stunning facts, reversing the president's fortunes. By the spring of 1973, the radiance of Nixon's triumphs in Beijing and Moscow had dimmed as his chessboard maneuverings came to seem academic beside the historic, constitutional questions raised by Watergate.

Nixon tried to use his public image as a peacemaker to defend himself during Watergate. He charged his opponents with mere pique at his achievements, accusing them of a petty wish to "wallow in Watergate." He preferred, he insisted, to "think of the ages ... think of the world—and ... realize that here in this office is where the great decisions are going to be made that are going to determine whether we have peace in this world for years to come.

We have made such great strides toward that goal."[47] More audaciously, Nixon insisted that his removal from office—an increasingly likely prospect from late 1973 onward—would upset the balance of world power and the fragile peace that he had personally attained. Thus, as the rapids of scandal churned harder, Nixon clung to the life raft of his statesman image with mounting desperation.

However cynical, it was natural that Nixon should fall back on foreign policy as Watergate engulfed him. He had always enjoyed his strongest support in the realm of international affairs. In 1972 he had little trouble convincing most of the nation that China and Russia mattered more than Watergate, and even when his overall approval rating fell to 26 percent, more than twice that portion of the electorate still professed admiration for his foreign policy. In the early 1970s, after all, with memories of the Cold War anxieties of the 1950s and early 1960s fresh, geopolitics still struck many as the single most important sphere of presidential leadership. In particular, many of the veteran journalists, politicians, and Washington insiders who had come to power with the Cold War were slow to appreciate that great-power politics had been displaced as the nation's most burning issue by deeper concerns about the integrity of the American system.[48] Their disposition allowed Nixon to rely on them for support during his crisis.

Ironically, many of these establishment figures were liberal. Few were fond of Nixon personally. "We didn't like the way Nixon looked; we didn't like the way he acted; we didn't like the way he talked," said Hugh Sidey of *Time*. "But we couldn't deny his achievements in foreign policy."[49] Nixon himself distrusted them—indeed, so intensely that he couldn't see that they were lending him valuable support. "The establishment is dying," he told his counsel, John Dean, in 1973, "and so ... despite the success we've had in foreign policy and in the election, they've got to show that it is just wrong."[50] But the "establishment" generally held fast to its view of the president as a master of great-power politics. In deference to his foreign policy achievement *Time* magazine named Nixon "Man of the Year" in 1971 and 1972, the second time bestowing the honor on Kissinger as well.

Awe of Nixon's peacemaking gripped these Cold War journalists and insiders even as their younger colleagues were glimpsing Watergate's magnitude. In *The Making of the President, 1972*, Teddy White veered back and forth between the scandal and Nixon's diplomacy, unsure which would prove more important. He concluded that a "national tragedy" would result if Americans "attempted to reverse the verdict of the people at the polls on the technicalities of a burglary, in a spasm of morality approaching the hysterical."[51] *New York Times* columnist James Reston, normally clear-eyed about Nixon, also was caught flat-footed. When Senator Philip Hart of Michigan raised the prospect of impeachment in April 1973, the *Times* columnist scoffed that the "eminently rational" Democrat must have been "smitten by the spring madness."[52] Stewart Alsop, who with his brother Joe ranked after only Lippmann in stature among the pundits, wrote in May that Nixon's "historic turnabout in the relations between the United States and the two chief Communist powers" was "in danger of being smashed" because of an "idiotic exercise in political dirty work" by "a bunch of amateur James Bonds."[53] Joe argued the same thing until the eve of Nixon's resignation, going so far as to tell Congressman Tom Railsback, one of the Judiciary Committee Republicans wavering on impeachment, that Nixon's ouster would imperil superpower relations by leaving the untested Gerald Ford in charge. Eventually, Alsop owned up to being "shocked by Nixon's transgressions," but he remained angry at the "hyenas around a corpse," as he described the president's critics. "After all," he wrote to the Herblock, "he is our president, son of a bitch though he may be. And although nobody seems to remember the fact except myself, his misfortunes may very well be our misfortunes."[54]

Nixon exploited this regard for his foreign policy skills. He counted on more of the good press of 1972 when he invited Brezhnev to visit to the United States in June of 1973—precisely when John Dean would be giving his explosive testimony before the Ervin Committee (after some grumbling, the much-awaited sessions were postponed as the media reveled again in heady talk of détente). Over the next year, Nixon's arguments about his indispensability grew more deliberate. In May 1974, in an eighty-minute interview with James J. Kilpatrick of the *National Review*, Nixon's grandiosity reached new heights. The president told the conservative journalist that he wouldn't resign because he had to maintain world stability, even suggesting that his ouster could have apocalyptic consequences. "We must seize the moment," Nixon asserted. "If we do not seize it, the world will inevitably move toward a conflagration that will destroy everything that we've made—everything this civilization has produced."[55]

Nixon matched the bombast with dramatic action. In April 1974, he took an unplanned trip to France for the funeral of President Georges Pompidou and found that he loved Paris in the springtime: he basked in flattering write-ups and cheering crowds, marred by none of the "Impeach Nixon" placards that were now dotting his domestic audiences. Noting how warmly world leaders greeted Nixon, Chief of Staff Alexander Haig, who had replaced the scandal-tarred Haldeman the previous spring, remarked that foreign heads of state considered Nixon "an essential factor" in building "a stable international environment." (The verdict was not quite unanimous; one French official upbraided Nixon for having "shamelessly substituted a publicity campaign for the mourning of an entire nation.")[56] Upon Nixon's return in May, the White House announced that he would not only be visiting Moscow, as planned, but would also travel to the Middle East and Europe, and later in the year would visit Japan. Nixon wanted to use these travels, as he noted in his diary, to regain moral authority, but the press scoffed that the excursions would shift attention away from impeachment. Cartoonist Paul Szep drew Nixon boarding Air Force One with a suitcase stickered with tags from Egypt, Israel, Moscow and Syria and a caption reading, "When the going gets tough, the tough get going." Pessimistically, Nixon predicted to Ziegler that the press would dwell on "the minuscule problems involved in Watergate" rather than "the momentous stakes" in the Middle East.[57]

In fact, the trip, begun on June 10 after a send-off gala organized by Rabbi Baruch Korff, one of Nixon's chief citizen defenders, went exceedingly well. In Cairo, the president was embraced by Egyptian leader Anwar Sadat, who had recently broken ties with the Soviet Union, while Egyptian citizens climbed rooftops and treetops to watch the official motorcade. Sadat endorsed the idea that Nixon's personal diplomacy was "vital to promote peace and tranquility in the area."[58] In Israel, too, Nixon drew cheers for having aided the Jewish state when it was attacked the previous fall. Journalists ingested a diet of parades and fanfare, and although some rued the sparse opportunities to ask Nixon about Watergate developments, they didn't deny him his customary good coverage. The president for his part stayed on message. In Moscow, he said in a toast to Brezhnev that détente stemmed from "a personal relationship" between the two leaders. "Any agreement is only as good as the will of the parties to keep it."[59]

But neither the trip nor foreign policy in general could rescue Nixon. On the contrary, his inveterate devotion to image-making had made the motives behind all his actions suspect. As early as April 1973, Kissinger and Nixon saw that rising public distrust would make it impossible to retaliate against North Vietnam for sending men and materiel into South Vietnam in contravention of the Paris accords, just months after their signing. By the time of the "Saturday Night Massacre" in October 1973—in which Nixon's top Justice Department officials resigned rather than fire the Watergate special prosecutor in a tension-filled weekend drama—skepticism of the president's foreign policy moves was rife. After the Soviet Union prepared to assist the

Egyptians during in the Yom Kippur War that month, leading Kissinger and Haig to put the military on high alert, journalists questioned whether the unusual step might have been taken to bury Nixon's troubles. One unnamed administration aide seemed to confirm the doubts, telling *Newsweek* winkingly, "We had a problem and we decided to make the most of it." The chatter infuriated Kissinger, who charged that the press had manufactured a "crisis of confidence." But Kissinger conceded that the administration's credibility, even in foreign affairs, was hurting. "It is a symptom of what is happening to our country," he said, "that it could even be suggested that the United States would alert its forces for domestic reasons."[60] Such suspicions never abated. In January, when Israel and Egypt reached a settlement, Dan Rather of CBS reported pointedly noting the timing of the agreement: it came just days after new headlines about the damning eighteen and one half-minute erasure on a key Watergate tape.[61] By Nixon's global tour in June 1974, newspapers were openly suggesting that he was trying to blot out Watergate with more staged happenings.

As his stature collapsed, critics grew bold. The Democratic Congress reasserted its primacy in international matters, cutting off funding for the wars in Southeast Asia and passing the War Powers Act, which mandated congressional approval of any sustained use of armed force. The right, meanwhile, seized on Nixon's weakness to prevent what Kissinger called the "full fruition" of détente and of Nixon's larger plan to "a new structure of international relations." Nixon's ace had not only failed; it had backfired.

Watergate thus undercut Nixon's foreign policy designs. And for the rest of his life if would constrain Nixon's bid for rehabilitation. In the two decades from his resignation to his death, he undertook a dozen strategies to restore his statesman image to the prominence it had enjoyed fleetingly in 1972. He courted journalists with intimate dinners, wrote treatises on foreign affairs and volumes of self-serving memoirs, bent the ear of presidents, staged stunts to showcase his ideas, set up a Nixon Center on international affairs, and gave learned speeches before friendly audiences. At the same time, he continued to minimize Watergate, fought in court to conceal his tapes and papers, withheld documents of historical import, tailored his foreign policy pronouncements to catch the prevailing winds, curated a spectacularly dishonest presidential library, and inscribed on his tombstone the line from his first inaugural that expressed his grand, unfulfilled dream: "The greatest honor that history can bestow is that of peacemaker."[62]

But it did not work. Despite bursts of indulgence at moments like his funeral, and reflexive praise from pundits and historians in the tradition of the Alsops and Hugh Sidey, Nixon never recovered. In June 2006, the Gallup organization found that just 28 percent of Americans surveyed approved of his performance as president—a scant four points higher than the 24 percent mark he earned in August 1974.[63] Most Americans knew him first and foremost as Tricky Dick.

Nixon understood why. When in 1990 he published *In the Arena*, his third memoir, he groused to his assistant that reviewers and readers dwelled on the material about Watergate at the expense of his foreign policy achievements. "None of the other stuff in there, like on the Russians or the other personal stuff, made it into the news or even the reviews," he sighed. "Watergate—that's all anyone wants." And when he saw the administration of George H. W. Bush struggle amid an ailing economy, he noted ruefully, "We tried to do what they are trying—to change the image during Watergate. It didn't work. Too phony."[64]

Notes

1. John Stacks and Strobe Talbott, "Paying the Price," *Time*, April 2, 1990, 46.
2. Earl Mazo, *Richard Nixon: A Political and Personal Portrait* (New York, 1959), 136.
3. *New York Times*, "Eisenhower vs. Stevenson: Campaign Debate," November 4, 1956, 200.
4. Herbert Block, *Herblock Special Report* (New York, 1974), 43.
5. Stanley I. Kutler, *Abuse of Power: The New Nixon Tapes* (New York, 1997), 8.
6. Richard Nixon to H. R. Haldeman, December 1, 1969, in Bruce Oudes, *From the President: Richard Nixon's Secret Files* (New York, 1989), 76.
7. Theodore H. White, *The Making of the President, 1968* (New York, 1969), 171.
8. Richard Nixon, *RN: The Memoirs of Richard Nixon* (New York, 1978), 770.
9. Melvin Small, *The Presidency of Richard Nixon* (Lawrence, Kans.: University Press of Kansas, 1999), 216.
10. Garry Wills, *Nixon Agonistes: The Crisis of the Self-Made Man* (Boston, 1970), 432.
11. Bruce Mazlish, *In Search of Nixon: A Psychohistorical Inquiry* (New York, 1972), 35.
12. Fawn Brodie, *Richard M. Nixon: The Shaping of His Character* (New York, 1981), 59–60; James David Barber, *Presidential Character: Predicting Performance in the White House* (Englewood Cliffs, N.J., 1972), 348.
13. Mark Feldstein, "Fighting Quakers: The 1950s Battle Between Richard Nixon and Drew Pearson," *Journalism History* 30 (Summer 2004): 77.

14. Meg Greenfield, "The Prose of Richard M. Nixon," *Reporter*, September 29, 1960, 18.
15. Norman Mailer, *Miami and the Siege of Chicago* (New York, 1968), 41–44.
16. Robert Dallek, *Nixon and Kissinger: Partners in Power* (New York, 2007), 180, 246, 381.
17. Richard M. Nixon, "Inaugural Address," January 20, 1969, *PPP, 1969*, 1–4.
18. Small, *Presidency of Richard Nixon*, 74.
19. *New York Times*, "Nixon Team Contrived Response to Speech," January 23, 1999, A14.
20. Dallek, *Nixon and Kissinger*, 261.
21. Tom Wells, *Wild Man: The Life and Times of Daniel Ellsberg* (New York, 2001), 1–31.
22. H. R. Haldeman, with Joseph DiMona, *The Ends of Power* (New York, 1978), 79.
23. Todd Gitlin, "Foreword," in Tom Wells, *The War Within: America's Battle over Vietnam* (Berkeley, 1994), xiv.
24. Henry Kissinger, *White House Years* (Boston, 1979), 284.
25. Dallek, *Nixon and Kissinger*, 465.
26. Small, *Presidency of Richard Nixon*, 64.
27. Richard Nixon, "Asia After Viet Nam," *Foreign Affairs* 46 (October 1967): 111–125.
28. Helen Thomas, *Front Row at the White House: My Life and Times* (New York, 1999), 186.
29. *Time*, "Nixon's Coup: To Peking with Peace," July 26, 1971, 11–17; *Newsweek*, "Nixon: I Will Go to China," July 26, 1971, 16–22.
30. H. R. Haldeman, *The Haldeman Diaries: Inside the Nixon White House* (New York, 1994), 293–294.
31. Kissinger, *White House Years*, 769.
32. Dallek, *Nixon and Kissinger*, 368.
33. http://www.earbox.com/W-nixoninchina.html, accessed on June 25, 2007; John Adams, and libretto by Alice Goodman, *Nixon in China: An Opera in Three Acts* (Amsterdam, 1988), 38.
34. Dallek, *Nixon and Kissinger*, 369.
35. William Bundy, *A Tangled Web: The Making of Foreign Policy in the Nixon Presidency* (New York, 1998), 311.
36. Richard Reeves, *President Nixon: Alone in the White House* (New York, 2001), 494.
37. Dallek, *Nixon and Kissinger*, 280.
38. William Safire, *Before the Fall: An Inside View of the Pre-Watergate White House* (New York, 1975), 442.
39. Richard Nixon, "Address to a Joint Session of the Congress on Return From Austria, the Soviet Union, Iran, and Poland," June 1, 1972, *PPP, 1972*, 660.
40. *Newsweek*, "After the Moscow Primary," June 12, 1972, 21.

41. John Osborne, *The Fourth Year of the Nixon Watch* (New York, 1973), 81, 88, 100.
42. *Newsweek*, June 12, 1972, 22.
43. *Time*, "What Nixon Brings Home from Moscow," June 5, 1972, 13.
44. Haldeman, *Haldeman Diaries*, 466.
45. Dallek, *Nixon and Kissinger*, 412.
46. C. L. Sulzberger, "Why Nixon Deserves to Win," *New York Times*, November 5, 1972, E15.
47. Richard Nixon, "Remarks to Members of the White House Staff on Returning from Bethesda Naval Hospital," July 20, 1973, *PPP, 1973*, 657.
48. *New York Times*, May 14, 1974, 22.
49. Hugh Sidey, "The Man and Foreign Policy," in *The Nixon Presidency*, ed. Kenneth W. Thompson (Lanham, Md., 1987), 305.
50. Richard Nixon, *The Presidential Transcripts* (New York, 1974), 88.
51. Theodore H. White, *The Making of the President, 1972* (New York, 1973), 493–494.
52. Kutler, *Wars of Watergate*, 471.
53. Stewart Alsop, "Poor Mr. Nixon," *Newsweek*, May 7, 1973, 112.
54. Bob Woodward and Carl Bernstein, *The Final Days* (New York, 1976), 231; Joseph Alsop, with Adam Platt, *I've Seen the Best of It: Memoirs* (New York, 1992), 478–479.
55. James J. Kilpatrick, "A Stout if Rambling Defense," *Time*, May 27, 1974, 16; *National Review*, "Nixon Interview," July 16, 1974, 632.
56. Dallek, *Nixon and Kissinger*, 574.
57. *New York Times*, May 27, 1974, 27; John Herbers, *No Thank You, Mr. President* (New York, 1976), 123; *New York Times*, May 26, 1974, 4; John Osborne, *The Last Nixon Watch* (Washington, 1975), 149.
58. *New York Times*, June 13, 1974, 1.
59. Richard Nixon, "Toasts of the President and Leonid Ilyich Brezhnev, General Secretary of the Central Committee of the Communist Party of the Soviet Union, at a Dinner in Moscow," June 27, 1974, *PPP, 1974*, 657.
60. Kutler, *Wars of Watergate*, 411.
61. Dallek, *Nixon and Kissinger*, 554.
62. Inaugural Address, *PPP, 1969*, 1.
63. Gallup poll, June 16, 2006. Accessed through Lexis/Nexis "Polls and Surveys" database, August 1, 2007.
64. Monica Crowley, *Nixon off the Record* (New York, 1996), 65; Monica Crowley, *Nixon in Winter* (New York, 1998), 286.

3

Henry Kissinger and American Grand Strategy

Jeremi Suri

The late 1960s mark a historical divide. In nearly every society, the tenor of life changed. Social and cultural traditions endured concerted attack. Authority figures faced direct challenges from "ordinary" citizens. Fears of worldwide chaos replaced assumptions about international order. Like balls of yarn, the stable lines of postwar geopolitics came undone as people pulled at them from multiple directions. This was an era of global revolution—from within and without.[1]

State leaders, particularly in the United States and Western Europe, were traumatized by this upheaval. They struggled to run their governments as the world collapsed around them. They grasped for political legitimacy when their inherited values lost public suasion. British Foreign Secretary Michael Stewart captured this sense of pervasive crisis in his private diary. "The 10:pm television news presents a depressing picture," he wrote. "The great difficulty of the world is the moral deficiencies of what should be the free world … Germany distracted, France selfish, ourselves aimless, U.S.A. in torment."[2]

Hamilton Fish Armstrong, the editor of *Foreign Affairs* and the figure who helped to articulate an American global vision at mid-century, echoed Stewart's foreboding. Armstrong explained to one of his younger associates—Henry Kissinger—that never since the days of President Warren Harding had "the prestige of the United States stood so low. We have the military power and we have the economic power … to command the world. But we do not have the moral prestige, because abroad governments and people know what we know in our hearts ourselves, that our life forces, the forces that we felt made us great, are dispersed and sullied."[3]

Kissinger shared Armstrong's sentiment. Working for both Lyndon Johnson and Nelson Rockefeller, he positioned himself in 1968 as a high-level adviser to Democrats and Republicans. He did not, however, expect great policy successes in the near future. He worried that the upheavals of the period would undermine rational decision making. He feared a return to the violence, chaos, and collapse of Weimar Germany in "the turmoil surely ahead of us." "The next Presidency is likely to be tragic," Kissinger predicted. "Nothing suggests that any of the prospective candidates can unify the country or restore America's position in the world. The next four years are likely to witness mounting crises—disorder at home, increasing tension abroad."[4]

"In the best of circumstances," Kissinger warned, "the next administration will be beset by crises. In almost every area of the world, we have been living off capital—warding off the immediate, rarely dealing with underlying problems. These difficulties are likely to multiply when it becomes apparent that one of the legacies of the war in Vietnam will be a strong American reluctance to risk overseas involvements." Like the democracies on the eve of the Second World War, the citizens of the transatlantic community had become weak, divided, and cowardly in Kissinger's eyes. The Cold War had encouraged a dangerous mix of strident rhetoric and stale policy.[5]

Watching the United States sink ever deeper into the military quicksand of Vietnam as citizens set American cities aflame, Kissinger believed that the nation needed imaginative leadership more than ever before. He agreed with protesters who argued that the old assumptions about containment and liberal politics no longer offered hope. The problem was not the content of American power—the United States had the military capability to destroy its adversaries in Vietnam and it had the resources to satisfy domestic grievances. The problem was the way power was organized, exercised, and judged. The United States needed to revise the basic concepts underpinning its policies. "The shape of the future," Kissinger wrote, "will depend ultimately on convictions which far transcend the physical balance of power."[6]

When asked in 1971 "where the administration wants to end up after four years?" Kissinger invoked both his sense of contemporary crisis and the strategic ideas he had articulated for more than a decade. "This administration came into office when the intellectual capital of US postwar policy had been used up and when the conditions determining postwar US policy had been altered," he explained:

> We had to adjust our foreign policy to the new facts of life. It is
> beyond the physical and psychological capacity of the US to make

itself responsible for every part of the world. We hope in the first term to clear away the underbrush of the old period. In the second term, we could try to construct a new international settlement—which will be more stable, less crisis-conscious, and less dependent on decisions in one capital.[7]

All of Kissinger's experiences—as a refugee, a counterintelligence officer, a scholar, and a strategist—prepared him to re-make foreign policy, "to clear away the underbrush of the old period." He rejected "ready made solutions" and encouraged the formation of a small, elite "directorate" of leaders that would craft new initiatives. Kissinger believed that this directorate could replace assumptions about a bipolar Cold War with an international system hinged on a redistribution of authority that increased local initiative, but also affirmed American power. Washington would exert its influence through diplomatic agreements and threats of force, not extended conflicts like the war in Vietnam.

Kissinger's contact with Richard Nixon began in May 1955 when he sent the vice president a letter of invitation to speak at Harvard's International Seminar. Nixon did not attend, although he did read Kissinger's book, *Nuclear Weapons and Foreign Policy*. The two men had at least one brief social encounter at a cocktail party in Washington during the 1960s, but they hardly talked to one another. They were, in fact, social outsiders who did not have much opportunity for interaction. Kissinger focused on building professional contacts with more respected Cold War figures, including Nelson Rockefeller. Nixon operated on the fringes of the Republican Party. As late as August 1968, Kissinger wrote of Nixon in distant and condescending terms. He doubted the former vice president's "suitability" for the highest national office. Kissinger's personal regard for Nixon was even lower. He told one of his regular correspondents in 1968: "I detest Nixon."[8]

These two estranged outsiders did not come together in later months out of common beliefs, affection, or a patron-client arrangement—as in all of Kissinger's other professional relationships. Despite their claims concerning the importance of grand strategy, there is no evidence they ever had a heart-to-heart conversation about their shared hopes for the future. They ranted about their perceived enemies—political insiders, liberal intellectuals, and the media—but they never outlined a future vision. How did they want to change the world? What was their desired legacy? Kissinger thought extensively about these matters alone, but he and the president never broached the subject together with any documented seriousness.

Theirs was not a collaboration for higher purposes. It was a marriage of convenience, filled with all of the suspicion, hostility, and jealousy that accompanies these dysfunctional alliances. Nixon and Kissinger respected and resented each other at the same time. They worked closely together, but remained strangers to one another. Looking back on his time in the White House, Kissinger remains amazed at how personally distant he was from the president who gave him so much power.[9]

Fears of democratic chaos and anxieties about pervasive threats—these were the anchors for Nixon and Kissinger's working relationship. They had a dark view of human nature and democratic society, born of their own experiences with social prejudice. Nixon never confronted the anti-Semitic virulence of Nazi Germany, but he faced the disdain of East Coast elites— like the Kennedys and Rockefellers—for a hard-working man from rural America, without polish or prestigious connections. He and Kissinger had to scrape and struggle for their advancement, and they viewed life in these terms. They did not believe that an expansion of freedoms would naturally make for a better society. Free citizens were often hateful and destructive, as the urban riots of the late 1960s seemed to prove once again. For Nixon and Kissinger, social improvement required firm national leadership to limit human excesses and restrict human hatreds. The same applied to the inter-national system, where competitive states would pummel one another to death without the force of imposed order from a superior power. Based on their own personal experiences, Nixon and Kissinger saw themselves as benevolent strong men, rather than Jeffersonian democrats. Their relation-ship was built on fear and frustration. Their policies were built on obsessions with toughness and secrecy.

Nixon and Kissinger inherited a mess in Vietnam. Writing less than a decade after he assumed his duties in the White House, Kissinger remem-bered: "When we came into office over a half-million Americans were fight-ing a war ten thousand miles away. Their numbers were still increasing on a schedule established by our predecessors. We found no plans for withdraw-als. Thirty-one thousand had already died. Whatever our original war aims, by 1969 our credibility abroad, the reliability of our commitments, and our domestic cohesion were alike jeopardized by a struggle in a country as far away from the North American continent as our globe permits." Despite evidence that the military situation was improving for the United States, the new administration was "determined to end our involvement in Vietnam."[10]

Throughout the 1960s Kissinger had defended America's commitment to South Vietnam, but he had also joined a chorus of opinion at the end of the decade that advocated a negotiated settlement to the war. Consistent with his broad strategic vision, Kissinger called for a combination of more effective military force, multilateral diplomacy involving the big regional powers, and serious proposals for compromise among the belligerents. As early as 1965 he explained that negotiations would "begin a new phase of the struggle rather than mark its end. The stakes remain high and the conduct of affairs grows more complicated because it depends on so many intangibles. Negotiations require as careful and thoughtful preparation as do our military campaigns." They were not an alternative to the use of force, but an opportunity to coordinate military and political capabilities—more firepower and more diplomatic maneuver.[11]

Although he believed that the United States could improve its military performance, Kissinger argued that the nation could not "win" in Vietnam by totally destroying the region with unremitting force. Brutality on this scale would further inflame domestic opinion. It would also antagonize neighboring China, as well as the Soviet Union. Kissinger vividly remembered the experience of the Korean War two decades earlier, when reckless expansion of the conflict sparked nearly three years of bloody fighting between American and Chinese soldiers, with the looming danger of nuclear escalation. Washington had to pursue a negotiated solution in Vietnam that avoided this dangerous course of events, while also preserving American strength. Force alone would not do the job.[12]

The United States could not shoot its way to victory, but it could not pick up tail and run either. For more than a decade, Washington had been the primary sponsor of South Vietnam. American leaders of both political parties had argued that success in the Cold War required an effective stand against communist expansion in Southeast Asia. Vietnam was a strategic fulcrum for the future of Asia, and it was a testing ground for American claims about containment. Efforts to transform South Vietnam into a vibrant capitalist economy during the 1960s further enhanced the U.S. stake in the region. If Washington admitted failure in South Vietnam, it would become harder for leaders to justify the pursuit of communist containment and capitalist transformation elsewhere. Perceiving weakness in U.S. determination, adversaries would become more likely to challenge America's assertions across the globe. "We could not," Kissinger explained, "simply walk away from an enterprise involving two administrations, five allied countries, and thirty-one thousand dead as if we were switching a television channel." Millions of Americans "opposed" the Vietnam War after 1968, but only a fraction of the public supported immediate and unconditional withdrawal. The strategic and ideological stakes were too high, even for those who wanted instant relief.[13]

American leaders struggled to preserve the nation's "credibility" as they accepted a major setback—perhaps the most damaging U.S. military experience in the twentieth century. They emphasized the importance of displaying continued resolve to defeat threatening enemies, and continued commitment to support loyal friends. The experiences of appeasement before the Second World War loomed large, when the fascist dictators came to believe their adversaries were weak and irresolute. Men like Hitler acted on this assumption and initiated a global conflagration. Policymakers from all backgrounds in the Cold War feared that evidence of American weakness in Vietnam would have a similar effect.[14]

The United States had to appear willing and able to deploy overwhelming force if it wished to forestall the need to use it. Threats of American retaliation underpinned deterrence of communist aggression, especially in Europe and Asia. In order to avoid fighting everywhere, Washington had to frighten its adversaries, convincing them that they faced an overwhelming response if they challenged local American vulnerabilities in places like West Berlin and South Korea. Although the United States was the most powerful nation in the world, it relied on intimidation (the prospect of force) as much as the actual use of force to protect its extensive interests. The perceived willingness to fight ferociously was necessary for war avoidance. Any apparent slackening in Washington's ability to fight, as in Vietnam, made it more difficult for the nation (and the Western alliance as a whole) to maintain an intrepid posture against challengers. Credibility was about appearing tough, and even brutal when necessary. It was about showing that American leaders would fulfill their commitments and put their force to use.

Thomas Schelling, Kissinger's former colleague at Harvard, explained the importance of credibility—what he called "face"—most effectively in the late 1960s: "If one side yields on a series of issues, when the matters at stake are not critical, it may be difficult to communicate to the other just when a vital issue has been reached." "It is undoubtedly true," Schelling admitted, "that false pride often tempts a government's officials to take irrational risks or to do undignified things—to bully some small country that insults them, for example. But there is also the more serious kind of 'face,' the kind that in modern jargon is known as a country's 'image,' consisting of other countries' beliefs (their leaders' beliefs, that is) about how the country can be expected to behave." Anticipating Kissinger's position on the Vietnam War, Schelling argued: "If the question is raised whether this kind of 'face' is worth fighting over, the answer is that this kind of face is one of the few things worth fighting over. Few parts of the world are intrinsically worth the risk of serious war by themselves, especially when taken slice by slice, but defending them or running risks to protect them may preserve one's commitments to action in other parts of the world and at later times. 'Face' is merely the interdependence of a country's commitments; it is a country's reputation for action, the expectations other countries have about its behavior."[15]

As much as Americans might have wished otherwise, the nation's credibility (its "face") was deeply entangled in Vietnam after more than a decade of intervention. For the United States to withdraw from the region and maintain its credibility as a superpower at the same time, it needed a settlement that recognized American strength. This meant coupling serious negotiation efforts with increased military pressure on North Vietnam. "Our military effort leaves a great deal to be desired," Kissinger wrote the president, "but it remains one of our few bargaining weapons." The White House's emerging "game plan" called for escalated attacks on enemy positions. Nixon wanted to "crack them pretty hard" with massive air strikes: "My inclination is to crack this one, and crack another one—plenty of places to hit." Nixon would send a signal of toughness to the world. Everyone, especially the North Vietnamese and their supporters in Moscow and Beijing, should "know that there's still a lot of snap left in the old boys."[16]

Air power offered the perfect mechanism for reducing American casualties and maintaining the credibility of U.S. force. Nixon blew hard about his desire to "*punish* the enemy in ways that he will really hurt." "I want you to get this spirit inculcated in all hands and particularly I want the military to get off its back side," he ordered Kissinger. "I think we have had too much of a tendency to talk big and act little. This was certainly the weakness of the Johnson Administration. … We have the power to destroy [the North Vietnamese] war making capacity. The only question is whether we have the *will* to use that power. What distinguishes me from Johnson is that I have the *will* in spades. … For once, I want the military and I want the NSC staff to come up with some ideas on their own which will recommend *action* which is very *strong, threatening,* and *effective.*"[17]

The president trumpeted his qualities as a tough guy. Kissinger had the difficult task of translating that sentiment into daily policy. He had to manage his boss, and he took the blame when toughness did not produce the desired outcomes. He also had to manage the Paris negotiations between the main belligerents—the North Vietnamese and South Vietnamese governments, the National Liberation Front for South Vietnam (the "Vietcong"), and the United States—as well as on-going discussions with the Soviet Union. Kissinger calibrated Nixon's pronouncements for various international audiences.

Mixing Nixon's invocations of toughness with diplomacy and force, Kissinger devised a three-point strategy. First, the White House would make it clear through public statements, private negotiations, and unilateral actions that it wanted to withdraw from Vietnam. The Nixon administration began reducing the American troop presence in the region soon after taking office—announcing the first removal of 25,000 soldiers (the "Vietnamization" of the war) in June 1969. Second, Washington would enlist support from the Soviet Union and other states to help the United States achieve favorable settlement terms. Kissinger would condition better relations with Moscow on the Kremlin's assistance in ending the war. Third, and most important, Nixon and Kissinger would display a disposition to act creatively—often in violation of the normal limits on American action. They would transcend the rules of the Cold War, and fight on their own terms if their enemies did not respect their wishes. This was a strategy of movement, uncertainty, and hope—in contrast to the policy stalemate of the late 1960s.[18]

Nixon had spoken of a "madman" approach to cowering his adversaries in the past, but the administration's Vietnam strategy was a more intricate and explicit application of Kissinger's long-standing thinking about foreign policy. Since the end of the Second World War, American leaders had alternated between the use of overwhelming force and the pursuit of negotiations. In the Korean War, for example, President Truman orchestrated a strong response to communist aggression, but he then accepted a more passive approach to the war after fighting bogged down and cease-fire discussions began. President Johnson had applied the same methods to Vietnam, escalating American operations in response to enemy attacks, but then curtailing bombing operations for the sake of negotiations. The Johnson administration never integrated fighting and diplomacy effectively in Vietnam. Kissinger broke out of this framework. More than Nixon, he pursued creative and flexible uses of American capabilities for the purpose of encouraging a mutually beneficial settlement.[19]

Applying his own writings as well as those of Thomas Schelling and others, Kissinger attempted to assert new leverage over events surrounding Vietnam. His approach presumed that war-fighting and diplomatic negotiation were integrated activities, part of the larger bargaining process that constituted military conflict. Kissinger emphasized the importance of seizing the initiative, rather than merely containing the enemy. Like Bismarck, he sought to bring transformative leadership and action to a moment of crisis. Nixon called this the "big play," but Kissinger saw it as a deeper reflection of the statesman's role in imagining a new future—a "conceptual" shift. Nixon was primarily concerned with ending the Vietnam War on favorable terms for political purposes; Kissinger sought to re-make the international system and the global positioning of the United States. Nixon focused on military and political tactics; Kissinger sought to address "the generally deteriorating strategic position of the United States" on a worldwide scale. Nixon was the pragmatist, Kissinger the revolutionary.[20]

Kissinger's effort to shape an international revolution reflected his accumulated thinking about politics and foreign policy since he fled Nazi Germany. He focused considerable energy on formulating military options for the United States. Traditional modes of behavior in a moment of crisis were self-defeating. A strong leader, according to Kissinger, was one who created new instruments of power for new challenges. In the context of the Vietnam War, this meant a rejection of the generally accepted confines for American activities.

In addition to the conventional bombing of North Vietnamese targets, the napalm attacks on Vietcong-controlled villages in the South, and the efforts to "pacify" the countryside, Kissinger advocated widening American operations into neighboring states—particularly Cambodia. The Johnson administration had already begun some limited raids against enemy "sanctuaries" across the border, but "Operation Breakfast" made it clear that the White House would now bring overwhelming force against communist forces operating in neutral countries. Washington would no longer allow its adversaries to hide behind claims of sovereignty, and it would no longer deploy its air power with careful restraint. In the year after the Cambodia bombings began in March 1969, the United States launched 3,650 B-52 attacks, dropping 110,000 tons of TNT in this nonbelligerent nation. On April 30, 1970, Nixon announced that in addition to the air strikes, 31,000 American soldiers had entered Cambodia to pursue North Vietnamese forces. Kissinger expressed some reservations about this expansion of ground operations— and two of his assistants, Roger Morris and Anthony Lake, resigned in protest—but he had strongly encouraged the president to seize control of the war by widening the terrain for American force. This was a calculated set of measures to send a "signal that things might get out of hand." Kissinger expected that the North Vietnamese and their supporters in Moscow and Beijing would now find themselves on the defensive.[21]

Conventional military raids into neutral territory were not enough. They failed to cut off enemy supply lines into South Vietnam. They did not intimidate America's adversaries; if anything the raids appeared to harden anti-American resolve in North Vietnam and surrounding territories. Most significant, the attacks on Cambodia had a minimal effect on North Vietnamese fighting strength. Hanoi continued to send waves of soldiers against American and South Vietnamese positions.

In response, Kissinger sought to widen the spectrum of weapons in play. He returned to his consistent calls for the United States to make its nuclear arsenal useful for diplomatic purposes. Kissinger did not advocate launching a nuclear attack, but he pushed for creative maneuvers with these weapons to frighten and cajole adversaries. This was a strategy of aggressive nuclear posturing and calculated risk-taking. It was an attempt to convert the prospect of total destruction into daily leverage over far away events.

In October 1969, Kissinger applied his ideas about nuclear posturing to the pursuit of a settlement in Vietnam. President Nixon demanded a negotiated cessation to the war by the end of the year; otherwise he would unleash a new set of massive and unprecedented attacks on North Vietnam. On Nixon's instructions, Kissinger warned Soviet Ambassador Anatoly Dobrynin: "the train had just left the station and was now headed down the track." Dobrynin and other observers assumed that "the train" referred to a prospective escalation of conventional forces, particularly aerial bombardments. Kissinger, however, encouraged the president to add a series of nuclear maneuvers to his conventional threats. He did not intend to initiate nuclear war over Vietnam, but to shock the Soviet leadership into pursuing a peace settlement for fear of dire and unpredictable consequences. Returning to his own writings and those of Thomas Schelling, Kissinger attempted to cower his adversaries by breaking out of the accepted rules for limited war, creating the prospect of "irrational" American behavior. This was what Nixon meant by his vague remarks about a "madman" posture. Kissinger devised a method for calibrating this to U.S. nuclear capabilities and the demands of the Vietnam War. As in the widening of the conflict into Cambodia, Kissinger sought to scare his adversaries by threatening a massive, perhaps irreversible, escalation of the conflict.[22]

On the morning of October 6, 1969, Kissinger triggered planning for American nuclear maneuvers when he asked Secretary of Defense Melvin Laird to increase the nation's preparations for war so that "the other side" will "pick this up." Later that evening Nixon ordered Laird to "initiate a series of increased alert measures designed to convey to the Soviets an increasing readiness by U.S. strategic forces." Nixon's charges were vague. Kissinger had to transform these cryptic comments into a specific set of actions. The president wanted to appear tough, but his National Security Council advisor had to figure out how to do this effectively with nuclear weapons. Kissinger and his assistant, General Alexander Haig, pressed the military bureaucracy to assemble a proposal that would:

1. be discernible to the Soviets and be both unusual and significant;
2. not be threatening to the Soviets;
3. not require substantial additional funding or resources;
4. not require agreement with the allies;
5. not degrade essential missions;
6. have minimum chance of public exposure.[23]

Senior military planners resisted this scheme because it violated standard assumptions about nuclear deterrence and it diverted American resources from other planned exercises and activities. It also appeared unlikely to frighten U.S. adversaries. Lieutenant General Robert Pursley, Secretary of Defense Laird's military aide, explained that without a real mobilization for nuclear war, this isolated act would look like a bluff—a "sham." Pursley attempted to convince Kissinger and Haig that they should find other ways of meeting the president's demand for symbolic acts of toughness.[24]

These objections gave Kissinger a compelling reason to call off the intended nuclear maneuvers, but he pushed forward. More than the president, the NSC advisor believed that nuclear weapons could compel favorable behavior around Vietnam. In particular, he anticipated that a strong signal of mounting frustration and potential belligerence in the White House would convince the Kremlin to help end the war on acceptable American terms. It would also set a precedent for constructive nuclear diplomacy in the future, rather than passive nuclear deterrence. Kissinger's thinking drew on ideas he articulated as early as the mid-1950s, and continued to advocate through three different presidential administrations. In 1969 he had the opportunity, for the first time, to put these ideas into action.

On October 9, Kissinger recommended that Nixon approve a series of specific nuclear maneuvers, including:

1. Communications silence in selected Strategic Air Command and Polaris nuclear submarine commands;
2. Cessation of regular combat aircraft exercises in select areas;
3. Increased surveillance of Soviet ships en route to North Vietnam;

4. Increased ground alert actions for Strategic Air Command bombers and tankers;

5. Dispersal of Strategic Air Command aircraft with nuclear weapons to forward positions.[25]

Nixon approved these recommended actions. Together they constituted a nuclear alert—preparations for a possible use of nuclear weapons against the Soviet Union. The alert did not make a nuclear attack likely, but it did reduce the time and preparation Washington would need to launch its weapons, if the president gave the order. Most significant, actions of this kind surely elicited the attention of the Soviet military, and they must have raised questions about American intentions. That was Nixon and Kissinger's point. They wanted to sow uncertainty in the minds of Moscow's leaders, encouraging them to accommodate the United States in Vietnam for the sake of international stability.[26]

Before its termination on October 30, the nuclear alert included the loading of thermonuclear weapons on B-52 aircraft stationed at March Air Force Base in Southern California and Fairchild Air Force Base in Washington State. Nuclear-armed B-52s flew 18-hour missions over the northern polar cap, toward the Soviet border, in a pattern they would use if they were indeed launching a nuclear strike. These were dangerous missions that could have initiated a direct clash between Washington and Moscow, especially if a nuclear-armed aircraft strayed into Soviet airspace or crashed near Soviet territory. Observers in the Kremlin also might have misconstrued this alert as the real thing. Fortunately that did not happen. Kissinger's calculated nuclear risk-taking did not have immediate policy costs.[27]

It did not produce positive results either. Kissinger expected that Soviet Ambassador Dobrynin would refer to the nuclear alert, and become more accommodating as a consequence. This reaction never materialized. Nonetheless, Kissinger continued to advocate the repositioning of nuclear weapons, and occasional nuclear threats, to throw adversaries off balance. He remained convinced that nuclear weapons could serve diplomatic purposes, intimidating enemies and encouraging favorable negotiations.[28]

Confronting the frustrating limits on American leverage in Vietnam, Kissinger reaffirmed his long-standing belief that the nation's overwhelming military power, including its nuclear arsenal, "is no better than the willingness to use it." Seeking to extricate the United States from a self-defeating war and preserve the nation's credibility, Kissinger attempted to bolster the American negotiating position by growling and flexing the nation's muscles, while offering adversaries an outstretched hand. He followed the same script in October 1973 when, threatened by the prospect of Soviet intervention in the Middle East, he raised the American nuclear alert status to "DEFCON 3"—the highest state of readiness in peacetime—while also encouraging political cooperation between Washington and Moscow. This was precisely the strategy Kissinger had long advocated; it was precisely the opposite of the "peace policies" endorsed by good democrats in the 1930s and the 1960s.[29]

Domestic protest over the Vietnam War and other deployments of American force convinced Kissinger that he had to pursue his maneuvers in secrecy, without public accountability. This explains the curious organization of the October 1969 nuclear alert as an action that would be obvious to Soviet officials, but hidden from American citizens. Drawing on his experiences in Germany during the 1930s and the United States during the late 1960s, Kissinger believed that democratic citizens were not prepared to manage the necessary uses of military power, especially during a period of extreme political turbulence. His policies of escalation in Vietnam attempted to end the war, as many protesters demanded, without diminishing America's global position, as many protesters hoped.

This was more than just a matter of strategy for Kissinger; it was a reflection of his own personal history as a German-Jewish immigrant to the United States. "The principles of America's honor and America's responsibility," he recounted,

> were not empty phrases to me. I felt them powerfully. I had been
> born in Germany in the Bavarian town of Fürth, six months before
> Hitler's attempted beerhall putsch in Bavaria's capital, Munich.
> Hitler came to power when I was nine years old … Until I emigrated
> to America, my family and I endured progressive ostracism and
> discrimination. My father lost the teaching job for which he had
> worked all his life; the friends of my parents' youth shunned them. I
> was forced to attend a segregated school … Even when I learned later
> that America, too, had massive problems, I could never forget what
> an inspiration it had been to the victims of persecution, to my family,
> and to me during cruel and degrading years.[30]

Connecting his personal history to his policymaking in Vietnam, Kissinger criticized the "self-hatred" of many protesters in the late 1960s. Despite American misdeeds, he still believed he had to defend the nation's global position for "its idealism, its humanity, and its embodiment of mankind's hopes." Kissinger had a responsibility, as he saw it, "to help end the war in a way compatible with American self-respect and the stake that all men and women of goodwill had in America's strength and purpose." "It seemed to me important," Kissinger explained, "for America not to be humiliated, not to be shattered, but to leave Vietnam in a manner that even the protesters might later see as reflecting an American choice made with dignity and self-respect."[31]

Kissinger was defending his American dream in Vietnam—his salvation as a Jewish immigrant from Nazism, his coming of age in the U.S. Army, his rise as a postwar intellectual, and his power as a Cold War policymaker. His American dream was threatened by international communists *and* domestic critics who sought to undermine the very institutions that made his career possible—the Army, the universities, and the government. To defend the moral vision he attached to the power of the American state, Kissinger implemented foreign policies that excluded public interference and accountability. He often acted against what he saw as dangerous domestic opinion. To do otherwise, in his eyes, would repeat the mistakes of the democratic purists in the 1930s, and bow to the weaknesses and extremes of mass politics. For Kissinger, the American dream was too important to be left to the people protesting in the streets.[32]

Kissinger's grand strategy was a product of the disorder and discontent that dominated the late 1960s. It sought to reestablish international stability and American strength. Although it furnished Washington with a number of new foreign policy initiatives, this grand strategy did not provide the United States with a favorable exit from the Vietnam War and other inherited conflicts. In its secrecy and centralization of power, it undermined basic democratic accountability. Despite his efforts, Kissinger's attempts to preserve the American dream intensified domestic and international challenges to it.

Notes

1. For analysis of the origins and nature of global revolution in the 1960s, see Jeremi Suri, *Power and Protest: Global Revolution and the Rise of Détente* (Cambridge, Mass., 2003); idem., *The Global Revolutions of 1968* (New York, 2007), x-xxiii. For more extensive analysis of Kissinger's intellectual and social background, and its influence on his foreign policy, see Jeremi Suri, *Henry Kissinger and the American Century* (Cambridge, Mass., 2007).
2. Michael Stewart, handwritten diary, April 17, 1968, STWT 8/1/5, Churchill Archives Centre, Churchill College, Cambridge, U.K.

3. Notes on conversation between Hamilton Fish Armstrong and Henry Kissinger, March 30, 1972, Folder: Kissinger, Henry A., 1963–1972, Box 39, Papers of Hamilton Fish Armstrong, Seeley Mudd Manuscript Library, Princeton, N.J. (hereafter Armstrong papers).

4. Handwritten letter from Henry Kissinger to Nelson Rockefeller, December 30, 1968, Folder 245, Box 10, Series P: Ann C. Whitman— Politics, Record Group 4, Nelson A. Rockefeller Papers (hereafter NAR), Personal, Rockefeller Archive Center, Pocantico Hills, New York (hereafter RAC); Kissinger to Rockefeller, August 20, 1968, Folder 110, Box 7, Series 35, Record Group 15, NAR, Gubernatorial, RAC.

5. Henry Kissinger, "Central Issues of American Foreign Policy," in *Agenda for the Nation*, ed. Kermit Gordon (Washington, D.C., 1968), 614.

6. Ibid., 602. Kissinger rejected the programs advocated by "New Left" and "New Right" radicals, but he sympathized with the protestors' criticisms of containment, liberal politics, and Cold War policies in general. See Kissinger to Rockefeller, May 31, 1968, Folder 91, Box 5, Series 35, Record Group 15, NAR, Gubernatorial, RAC; Kissinger article draft to be published under Rockefeller's name, 1967, Folder 246, Box 10, Series P, Record Group 4, NAR, Personal, RAC. This draft text, authored by Kissinger, was the basis for Nelson A. Rockefeller, "Policy and the People," *Foreign Affairs* 46 (January 1968): 231–241.

7. Memorandum of conversation between Henry Kissinger and Fellows from the Harvard Center for International Affairs, December 7, 1971, Digital National Security Archive Document Database (hereafter NSA), http://nsarchive.chadwyck.com.ezproxy.library.wisc.edu (accessed 26 July 2006).

8. Henry Kissinger to William Elliott, May 12, 1955, with attached letter to Vice President Richard Nixon, May 12, 1955, Folder: International Seminar, Harvard, 1951–1959, Box 2, William Y. Elliott Papers, Hoover Institution, Stanford, California; Kissinger to Rockefeller, August 20, 1968, Folder 110, Box 7, Series 35, Record Group 15, NAR, Gubernatorial, RAC; Henry Kissinger to Ernst Van der Beugel, August 14, 1968, Papers of Ernst Hans Van der Beugel, National Archive, the Netherlands. See also Henry Kissinger, *White House Years* (Boston, 1979), 9–10.

9. Author's interview with Henry Kissinger, July 27, 2004; Henry Kissinger, *Years of Renewal* (New York, 1999), 54–63.

10. Kissinger, *White House Years*, 226–227. On the improving military situation for the United States in Vietnam, see Special National Intelligence Estimate, SNIE 14–69, January 16, 1969; Memorandum from Chairman of the Joint Chiefs of Staff Earle Wheeler to Secretary of Defense Melvin Laird, July 21, 1969, *FRUS, 1969–1976*, vol. VI, documents 1 and 100; Lewis Sorley, *A Better War: The Unexamined Victories and Final Tragedy of America's Last Years in Vietnam* (New York, 1999).

11. Henry Kissinger to Henry Cabot Lodge, U.S. Ambassador to South Vietnam, September 7, 1965, Reel 20, Part 5, Papers of Henry Cabot

Lodge II, Massachusetts Historical Society, Boston, Mass. For the same argument, see Kissinger, "Central Issues of American Foreign Policy," 585–614; and idem, "The Viet Nam Negotiations," *Foreign Affairs* 47 (January 1969): 211–234.

12. See Kissinger to Nixon, undated (circa late March 1969), *FRUS, 1969–1976*, vol. VI, document 46.

13. Kissinger, *White House Years*, 227–228. For more on the depth of American liberal commitments in Vietnam, see Michael E. Latham, *Modernization as Ideology: American Social Science and "Nation-Building" in the Kennedy Era* (Chapel Hill, N.C., 2000), esp. 69–108; Lloyd C. Gardner, *Pay Any Price: Lyndon Johnson and the Wars for Vietnam* (Chicago, 1995), esp. 40–64; Suri, *Power and Protest*, 131–163. For more on American public opinion regarding the Vietnam War, see John E. Mueller, *War, Presidents and Public Opinion* (New York, 1973), 42–167; Robert D. Schulzinger, *A Time for War: The United States and Vietnam, 1941–1975* (New York, 1997), 280–283; and Melvin Small, *Johnson, Nixon, and the Doves* (New Brunswick, N.J., 1988), esp. 162–224.

14. For an excellent discussion of "credibility" and American foreign policy, see Robert J. McMahon, "Credibility and World Power," *Diplomatic History* 15 (Fall 1991): 455–472.

15. Thomas C. Schelling, *Arms and Influence* (New Haven, 1966), 124–125. Like Kissinger, Schelling generally supported American actions in Vietnam during the 1960s. After the American invasion of Cambodia in 1970, however, Schelling strongly opposed Nixon and Kissinger's policies.

16. Kissinger to Nixon, March 8, 1969; transcript of telephone conversation between Nixon and Kissinger, April 5, 1969, *FRUS, 1969–1976*, vol. VI, documents 34 and 55.

17. Nixon to Kissinger, May 9, 1972, Folder: Memos, May 1972, Box 4, President's Personal File, White House Special Files, Nixon Presidential Materials Project, National Archives, College Park, Md. Emphasis in original.

18. For Kissinger's clear articulation of this strategy for Vietnam, see Kissinger to Nixon, April 3, 1969, *FRUS, 1969–1976*, vol. VI, document 52; handwritten notes on Kissinger's conversation with Henry Cabot Lodge, February 28, 1969; handwritten notes on Kissinger's conversation with Lodge, August 1969, Reel 9, Part 1, Lodge papers. See also Jussi Hanhimäki, *The Flawed Architect: Henry Kissinger and American Foreign Policy* (New York, 2004), 46–48.

19. On Nixon's "madman" ideas, and their influence on the administration's foreign policy, see Jeffrey Kimball, *Nixon's Vietnam War* (Lawrence, Kan., 1998), 63–86; idem, ed., *The Vietnam War Files: Uncovering the Secret History of Nixon-Era Strategy* (Lawrence, Kans., 2004), 11–24, 53–120; William Burr and Jeffrey Kimball, "Nixon's Secret Nuclear Alert: Vietnam War Diplomacy and the Joint Chiefs of Staff Readiness Test, October 1969," *Cold War History* 3 (January 2003): 113–156; Scott D. Sagan and

Jeremi Suri, "The Madman Nuclear Alert: Secrecy, Signaling, and Safety in October 1969," *International Security* 27 (Spring 2003): 150–183.

20. Kissinger to Nixon no date (circa early October 1969), with attached paper on "The Modern World: A Single 'Strategic Theater'" by Kissinger's old mentor, Fritz Kraemer, September 29, 1969, Folder: Kraemer, Fritz G., Box 822, NSC Files, Nixon papers. For Nixon's thinking about the "big play," see William Safire, *Before the Fall: An Inside View of the Pre-Watergate White House* (Garden City, N.Y., 1975), 97–106.

21. Kissinger to Nixon, March 16, 1969; Nixon to Kissinger, April 22, 1970; Kissinger to Nixon, no date (circa April 23, 1970); National Security Council Decision Memorandum 57, April 26, 1970, *FRUS, 1969–1976*, vol. VI, documents 40, 245, 253, 260; Kissinger, *White House Years*, 489–499. The literature on the United States attacks on Cambodia during the Vietnam War, and their tragic effects, is enormous. The most moving account remains, William Shawcross, *Sideshow: Kissinger, Nixon and the Destruction of Cambodia* (New York, 1979). See also David P. Chandler, *The Tragedy of Cambodian History: Politics, War, and Revolution since 1945* (New Haven, 1991); Schulzinger, *A Time for War*, 284–287; and Kimball, *Nixon's Vietnam War*, 131–145, 197–212.

22. Kissinger recounts that he first brought the idea of a nuclear alert to Nixon. The president was making threats about the need to end the war in Vietnam soon, and something had to be done. Kissinger reiterates that the alert was meant to be seen by the Soviets, but not threatening. This was a warning, not a provocation for war, he explains. Author's interview with Kissinger, July 27, 2004. See also memorandum of conversation between Kissinger and Dobrynin September 27, 1969, Folder: Dobrynin/Kissinger 1969 (Part 1), Box 489, Henry Kissinger Office Files, NSC files, Nixon Papers; Kissinger to Nixon, March 16, 1969, *FRUS, 1969–1976*, vol. VI, document 40; Sagan and Suri, "Madman Nuclear Alert," 150–183; Burr and Kimball, "Nixon's Secret Nuclear Alert," 113–156. For Schelling's influence on Kissinger's manipulation of risk and uncertainty, see Thomas C. Schelling, *The Strategy of Conflict* (Cambridge, Mass., 1960), 187–203; idem., *Arms and Influence*, 92–125. Daniel Ellsberg offered a similar analysis in the late 1950s. See Daniel Ellsberg, "The Theory and Practice of Blackmail," RAND P-3883, July 1968 (originally delivered as a lecture at the Lowell Institute at the Boston Public Library, March 1959), available at http://www.rand.org/pubs/papers/2005/P3883.pdf (accessed September 10, 2006).

23. Alexander Haig to Kissinger October 14, 1969, Folder: Haig Chron., October 1–15, 1969 (1 of 2), Box 958, NSC files, Nixon papers. The account of Kissinger's October 6, 1969, telephone conversation with Laird comes from William Burr and Jeffrey Kimball, "New Evidence on the Secret Nuclear Alert of October 1969: The Henry A. Kissinger Telcons," *Passport: The Newsletter of the Society for Historians of American Foreign Relations* (April 2005).

24. Lieutenant General Robert Pursley to Haig, October 9, 1969, Folder: Items to Discuss with President, 8/13/69–12/30/69, Box 334, NSC files, Nixon papers; Pursley telephone interview with Scott Sagan, November 4, 2002.

25. Kissinger to Nixon October 9, 1969, Folder: Schedule of Significant Military Exercises, Volume 1, Box: 352, NSC files, Nixon papers; Haig to Kissinger October 9, 1969, Folder: Items to Discuss with President, 8/13/69–12/30/69, Box 334, NSC files, Nixon papers.

26. Haig to Kissinger October 17, 1969, Folder: Items to Discuss with President, 8/13/69–12/30/69, Box 334, NSC files, Nixon papers.

27. History of the 92nd Strategic Aerospace Wing (Heavy) and 92nd Combat Support Group, 14 September–31 December 1969, KWG-92-HI, AFHRC, Maxwell Air Force Base; Strategic Air Command to Eielson, March, and Fairchild Air Force Bases 21 October 1969, FOIA; Sagan and Suri, "Madman Nuclear Alert," 173–179. The risk of Moscow misconstruing an alert or exercise as the start of a real war was serious. In 1983 Soviet leaders apparently misconstrued a NATO nuclear exercise— codenamed Able Archer 83—as a possible initiation of nuclear war. The KGB began to prepare for imminent conflict. See Benjamin B. Fischer, "A Cold War Conundrum," History Staff of the Center for the Study of Intelligence, CIA, 1997, https://www.cia.gov/csi/monograph/coldwar/ source.htm (accessed August, 18, 2006); Christopher Andrew and Oleg Gordievsky, *KGB: The Inside Story* (New York, 1990), 583–605; Jeremi Suri, "Explaining the End of the Cold War: A New Historical Consensus?" *Journal of Cold War Studies* 4 (Fall 2002): 69–70.

28. Kissinger confirms that to his knowledge the Soviet Union never reacted to the October 1969 U.S. nuclear alert: "They must have seen it, but what were they going to do?" Kissinger recounts that he never discussed the nuclear alert with Soviet officials. He does not, however, reject the logic behind using nuclear maneuvers to signal and intimidate adversaries. Author's interview with Kissinger, July 27, 2004.

29. Henry Kissinger, Memorandum to Arthur Schlesinger, Jr., December 8, 1954, Folder: Kissinger, Henry A., 1954–57, Box 39, Armstrong papers; Kissinger, *Years of Upheaval*, 575–599. On Kissinger's attempts to create new limited nuclear strike options for diplomatic leverage, see William Burr, "The Nixon Administration, the 'Horror Strategy,' and the Search for Limited Nuclear Options, 1969–1972," *Journal of Cold War Studies* 7 (Summer 2005): 34–78; Terry Terriff, *The Nixon Administration and the Making of U.S. Nuclear Strategy* (Ithaca, 1995), esp. 51–96, 159–203.

30. Kissinger, *White House Years*, 228–229.

31. Ibid.

32. For more on the isolation of foreign policy from popular interference and accountability in this period, see Suri, *Power and Protest*, 213–259.

4

Salesmanship and Substance: The Influence of Domestic Policy and Watergate

Dominic Sandbrook

Richard Nixon took office in January 1969 after one of the most turbulent years in recent American history, marked by assassinations, race riots, student protests, a crippling gold crisis and a bloody stalemate in South Vietnam. Many ordinary Americans had voted for Nixon because he stood for old-fashioned stability and respectability in bewildering, disorderly times. Yet as he contemplated the challenges of the 1970s, from campus unrest and drug use to rising crime and soaring inflation, Nixon could have been forgiven a shudder of trepidation. Deeply rooted in the changing social and cultural landscape of the postwar years, these problems were beyond the scope of any one man to solve. Since they had already consumed the ambitions of his predecessor Lyndon Johnson, there seemed every chance that they would frustrate Nixon too. The last president to face such enormous challenges had been Harry Truman; ominously, his presidency had ended in corruption, paralysis, and record unpopularity.[1]

In 1968, Nixon's campaign had been notable for careful moderation rather than robust conservatism, and his record in office was no less ambiguous. On one hand, he clearly anticipated the conservatism of the 1980s and beyond, not least in his appeal to the Southern white middle classes, his patriotic populism and his aggressive antielitist rhetoric. Yet there is also a persuasive case for treating Nixon as the last representative of the New Deal order. He famously told his staff that he was simply not interested in most domestic issues, but at the same time he fancied himself an American Benjamin Disraeli, a "Tory man with liberal measures."[2] Indeed, Nixon's progressive domestic accomplishments belied his image as an unfeeling reactionary: poverty continued to decline during his presidency, while domestic spending rose by 44 percent. On this evidence, it is easy to see why he is often regarded as the last liberal president.[3]

A crucial factor in all this, of course, was Congress. Nixon was the first president since 1853 to take office without a majority in either house, which boded ill for the passage of his policies. What was more, the Democratic Party remained a formidable electoral outfit. Despite slight losses in 1968, the Democrats still controlled the House by 248 seats to 187 and the Senate by 58 votes to 42. Nationwide, 55 percent of Americans said that they identified with the national Democratic Party, compared with 34 percent preferring the Republicans. Since Nixon had won the presidency by less than 1 percent and took office with an approval rating of just 59 percent, it was hardly surprising that he was deeply anxious about his prospects for reelection. It is hard to imagine a more challenging situation: a Republican president, elected with the most fragile of mandates, compelled to work closely with a Democratic Congress in the context of social unrest, cultural change, economic deterioration, and the stalemate in Vietnam.[4]

Throughout his presidency, Nixon's relations with Congress were simply dreadful. The Democratic majorities meant that even if he had wanted to push through a radically conservative agenda, it would have been impossible for him to do so. And since Nixon showed little interest in cultivating the Democrats or even building a close alliance with his fellow Republicans, it was hardly surprising that in his second term the Senate pursued the Watergate scandal so keenly. On the domestic front, he used pocket vetoes to block legislation he disliked, invoked executive privilege on a record twenty-seven occasions, and impounded congressional funds relating to more than 100 different programs. And in every major foreign policy dilemma of his presidency, Nixon consistently tried to keep Congress in the dark. As he explained in his memoirs, Congress was "cumbersome, undisciplined, isolationist, fiscally irresponsible, overly vulnerable to pressures from organized minorities, and too dominated by the media."[5] Even the congressional Republicans, Nixon explained to his chief of staff Bob Haldeman in 1973, were "nothing but a bunch of asses."[6]

Nixon's deep distrust of Congress helps to explain his enduring obsession with leaks, even when, as in the case of the Pentagon Papers in 1971, the information being leaked actually concerned his predecessors. In tandem

with Henry Kissinger, he created an extremely tight and personalized foreign policy apparatus, steeped in suspicion and secrecy, that observers came
to associate with the much-criticized "imperial presidency." In fairness to
Nixon, the imperial presidency clearly developed over a long period of time,
not least under his immediate predecessors.[7] But it reached its apogee during
the early 1970s, fuelled above all by his insistence on seeing politics in terms
of conflict, conspiracy, secrecy, and surprise. Like Kissinger, Nixon feared
that Congress would rush to close down the Vietnam War in a disorderly
manner, and fancied himself as a Lone Ranger in the international arena.
In one revealing note to himself, he scribbled: "Foreign Policy=Strength ...
Must emphasize—Courage. Stands alone ... Knows more than anyone else.
Towers above advisers. World leader."[8]

Foreign policy, of course, is never made in a vacuum: no president can
afford to ignore public opinion, social trends, the electoral calendar, and
the balance of power in Congress. The Nixon White House, however, was
notorious for its compulsive attention to opinion polls and press coverage.
A remarkably thin-skinned man, smarting from his treatment by the press
during the 1950s and 1960s, Nixon was obsessed by the treatment of foreign
policy in the newspapers, often reading fifty closely typed pages of news
summaries a day. The very first thing he did on his first full day in China,
for example, was to ask Haldeman to review the American coverage of his
arrival. The press, he reminded his cabinet in 1971, "aren't interested in liking you, they're only interested in news or in screwing me."[9] In a memo
later the same year, he unburdened himself further: "Ninety-five percent of
the members of the Washington press corps are unalterably opposed to us
because of their intellectual and philosophical background. Some of them
will smirk and pander to us for the purpose of getting a story but we must
remember that they are just waiting for the chance to stick the knife in deep
and to twist it."[10]

Nixon's fear of the press proved both infectious and corrosive: after a
brief public spat about casualties in Laos, for example, Haldeman recorded
that "the whole episode shows more clearly than anything else yet how the
White House press is totally dedicated to screwing us rather than getting
the facts and reporting them." And while this climate of suspicion undoubtedly contributed to the criminal excesses of the Plumbers and the Watergate
operation, it also encouraged Nixon's determination to keep diplomatic
decision making inside the White House. In this respect, Nixon had an ideal
partner in the similarly conspiratorial Henry Kissinger. Both were convinced
that their own administration was stuffed with liberals awaiting the chance

to stab them in the back. As early as 1969, Haldeman recorded a dinner at Camp David where the president's guests discussed "the bad guys 'they' have infiltrated into everywhere, especially State." Nixon even told his cabinet that "down in the government are a bunch of sons of bitches ... We've checked and found that 96 percent of the bureaucracy are against us; they're bastards who are here to screw us."[11]

Of modern presidents, perhaps only Nixon's former patron, Dwight D. Eisenhower, was better prepared to handle American foreign relations when he took office. As vice president, Nixon had made frequent trips abroad and built up an impressive network of foreign contacts, including the likes of Charles de Gaulle and Konrad Adenauer. It was this experience that gave him the confidence to develop his own vision of foreign affairs, breaking through the narrow anti-Communism that originally had made his name. He was also unusual among twentieth-century presidents in terms of his sheer enthusiasm for foreign policy. While always conscious of the constraints on his freedom to act, notably Congress and public opinion, he was determined to take an active role in the conduct of diplomacy. Chatting to the journalist Theodore H. White during his presidential campaign, he mused: "I've always thought the country could run itself domestically without a President. All you need is a competent Cabinet to run the country at home. You need a President for foreign policy."[12]

Of course it was impossible for Nixon to leave domestic policy to his cabinet: if nothing else, he was an obsessive micromanager, issuing memos on everything from the design of the Cabinet Room chairs to the wine to be served at state dinners. But he always insisted that foreign policy was his chief priority, dismissing domestic concerns as merely "building outhouses in Peoria."[13] In March 1970, for instance, he sent Haldeman, Kissinger, and John Ehrlichman a long memo explaining that the only domestic issues he wanted to handle personally were the economy, crime, and school integration. But he had rather more enthusiasm for foreign policy, listing five major priorities: "East-West relations"; "Policy towards the Soviet Union"; "Policy towards Communist China"; "Policy towards Eastern Europe, provided it really affects East-West relations at the highest level"; and "Policy towards Western Europe, but only where NATO is affected and where major countries (Britain, Germany and France) are affected." Apparently nothing else, apart from Vietnam, really mattered.[14]

Even before the Watergate scandal, Nixon's critics described him as outrageously partisan, a dirty fighter who would subordinate all other interests to his own electoral fortunes. In 1968, however, Nixon presented himself as a born-again statesman, and for the rest of his life both he and Kissinger insisted that their goal had been to protect foreign policy from the passions of everyday partisanship. Kissinger claimed in his memoirs that "in the Nixon White House there was an almost complete separation between the domestic and foreign policy sides."[15] And Nixon made the same point in private, complaining in February 1969 that he was sick of seeing State Department papers referring to "domestic political considerations" affecting American policy in the Middle East. "Under no circumstances will domestic political considerations have any bearing on the decisions I make with regard to the Mideast," Nixon wrote. "The only consideration which will affect my decisions on this policy will be the security interests of the United States ... In the future, I want no reference to domestic political considerations to be included in any papers."[16]

This is not the whole story, however. When Nixon referred to "domestic political considerations," he clearly meant Jewish support for Israel, a phenomenon he regarded with irritation and distaste. Similar "domestic political considerations" might also include the labor movement, the Democratic Party, the antiwar movement, and Congress, all of which both Nixon and Kissinger treated as adversaries bent on exercising illegitimate influence over foreign policy.[17] On the other hand, Nixon's own domestic considerations fell into a very different category. As early as October 1970, the journalist Elizabeth Drew wrote that in the Nixon administration, "more than in any other within memory, policy and politics intermix."[18] Indeed, electoral factors clearly had great influence on administration policy, especially in such areas as crime or the economy. In July 1970, for example, Haldeman recorded Nixon's order to put "more emphasis on basing all scheduling and other decisions on political grounds." And a year later, looking forward to his reelection campaign, Nixon told his staff to "make a shift, as of now, throughout our entire shop to being a totally oriented commitment to relating everything we do to the political side, without appearing to do so ... The question to be asked in weighing every answer is, 'Does this help us politically?' "[19]

In general, electoral considerations weighed less heavily on foreign policy than on domestic decisions. For one thing, voters were consistently less interested in foreign affairs (apart, of course, from Vietnam) than they were in such bread-and-butter issues as crime and inflation, so there was less incentive for Nixon to tailor his diplomatic policies accordingly. What was more, he was frequently distracted by immediate domestic concerns and allowed Henry Kissinger enormous leeway to negotiate with the Chinese, the Vietnamese, and so on. Although Nixon's critics often compared him with a used-car salesman, Kissinger suffered from the opposite problem. He had never run for elected office and lacked Nixon's extreme political sensitivity: fancying himself a latter-day Metternich, he treated domestic pressures as irritating intrusions on the lofty business of international diplomacy. In May 1970, Nixon even ordered that Kissinger should be taken off press "backgrounders," because he "goes into so much detail about the philosophy and the procedures, etc., that the main [i.e., political] thrust doesn't come through."[20] As Jussi Hanhimäki puts it, Kissinger was a "poor salesman," indifferent to domestic issues and incapable of winning "broad support from heartland audiences," which would cost him dearly when détente came under attack after 1973.[21]

The most obvious way in which domestic political considerations affected foreign policy was Nixon's obsession with presentation. Selling foreign policy to the public mattered enormously to him: returning from Romania in August 1969, Haldeman noted that he was "still really concerned that we aren't adequately selling the accomplishments, keeps grinding away on this. Got heavily into the need for a PR man again." A year later, Nixon complained that "we now have the image of a PR-oriented Administration, but we've totally failed in our real PR," citing "the foreign policy area where we had three major accomplishments: Cambodia, the Middle East, and the [November 1969] Vietnam speech, but we don't get across the courage, the independence, the boldness, standing alone, overruling advisors, that go into this."[22] As Nixon explained to John Ehrlichman in April 1972, salesmanship was crucial to secure public and congressional backing:

> In the case of foreign policy, selling the policy is very important just
> like making the policy is important. Without selling the policy, public
> support for it which is so essential to get the approval of funds where
> necessary in Congress, is not generated. On the other hand, substance
> in the case of foreign policy is infinitely more important than
> substance is in the case of domestic policy, insofar as long-range
> consequences are concerned. For example, I could easily have
> rejected the Cambodian and Laotian operations and not ordered
> a response by air to the current North Vietnamese offensive. This
> would have been an easy policy to sell. It would have been disastrous
> from the standpoint of substance, however.

"In other words," he concluded, "while selling foreign policy is important, substance is indispensable."[23]

The area of foreign policy in which salesmanship was most critical was, of course, Vietnam. By 1969, a majority of Americans thought that entering the war had been a mistake, and although polls showed that only a minority favored an immediate withdrawal, Nixon's diplomatic priority was to get the troops home. "I'm not going to end up like LBJ, holed up in the White House, afraid to show my face on the street," Haldeman recalled Nixon saying. "I'm going to stop that war. Fast."[24] Unfortunately, although Nixon had promised an "honorable peace" during his presidential campaign, he had no very clear idea how to bring it about and greatly overestimated how long it would take.[25] As early as July 1969, in fact, Kissinger was gloomily reporting that his "plans for ending [the] war aren't working fast enough," and was pushing for "some escalation, enough to get us a reasonable bargain for a settlement within six months," which, as we now know, was still an unrealistically optimistic scenario.[26]

Three months later, Kissinger was still talking about a similar schedule, but was "very concerned" whether Nixon "can hold the government and people together for the six months it will take." Haldeman noted that "his contingency plans don't include the domestic factor," and Ehrlichman suggested preparing "several routes on a PR basis." Yet the really striking thing about the administration's policy in Vietnam is how *little* domestic politics intruded. If Nixon had been as ruthlessly self-serving as his critics suggest, he would have surely pulled American troops out more quickly, and certainly would have not taken the controversial gamble of sending troops into Cambodia. It is worth remembering that at home he was under tremendous pressure to wind up the war more quickly, not least from Congress, where the influential Senate Foreign Relations Committee had long since turned against the war. As early as March 1969, the committee approved a resolution that would inhibit the president from sending troops abroad without a declaration of war, while in June 1970 the Senate both repealed the Gulf of Tonkin Resolution and passed the Cooper-Church Amendment, which would have cut off all funds for Cambodian operations by the end of the month had it not been rejected by the House. As the next presidential election approached, various Democrats competed to take the fiercest line: in February 1971, for example, Haldeman noted that "the Democratic attacks on the war ... are becoming strong and very partisan," although there is no evidence that Nixon took much notice.[27]

Nixon certainly took little notice of the strident antiwar movement, later calling it "a brotherhood of the misguided, the mistaken, the well-meaning, and the malevolent."[28] Like many conservatives, he feared that the protests encouraged the North Vietnamese to put off a settlement on the assumption that American will was weakening, but even if there is some truth in this, it was hardly a decisive factor. And although he certainly tried to minimize the effect of public dissent, if this had been his priority he would presumably have adopted very different policies. As it was, he ordered bombers into Laos, Cambodia and Vietnam, sent American troops into Cambodia, and presided over four more years of warfare, hardly the behavior of somebody terrified by protests and public opinion. It is revealing that on November 13, 1969, when marchers held a candlelit vigil outside the White House, Nixon refused to watch and spent two hours in his private bowling alley.[29]

What allowed Nixon to ignore the peace movement was the plain fact that his policies were broadly popular with the American public. By the end of 1972, the draft had been scrapped, Vietnamization had reduced American troop numbers from 543,400 to 24,200, American combat deaths had virtually ceased, and the antiwar movement had fallen silent. Draft reform acted as a crucial brake on the momentum of antiwar protest; indeed, the movement had effectively fizzled out as early as the fall of 1969, when Nixon's "silent majority" speech rallied public opinion behind Vietnamization.[30] What temporarily revived the movement was the invasion of Cambodia, in which domestic politics may well have played a role. As early as April 1969 Kissinger told Nixon that a "really strong overt act" was "essential to galvanize people into overcoming slothfulness and detachment arising from general moral decay." At the time, Nixon disagreed.[31] But it is worth noting that when he changed his mind, in the spring of 1970, it was against the background of falling approval ratings (down ten points in two months) and the humiliating rejection of his Supreme Court nominees Harrold Carswell and Clement Haynsworth.[32] Of course the invasion had been long planned; even so, Haldeman noted that Kissinger "would go ahead even if plan is wrong, just to prove P can't be challenged."[33] Ehrlichman even told Kissinger that Nixon needed a "bold stroke" because of his troubles "on [the] domestic side."[34]

Yet this picture is more complicated than it looks. Nixon was taking a tremendous gamble by widening the war, and he told Haldeman that he would have to do "a masterful job of explanation to keep the people with him." From the domestic perspective, the gamble handsomely paid off. Despite enormous anger on the campuses and intense controversy over the Kent State shootings, Nixon's ratings showed a healthy increase after it was all over, reaching an impressive 61 percent in July 1970: "darn good in normal times," wrote Haldeman, "unbelievable now, in spite of Cambodia, the economy, the students, and the press."[35] Polls consistently found that most Americans approved of Nixon's approach, deplored student protests, and blamed the demonstrators themselves for the killings at Kent State University.[36]

In reality, Cambodia marked the climax of the antiwar movement. Although the events of the following year—notably the failure of secret negotiations with the North Vietnamese in Paris and the hapless South Vietnamese invasion of Laos—brought more frustration for Nixon, he paid no domestic price. With Vietnamization and draft reform continuing apace, the peace movement simply ran out of steam.[37] In March 1971, when William Calley was sentenced to imprisonment for his role in the My Lai massacre, a majority of Americans, like Nixon himself, sympathized with him. A month later, thousands of Vietnam veterans marched on the Capitol, but this was a dying, futile hurrah, and had no discernible impact on Kissinger's negotiations with the Vietnamese. Although Nixon was briefly worried about the veterans, he treated them as a public relations problem. On the day of the great march, according to Haldeman, he was "mainly interested … in seeing that it was downplayed as much as possible" and "didn't seem to be particularly concerned about it."[38] Nixon's complacency was understandable: by the year's end, even though peace remained elusive, the movement had effectively disappeared.

Although Nixon and his aides hoped that the Cambodian incursion would count in his favor in the 1970 midterm elections, the truth is that foreign policy was simply not a factor. In the final days of the campaign, when Nixon took to the stump in a rare presidential effort to rally support for his fellow Republicans, foreign affairs were barely mentioned at all. Both Nixon's own election-eve broadcast and Democratic Senator Edmund Muskie's reply concentrated on crime and the economy. Nixon himself was puzzled that foreign policy seemed to make no difference when voters chose their congressmen: the reason, of course, was that voters cared much more about pocketbook issues.[39] Reporting on the disappointing results, which showed the Republicans losing nine House seats, gaining two in the Senate and losing eleven governorships, Charles Colson reminded Nixon that although "people are generally satisfied with your handling of the war," it had "become something of a non-issue," neither hurting the Democrats nor bolstering the Republicans.[40]

Even so, in terms of foreign policy the 1970 midterm elections still represented a significant moment, confirming the enduring strength of the Democrats and the constraining presence of opposition in Congress. If Nixon's mandate had been desperately slim in 1968, it was not much greater two years later. From this point onward, the next presidential election assumed vast significance in Nixon's thinking. And despite its general irrelevance in 1970, foreign policy would more than ever be treated as an opportunity to impress his domestic audience.

The quintessential examples of this approach were Nixon's extraordinary expeditions to Beijing and Moscow, which were so closely interwoven with his reelection drive as to become virtually indistinguishable from campaign events. The trip to Moscow, for example, was a classic piece of political theater, consciously planned to boost Nixon's domestic popularity: on his return on June 1, for example, he immediately flew to the floodlit Capitol where, live on network television, he walked straight into a joint session of Congress. The point, Colson told his staff, was "not to achieve greater public support for SALT, but rather to strengthen the president's image as one of the great world leaders of the century."[41] Had Nixon spent more time selling SALT to the American people instead of bolstering his own image, then détente might have stood more chance of weathering the storms of the mid-seventies. Yet given the advice he was getting from his subordinates, his address to Congress was a model of restraint. Ehrlichman had told him to turn it into "a campaign kickoff speech." Haldeman records that Nixon "thought that was ridiculous ... and totally rejected the idea." But public relations were never far from his mind: a few moments later, Nixon reflected that "it's not domestic issues that we should spend our time on, that's their issue, not ours. We should concentrate on the international, which is where we make the gains."[42]

Even the trip to Moscow paled by comparison with Nixon's breathtaking visit to China earlier that year. As in Moscow, the actual negotiations were left to Henry Kissinger, while Nixon's staff fretted about public relations. Discussing the trip in October 1971, Nixon insisted on "having maximum TV coverage available, in spite of Henry's objections to all that." Here, as so often, their priorities differed: despite his usual enthusiasm for press coverage, Kissinger wanted nothing to interfere with his delicate negotiations with the Chinese, while Nixon preferred to impress the American public with his globe-trotting statesmanship. According to Haldeman, Kissinger "sat and sulked" when Nixon overruled him about coverage of the summit. "Henry's concern on all this is that we not make a circus out of it," he noted, "and that we not appear to be staging the whole thing for the benefit of domestic TV." Haldeman himself shared Nixon's view that "we need maximum coverage in order to get the benefit from it, especially in the short term." Nixon got his way, but still spent much of the trip demanding reports on the television coverage. Even on the flight home, Haldeman had to persuade him "that we were really in very good shape," although "it was hard to convince him of that ... he was afraid we were dealing with a bad story and we'll have to move hard and fast on it to avoid getting really clobbered."[43]

Nixon's fears of a "bad story" reflected his anxiety at the possibility of an angry reaction within the Republican Party. Ever since the 1960 presidential election, when he had handed over the party platform to the liberal Nelson Rockefeller, Nixon had been regarded with deep suspicion by the conservative wing of the Republican Party. Even in 1968, Southern conservatives had greatly preferred the candidacy of Ronald Reagan, and well before his rapprochement with the Chinese, Nixon's domestic policies had alarmed right-wing observers like the magazine *Human Events*, the publisher William Loeb and the *National Review* founder William Buckley.[44] Given the conservatives' abhorrence of communist China, Nixon's anxiety about their reaction to his trip to Beijing is perfectly understandable. His speechwriter Pat Buchanan came close to resignation, while Loeb called the visit "immoral, indecent, insane and fraught with danger for the survival of the United States." Buckley, meanwhile, publicly abandoned Nixon in December 1971 and supported the Ohio conservative John Ashbrook in the Republican primaries.[45]

Yet the striking thing is how little all this actually mattered. Nixon himself told Haldeman that "we don't need to worry too much about the right-wing nuts on this."[46] Ashbrook's campaign went nowhere; as the historian Robert Mason puts it, the right-wing challenges "remained irritants of no more than a minor nature" and had no immediate impact on détente.[47] Kissinger recalls that Nixon was "beside himself" with anxiety about the concessions in the Shanghai Communiqué, but the fact that they had agreed on a communiqué at all spoke volumes about the impotence of the right-wingers.[48]

Nixon's trips to China and the Soviet Union marked the last time that he was able to give foreign policy his full attention; after the summer of 1972, he was distracted first by his reelection campaign and then by the Watergate scandal. In the presidential campaign, Nixon and his advisers were keen to make foreign policy a major issue, but as before, they found it hard going. In November 1971 a poll of newspaper editors found that only nine expected "international affairs" to be the principal issue of the campaign, compared with 107 who nominated the economy. Nixon furiously scribbled on his news summary: "They must not be allowed to get away with this—International affairs is *our* issue; Economy is theirs regardless of what happens to it because Libs can always promise more."[49] As it turned out, however, his economic team was able to engineer a small boom before the 1972 election—a much more obvious example of popularity-driven policy than any comparable case in foreign affairs—while the Democrats' disastrous nomination of George McGovern effectively allowed Nixon to run on whichever issues he chose.

With McGovern widely regarded as a radical extremist, Nixon delightedly played up his image as an international statesman, glossing over the economic record of the last four years. "The real issue is patriotism, morality, religion," he told his aides, "not the material issues of prices and taxes. If those were the issue, the people would be for McGovern rather than for us."[50] Indeed, foreign policy was one of Nixon's greatest strengths in 1972. While his diplomatic achievements drew praise from the likes of the AFL-CIO labor baron George Meany and Chicago's working-class mayor Richard Daley, they also allowed him to reach out to the Democrats' moderate congressional leaders Carl Albert and Hale Boggs, both of whom promised to back Nixon on national security issues. The press, meanwhile, was almost uniformly complimentary about Nixon's foreign policy, with news broadcasts showing clips of his visits to China and the Soviet Union, and editorials praising his moderation and statesmanship.[51] Polls indicated broad public approval of Nixon's diplomatic initiatives, and even though he had still not obtained a settlement of the Vietnam War—his declared priority four years earlier—he still led McGovern on the issue by a stunning 32 percent. On foreign affairs, said the *New York Times*, Nixon was "invincible."[52]

Foreign policy clearly played a much greater role in the 1972 election than in 1970, and Nixon's pollster Robert Teeter consistently urged him to emphasize the issue. After Nixon's landslide victory, Teeter was vindicated: polls showed that the president's greatest strength had been his policy in Vietnam, while his greatest weakness had been the economy.[53] Even so, foreign policy was far from Nixon's only weapon, and even if it had been eliminated as an issue, he would surely still have trounced his opponent. By his reckoning, the "gut" issues, the ones that really mattered, were "crime, busing, drugs, welfare, inflation," and he was almost certainly right.[54] For all his eye-catching accomplishments, as Nixon told his aides, foreign policy only really mattered "to Henry's country, the intellectuals and the social jet set." By contrast, "the plain folks in the middle of America, they don't know anything about what you're doing on SALT and all these other things, they just want things to simmer down and be quiet."[55]

In March 1973, when the last American troops left Vietnam, Nixon's approval rating peaked at 70 percent. From this point onwards, however, his presidency was consumed in the fall-out from the Watergate scandal. Within a month, as rumors of sensational disclosures swept Washington, Nixon's rating plummeted by a staggering 22 points. By July, after the resignations of Haldeman and Ehrlichman and the defection of John Dean, it stood at a mere 39 percent, and after October's botched "Saturday Night Massacre," when Nixon controversially fired the Watergate special prosecutor Archibald Cox only to provoke the resignation of his own attorney general, it reached a new low of 27 percent. No president in history had suffered such a rapid and complete collapse of his credibility. To make matters worse, with inflation touching double digits and unemployment rising, the economic picture was bleaker that at any point since the Depression. This alone would have severely eroded Nixon's popularity, but the combination of stagflation and scandal was too much to bear. By the end of 1973, roughly three-quarters of the population, including many Republican voters and elected officials, had lost faith in their president. In November an unprecedented editorial in *Time* magazine called for Nixon to resign: it was clear that however long he lingered, the game was up.[56]

Nixon's defenders often argue that the Watergate scandal was, above all, a product of the domestic tensions surrounding the Vietnam War. Joan Hoff, for example, opens her account with Nixon's fear of the antiwar movement, his domestic surveillance program and the furor over the leak of the Pentagon Papers in 1971. "As far as the White House was concerned," she writes, "a wartime atmosphere prevailed that warranted traditional wartime violations of the Constitution."[57] Even so, there was far more to it than that. Nixon's own tapes show that the "dirty tricks" campaigns were largely driven by his personal insecurities about the media, the so-called liberal establishment and his Democratic opponents. The war may have pushed Nixon's insecurities to fever pitch, but it did not create them.[58]

Yet Nixon himself never missed an opportunity to bring in foreign affairs, frequently arguing that Watergate arose out of the pressures of Vietnam and that the investigations were undermining the country's sensitive global position. Reprimanding the special prosecutor Archibald Cox in October 1973, for instance, Nixon insisted that his investigation was damaging "our ability to act" in the Arab-Israeli conflict.[59] Having sent Kissinger to Moscow, Nixon was outraged when Cox refused to drop his demands for White House tapes. "I thought of Brezhnev," he wrote in his memoirs, "and how it would look to the Soviets if in the midst of our diplomatic showdown with them I were in the position of having to defer to the demands of one of my own employees."[60] He used a similar argument when trying vainly to dissuade

Elliot Richardson from resigning as Attorney General.[61] Yet Nixon remained convinced that foreign affairs offered a way out of Watergate. After arranging Brezhnev's American visit for June 1973 to overshadow John Dean's testimony to the Ervin Committee, he spent much of the following year touring foreign capitals, hoping that international acclamation would drown out the discontent at home. As so often happens, however, foreign affairs were easily outweighed by domestic factors, for Nixon's overseas jaunts had no discernible effect on his dreadful public standing.[62]

In later years, Nixon contradicted himself about the impact of Watergate on foreign policy. At times he claimed that the scandal had destroyed his ability to protect détente and South Vietnam; at others he denied that it had had any effect at all.[63] But Watergate clearly had an impact in three distinct areas: the institution of the presidency, the collapse of South Vietnam, and the decline of détente. In the first case, it manifestly played a large part in the reassertion of congressional power and weakening of the imperial presidency. Haldeman's diary shows that by the middle of March 1973, Nixon's chief advisers were spending every available moment on Watergate, and after Haldeman and Ehrlichman left the White House, Nixon himself seems to have sunk into a deep depression, often musing about resignation or suicide.[64] Aides and visitors later remarked on the president's apparent instability, and he certainly lost interest in the basic tasks of government, spending hours closeted with his tapes and hardly bothering to comment on the documents that crossed his desk. In the historian Stanley Kutler's words, "Richard Nixon himself seems to disappear from his own papers."[65]

In the short term, this meant that foreign policy became even more the personal province of Henry Kissinger, who from September 1973 combined the posts of national security advisor and secretary of state. Oddly enough, Kissinger believed that had it not been for Watergate, Nixon would have forced him out. As it was, he wrote, "a foreign-born American wound up in the extraordinary position of holding together our foreign policy and reassuring our public."[66] Yet the corrosive effects of Watergate, coupled with Nixon's disconcerting instability, meant that Kissinger faced an unequal struggle. Congress had been seeking to reassert its influence in foreign policy ever since the mid-1960s, and the collapse of Nixon's position gave it a rare opportunity. In August 1973, Senate pressure forced Nixon to end the bombing of Cambodia, and in November both houses voted to pass the War Powers Resolution over Nixon's veto, compelling the president to report to Congress within two days of sending troops into combat. It was a compelling symbol of congressional self-assertion at the expense of presidential power.[67]

Both Nixon and Kissinger blamed the congressional revival, and therefore the Watergate scandal that had enabled it, for the collapse of South Vietnam in April 1975. Nixon insisted that without Watergate "we would not have lost the war in Vietnam. I would have seen to it that we would have forced the North Vietnamese to keep the Paris peace agreement."[68] It is certainly true that Watergate eroded public confidence in the Nixon administration, destroyed his relationship with Congress and made it inconceivable that he could win support for renewed hostilities in Indochina. Whether or not this really matters, however, depends upon one's broader interpretation of the last years of the Vietnam War. Larry Berman, for instance, argues that Nixon and Kissinger consciously planned a "permanent war" in the skies to preserve their allies in the South; however, "Watergate derailed the plan."[69] By contrast, Jeffrey Kimball suggests that they knew South Vietnam was lost and hoped only for a "decent interval" before it finally collapsed, in which case Watergate looms rather less large.[70] In fact, South Vietnam put up such a feeble military performance between 1973 and 1975 that had Nixon been free to intervene there is still no guarantee that it would have survived. And even without Watergate the public and congressional mood would still have made it difficult to mount a "permanent war." Nixon was, after all, a lame-duck president struggling with dreadful economic circumstances: in this context, the congressional backlash against renewed warfare might well have come anyway.

A similar debate surrounds the decline of détente, which came under severe attack from both conservatives and liberals during Nixon's second term. The passage of the Jackson-Vanik Amendment in December 1973, which made Soviet trading privileges dependent upon Jewish emigration, was only the most obvious reflection of the changing climate. By the beginning of 1976, when both Reagan and Carter denounced Kissinger in the presidential primaries, the pendulum had swung decisively against détente. On the advice of his pollsters, Gerald Ford dropped the very word from his speeches, a far cry from Nixon's enthusiastic embrace of Brezhnev and Mao four years before.[71] As with the collapse of South Vietnam, there is a good case that all of this would have happened anyway. Nixon himself blamed the presidential ambitions of Henry Jackson, pressure from interest groups and "domestic political fluctuations" within both parties, problems that "would have existed regardless of Watergate."[72] And since détente was arguably oversold, it is plausible that a lame-duck president would have struggled to sustain it even without the Watergate scandal.

Still, while South Vietnam was surely doomed even before the Watergate revelations, this was not the case for détente. Henry Kissinger, who had more to lose from its demise than anyone, wrote that it had fallen victim to "the ugly suspicions of Watergate," and he was probably right.[73] By monopolizing Nixon's interest and destroying his domestic standing, Watergate made it impossible for him to mount an effective counter-attack against Jackson's campaign during the crucial period for public opinion. By the summer of 1974, Nixon was tempering his enthusiasm for détente so as not to alienate conservative congressmen before a possible impeachment vote. Returning from Moscow in July, he cancelled a planned speech explaining the development of détente, a sure sign that he was afraid to antagonize Republican supporters.[74] Instead, the job of explaining détente to the American people was left to Kissinger, who was ill suited to the task. As Hanhimäki has pointed out, Kissinger was simply not very good at selling détente to ordinary Americans in the heartland: for all his vaunted political skills, he proved no match for Henry Jackson, whose honest, all-American image made a powerful contrast with Kissinger's wily reputation and thick Germanic accent. The fact that in 1976 Kissinger was an easy target for both Reagan in the Republican primaries and Carter in the general election testifies to his failure as a political salesman.[75]

"In the case of foreign policy," Nixon had said, "selling the policy is very important just like making the policy is important." Other presidents had found exactly the same: the examples of Woodrow Wilson, Franklin D. Roosevelt, and George W. Bush provide compelling illustration of the narrow divide between the statesman and the salesman. To Nixon, who was fascinated by the media and public relations, statesmanship and salesmanship were often the same thing. This was not simply a matter of subordinating his foreign policy to the demands of the electoral calendar: as the fate of détente suggests, "selling the policy" was often a crucial element of securing its success. And if Nixon kept a close eye on his personal popularity, arranged diplomatic showpieces for the benefit of the media and carefully calibrated the domestic impact of overseas developments, then this was no surprise: so, after all, had Roosevelt.

The obvious weakness of Nixon and Kissinger in terms of foreign policy and domestic affairs, in fact, was not that they were *too preoccupied* with salesmanship, but that they were simply *not very good* at it. Where Vietnam was concerned, Nixon proved very skillful at neutering the peace movement, buying Kissinger far more time than many people had thought possible to reach a deal with the Vietnamese. But in the case of détente, public support proved ephemeral, and by 1976 Kissinger was being assailed on all sides. Clearly Watergate was a crucial factor here, but it is an indictment of

Nixon and Kissinger that détente had put down such shallow roots. A more open approach to foreign policy might have won broader and more enduring popular support, but then that would have required completely different architects. "We didn't have the Congress with us," Nixon told Kissinger emotionally as his presidency collapsed. "We didn't have the press with us. We didn't have the bureaucracy with us. We did it alone, Henry."[76] But this was partly their own fault; and in the final analysis, it was their greatest failing.

Notes

1. For the Truman analogy, see Melvin Small, *The Presidency of Richard Nixon* (Lawrence, Kans., 1999), 33–34.
2. Iwan Morgan, *Nixon* (London, 2002), 67ff. See also Joan Hoff, *Nixon Reconsidered* (New York, 1994), 77–146.
3. Small, *Presidency of Richard Nixon*, 154, 214; David Greenberg, *Nixon's Shadow: The History of an Image* (New York, 2003), 306.
4. See Small, *Presidency of Richard Nixon*, 30, 155; and Robert Mason, *Richard Nixon and the Quest for a New Majority* (Chapel Hill, N.C., 2004), 35.
5. Richard Nixon, *RN: The Memoirs of Richard Nixon* (New York, 1978), 770.
6. H. R. Haldeman, *The Haldeman Diaries: Inside the Nixon White House* (New York, 1995), 712.
7. See Arthur M. Schlesinger, Jr., *The Imperial Presidency* (New York, 1973).
8. Quoted in Richard Reeves, *President Nixon: Alone in the White House* (New York, 2001), 22.
9. Haldeman, *Haldeman Diaries*, 506, 375.
10. Nixon to Haldeman, May 9, 1971, reprinted in Bruce Oudes, ed., *From—The President: Richard Nixon's Secret Files* (London, 1989), 250–254.
11. Haldeman, *Haldeman Diaries*, 163, 66, 375.
12. Theodore H. White, *The Making of the President, 1968* (New York, 1969), 147.
13. Reeves, *President Nixon*, 33.
14. Nixon to Haldeman, et al., March 2, 1970, reprinted in Oudes, *From—The President*, 99–102.
15. Henry Kissinger, *Years of Upheaval* (Boston, 1982), 77.
16. Quoted in Reeves, *President Nixon*, 42.
17. See Nixon, *RN*, 770–771; Henry Kissinger, *Years of Renewal* (New York, 1999), 92–112.
18. *Atlantic Monthly*, October 1970.
19. Haldeman, *Haldeman Diaries*, 218, 361.
20. Nixon to Haldeman, May 11, 1970, reprinted in Oudes, *From—The President*, 126–127.

21. Jussi Hanhimäki, *The Flawed Architect: Henry Kissinger and American Foreign Policy* (New York, 2004), xvii.
22. Haldeman, *Haldeman Diaries*, 95, 256.
23. Nixon to Ehrlichman, April 9, 1972, reprinted in Oudes, *From—The President*, 410–411.
24. H. R. Haldeman, with Joseph DiMona, *The Ends of Power* (New York, 1978), 81.
25. See Jeffrey Kimball, *Nixon's Vietnam War* (Lawrence, Kans., 1998).
26. Haldeman, *The Haldeman Diaries*, 84–85. See also Henry Kissinger, *White House Years* (Boston, 1979), 226–311.
27. Haldeman, *Haldeman Diaries*, 114, 302.
28. Richard Nixon, *No More Vietnams* (New York, 1985), 15.
29. Haldeman, *Haldeman Diaries*, 128.
30. Hoff, *Nixon Reconsidered*, 229–230; Small, *Presidency of Richard Nixon*, 74–75; Mason, *Richard Nixon and the Quest for a New Majority*, 63–64.
31. Haldeman, *Haldeman Diaries*, 65.
32. Nixon's Gallup approval ratings are at http://www.ropercenter.uconn. edu/cgi-bin/hsrun.exe/Roperweb/PresJob/PresJob.htx;start=HS_ fullresults?pr=Nixon
33. Haldeman, *Haldeman Diaries*, 18.
34. Quoted in Small, *Presidency of Richard Nixon*, 78.
35. Haldeman, *Haldeman Diaries*, 184, 204.
36. See Mason, *Richard Nixon and the Quest for a New Majority*, 70.
37. William Bundy, *A Tangled Web: The Making of Nixon's Foreign Policy, 1968–1974* (New York, 1998), 296–298.
38. Haldeman, *Haldeman Diaries*, 337.
39. Mason, *Richard Nixon and the Quest for a New Majority*, 106–109.
40. Colson to Nixon, November 6, 1970, reprinted in Oudes, *From—The President*, 166–170.
41. Quoted in Reeves, *President Nixon*, 494.
42. Haldeman, *Haldeman Diaries*, 567.
43. Ibid., 441, 514–515; see also 504–506ff.
44. Greenberg, *Nixon's Shadow*, 311–312.
45. *New York Times*, December 7, 1971; Mason, *Richard Nixon and the Quest for a New Majority*, 137–138.
46. Haldeman, *Haldeman Diaries*, 403.
47. Mason, *Richard Nixon and the Quest for a New Majority*, 139.
48. Kissinger, *White House Years*, 1083.
49. Reeves, *President Nixon*, 388.
50. Haldeman, *Haldeman Diaries*, 631–632.
51. Greenberg, *Nixon's Shadow*, 275–276.
52. *New York Times*, September 27, 1972.
53. Mason, *Richard Nixon and the Quest for a New Majority*, 190–191.
54. Dan T. Carter, *From George Wallace to Newt Gingrich: Race in the Conservative Counter-Revolution* (Baton Rouge, La., 1996), 53.

55. Haldeman, *Haldeman Diaries*, 354–355.

56. *Time*, November 12, 1974.

57. Hoff, *Nixon Reconsidered*, 281.

58. See Stanley Kutler, ed., *Abuse of Power: The New Nixon Tapes* (New York, 1997), 3–42.

59. *New York Times*, October 20, 1973.

60. Nixon, *RN*, 933–934.

61. Kutler, *The Wars of Watergate: The Last Crisis of Richard Nixon* (New York, 1990), 405–406.

62. See the Gallup polls at http://www.ropercenter.uconn.edu/cgi-bin/hsrun.exe/Roperweb/PresJob/PresJob.htx;start=HS_fullresults?pr=Nixon

63. See Nixon, *Memoirs*, 887–89; and Richard Nixon, *No More Vietnams* (New York, 1985), 165.

64. See Haldeman, *Haldeman Diaries*, 716, 782; Kutler, *Abuse of Power*, 601–602.

65. Kutler, *Wars of Watergate*, 437–438.

66. Kissinger, *Years of Upheaval*, 125–126.

67. See Kutler, *Wars of Watergate*, 601–603.

68. Excerpt from "Meet the Press" (NBC), April 10, 1988, in Oudes, *From—The President*, 621.

69. Larry Berman, *No Peace, No Honor: Nixon, Kissinger, and Betrayal in Vietnam* (New York, 2001), 8–9.

70. Kimball, *Nixon's Vietnam War*, passim.

71. Raymond L. Garthoff, *Détente and Confrontation: American-Soviet Relations from Nixon to Reagan*, rev. ed. (Washington, 1994), 604.

72. Quoted in Kutler, *Wars of Watergate*, 606–607.

73. Kissinger, *Years of Upheaval*, 983.

74. Kutler, *Wars of Watergate*, 489.

75. Hanhimäki, *Flawed Architect*, 427–456.

76. Kutler, *Abuse of Power*, 459.

Part II

Openings

5

Nixon, Kissinger, and the Opening to China

Margaret MacMillan

The opening of relations between the United States and the People's Republic of China in 1972 was one of those startling changes that seem inevitable once they have occurred. True, the two countries had been divided by the Cold War and by actual fighting in Korea, but there were several good reasons why, at the very least, they should be in contact with each other. Both countries had a strong interest in stability in the Northeast Pacific and in Asia more generally, and both regarded the Soviet Union with suspicion and even fear. Although it was impossible to gauge public opinion in Mao's China, it is clear that among the elites in the party, the military, and the government, there were those who would have welcomed an end to the long freeze in Sino-American relations, and did so when it finally came about. The worst phase of the Cultural Revolution was over by the start of the 1970s, and China was moving with dispatch to open up its foreign embassies again. In the United States, much of the old passion had gone out of the hostility to "Red" China. Moreover, a number of American allies were breaking ranks with the United States, not only in establishing diplomatic relations with China but in switching their support away from Taiwan as it tried to remain in the United Nations as the legitimate representative of the Chinese people.

The conditions were right for the opening but it took President Richard Nixon and Chairman Mao Zedong to make it happen. Nixon had the stature as a statesman and the political capital which came from being a known anti-communist and "Cold Warrior." He did not have as much to fear, as a Democrat president might have, the accusations from the Right that he was selling out to the enemy. In Mao, he was dealing with someone who had established an unchallenged primacy over China's policies, both internal and external. The Standing Committee of the Politburo, in theory responsible for setting policy directions, in reality existed to approve Mao's decisions.[1]

To the end of his life, Nixon regarded his trip to China in 1972 as one of the greatest moments of his presidency. His initiative, he firmly believed, had brought the United States and China into a mutually beneficial relationship, which helped to bring greater stability to Asia and indeed the world. As he said shortly before he died, "I will be known historically for two things. Watergate and the opening to China ... I don't mean to be pessimistic, but Watergate, that silly, silly thing, is going to rank up there historically with what I did here."[2]

And it was Nixon's initiative, although Henry Kissinger has since laid claim to what one of the high points of Nixon's presidency.[3] In his memoirs and interviews, Kissinger refers to "our China initiative" and leaves the impression that he and Nixon reached the same conclusions about the need for an opening to China independently.[4] When Nixon, by contrast, refers "the China initiative" in his memoirs, he leaves no doubt that he was issuing the instructions and that Kissinger was following them.[5] The evidence bears out Nixon's version. He had been considering the possibility of mending fences with China for some years before he ran for president in 1968. The Sino-Soviet split of the early 1960s had demonstrated to him that the communist world was no longer monolithic. In his extensive travels in Asia in those years between 1960 and 1968 when he was out of office, he made a point of informing himself about China.[6] In his well-known 1967 article in *Foreign Affairs*, he warned of the dangers of leaving an angry and hostile China outside the family of nations.[7]

Kissinger, it is true, had considered the possibility that one day the United States might be able to improve its relations with China. In a speech he wrote for Nelson Rockefeller in the 1968 campaign, he included a phrase about "a subtle triangle with Communist China and the Soviet Union," but his main focus as an academic and then policy adviser had always been on Europe and, above all, on American relations with the Soviet Union.[8] He barely knew Asia; he did not, for example, visit Taiwan until after he became national security adviser. Moreover, most observers agree that Nixon generally determined the strategy in American foreign policy while Kissinger worked out the tactics.[9] As the presidential speechwriter Raymond Price put it, "In the final analysis, each major turn got down to a presidential decision, and Nixon gave more care to these decisions than to anything else in his presidency."[10]

Kissinger's reaction, according to others in the administration, when Nixon first talked of an opening to China in February 1969 was one of incredulity. "Our Leader has taken leave of reality," he told his aide Alexander Haig. "He has just ordered me to make this flight of fantasy come true."[11] In the late summer of 1969, when Nixon and his party were flying back from a world tour in the course of which the Americans had done their best to establish contact with the Chinese through intermediaries such Pakistan and Romania, Kissinger, at least with his colleagues, remained skeptical. "Fat chance," he told H. R. Haldeman, Nixon's chief of staff, when the latter said that Nixon was determined to visit China.[12] In the end, Kissinger, who had little independent power base of his own, had no choice but to support Nixon's initiative, and he did so with energy and determination. According to American foreign service officers who worked with Kissinger, he saw the China opening primarily as a way of putting pressure on the Soviet Union, for him still the central issue in American foreign relations.[13]

It is no wonder, of course, that both men would want to take full credit for a bold move that transformed international relations—and which was one of the good news stories of a troubled presidency. It was, moreover, a pattern in their relationship, which was marked by both an extraordinarily close collaboration and mutual jealousy. Although in moments when Kissinger was being particularly tiresome Nixon frequently talked to Haldeman and others about getting rid of him, the president recognized that he had, in Kissinger, someone who was not only an intellectual equal but who had the necessary drive and stamina to carry out his foreign policy goals.

Both men also shared a firm belief in the value of diplomacy (although they did not always trust their own diplomats), in meticulous preparation, and in face to face meetings with foreign leaders. "Knowledge," Kissinger once told a journalist, was essential. "Knowledge of what I am trying to do. Knowledge of the subject. Knowledge of the history and psychology of the people I am dealing with. And some human rapport ..."[14] In *The Real War*, written after he had left office, Nixon offered his successors advice. "There is one cardinal rule for the conduct of international relations," he wrote. "Don't give anything to your adversaries unless you get something in return".[15] "Nixinger diplomacy," as one academic has called it, analyzed the world in terms of how the United States and its interests could be furthered and used a wide array of tactics from persuasion to force or the threat of force to achieve those ends.[16]

The opening to China appealed to both Nixon's and Kissinger's sense of drama: the secrecy; the back channels; the surprise sprung on the American people and the world when Nixon went on television in July 1971 to announce that Kissinger had just come back from Beijing bringing him an invitation to visit China; and, above all, the visit itself, the first one ever by an American president to a country Nixon described as being as unknown as the far side of the moon. Both men had studied and hoped to emulate the great leaders who made great decisions. Nixon's heroes, for example, were Winston Churchill and Charles de Gaulle, men who defied their contemporaries and overcame enormous odds to achieve victory; Kissinger's were Bismarck and Metternich, or as he once said in a notorious interview with Oriana Fallaci, the "lone gunslinger."[17] Both Nixon and Kissinger wanted to be ranked by posterity among those who had changed the world.

Of course, the opening to China made eminent sense from the perspective of furthering American interests. Nixon and Kissinger were both aware that the relative power of the United States had been slipping since the start of the 1960s. "Power of the United States," he told Haldeman in his first year in office, "must be used more effectively, at home and abroad or we go down the drain as a great power. Have already lost the leadership position we held at the end of WW II, but we can regain it, if fast!"[18] The United States had lost ground internationally in the 1960s, partly because other nations had grown in power and partly because it was shouldering too much of the burden for the maintenance of the international order. The time had now come, as Nixon tried to make clear in what became known as his "doctrine," for American allies to take responsibility for their own defense rather than relying on the United States. "In the forties and fifties," Kissinger wrote in a 1968 essay, "we offered remedies; in the late sixties and in the seventies our role will have to be to contribute to a structure that will foster the initiative of others. We are a superpower physically, but our designs can be meaningful only if they generate willing cooperation."[19]

Willing cooperation was in short supply, particularly when it came to the Soviet Union. Managing relations with the other superpower was the long term and central preoccupation of Nixon's and Kissinger's foreign policy but the Soviets were proving to be difficult in Nixon's first year in office. Flush with oil money, under Brezhnev's leadership the Soviet Union was spending huge amounts on their military and on foreign aid. The Soviets were pushing ahead with the development of advanced nuclear weapons and were expanding their navy. In the Middle East, the Soviets were supplying huge amounts of weaponry and sending thousands of advisers to radical Arab states such as Egypt and Syria. Soviet influence was spreading in Africa, and—so Nixon and Kissinger feared—in Latin America. The Soviet

invasion of Czechoslovakia in 1968 to crush a moderate reforming communism seemed to demonstrate a new Soviet willingness to use its arms
to crush dissent. The subsequent Soviet justification in the shape of the
Brezhnev Doctrine, to the effect that the Soviet Union would determine
when it needed to intervene in other socialist countries promised an uneasy
future. (It also worried the Chinese leadership although the Americans
could not know that.) Furthermore, the Soviets were dragging out the arms
control negotiations which were such an important part of the wider policy
of détente, and they would not be pinned down on a date for the summit
with Brezhnev that Nixon badly wanted.

In addition, the Soviet Union and its allies, infuriatingly, continued to
support North Vietnam in its war with the United States. Vietnam was the
chief symbol of the decline in American power. Both Nixon and Kissinger
were painfully aware that the international position of the United States
had been badly damaged and continued to be damaged by the war. The
key Cold War alliance of NATO was, as Kissinger put it, in "a state of malaise."[20] The faith of American allies had been shaken by the inability of the
leader of the Western alliance to deal with a small and backward power and
their publics had increasingly turned sour on the United States. Much of the
criticism, and not just from the left, was disturbingly anti-American. The
United States was portrayed as an international bully in which the forces of
capitalism ran uncontrolled. In the Third World, American imperialism was
routinely condemned while little was said of the Soviet empire.

Nixon was deeply concerned as well that the experience of Vietnam and
the preoccupation of the country's elites with domestic problems would
make the United States increasingly parochial.[21] As he told Kissinger,
"nations must have great ideas or they cease to be great."[22] Nixon intended
to deal with the great strategic issues, of détente, rebuilding relations with
American allies, and strengthening the forces of international order and stability but until he could get the United States out of Vietnam, he would be
handicapped. Moreover, he did not want his presidency destroyed by the
war as Johnson's had been. "No matter what facet of the Nixon presidency
you're considering," Haldeman told an audience in the late 1980s, "don't
ever lose sight of Vietnam as the over-riding factor in the first Nixon term.
It overshadowed everything else, all the time, in every discussion, in every
opportunity, in every problem."[23] The problem was how to end the war and
in a way that did not look like an ignominious American defeat. The North
Vietnamese leadership, sensing victory, had shown no interest in serious
negotiations or in saving American face.

When Nixon and Kissinger contemplated a rapprochement with China, they did so in terms of the advantages that it would bring to the United States. Great powers always looked out for their own national interests, he told his White House staff just after the announcement that he was to visit China, "or else they're played for suckers by those powers that do."[24] Interests could coincide and it was the wise statesman who could see this and be ready to negotiate. Since Nixon and Kissinger believed, as Nixon put it in a letter to Melvin Laird, his Secretary of Defense, "the great issues are fundamentally interrelated," they also saw ways in which the offer of American relations with China might persuade the Chinese to offer assistance in other areas.[25] In particular, China might put pressure on the North Vietnamese to come to an agreement with the Americans.

In the longer run, a new relationship between the United States and China would take advantage of the Sino-Soviet split. "We moved to China," Kissinger wrote in his memoirs, "not to expiate liberal guilt over our China policy of the late 1940s but to shape a global equilibrium."[26] Or, as he put it in his own inimitable way to Nixon in 1973, "With conscientious attention to both capitals, we should be able to continue to have our mao tai and drink our vodka too."[27] An opening to China would shake the Soviets and, so it was hoped, encourage them into a more amenable frame of mind. The existing bilateral relationship between the United States and the Soviet Union would become a triangular one with, so Kissinger and Nixon assumed, the United States holding the balance between the two great communist powers, each of which would now have a stake in dealing with the United States "constructively." Ideally the United States could exploit the mutual hostility between the Soviet Union and China and maintain closer relations with each than they had with each other. This, Kissinger always maintained, should not be seen as a crude attempt to play a China card against the Soviet Union, or vice versa, but in fact that is exactly what it was.[28] Moreover, the Chinese were, as it turned out, thinking along very much the same lines by the end of the 1960s.

In the first two years of his presidency, Nixon and a small group of senior officials started to prepare American opinion and American policymakers for the shift in policy toward China, which necessarily meant abandoning or at least cutting back on support for Taiwan, long the darling of the American right. Typically, Nixon did not inform his own State Department, nor his allies, of the impending change. The State Department therefore spoke reprovingly to the Canadians when the new Trudeau government moved to recognize China in 1969 and 1970. The Secretary of State, William Rogers, apparently told his Canadian counterpart, "We hate like hell what you are doing but you are still our best friends."[29]

One of Nixon's first moves as president was to direct the National Security Council (NSC) to undertake a study of current U.S. policies toward both Chinas, of possible communist Chinese intentions in Asia, and "alternative U.S. approaches on China and their costs and risks."[30] As well, he instructed Kissinger quietly to let senior government and political figures know that the administration was exploring the possibilities of a rapprochement with China.[31] Kissinger duly talked to, among others, leading hardliners on China such Walter Judd, a congressman from Minnesota, and Senator Karl Mundt.[32] Nixon himself told Mike Mansfield, the Senate majority leader, that the time had come to involve China in "global responsibility."[33] Later that June, Mansfield used Prince Sihanouk of Cambodia to contact Zhou Enlai to ask whether he could visit China, a move the Chinese noted with interest although they did not send a reply.[34] In December 1969, Kissinger gave a press briefing in which he said, "We have always made it clear that we have no permanent enemies and that we will judge other countries, and specifically countries like Communist China, on the basis of their actions and not on the basis of their domestic ideology."[35]

Timing is important in history, and what would have seemed outrageous to American opinion in the aftermath of the Korean War now seemed increasingly reasonable. By the time Nixon became president, much of the passion of his anti-communism had evaporated, as it had among many Americans. The Soviet Union was home to a repugnant ideology and was a hostile power, but the United States had been obliged to deal with it, in Europe where the division into East and West had achieved a sort of permanence and stability, in other parts of the world such as the Middle East, and, above all, in the nuclear arms race. The Cuban Missile Crisis had shown all too starkly what would happen if the two superpowers failed to manage their relationship.

Since the United States already had a relationship with one great communist power (and a host of smaller ones), it was not unthinkable to approach China. American public opinion, or so Nixon hoped, was already prepared for this. Americans, by and large, no longer felt the same antipathy and fear toward Chinese communism that had been such a feature of American politics in the 1950s. Where the China Lobby, that collection of Cold Warriors who steadfastly opposed recognition of the People's Republic, had once thrown its weight around to effect, it had run out of steam by the late 1960s. Many of its initial supporters, such as Henry Luce, had disappeared from the scene, and in 1969, its chief organizer abruptly resigned and moved to London to take up producing plays. The *New York Times* referred to the "once powerful China Lobby."[36] Significantly, by the late 1960s people in business were calling for trade relations.[37]

Although he liked to see himself as the target of liberals, including those in the big East Coast universities, Nixon actually could count on considerable support from the academic community who were increasingly calling for opening up contacts with their counterparts in China. Although he had trouble believing it, he also had support within the State Department. John Holdridge, whom Kissinger brought in from the State Department to work on China policy at the NSC, had seen the various abortive attempts to make contact between China and the United States in the 1950s and 1960s: "We always had this feeling in the back of our minds—through the Geneva talks, the ambassadorial-level talks, and in various ways—that we didn't want to foreclose any opportunities which might open in the future. We wanted some kind of a relationship."[38] Most of the old hardliners had retired by the time Nixon became president and a younger generation of diplomats felt, as one said, "we should be moving in the direction of rapprochement with Peking".[39]

The problem, of course, was how to signal to the Chinese that American attitudes had changed. Years of nonrecognition, of insults hurled back and forth, and of conflict in Korea and now in Vietnam stood in the way. Moreover, China, which was always opaque to outsiders, had become virtually inaccessible during the Cultural Revolution. It was not clear who was in charge of foreign policy and there was no way for American statesmen to gauge what the likely reaction of the Chinese leadership was likely to be to an overt American offer of rapprochement. If Nixon had publicly called on the Chinese to negotiate a new relationship, he ran the risk of a public rebuff from Beijing which could have infuriated American public opinion and damaged American prestige still further. There was also the question of national pride. Even when the secret channel to Beijing had started to produce results, Nixon from time to time worried that the United States was showing itself to be too eager.[40] What Lawrence Eagleburger, a Kissinger aide who later became secretary of state for the first President Bush, called Nixon's and Kissinger's "conspiratorial approach to foreign policy management" was not just effective but essential in achieving the breakthrough with China.[41] The opening to China required two years of delicate negotiations between two powers who had no reason to trust each other and many reasons to be suspicious.

Kissinger later described the steps by which the United States and China inched toward each other as an intricate minuet, "so delicately arranged that both sides could always maintain that they were not in contact, so stylized that neither side needed to bear the onus of an initiative, so elliptical that existing relationships on both sides were not jeopardized."[42] On the other hand, the failure, once contact had been established, to properly brief the other executive branches of the American government, notably the State Department, led to alienating allies such as Japan unnecessarily or to missteps such as the one over the writing of the Shanghai communiqué, which could have had serious consequences.

It was fortunate that, as Nixon and Kissinger decided on an opening to China, the Chinese leadership was reaching a similar conclusion. Both Mao and Zhou Enlai, his closest foreign policy collaborator, were deeply concerned, with reason, about the weak and friendless situation their country found itself in. The Cultural Revolution had damaged China greatly: its educational system was in disarray, its industries floundering, and much of its military had been diverted to maintaining order in the cities. China's foreign policy had virtually shut down as diplomats were recalled to be "struggled against" (as the communists referred to their persecutions) and reformed. China, in any case, had few friends in the world. Its relationships with its Asian neighbors were cool, as in the case of Japan and South Korea, and positively hostile, as, for example, with India and Taiwan.

One country, above all, figured in the Chinese decision to move toward opening relations with the United States. In their talks with the Americans, both during Kissinger's preliminary visits and Nixon's, they referred to the Soviet Union only obliquely and in passing, mentioning "our northern neighbor" or "another big power" occasionally or making jokes about polar bears. During his one-hour conversation with Nixon in 1972, Mao refused to be drawn on the subject at all.[43] In fact, the Soviet Union was central in his thinking about China's position in the world.

The Sino-Soviet dispute, which had broken out into the open at the start of the 1960s, was, as the Americans and indeed the whole world knew, bitter and far-reaching. Both sides accused the other of being poor communists and both endeavored to draw other communist nations and the nonaligned of the Third World to their side. By the end of the 1960s, the Chinese leadership was increasingly concerned, with good reason, about what the Soviet Union might be planning. If the Americans were hoping to play the China card against the Soviets, the Chinese saw an America card as serving precisely the same purpose.

In December 1971, to prepare the Chinese leadership for Nixon's forth-coming visit, Zhou outlined the advantages to China in an improved relation-ship with the United States. With Nixon's visit, China had the opportunity to use the contradictions between the United States and the USSR and to magnify them." The United States needed China because it had got itself stuck in Vietnam and this had given the Soviet "revisionists" and "imperi-alists" the opportunity to expand their sphere of influence in Europe and the Middle East. "When [Nixon] comes, he has to bring something in his pocket." China also, although Zhou seems not to have spelled it out, could now use friendship with the United States as a means with which to deter the Soviet Union from threats or worse.[44]

The relationship between the two great communist powers had never been an easy one, partly for cultural and historical reasons, and partly because the Chinese communists represented a challenge to Soviet domination of the world communist movement. By the time Nixon became president, Mao, and what was left of the foreign policy establishment in Beijing, were increasingly coming to see the Soviet Union as a more immediate threat than the United States. The invasion of Czechoslovakia and the Brezhnev Doctrine deeply alarmed them. Official reaction in Beijing described the events of 1968 as: "The most barefaced and typical specimen of fascist power politics played by the Soviet revisionist clique against its so-called allies."[45] China, on Mao's orders, began to prepare against a possible invasion and for civil defense against aerial attack.[46]

Soviet words and actions fed Chinese fears. The Soviet Union had been openly critical of Mao's policies from the Great Leap Forward of the 1950s onwards. Soviet leaders condemned the Cultural Revolution of the 1960s as fanaticism and were enraged when Soviet diplomats and their families in Beijing were roughed up and humiliated by crowds of Red Guards. Soviet radio broadcast calls to the Chinese people to overthrow Mao and a Soviet military newspaper claimed that the Soviet Union stood ready to help.[47]

Between 1965 and 1969, the Soviets increased the number of their army divisions along the common border with China in the Far East from about seventeen to twenty-seven and deployed bombers and rockets capable of carrying nuclear warheads to the major cities of north China. Although the People's Republic did not yet have a comparable nuclear force, it responded by increasing its military on the ground.[48] In 1969 open hostilities broke out, first in the spring along the Ussuri River border in the Soviet Far East and then in August on China's western border in Xinjiang province. Soviet hard-liners, including the defense minister, were for dealing firmly with China, even if it meant using nuclear weapons.[49] Alarming reports reached the Chinese leadership that Soviet diplomats were sounding out their American and Warsaw Pact counterparts to see what the reaction would be if the Soviets attacked Chinese targets with nuclear weapons.[50] In August 1969, Nixon and Kissinger were briefed by Allen Whiting, a respected China specialist, who warned that the Soviet Union was laying the groundwork for a successful attack on China. It may well be that this was the moment when Kissinger finally came to agree fully with Nixon that the United States ought to move toward China.[51]

Where earlier American administrations might have welcomed the prospect of war between the two great communist powers, the Nixon administration regarded it with deep concern. Asia was already tense enough, with the Vietnam war and worsening relations between India and Pakistan. Moreover, the Americans assumed that China would almost certainly lose, an outcome which would leave the Soviet Union in a commanding position in North Asia. In late August 1969 Richard Helms, Director of Central Intelligence, gave diplomatic correspondents a confidential briefing undoubtedly intended for wider consumption in which he warned that the Soviet Union might be intending to attack China. Elliott Richardson, the undersecretary of state, shortly afterward told an academic conference that while the United States had no interest in exploiting the antagonism between the two communist powers, "We could not fail to be deeply concerned, however, with an escalation of this quarrel into a massive breach of international peace and security."[52]

In Beijing, Mao, who had done so much to stir up antagonism with the Soviet Union and whose Cultural Revolution had set China at odds with many of its former friends, was now thinking seriously about the consequences of China's isolation in the world. There is an old Chinese saying that "When the extreme is reached, the reverse will set in."[53] Mao, although few Chinese knew it, was starting to think about a dramatic shift in China's foreign relations. In February 1969, he established a special advisory group to study the international situation. Its four members, all marshals in the People's Liberation Army, had a free hand to read whatever they wanted and to raise even heretical questions. Cautiously, for Mao's China was not tolerant of heresy, they examined one of the main assumptions of China's foreign policy—that the Soviet Union and the United States were equally hostile to China—and suggested that China might be able to maneuver between them. Chen Yi, a former foreign minister, was the boldest. "Why can't we play the America card?" China and the United States had very different social and political systems but in international relations, alliances were made out of necessity and shared interests. American policy, Chen argued, appeared to be subtly shifting and becoming less antagonistic to China.[54]

The Four Marshals submitted several reports over the next months. In July, they pointed to the hostility between the United States and the Soviet Union and argued that neither was likely to attack on China for fear of what the other might do.[55] In September, as Chinese fears of a sneak Soviet attack built, they stressed that the United States would not stand by while the Soviet Union tried to increase its empire. Although in the long-term China had to regard both powers as enemies, its shorter term strategy should be to use the one against the other.[56] In a separate and even franker memorandum, Chen Yi suggested that China should consider an opening to the United States.[57]

Mao received the reports but kept his own counsel. Apparently, although the record remains fragmentary, he was still working out his own thoughts on the correct strategy for China.[58] Zhou, as he invariably did, waited for the Chairman's directions. When the Swedish ambassador pressed him on whether the Soviet Union or the United States was the greatest threat, Zhou refused to commit himself.[59] Chinese history, however, which still affected the thinking of even communist leaders, offered a well-known and instructive lesson. In the third century A.D., in a period of disunity, one of China's greatest strategists had allied his kingdom with a second to defeat a third. He had chosen the one furthest away as an ally over the nearest on the grounds that it could be dangerous to become too closely allied with a neighbor.

We have few records yet available of Mao's conversations with his intimates but his personal physician later wrote memoirs whose authenticity is generally accepted. That autumn, Mao posed Dr. Li a problem. "We have the Soviet Union to the north and the west, India to the south, and Japan to the east. If all our enemies were to united, attacking us from the north, south, east, and west, what do you think we should do?" Doctor Li was at a loss. "Think again," Mao said. "Beyond Japan is the United States. Didn't our ancestors counsel negotiating with faraway countries while fighting with those that are near?" Unlike the Soviet Union, Mao went on, the United States had never occupied Chinese territory. He had no objections to dealing with President Nixon. On the contrary. "I like to deal with rightists. They say what they really think—not like the leftists, who say one thing and mean another."[60]

Although the Chinese may not have known it, Nixon was already conducting his own study in Washington in 1969.[61] In the May meeting of the Senior Review Group, which included representatives from the State Department, the Central Intelligence Agency, the NSC, and Defense among other government agencies, Kissinger remained cool to the idea of a sudden shift in American policy. Even a weak and inward-looking China, he argued, by its very size represented a potential threat to its smaller neighbors. The issue, though, for the United States was "whether we care if China maintains her policy of isolation so long as this is coupled with a relatively low level of aggression." Did the United States really want China to emerge onto the world scene as a world power, capable of competing with it as the Soviet Union now did? "Why is bringing China into the world community inevitably in our interest?" On the other hand, as he had done in his 1968 speech for Nelson Rockefeller, he returned to the prospect of a triangular relationship between the USSR, China, and the United States with the last playing the China card against the first. "History suggested to him," he said, "that it is better to align yourself with the weaker, not the stronger of two antagonistic powers." Nor did he think, as some Kremlinologists feared, that a more conciliatory policy toward China would ruin American relations with the Soviet Union.[62]

The resulting document, NSC Memorandum 14, made its way slowly through the Washington bureaucracy, and the final version was presented to the president at San Clemente on August 14. It was a cautious document reflecting the concerns of Kissinger and his fellow officials. Its underlying assumptions were pessimistic: "Peking's policies towards the United States may moderate somewhat under a post-Mao leadership, but Chinese efforts to assert their influence in Asia will result in rivalry with the US regardless of the nature of the Peking regime." It cautiously laid out three options: continuing the present strategy of isolation, intensifying it with increasing aid to China's neighbors and a more visible and aggressive American deterrent capacity, or moving toward reducing China's isolation and removing some of the points of friction with it. The study leant toward the third option arguing that it was unlikely that the existing level of conflict and antagonism with China would last indefinitely. "US long-range objectives and interests can, therefore, plausibly be set in more flexible terms and in the direction of the achievement of an improved and more relaxed relationship with the PRC."[63] The available records of the San Clemente meeting do not reveal whether Nixon told his cabinet colleagues which option he preferred.[64] According to Kissinger's memoirs, though, Nixon startled the meeting by making it clear that the United States had strong interest in seeing that China was not defeated in a war with the Soviet Union. "It was a major event in American foreign policy," wrote Kissinger, "when a President declared that we had a strong interest in the survival of a major communist country, long an enemy, and with which we had no contact."[65] It is unlikely that Nixon would have made his views clear at this point since he feared premature leaks of his intentions toward China and he did not trust most of his cabinet.

Nixon had been sending cautious signals to the Chinese. In his first month in office, he ended the provocative high-speed patrols by U.S. naval vessels near the coast of China in the Taiwan Straits and that fall he ended the Seventh Fleet's regular patrols through the straits. In the spring, Secretary of State Rogers announced in a public speech, "we shall take initiatives to re-establish more normal relations with Communist China and we shall remain responsive to any indications of less hostile attitudes from their side."[66] Although Nixon made reference at his press conference in Guam in late July 1969 to the "very belligerent" foreign policy of China, the announcement of the Nixon Doctrine—that the United States had learned from its mistakes in Vietnam and was no longer going to support its allies militarily—also sent a signal of reassurance to the Chinese.

That same month, the National Security Council recommended that the United States move unilaterally to improve its relationship with China. A whole series of measures followed: restrictions on trade and travel between the United States and China were loosened. American passport holders from designated professions such as the academic world or medicine were now allowed to travel to China. American companies would no longer face penalties in the United States if their foreign subsidiaries sold goods to China. Significantly, in the fall of 1970 Nixon used the term People's Republic of China for the first time in a public speech, at a banquet for President Nicolae Ceaucescu of Romania, one of the foreign leaders he had been hoping could open up a communication channel to China.

Nixon had tried a variety of ways besides Romania, through Poland, Cambodia, and France, to get through to the Chinese leadership that the United States wanted a rapprochement.[67] During a brief stay in Pakistan on his 1969 Asian tour, Nixon asked its dictator, General Yahya Khan, who was on good terms with the Chinese to be his intermediary and it was this channel that finally paid off for the Americans.[68] At the end of December 1969, the American ambassador in Warsaw, Walter Stoessel, also managed to make contact with Chinese diplomats as they all were leaving a Yugoslav fashion show to say that he had an important message for them. Mao and Zhou were not only reassured that the American overtures were genuine but felt that Chinese national pride had been satisfied. "It is the Americans who need something from us, not the other way around." It was a story that Mao and Zhou loved to recount.[69]

What Kissinger described as a delicate minuet started in the spring of 1970 as messages laboriously made their way to and from Washington and Beijing through Pakistan's emissaries. The negotiations had to overcome more than twenty years of suspicion and fear and there were several occasions when they came close to being broken off altogether, for example when the United States backed Lon Nol's coup in Cambodia in the spring of 1970. Another major stumbling block was China's initial insistence that it would only accept a visit from a special American envoy in order to discuss the withdrawal of American forces from Taiwan.[70] The Chinese eventually dropped the demand but Taiwan remained central on the list of subjects they wished to discuss.

The final breakthrough came in the spring of 1971. In April, the Chinese government made an extraordinary public gesture when it suddenly invited an American table tennis team, which had been taking part in an international tournament in Japan, to visit China. Team officials and a group of bewildered players found themselves as the first official American representatives to visit China since 1949. (Zhou Enlai ordered the Chinese players to allow the Americans to win a few games.) At a reception, he toasted the Americans. "Your visit", he said, "has opened a new chapter in the history of the relations between Chinese and American peoples." And he went on: "With you having made the start the people of the United States and China in the future will be able to have constant contacts."[71]

The messages through the secret Pakistan channel increased in number and in warmth. Finally, on June 2, 1971, the Pakistani ambassador to Washington brought in the one that Nixon and Kissinger had been waiting for. Zhou extended a warm invitation to Kissinger to come to Beijing in June to prepare the way for Nixon's visit. "It goes without saying," Zhou added, "that the first question to be settled is the crucial issue between China and the United States which is the question of the concrete way of the withdrawal of all the U.S. Armed Forces from Taiwan and Taiwan Straits area." In fact, as Kissinger was quick to recognize, the Chinese had backed away from their original position that the forces must be withdrawn before talks could take place.[72]

Nixon, according to his memoirs, proposed a toast. "Henry, we are drinking a toast not to ourselves personally or to our success, or to our administration's policies which have made this message and made tonight possible. Let us drink to generations to come who may have a better chance to live in peace because of what we have done."[73] For once, Nixon was not exaggerating. The opening to China transformed the Cold War from a bipolar one into something much more complex and did much to bring China back into the community of nations. Once Mao and his radical successors had disappeared from the scene by the late 1970s, Deng Xiaoping and President Jimmy Carter moved rapidly to establish full diplomatic relations between their two countries. China was able to draw on the resources of the United States from technology to capital, first to repair the damage caused by the Cultural Revolution and Mao's other policies and then to embark on the extraordinary and rapid development of the 1980s and 1990s. Nixon's visit to China started a process, the consequences of which we see today.

Notes

1. See Yafeng Xia, "China's Elite Politics and Sino-American Rapprochement, January 1969-February 1972," *Journal of Cold War Studies* 8 (Fall 2006): 4–5 and passim.
2. Monica Crowley, *Nixon in Winter* (New York, 1998), 159.
3. Author interview with Henry Kissinger, May 15 and 18, 2003; Henry Kissinger, *White House Years* (Boston, 1979), 163–165.
4. Kissinger, *White House Years*, 163, 194.
5. Richard M. Nixon, *RN: the Memoirs of Richard Nixon* (New York, 1978), 544–550.
6. Robert J. Nichols and Marshall Green interviews, *Frontline Diplomacy: The US Foreign Affairs Oral History Collection*, ed. Marilyn Bentley and Marie Warner (Arlington, Va., 2000) Hereafter USOH.
7. Richard M. Nixon, "Asia After Viet Nam," *Foreign Affairs* 46 (October 1967): 121–123.
8. Walter Isaacson, *Kissinger: A biography* (New York, 1992), 126.
9. See, for example, Viktor Sukhodrev in Gerald S. and Deborah H. Strober, *Nixon: An Oral History of his Presidency* (New York, 1994), 119.
10. Raymond Price, *With Nixon* (New York, 1977), 305. See also Joan Hoff, *Nixon Reconsidered* (New York, 1994), 152–153.
11. Alexander Haig, with Charles McCarry, *Inner Circles: How America Changed the World: A Memoir* (New York, 1992), 257.
12. H. R. Haldeman, *The Ends of Power* (Montreal, 1978), 91.
13. See, for example, Paul Kreisberg interview, USOH.
14. Quoted in Robert Dallek, *Nixon and Kissinger: Partners in Power* (New York, 2007), 151.
15. Richard Nixon, *The Real War* (New York, 1980), 267.
16. Joan Hoff, *Nixon Reconsidered* (New York, 1994), chapter 5.

17. Oriana Fallaci, *Interview with History*, trans. John Shepley (New York, 1976), 41.
18. H. R. Haldeman, *The Haldeman Diaries: Inside the Nixon White House* (New York, 1994), 73.
19. *FRUS, 1969–72*, vol. I: 45–46.
20. Ibid., 110.
21. Ibid., 352.
22. Ibid, 142.
23. Jonathan Aitken, "The Nixon Character," *Presidential Studies Quarterly* 26 (Winter 1996): 244.
24. Memorandum for the President's Files, "Briefing of the White House Staff on the July 15 Announcement of the President's Trip to Peking," July 19, 1971, Electronic Briefing Book No. 66, Doc. 41, National Security Archive, http://www.gwu.edu/~nsarchiv/index.html (hereafter NSA).
25. Nixon to Melvin Laird, February 4, 1969, *FRUS, 1969–1976*, I: 57.
26. Kissinger, *White House Years*, 192.
27. Henry Kissinger, *Years of Upheaval* (Boston, 1982), 70.
28. Kissinger, *White House Years*, 164, 712, 763–770.
29. Author interview with John Fraser, February 2004.
30. National Security Study Memorandum 14, February 5, 1969, NSA.
31. Kissinger, *White House Years*, 169.
32. James Mann, *About Face: A History of America's Curious Relationship with China from Nixon to Clinton* (New York, 1999), 22.
33. Hoff, *Nixon Reconsidered*, 196–197.
34. Jisen Ma, *The Cultural Revolution in the Foreign Ministry of China* (Hong Kong, 2004), 298.
35. *FRUS*, 154.
36. Stanley D. Bachrack, *The Committee of One Million: "China Lobby" Politics, 1953–1971* (New York, 1976), 261, 265; Nancy Bernkopf Tucker, "Taiwan Expendable? Nixon and Kissinger Go to China," *Journal of American History* 92 (June 2005): 129.
37. Rosemary Foot, "Redefinitions: the Domestic Context of America's China Policy in the 1960s", in *Re-examining the Cold War: U.S.-China Diplomacy 1954–1973*, ed. Robert S. Ross and Jiang Changbin (Cambridge, Mass., 2001), 277–278, 280.
38. John H. Holdridge interview, USOH.
39. Robert L. Nichols interview, USOH.
40. See, for example, Dallek, *Nixon and Kissinger*, 266.
41. Isaacson, *Kissinger*, 140.
42. Kissinger, *White House Years*, 187.
43. For the transcripts and summaries of Kissinger's talks with the Chinese on his two visits in 1971 and Nixon's meeting with Mao in 1972, see *FRUS, 1969–1976*, vol. XVII: 359–452, 498–558, 677–684.
44. Barbara Barnouin and Changgen Yu, *Chinese Foreign Policy During the Cultural Revolution* (London and New York, 1998), 108–109.

45. Ibid., 86.

46. James R. Lilley, with Jeffrey Lilley, *China Hands: Seven Decades of Adventure, Espionage and Diplomacy in Asia* (New York, 2004), 146.

47. John W. Garver, *Foreign Relations of the People's Republic of China*, (Englewood Cliffs, N.J., 1993), 304–305.

48. Lyle J. Goldstein, "Return to Zhenbao Island: Who Started Shooting and Why It Matters," *China Quarterly* 168 (December 2001): 992–994.

49. Christian F. Ostermann, "New Evidence on the Sino-Soviet Border Dispute 1969–71," in *The Cold War in Asia: Cold War International History Project Bulletin* 6–7 (Winter 1995–96), 187–188; Michael Schaller, "Détente and the Strategic Triangle, Or "Drinking Your Mao Tai and Having Your Vodka Too," in Ross, ed., *Re-Examining the Cold War*, 368.

50. Kuisong Yang, "Changes in Mao Zedong's Attitude towards the Indochina War, 1949–1973," *Cold War International History Project Working Paper* 34 (February 2002), 34; Elizabeth Wishnick, *Mending Fences: the Evolution of Moscow's China Policy from Brezhnev to Yeltsin* (Seattle, 2001), 35.

51. Hoff, *Nixon Reconsidered*, 197; Allen S. Whiting, "Review: Sino-American Détente," *China Quarterly* 82 (June 1980): 226.

52. Kissinger, *White House Years*, 184.

53. Chün-tu Hsüeh and Robert C. North, "China and the Superpowers" Perception and Policy," in *China's Foreign Relations: New Perspectives*, ed. Chün-tu Hsüeh (New York, 1982), 25.

54. Yingcai Luo, *Chen Yi De Feichang Zhilu* (Beijing, 2004), 272–273.

55. Chen Jian and David L. Wilson, "'All Under the Heaven is Great Chaos': Beijing, the Sino-Soviet Border Clashes, and the Turn Toward Sino-American Rapprochement, 1968–69", *Cold War International History Project Bulletin* 11 (Winter 1998), 166–168.

56. Ibid., 170.

57. Ibid., 171; Ma, *Cultural Revolution in the Foreign Ministry of China*, 301.

58. Baijia Zhang, "The Changing International Scene," in Ross, ed., *Re-examining the Cold War*, 71.

59. Yang, "Changes in Mao Zedong's Attitude towards the Indochina War," 43.

60. Zhisui Li, *The Private Life of Chairman Mao: The Memoirs of Mao's Personal Physician* (New York, 1994), 514.

61. National Security Study Memorandum 14, February 5, 1969, NSA.

62. Minutes of the Senior Review Group Meeting, May 15, 1969, *FRUS*, 1969–1976, vol. XVII: 33, 36–37.

63. "Response to National Security Study Memorandum 14," August 8, 1969, ibid., 56–62.

64. See ibid., 67n1.

65. Kissinger, *White House Years*, 182.

66. *FRUS, 1969–1976*, vol. I: 79

67. Department of State, "Next Steps in China Policy," October 6, 1971, NSA.

68. John H. Holdridge, *Crossing the Divide: An Insider's Account of the Normalization of U.S.-China Relations* (Lanham, Md., 1997), 32;

F.S. Aijazuddin, *From a Head, Through a Head, To a Head: The Secret Channel between the US and China through Pakistan* (Karachi, 2000), 3.

69. Yafeng Xia, "China's Elite Politics and Sino-American Rapprochement," 11.
70. Aijazuddin, *From a Head, Through a Head, to a Head*, 42–43.
71. *Globe and Mail* (Toronto), April 15, 1971.
72. Kissinger, *White House Years*, 726–727; Haldeman, *Diaries*, 295; Nixon, *RN*, 551–552; Mann, *About Face*, 29.
73. Nixon, *RN*, 727.

6

Nuclear Nixon: Ironies, Puzzles, and the Triumph of Realpolitik

Francis J. Gavin

In the nuclear field, the Nixon presidency has long been known for, above all else, the landmark Anti-Ballistic Missile Treaty (ABM) and the Strategic Arms Limitation Treaty (SALT) negotiated with the Soviet Union and signed in 1972. Arms control advocates hailed these treaties as the cornerstone of strategic stability, formally recognizing that nuclear weapons offered no military and scant political utility in a world of superpower parity and mutually assured destruction. For those analysts who saw the nuclear arms race as one of the leading causes of tension during the Cold War, Nixon's arms control policies removed the major irritant in U.S.-Soviet relations, recognized the equality of the superpowers, and ushered in a period of cooperative relations often referred to as détente.

This focus on ABM and SALT, however, has obscured other key arms control events during the Nixon administration, including a treaty to ban biological weapons and the beginning of mutual conventional force reduction negotiations. In addition, the administration signed the Prevention of Nuclear War Treaty with the Soviets, and its officials were among the first to recognize the dangers of nuclear terrorism. Two other key policies in the nuclear realm proved even more important: the ratification of the Nuclear Nonproliferation Treaty (NPT), and a transformation of U.S. nuclear strategy. Taken as a whole, these Nixon era policies were impressive. When viewed through the widely shared perspective that saw arms control as the best (and only) option to curtail the instabilities and dangers of nuclear arms racing, Nixon's presidency was, despite other failings, a great success.

This view, however, suffers from a fatal flaw: Nixon and his powerful foreign policy advisor, Henry Kissinger, did not accept the worldview of the arms control community, nor did they share the enthusiasm of the previous two administrations for limiting the vertical and horizontal spread of nuclear weapons. Neither saw the nuclear arms race as the *cause* or *key* factor in the Cold War conflict with the Soviet Union. For Nixon and Kissinger, *geopolitical competition*, and not the arms race, remained the core driver of international politics, much as it had in the time of Metternich and Bismarck. Treaties would be violated if it were in a state's interest to do so.

Despite some overheated rhetoric, Nixon and Kissinger had a coherent, if controversial, set of theories about the nuclear age. They did not, as has often been portrayed, simply rely on the "madman" theory or desire to subsume all policy to political expedience. Their framework was based on years of experience participating in and observing U.S. national security policy, and provided a credible if at times harrowing alternative to the more conventional views of those in the arms control community.

What was the substance of their philosophy? Neither accepted many of the core ideas around the so-called nuclear revolution. First, neither Nixon nor Kissinger thought that nuclear weapons transformed the way people thought and the way nations behaved. While these fearsome weapons were extraordinarily important, they did not fundamentally alter more powerful political forces. Second, nuclear weapons had value far beyond simply deterrence, offering military and political utility, even in an age of superpower parity. Nixon and Kissinger believed strategic nuclear superiority mattered, and should be regained if at all possible. If it was not possible to reclaim numerical advantage, other tactics including flexible nuclear options and strategies based on what Thomas Schelling had called "manipulation of risk" and threats that left something to chance, could be employed to gain advantage against an adversary. Third, given their political and military utility, other nations would want these powerful weapons. Neither Nixon nor Kissinger thought halting nuclear proliferation merited sacrificing other geopolitical goals. More states with nuclear weapons were not only inevitable, but also potentially desirable. In sum, this was a strategy built upon the puzzles and ironies of making policy in the nuclear age. As Kissinger stressed to Nixon: "And we've got to play it recklessly. That's the safest course."[1]

Why did Nixon and Kissinger pursue arms control arrangements that appeared to contradict their core beliefs about the world? Nixon and Kissinger had ambitious geopolitical goals at a time of declining U.S. power, shrinking military budgets, and decreased domestic support for American engagement in the world. American prospects in the global order were dim: the administration inherited a disastrous war in Southeast Asia and pressure for retrenchment in East Asia; conflict and Soviet encroachment in the Middle East; and malaise and drift among America's closest European allies. These issues shaped the Nixon administration's views on nuclear questions. In order to reverse these trends, arms control was a useful tool, but not an end in itself. At the same time, Nixon and Kissinger believed that—in the absence of strategic superiority—nuclear threats, and the strategies that gave them credibility, could be deployed to advance U.S. interests. And in a dangerous world, neither Nixon nor Kissinger saw much to gain spending valuable political capital trying to prevent states from acquiring their own nuclear weapons.

Before exploring Nixon and Kissinger's nuclear philosophy, it is important to lay out how most other analysts, policymakers, and arms control participants viewed the influence of nuclear weapons on international politics and the importance of arms control. As remarkable as the ABM and SALT treaties were, many believed their negotiation was not only necessary, but also practically inevitable. Since the beginning of the atomic age, strategists puzzled over the influence of these fearsome weapons on international politics. Nuclear weapons presented an obvious dilemma—their terrifying power, if used, could kill tens of millions and destroy civilized life. It was this very feature, however, that strategists believed could prevent a third world war. If two adversaries both possessed these weapons, they might think twice before initiating hostilities. This idea—that nuclear weapons could make war between great powers *less likely*—was at the heart of the concept of deterrence and the "nuclear revolution."[2]

As strategists puzzled over the dynamics of nuclear weapons, they soon recognized that mere possession of a handful of atomic bombs might not be enough to achieve deterrence, which required two additional characteristics. First, a state had to be able to deliver their weapons against its adversaries. In many ways, developing the technology to deliver nuclear weapons became as important as developing the weapons themselves. As a result, the Soviet Union and the United States spent billions on long-range bombers, land-based intercontinental ballistic missiles, and submarine-launched weapons that could hit each other. Second, a state's nuclear force had to be robust enough, or invulnerable enough, to withstand a surprise attack with enough weapons left over to threaten the attacker with unacceptable damage. For nuclear deterrence to be effective on both countries there had to be *strategic stability*; in other words, both the Soviet Union and the United States had to possess secure "second-strike" forces. If one side's nuclear forces were in any way vulnerable, if they could be wiped out by a surprise attack, the balance would be unstable and dangerous. The policy goal of both superpowers, according to strategists and arms control advocates, should be to construct nuclear forces and strategies that accepted mutual vulnerability and did not seek a first-strike advantage.

Would the United States and the Soviet Union accept the logic of nuclear deterrence and the profound effect it would have on world politics? Looking to the past, strategists noted the natural tendency of rival states to accumulate more and more weapons, ostensibly for defensive purposes. They believed this often unleashed a dangerous competition for arms between rival states that these analysts argued could spiral out of control and lead to war. Plans for disarmament were naïve and overlooked the deterrent benefits a stable nuclear order might bring. According to this view, these dangerous arms races could only be stopped by mutually agreed upon restraints, in other words, arms control.

The arms controllers and strategists found a policy champion in Robert McNamara, the secretary of defense from 1961 until 1968. He eschewed the search for nuclear superiority, and embraced the idea of mutual assured destruction, or MAD. He belittled defensive forces, arguing that cheaper offensive forces could easily overwhelm proposed antiballistic missile forces. And he became a forceful advocate of negotiating treaties with the Soviet Union to stem both arms races in both defensive and offensive nuclear weapons.

These views dominated the policy landscape that Nixon and Kissinger inhabited, and it has long been assumed that they reluctantly accepted them as reality. One of the key arms control officials of the period has argued, "Nixon surprised both critics and supporters by vigorously pursuing Johnson's initiatives on capping strategic nuclear arms and nuclear proliferation."[3] Another scholar claims the SALT treaties "were given enormous importance in American thinking and were the legacy of Richard Nixon and Henry Kissinger."[4] These arms control treaties have been accorded enormous historical importance, even by analysts inclined to dislike both Nixon and Kissinger. Even a critic like McGeorge Bundy applauded the Nixon administration for "arms control arrangements ... [that] were by far the largest achieved in the nuclear age" and laid the foundation for a "bilateral rhetoric of détente that had worldwide appeal."[5] Sidney Drell, a prominent scientist and arms control advocate, summed up the conventional wisdom when he declared that he considered the ABM treaty negotiated by the Nixon administration "to be our most important arms control achievement to date."[6] Nixon biographer Joan Hoff contends that "in the areas of arms control,

Nixinger détente policy contained the potential not only to substitute for containment" but to transcend the "procrustean ideological constraints" that animated the Cold War.[7] Judging from their memoirs written after they had left office, the president and his national security advisor appeared to share these views. Nixon stated "the ABM treaty stopped what inevitably would have become a defensive arms race, with untold billions of dollars being spent on each side." The treaty made "permanent the concept of deterrence through 'mutual terror.' "[8] Kissinger claimed, "the fundamental achievement was to sketch the outline on which coexistence between the democracies and the Soviet system must be based. SALT embodied our conviction that a wildly spiraling nuclear arms race was in no country's interest and enhanced no one's security."[9]

The documents, however, reveal that Kissinger and especially Nixon had a different notion of how nuclear weapons affected international relations. Nixon and Kissinger did not share the view of the arms controllers or liberal internationalists who put their faith in global organizations, international law, and treaties. Theirs was a realist view—world politics was driven, as it had been for centuries, by geopolitical competition between great powers. The "nuclear revolution" had not changed this core feature of the international system. In relations with the Soviets, the message to their opponents was clear: "look we'll divide up the world, but by God you're going to respect our side or we won't respect your side."[10]

Their belief in the supremacy of geopolitics influenced Nixon and Kissinger's skepticism of arms control. There was to be no rush to negotiations with the Soviet Union, and, in fact, the SALT discussions were shelved during the first months of the administration. For the president and his national security advisor, the subject of armaments could not be separated from the question of their political use. Arms races did not lead to war: "Our reading of history indicates that all crises have been caused by political conditions, not by the arms race as such."[11] In his first official meeting with the Soviet ambassador to the United States, Anatoly Dobrynin, Nixon cautioned that "there is no guarantee that freezing strategic weapons" would bring about peace. "History makes it clear that wars result from political differences and problems."[12] Just as in the age of Metternich and Bismarck, hardnosed, personal diplomacy mattered far more than treaties or idealism:

> Finally, it comes down to the men involved. It is the will of the men rather than the treaties. We have had treaties such as the Hitler-Stalin pact—but all wars have started with broken treaties, World War I

and World War II. I approach Soviet-American relations in a totally pragmatic fashion.[13]

Nixon and Kissinger actually feared that arms control, in certain circumstances, could be a bad thing. During a briefing for the president, Kissinger stated that the prevailing view among American policymakers and intellectuals was that the Soviet Union and the United States shared a common interest in survival and the prevention of war. This led to the belief that "every effort should be made to engage the Soviets in negotiations wherever common interests occur and especially arms control." Even if unsuccessful, these analysts believed arms control talks could "serve as a firebreak to prevent confrontations from getting out of hand." Kissinger disagreed with this view: "arms per se rarely cause wars," and narrowly focusing on these issues risks "the danger that the Soviets will use the bait of progress in one area in order to neutralize our resistance to pressure elsewhere."[14] Nixon cautioned his secretary of state, William Rogers, that arms control was not simply a matter of "purely technical and military matters" and that he had to be wary that the Soviets did not use "talks on arms as a safety valve on intransigence elsewhere." The President reminded Rogers that "the invasion of Czechoslovakia was preceded by the exploration of a summit conference."[15]

Nixon and Kissinger were always suspicious the Soviets were trying to dupe them into an arms control agreement that would tie down the United States while Russia moved elsewhere. Right before the Moscow summit, Kissinger told the president he believed the Soviets "were determined to hit China next year" and that they wanted to sign SALT so that they could "get their rear cleared."[16] On many occasions, they lamented the attention arms control received over what they considered more important issues. During the bombing of Cambodia, Nixon stated that "looking back over the past year we have been praised for all the wrong things: Okinawa, SALT, germs, Nixon Doctrine. Now [we are] finally doing the right thing."[17]

Neither saw any value in arms control for its own sake. With the Vietnam War still unresolved, Nixon told Kissinger, "I don't give a damn about SALT; I just couldn't care less about it."[18] The president was regularly dismissive of his negotiating team: "The arms control people will support anything."[19] Nixon was uninterested in discussions that focused on the technical minutiae of arms control. On the controversial question of the number and performance of Soviet radars, Nixon told Kissinger that as "you and I both know, it doesn't make a hell of a lot of difference."[20] Both agreed a debate over the number of missile interceptors was "just of no consequence. ... I don't think it makes a hell of a lot of difference."[21] Nixon told Kissinger to "do the best you can" because they could not have an arms control treaty that "looks as if we got took. They're going to analyze that son-of-a-bitch right down to its wire teeth." The president adamantly opposed having an ABM site protect the capital, whose purpose was to prevent a "decapitating" nuclear strike against American command, control, communication and intelligence centers, a contingency arms controllers greatly feared. "I don't want Washington. I don't like the feel of Washington. I don't like that goddamn command airplane or any of this. I don't believe in all that crap. I really don't.... I think the idea of building a new system around Washington is stupid."[22] At the end of the day, Nixon felt that none of these technical issues or treaty agreements had any worth if the core, underlying geopolitical tensions remained unresolved. As the president pointed out:

> What sense does it make to sit there with the Soviet Ambassador at a time they're raiding South Vietnam and say that they made a great contribution to peace by signing the silly biological warfare thing, which doesn't mean anything? Now, you know it and I know it.[23]

So why pursue the arms control negotiations and treaties with the Soviet Union in the first place? The president told his General Advisory Committee on Arms Control that while the public message was "let us curb the arms race and prevent nuclear war," the real reasons for negotiations could be found elsewhere. From the Soviet side, Nixon thought the motivations were at best temporary. "The arms race is burdensome, the Soviet economy has been flat, their neighbor to the East could be a big problem in 20 years, so that may be a good opportunity to deal with the US." Other, more sinister motives might also be involved. Arms control might help the Soviets "break up NATO" by coupling "SALT with a European Security Conference." It could also help them keep "Eastern Europe under control."[24] The Soviets were not to be trusted. As Kissinger told the president, "[I]f the Soviets believe they have strategic predominance then, of course, this document will be meaningless."[25] From Nixon's perspective, "If the balance shifts, we are all in deep trouble."[26]

Proving equally complex were U.S. motivations: Nixon and Kissinger wanted a return to nuclear superiority, but because of domestic politics and the world situation, it was simply not in the cards. "The possibility of our going into a massive arms build-up is no longer what is was." Perhaps they could "frighten the U.S. people" into something but "time was running out."

The Soviet and Americans were now equal, but the United States was no longer "credible" when it threatened to keep up with further Soviet increases. Nixon reminded his advisory committee "in this room we know—and Soviet intelligence knows—that we have weaknesses."[27] The president reminded his White House advisor Alexander Haig that while he shared the right-wing's aversion to arms control, he understood that "we simply can't get from the Congress the additional funds needed to continue the arms race with the Soviets in either the defensive or offensive missile category."[28] Nixon recognized that after more than two decades of an expensive commitment to the Cold War, and years of a bloody, failing war in Southeast Asia, Americans did not have the stomach for escalating the strategic arms race with the Soviets. "We face the reality of a change in strategic relations. We face the reality of a complex domestic situation."[29] The Nixon administration had its hands full simply staving off isolationism. "The real question is whether the Americans give a damn any more. Americans don't care about Cambodia, Laos, Thailand and the Philippines. No President could risk New York to save Tel Aviv or Bonn."[30]

Kissinger and especially Nixon believed nuclear weapons had powerful military and political utility beyond simple deterrence, and that the strategic nuclear balance mattered. United States nuclear superiority was not, as the arms controllers would have it, either useless or even dangerous. To their mind, America's numerical advantage had held the Soviets at bay and allowed earlier administrations to prevail during crises in the past. Time and time again, they lamented the conditions of nuclear parity and highlighted how much more freedom the United States had during an earlier period. The new strategic balance explained what Kissinger labeled "the aggressiveness" of Soviet foreign policy. Nixon was obsessed with the strategic superiority the United States had during the Cuban Missile Crisis and the leverage it provided John F. Kennedy. "Kennedy saw 5–1 in 1962, [and] had confidence. We can't do this today ... We may have reached a balance of terror."[31] Three years later, the president stated "[I]n 1962, at the time of the Cuban missile crisis, it had been 'no contest,' because we had a ten to one superiority."[32] At a meeting with NATO Ambassadors over a year later, Nixon again brought up how different the U.S. situation was eleven years after Kennedy's showdown with the Russians:

> We also have had to consider that we are conducting foreign policy under extremely difficult circumstances. We did not invent the new strategic balance. We inherited a changed strategic relationship.

Whereas the Kennedy administration dealt with the Soviet Union when the Soviets had 80 ICBMs [intercontinental ballistic missiles] that were liquid fueled and took ten minutes to prepare, we face over 1,000 ICBMs that can be fired immediately.[33]

Nixon and Kissinger would have preferred to recapture U.S. nuclear superiority, but the obstacles were simply too great. Kissinger, in a briefing paper on nuclear options early in the president's first term, pointed out that unlike in 1962, "now we have no first strike capability," and that it would be "hard to recapture 5 to 1 superiority."[34] During the same meeting, Chairman of the Joint Chiefs Earle Wheeler stated if the United States could develop an ABM system which "gave first strike capability, I would advocate it, destabilizing or not ... [It] wouldn't bother me." Nixon agreed: "Wouldn't bother me either." Nixon pushed the point on his arms control chief and undersecretary of defense:

> Nixon: Suppose you could defend cities. Really means credible threat of first strike would be much greater if they are screwing with Allies.
>
> Packard: Wouldn't really give you first strike.
>
> Smith: Population protection is historically a signal of going for first strike. Would be more threatening.
>
> Nixon: We say glibly we will fire on warning. Who's sure? As soon as you do, you are risking great destruction.[35]

Nixon and Kissinger recognized what the arms control community often chose to ignore: that the U.S. commitment to defend Western Europe and other allies was only really credible if the United States had nuclear superiority. In an age of parity, the president declared the "nuclear umbrella in NATO a lot of crap." As Kissinger recognized, "Europeans don't realize American nuclear umbrella depended on first strike. No longer true." The administration had to undertake a review of nuclear options, as they felt the strategy they inherited from Kennedy and Johnson was bankrupt. "Flexible response is baloney. They have possibility of conventional options, greater options. We remember our massive retaliation, gave us freedom to act. This has changed." The age of parity meant that the Soviets' "assured destruction edge affects their willingness to be aggressive." This might push the Soviets to more "local aggression." The president felt with the nuclear umbrella diminished, America's "bargaining position has shifted. We must face facts."[36]

Neither Nixon nor Kissinger wanted to accept either the logic or reality of MAD, and both sought ways out of the limitations imposed by strategic nuclear parity. This effort had two parts. First, the administration sought changes in nuclear strategy that would provide more flexible, "useable," options. The second strategy was to pursue what Nixon, his aides, and scholars have called the "madman" strategy, which was in fact a variation on Thomas Schelling's idea of the manipulation of risk.[37] Both Nixon and Kissinger saw great political utility in engaging in nuclear brinkmanship in order to prevail in a crisis. With the American public unwilling to support the increases necessary to support a strategy of nuclear superiority, Nixon and Kissinger had to find other ways to exploit what they saw as the military and political utility of nuclear weapons to advance U.S. interests.

Scholars William Burr and Terry Terriff have admirably chronicled the Nixon administration's efforts to create more flexible nuclear war plans that gave the president more options in a crisis.[38] Nixon and Kissinger were stunned by their inheritance from previous Democratic administrations. Robert McNamara had, with great fanfare, announced the Kennedy administration's ambition to construct a more supple strategy in 1962. This new doctrine, dubbed "flexible response," was supposedly a reaction to the Eisenhower administration's "massive retaliation" plan. Massive retaliation, it was argued, relied exclusively on a large, preordained strategic nuclear response against thousands of targets throughout the communist world in the event of Soviet aggression. In a crisis, critics argued, the plan's inflexibility gave the president only two options—capitulation or launching a nuclear attack that would leave tens of million of people dead. Flexible response was supposed to provide U.S. decision makers with an array of less extreme options, and the ability to deploy effective forces on any rung of the so-called escalation ladder.

In retrospect, it is clear that the strategy of flexible response was a rhetorical policy and nothing more.[39] Under McNamara, there was some minor tinkering with the nuclear war plan, but the general thrust of the strategy—massive, preprogrammed, inflexible strategic nuclear strikes against thousands of targets—remained in place. Nixon and Kissinger demanded changes that would give the president politically plausible options that did not involve appalling outcomes. Not only was a strategy that relied upon killing tens of millions of Russians immoral—even the realist Kissinger said that to "have the only option that of killing 80 million people is the height of immorality"[40]—it was of questionable credibility.

The administration pushed the military establishment to dramatically revise its war plans and provide more options. Kissinger demanded to know if "all-out thermonuclear war became too dangerous, would limited applications of nuclear forces still be feasible?"[41] The military bureaucracy, however, presented enormous resistance to deviations from the large, preprogrammed attacks.[42]

The Defense Department, led by Melvyn Laird, did not begin a serious effort to alter the war plans until January 1972, when a committee led by Director of Defense Research and Engineering John Foster was tasked with producing a nuclear attack and targeting policy to guide the Joint Chiefs of Staff. While much of the background of the report remains classified, it appears that the committee did go some way toward recommending the flexibility that Nixon and Kissinger desired. An aide to Kissinger described the recommendations as a "radical departure" from the current war plan. Instead of trying to "win the war through the destruction of the enemy's forces and military capability," the new plan would aim to control escalation and "re-establish mutual deterrence."[43] In addition to the major, general war attacks, the plan called for selected, regional, and limited attack options. President Nixon took almost two years to sign the National Security Action Memorandum 242, authorizing the military to make the changes the Foster Panel recommended. Despite the national security decision memoranda (NSDM) and the public pronouncements of Laird's successor, James Schlesinger, that the United States sought flexible nuclear options, evidence indicates that the new single integrated operational plan (SIOP) was only marginally different than those that preceded it.[44]

The other aspect of Nixon and Kissinger's nuclear strategy was what Nixon himself called his "madman" strategy. The idea—which has been previously laid out by participants like H. R. Haldeman and scholars such as Jeffrey Kimball—was to convey the impression that the administration was willing, in a crisis, to use "excessive" force, and to threaten, often implicitly, that nuclear weapons might be used.[45] As Kissinger told the National Security Council during the first month of the administration, "for deterrence, what the other side thinks is as important as what we think" because in the nuclear age "bluff[s] [are] taken seriously."[46] What is perhaps more interesting is that conversations between Nixon and Kissinger hint these may have been more than threats, and the use of nuclear weapons was not completely off the table.

Excellent research by Jeremi Suri, Scott Sagan, Jeffrey Kimball, and William Burr has made clear that one of the first and most important tests of the "madman" theory occurred in the fall of 1969. Nixon ordered an increase in U.S. nuclear readiness to signal to the Soviets the possibility that he might use extreme force to bring the Vietnam conflict to an end.[47] These scholars argue Nixon and Kissinger hoped to convey the possibility that the president might not be entirely rational in his application of force. No evidence exists that the Soviets made any changes in policy as a result of worldwide alert.

Nixon and Kissinger engaged in veiled or explicit brinkmanship in several other cases. In late 1971, India intervened in Pakistan's bloody civil war that saw East Pakistan become an independent country, Bangladesh. The administration feared India would destroy what remained of Pakistan in the west, humiliating an American ally and providing what Nixon and Kissinger believed would be an unacceptable victory to their Cold War rival, the Soviets. Less than half a year later, Nixon and Kissinger appeared willing to scuttle the Moscow summit and end any possibility of SALT by threatening massive escalation after a spring offensive by North Vietnam into the south.[48] Kissinger claimed that during the dispute over the Soviet submarine base at Cienfuegoes in 1970, the Nixon administration "used more or less the same tactics [as Kennedy had used in 1962] and we achieved more or less the same result."[49] The most explicit case of nuclear brinkmanship occurred in October 1973. After Israel had reversed its initial losses from Egypt and Syria's surprise attack, the Soviet Union pressed the United States to jointly deploy a peacekeeping force to prevent the Israeli military from destroying Arab military forces. After Kissinger rejected this suggestion, the Soviets appeared as if they might intervene unilaterally. With Nixon supposedly in a debilitated physical and emotional state due to Watergate and the aftermath of the "Saturday Night Massacre," Kissinger ordered U.S. military forces to a high alert, DEFCON 3. While it is unclear how the Soviets interpreted and responded to the alert, they ceased pushing for a joint or unilateral superpower military intervention in the conflict.[50]

Kissinger and especially Nixon had developed this idea based on their views of past. Nixon may have believed Eisenhower's claim that nuclear threats had brought the Korean conflict to an end in 1953 and allowed the United States to protect Taiwan's interests in their crises in the straits. Even more impressive to Nixon was Nikita Khrushchev's use of brinkmanship during the Suez and Berlin crises while the Soviets were in a position of strategic nuclear inferiority. Regardless of the source, both believed it was effective for them. Kissinger believed these threats were "how we broke the India-Pakistan situation last year."[51] And Nixon argued that brinkmanship in October 1973 had been successful. "The Soviets had a hard choice to our alert—to go back to the Cold War and risk the United States relationship, or to back off. They joined us in the UN and called for a cease-fire."[52]

More interesting than the threats to manipulate risk during crises are the examples when Nixon appeared at least willing to contemplate employing nuclear weapons. Consider this remarkable exchange between Nixon and Kissinger at the height of the 1971 Indo-Pakistani conflict. When Kissinger argued if "the Soviets move against them and we don't do anything, we'll be finished," the president asked, "So what do we do if the Soviets move against them? Start lobbing nuclear weapons?" While not answering the question, Kissinger suggested that if "Pakistan is swallowed by India, China is destroyed, defeated, humiliated by the Soviet Union, it will be a change in the world balance of power of such magnitude that the security of the United States may be forever [weakened], certainly for decades."[53] During the North Vietnamese spring 1972 offensive, weeks before the scheduled Moscow summit with the Soviet Union, Nixon fumed: "We're going to do it. I'm going to destroy the goddamn country, believe me, I mean destroy it if necessary. And let me say, even the nuclear weapons if necessary. It isn't necessary. But, you know, what I mean is, that shows you the extent to which I'm willing to go. By a nuclear weapon, I mean that we will bomb the living bejeezus out of North Vietnam and then if anybody interferes we will threaten the nuclear weapons."[54] A week later, Nixon repeated the threat. "I'd rather use a nuclear bomb. Have you got that ready?" When Kissinger appeared to protest, Nixon asked "A nuclear bomb, does that bother you? ... I just want you to think big, Henry, for Christ's sake!"[55]

How did Nixon and Kissinger's theories about nuclear weapons affect their attitudes toward the atomic aspirations of other powers? While the primary focus of arms control experts and U.S. officials were on the strategic nuclear balance between the United States and the Soviet Union, a new concern arose in the 1960s. States other than the superpowers were expressing an interest in acquiring their own atomic weapons. How would this issue of new nuclear powers—"the nth country problem," in the parlance of the day—affect international politics? Once again, Nixon and Kissinger had different views than most.

The Kennedy and Johnson administrations recognized the need for policies to slow the threat of nuclear proliferation. China's detonation of a nuclear device in October 1964 led to concerns about a "chain reaction" of nuclear proliferation. India, Japan, Pakistan, Taiwan, Indonesia, and Australia, it was feared, would acquire atomic weapons. East Asia was not the only region where fears of nuclear spread existed. In the Middle East, Israel was suspected of developing nuclear weapons. And in Europe, there was great concern that West Germany, at the frontline of the Cold War, would want to defend itself with the same weapons its closest allies, the United States, Great Britain, and France possessed. A nuclear armed Bundeswehr, however, worried all of West Germany's neighbors, allies and adversaries alike.[56]

Nixon's predecessors saw promising opportunities for cooperation with their Cold War enemy, the Soviet Union, to slow the spread of nuclear weapons. In the summer of 1968, the two sides completed over two years of intense, detailed negotiations and announced the signing of the NPT. The NPT forbid signatories who already had nuclear weapons from helping states acquire these weapons; it also committed nuclear states to reduce and eventually eliminate their nuclear stockpiles. Nonnuclear signatories waived their rights to these weapons. While the treaty was considered a great success, the Soviet invasion of Czechoslovakia prevented Johnson from sending it to the U.S. Senate for approval.

What was the attitude of the new Nixon administration to nuclear nonproliferation? Nixon opposed the treaty during the campaign. Neither Nixon nor Kissinger believed proliferation could be halted if states really wanted to go nuclear. As early as 1957, Kissinger argued that a nonproliferation treaty would be unenforceable.[57] The president himself argued that "treaties don't necessarily get us very much" and that if a country wanted to "make their own weapons" they could "abrogate the treaty without sanction."[58] Some in the administration actually argued that the United States should help friendly states acquire atomic weapons. If it were decided, "the NPT was not in the US interest," a formal disengagement would "have considerable support in the FRG and in some circles in Italy, Japan, India, Brazil, and Israel."[59] When Nixon did finally send the NPT to the Senate for ratification, he told his staff to downplay its importance, and that the United States should not pressure other countries, especially the Federal Republic of Germany, to also ratify it.[60]

The ambivalence the Nixon administration displayed to broader nuclear nonproliferation policy turned to outright hostility in specific cases. Soon after de Gaulle left office, the administration decided they would "like to give assistance" to France's nuclear program.[61] Kissinger told the French ambassador, "It is too dangerous to have one country as the repository of nuclear weapons. We would like France to be a possessor."[62] The United States also ended pressuring Israel to get rid of its nuclear weapons. This policy change emerged after an apparently unrecorded, undocumented meeting between Nixon and Israeli Prime Minister Golda Meir led to a secret, mutual, and as yet unrevealed understanding on Israel's nuclear weapons program.[63]

Time and time again, Nixon and Kissinger placed geopolitical goals well ahead of the aim of staunching nuclear nonproliferation. When Secretary of State William Rogers argued the NPT required the United States to pursue nuclear arms reductions, Nixon rejected this view.[64] When Winston Lord, a Kissinger national security council staffer, asked of the Nixon Doctrine, which "is the lesser of two evils—nuclear proliferation or the extension of more concrete American nuclear assurance?" the answer was clear. Looking at Asia, Lord asked, would Japan going nuclear "necessarily be against our long range interests?"[65]

The Nixon administration pursued other policies that, intentionally or not, increased the incentives and opportunities for nuclear proliferation. According to Raymond Garthoff, the administration's tilt toward Pakistan in 1971 "may have had one critical effect—it may have influenced India to develop nuclear weapons."[66] Furthermore, Nixon's opening to China, which gave the United States new leverage in its conflict with the Soviets, set America's East Asian allies on edge. Taiwan, in particular, stepped up its efforts to acquire nuclear weapons. Reversing weapons programs in South Africa, Brazil, and Argentina were given relatively low priority. Finally, his crusade to privatize the nuclear power industry diluted U.S. control over world nuclear fuel production and led countries to replace U.S. agreements with ones less focused on preventing nuclear proliferation.

It is perhaps not unexpected that Nixon and his close advisor Kissinger disagreed with the views of the Democratic administrations that preceded them, nor with the ideas espoused by academic strategists and arms controllers. What is surprising, however, is that they had a broad, consistent, and intellectually defensible (if controversial) view of the influence of nuclear weapons on modern statecraft. Scholars have not seen it this way, choosing instead to emphasize Nixon and Kissinger's expediency and personality. The historian Robert Dallek, for example, argues that during the SALT negotiations Nixon was most concerned about "personal credit and domestic politics."[67] Jeffrey Kimball, an important scholar of Nixon's decision making in the Vietnam War, and particularly the "madman" strategy, emphasizes Nixon's "peculiar psychology" and his "odd relationship" with Kissinger.[68] While these assessments—and many others like them—contain a certain amount of truth, they underestimate the coherence and validity of a philosophy toward the nuclear age that had been developed in their years as policymakers and observers. Nixon and Kissinger's theories about statecraft in a nuclear age, and how they manifested themselves in their policy choices, should be taken seriously and judged on their merits.

Consider their views on nuclear strategy. Nixon and Kissinger believed that strategic nuclear superiority mattered, and that President Kennedy was able to prevail in his showdown with the Soviets because the United States had what almost amounted to a first-strike capability in October 1962. Members of Kennedy's inner circle have vigorously denied that nuclear superiority, if it even existed, played any role in the outcome of the Cuban Missile Crisis. Who was right? The answer is not as clear-cut as many proponents of the "nuclear revolution" thesis would suggest.[69] While Nixon and Kissinger recognized that neither the domestic nor the international political factors they faced in office would allow for the massive strategic build-up necessary to recapture their vision of "nuclear superiority," it does not mean they would not have pursued such a strategy if circumstances were different.

When judged on their merits, Nixon and Kissinger's nonconventional views are at least credible. No conclusive evidence exists that arms races cause wars, and the strategic studies literature can be justly criticized for emphasizing autonomous military factors over more important developments in global politics.[70] The massive study, *History of the Strategic Arms Competition, 1945–1972*, concluded the "facts will not support the proposition that either the Soviet Union or the United States developed strategic forces only in direct immediate reaction to each other."[71] Nixon and Kissinger's policies certainly cast doubt on the widely held belief that the possession of nuclear weapons diminished "the tendency of nations to take risks."[72] And there is certainly an intellectually credible case that the United States should not sacrifice core political interests in the world in order to vigorously impede nuclear proliferation.[73]

This is not to justify Nixon and Kissinger's nuclear philosophies or praise their statecraft. While assessing the results for each crisis remains difficult, the Nixon administration's attempts to manipulate risk (or employ the "madman" strategy) often proved ineffective, and at times, reckless. Nixon's discussions of actually using nuclear weapons were irresponsible. For those who consider nuclear proliferation the greatest threat to U.S. interests, the Nixon period represents lost years, years that did great damage. The case for and against their worldview and policies could be argued in many ways. But before doing so, it is important to recognize Nixon and Kissinger's worldview for what it was. Before the Nixon period can be analyzed correctly, it is important to note that Nixon and Kissinger had distinct, well-thought out ideas about how international politics functioned in a world with nuclear weapons, views that stood in sharp contrast to the beliefs of most other policymakers and analysts of their day.

Notes

1. Conversation between Richard Nixon and Henry Kissinger, April 4, 1972, *FRUS, 1969–1976*, vol. XIV: 258.
2. For a fascinating history of the development of these ideas, see Fred Kaplan, *The Wizards of Armageddon* (New York, 1983). For the best intellectual treatment of the nuclear revolution and its significance for world politics, see Robert Jervis, *The Meaning of the Nuclear Revolution: Statecraft and the Prospect of Armageddon* (Ithaca, 1989).
3. Spurgeon M. Keeny, Jr., "Fingers on the Nuclear Trigger," *Arms Control Today* (October 2006) http://www.armscontrol.org/act/2006_10/ BookReview.asp?print (accessed June 16, 2007).
4. David Hoffman, "1983: Turning Point of the Cold War," *Security Index*, No. 1, 81 (Spring 2007): 135–146.
5. McGeorge Bundy, *Danger and Survival: Choices about the Bomb in the First Fifty Years* (New York, 1988), 552.
6. Sidney D. Drell, "The Impact of a US Public Constituency on Arms Control," in *Breakthrough*, ed. Anatoly Gromyko and Martin Hellman (New York, 1988).
7. Joan Hoff, *Nixon Reconsidered* (New York, 1994), 201.
8. Richard Nixon, *RN: The Memoirs of Richard Nixon* (New York, 1978), 617–618.
9. Henry Kissinger, *White House Years* (Boston, 1979), 1253–1254.
10. Conversation between Nixon and Kissinger, April 19, 1972, *FRUS, 1969–1976*, vol. XIV: 439.
11. Memorandum Kissinger to Nixon, February 15, 1969, *FRUS, 1969–1976*, vol. XII: 33.
12. "Ambassador Dobrynin's Initial Call on the President," February 17, 1969, *FRUS, 1969–1976*, vol. XII: 40.
13. "Richard Nixon's Meeting with NATO Ambassadors," June 30, 1973, Digital National Security Archive (hereafter DSNA), Kissinger Transcripts, item #KT00767, 12.
14. Kissinger to Nixon, February 18, 1969, *FRUS, 1969–1976*, vol. XII: 51.
15. Nixon to William Rogers, February 4, 1969, ibid., 27.
16. Memo of telephone conversation, Nixon and Kissinger, May 14, 1972, *FRUS, 1969–1976*, vol. XIV: 841.
17. H. R. Haldeman, diary entry, April 27,1970, in Jeffrey Kimball, *The Vietnam War Files: Uncovering the Secret History of Nixon-Era Strategy* (Lawrence, Kan., 2003), 132.
18. Transcript of telephone conversation between Nixon and Kissinger, May 6, 1972, *FRUS, 1969–1976*, vol. XIV: 752.
19. Meeting between Nixon and Committee on Arms Control and Disarmament, March 21, 1972, in editorial note, *FRUS, 1969–1976*, vol. XIV: 218.
20. Memorandum of telephone conversation between Nixon and Kissinger, May 14, 1972, ibid., 835.

21. Conversation between Nixon and Kissinger, April 19, 1972, ibid., 243.

22. Ibid., 444

23. Conversation, Nixon and Kissinger, April 10, 1972, in editorial note, ibid., 281.

24. Meeting between Nixon and Committee on Arms Control and Disarmament, March 21, 1972, in editorial note, ibid., 219.

25. Nixon's Meeting with NATO Ambassadors, June 30, 1973, DNSA item# KT00767, 7.

26. Ibid., 12.

27. Meeting between Nixon and Committee on Arms Control and Disarmament, March 21, 1972, in editorial note, *FRUS, 1969–1976,* vol. XIV: 218.

28. Nixon to Haig, May 20, 1972, ibid., 965.

29. Nixon's meeting with NATO Ambassadors, June 30, 1973, DNSA item# KT00767, 2.

30. Memo for the President's Files, May 8, 1972, *FRUS, 1969–1976,* vol. XIV, 769.

31. Notes on NSC Meeting, February 14, 1969, DSNA, item # KT00006, 3.

32. Meeting between Nixon and Committee on Arms Control and Disarmament, March 21, 1972, in editorial note, *FRUS, 1969–1976,* vol. XIV, 218.

33. Nixon's Meeting with NATO Ambassadors, June 30, 1973, DNSA item# KT00767, 2.

34. NSC Meeting, February 19, 1969, DNSA, item #KT00006, 1.

35. Ibid., 3–5.

36. Notes on NSC Meeting, February 14, 1969, DSNA, item# KT00003, 5.

37. For an early, scholarly description of Nixon's use of "the madman theory," see Raymond L. Garthoff, *Détente and Confrontation: American-Soviet Relations from Nixon to Reagan* (Washington, 1985), 251. For "manipulation of risk," see Thomas Schelling, *Arms and Influences* (New Haven, 1966), 92–125. For "the threat that leaves something to chance," see idem, *The Strategy of Conflict* (Cambridge, Mass., 1960), 187–204. For an interesting analysis, see Jeffrey Kimball, "Did Thomas C. Schelling Invent the Madman Theory?" *History News Network*, October 24, 2005, http://hnn.us/articles/17183.html (accessed July 10, 2007).

38. William Burr, "The Nixon Administration, the 'Horror Strategy,' and the Search for Limited Nuclear Options, 1969–1972," *Journal of Cold War Studies* 7 (Summer 2005): 34–78; Terry Terriff, *The Nixon Administration and the Making of U.S. Nuclear Strategy* (Ithaca, 1995).

39. Francis J. Gavin, "The Myth of Flexible Response: American Strategy in Europe During the 1960s," *International History Review* 23 (December 2001): 847–875.

40. Minutes, Verification Panel Meeting, "Nuclear Policy (NSSM 169)," August 9, 1973, with cover memorandum from Jeanne W. Davis to Kissinger, August 15, 1973, National Security Archive Electronic Briefing

Book No. 173, accessed at http://www.gwu.edu/~nsarchiv/NSAEBB/NSAEBB173/index.htm

41. Kissinger, *White House Years*, 198.

42. See Burr, "The Nixon Administration, the "Horror Strategy," and the Search for Limited Nuclear Options"; and Terriff, *Nixon Administration and the Making of U.S. Nuclear Strategy*.

43. Burr, "The Nixon Administration, the "Horror Strategy," and the Search for Limited Nuclear Options," 71.

44. NSDM 242 can be found at http://www.gwu.edu/~nsarchiv/NSAEBB/NSAEBB173/SIOP-24b.pdf (accessed September 12, 2007).

45. Jeffrey Kimball, *Nixon's Vietnam War* (Lawrence, Kan., 1998), esp. 23, 27, 68–69. For Haldeman's views, see ibid., 76–77; and Kimball, *Vietnam War Files*, 132.

46. NSC Meeting, February 19, 1969, DNSA, item# KT00006, 1.

47. See William Burr and Jeffrey Kimball, "Nixon's Nuclear Ploy, To Help End the War in Vietnam, the United States Thought a Secret, yet Massive, Nuclear Alert Would Get the Soviets' Attention and Assistance," Bulletin of the Atomic Scientists 59 (2003): 28–39; and Scott Sagan and Jeremi Suri, "The Madman Alert: Secrecy, Signaling, and Safety in October 1969," International Security 27 (Spring 2003): 150–183.

48. This is a consistent theme throughout *FRUS, 1969–1976*, vol. XIV, documents 73–124.

49. Kissinger quoted in Jervis, *Meaning of the Nuclear Revolution*, 43.

50. For an excellent, early treatment of this episode, see Barry Blechman and Douglas Hart, "The Political Utility of Nuclear Weapons: The 1973 Middle East Crisis," in *Strategy and Nuclear Deterrence*, ed. Steven E. Miller (Princeton, 1984), 273–297. For an excellent treatment of the efficacy of nuclear threats during the Cold War, see Richard K. Betts, *Nuclear Blackmail and Nuclear Balance* (Washington, D.C., 1987).

51. Conversation between Nixon and Kissinger, April 4, 1972, *FRUS, 1969–1976*, vol. XIV: 258.

52. "President Nixon's Meeting with Bipartisan Congressional Leadership," June 20, 1974, DSNA, item #KT01227, 2.

53. Oval Office Conversation no. 637–3, between 8:45 and 9:42 a.m., December 12, 1971, in editorial note, *FRUS, 1969–1976*, vol. XIV: 74.

54. Conversation between Nixon and Kissinger, April 19, 1972, ibid., 433.

55. Executive Office Building Conversation no. 332–35, Nixon and Kissinger, between 12 and 12:28 p.m., April 15, 1972, in Kimball, *Vietnam Wars Files*, 217.

56. For an account of these policies, see Francis J. Gavin, "Blasts from the Past: Nuclear Proliferation and Rogue States Before the Bush Doctrine," *International Security* 29 (Winter 2004–05): 100–135.

57. Henry Kissinger, Nuclear Weapons and Foreign Policy (New York, 1957), 213.

58. Minutes of the NSC, January 29, 1969, Box H-12, NSC Draft Minutes, NPMP.

59. Summary of NPT Issues Paper, January 28, 1969, Box H-019, NSC Meetings File, NPMP.
60. Roger Kelly Smith, "The Origins of the Regime, Nonproliferation, National Interest, and American Decision-making, 1943–1976," Ph.D. dissertation, Georgetown University, 1990, 370.
61. Minutes of NSC Meeting on Post-de Gaulle France, February 23, 1970, DNSA, item #KT00101, 2.
62. "Discussion with Ambassador Kosciusko-Morizet of U.S. Relations with France and Western Europe," April 13, 1973, DNSA, item # KT00702, 9.
63. The leading scholar on Israel's nuclear program, Avner Cohen, has put together an excellent briefing book on this question, which can be found on the National Security Archive's web site. See http://www.gwu.edu/~nsarchiv/NSAEBB/NSAEBB189/index.htm
64. NSC Meeting, February 19, 1969, DNSA, item # KT00006, 7.
65. Winston Lord, "The Nixon Doctrine for Asia: Some Hard Choices," January 23, 1970, DSNA, item # KT00182, 4.
66. Garthoff, *Détente and Confrontation*, 286.
67. Robert Dallek, *Nixon and Kissinger: Partners in Power* (New York, 2007), 139.
68. Kimball, *Nixon's Vietnam War*, xii.
69. For the best discussion of this fascinating question, see Marc Trachtenberg, *History and Strategy* (Princeton, 1991), 235–260.
70. For this critique, see Marc Trachtenberg, "The Past and Future of Arms Control," *Daedalus* 120 (Winter 1991): 203–216; and "Comment on Robert Jervis, Security Studies: Ideas, Policy, and Politics," in *The Evolution of Political Knowledge: Democracy, Autonomy, and Conflict in Comparative and International Politics*, ed. Edward D. Mansfield and Richard Sisson (Columbus, Ohio, 2004). Both articles can be accessed at http://www.polisci.ucla.edu/faculty/trachtenberg/cv/cv.html
71. Ernest R. May, John D. Steinbruner, and Thomas Wolfe, *History of the Strategic Arms Competition, 1945–1972, Part II* (Washington, D.C., 1981), 810, available on DNSA.
72. John Lewis Gaddis, *The United States and the End of the Cold War: Implications, Reconsiderations, Provocations* (Oxford, 1992), 110.
73. The best articulation of this idea can be found in the essay by Kenneth N. Waltz, "More May Be Better," in Scott D. Sagan and Kenneth N. Waltz, *The Spread of Nuclear Weapons: A Debate* (New York, 1995).

7

The Frailties of Grand Strategies: A Comparison of Détente and Ostpolitik

Mary Elise Sarotte

Ostpolitik, or Eastern policy, is the name given to the negotiated process of partial reconciliation between West Germany and its Warsaw Pact neighbors in the middle years of the Cold War. Like the word détente, it is a vague term comprising everything from very specific, formal treaties to very general declarations of interest in using diplomacy and high-level visits to reduce tensions. To complicate matters, analysts sometimes further subdivide Ostpolitik into contrasting categories. One expert on the topic, Timothy Garton Ash, has suggested that there are three: relations between the two halves of Germany (or *Deutschlandpolitik*), West German relations with other East European Warsaw Pact member states, and West German relations with Russia. This tripartite division, while useful for specialists, is somewhat artificial—West German efforts at improving relations across the Iron Curtain were part of a single whole. At first glance, these efforts may not seem central to the course of American foreign policy in the Nixon/ Kissinger era.[1] However, a comparison of Ostpolitik with détente provides highly relevant information about the profound challenge of reconciling Realpolitik with idealism in policymaking.

This chapter asks the following questions: To what extent did the primary authors of détente and Ostpolitik, namely President Richard Nixon and National Security Adviser Henry Kissinger on the American side, and Federal Chancellor Willy Brandt and State Secretary Egon Bahr on the West German side, agree or differ on style and substance? Did détente and Ostpolitik work together or compete with each other (or both)? Did the two policies undermine or support each other (or both at different times)?

Comparing the two policies is particularly useful because, in effect, they represent alternate models for achieving the same goal: reducing and restructuring tensions in the middle Cold War period. A comparison highlights what worked in one model versus the other. By looking at the origins of Ostpolitik, then at the American and West German leaders who created or tolerated it, and finally at its interaction with détente, we can see how the two policies differ. It appears that Ostpolitik, while hardly flawless, nonetheless proved to be a sustainable manner of conducting relations in a region formerly prone to constant crisis. Its formal accords endured through a variety of vicissitudes, until the passing of the Cold War rendered them irrelevant. Because West German leaders chose to focus not on global but on regional strategy—a suitable choice, given their capabilities—they showed how a close-focus, small-bore approach could improve relations with political enemies and conditions for those subjected to them. This emphasis on achievable regional goals—as contrasted with ambitious but ultimately fragile grand strategies—holds lessons relevant to more than just our understanding of the Cold War.

What are the origins of Ostpolitik? Put differently, where did the idea of an independent European strategy of détente begin? Certainly the French felt that the answer was clear: it was Charles de Gaulle who had originated the idea of a "European Europe."[2] Going further back, it might even be possible to see its origins in the hopes raised in Eastern Europe the wake of the death of Stalin. This speculation notwithstanding, Ostpolitik remains most firmly associated with Brandt and Bahr. Whatever their debts to their precursors (particularly to other West German leaders before them), it was they who translated thoughts into treaties and accords. As a result, it is worth examining the personalities of both men in detail.

Brandt, a future Nobel laureate, was born Herbert Frahm in the northern German town of Lübeck. He entered the world in the same year, 1913, as Richard Nixon. His unwed mother, a shop assistant, concealed the identity of his father (whom Brandt would never meet) until he was an adult. A passionate believer in the ideals of social democracy, she transferred her political allegiances to her son early on. He became an active opponent of the Nazis and adopted the name "Willy Brandt" to escape detection by the Gestapo. When Germany descended into tyranny, Brandt fled to Norway; he was stripped of his German citizenship in 1938. Brandt began establishing a life for himself in the north, entering into two subsequent marriages with Norwegian women and becoming a father.[3] After the defeat of the Nazis, however, he decided to return and contribute his political talents to the

Social Democratic Party (known by its German initials, SPD) and the reconstruction of at least part of Germany. He became member of the Bundestag
in 1949, was mayor of West Berlin by 1957 (and saw the wall go up on his
watch in 1961), went on to serve as foreign minister in a coalition government from 1966–1969, and became the first-ever SPD chancellor of West
Germany in 1969.[4]

From his days as mayor of Berlin onward, Brandt consistently relied on
the advice of Egon Bahr, called the West German Kissinger by none other
than Kissinger himself.[5] Bahr was born in Thuringia on March 18, 1922,
one year before Kissinger. During the Second World War, Bahr served in
the Wehrmacht, but was discharged when it was discovered that he had
Jewish ancestry. After the end of hostilities, he worked as a journalist, and in
1960 became press adviser to the then-mayor of West Berlin, namely Willy
Brandt.

Following the tragedy of the construction of the Berlin Wall in 1961, Bahr
implemented Brandt's on-going efforts to mitigate its inhumanity, mainly by
negotiating accords that de facto opened cracks in the wall. Thanks to Brandt
and Bahr, divided German families gained fleeting, irregular opportunities to
see each other, if only on a few specific holidays. For example, in the cold,
dark December days of 1963, an estimated 730,000 western Germans stood
in lines that wound out building doors and down city streets in order to gain
Christmas passes to visit East Germany—a moving sight, and clear a indication of the strength of cross-border affections.[6]

When Brandt became chancellor, he gave Bahr the post of "state secretary."
This relatively unimportant title, which Bahr and Brandt chose to preserve
the possibility of disavowing Bahr's actions if necessary, concealed Bahr's
full significance: he implemented all central aspects of Brandt's foreign policy. Together, they decided to use Brandt's chancellorship to pursue on a
European scale the same goals they had sought in Berlin: increasing German-
German contacts and decreasing human suffering where possible, even if
only with small measures such as visas for border crossings or establishing
postal connections. They wanted to save what could be saved of a sense of
German unity, both out of a sense of nationalism and humanitarianism.[7]

In particular, they correctly recognized that, as a result of the bloody history of conflict between Germany and Russia, the Soviet Union would attach
particular historical significance to reaching formal agreements designed to
guarantee the borders achieved by war. As a result, Brandt and Bahr were in
a unique position to try to move international relations in a direction conducive to improved relations across the Iron Curtain. This drive represented

one of the first independent efforts by European, as opposed to American or Soviet, political leaders to ease tensions.[8]

Having established some basic background on Brandt, Bahr, and the ideas behind the start of Ostpolitik, it is now possible to begin to draw comparisons with their American counterparts. The extent of the similarities between the Nixon-Kissinger and Brandt-Bahr relationships and leadership styles is remarkable, even if the former pair were Republicans and the latter Social Democrats.

Although they would all eventually become players on a global stage, a circle with a radius of just 150 miles would encompass the birthplaces of three out of the four: Fürth (Kissinger), Lübeck (Brandt), and Treffurt (Bahr). All four emerged from the same generation, born either in 1913 (Nixon and Brandt) or 1922–1923 (Bahr and Kissinger), and they came to political consciousness as the interwar peace crumbled. All became successful political leaders, and in the same way: Nixon and Brandt via election, Kissinger and Bahr via appointment. Both sets of leaders replaced the opposing party in office in the exact same year, 1969, by making the exact same bet—namely, that they could redefine the Cold War via their overtures to the communist world. Once in office, both Nixon and Brandt chose to entrust the execution of foreign policy to a close confidante, bypassing the relevant departments and ministries. Kissinger and Bahr thereby obtained de facto control over the key elements of foreign policy without being named officially to the post of foreign secretary.

In terms of policy, both teams were willing to use their new authority to take risks rather than accept the status quo (and members of both sides won Nobel Peace Prizes for their efforts: Brandt in 1971 and Kissinger in 1973). Both felt that they could reduce hostilities and increase the security of their respective states by negotiations with the other side. Both believed that face-to-face summits and treaties (not to mention a lot of publicity, once matters were decided) were the keys to success.

For Nixon and Kissinger, this meant reaching out not only to Moscow but also to Beijing, and holding summits and signing accords with both (albeit initially more with the Soviets than the Chinese). Brandt and Bahr prioritized relations with Moscow as well. Bahr was the key negotiator on the first major Ostpolitik accord, the Moscow Treaty, which Brandt signed on August 12, 1970, in the Soviet capital. The final treaty stated that both parties renounced the use of force in their dealings with each other in the future. Given the bloody context of German-Soviet relations in the twentieth century, this represented an important milestone.

In short, there are clearly similar and cooperative elements in the leadership styles and goals of the two pairs. If one set had been committed to the status quo, it would have created a great deal of friction. If another had balked at the idea of dealing with communist governments in the service of achieving change, that too would have created roadblocks. Even if one pair had insisted on working through the appropriate channels of the State Department or Foreign Ministry, that would have irritated the secrecy-loving opposite pair. But none of these issues arose.

But the similarities have their limit. Nixon and Kissinger were leaders of a large and powerful country, one that had emerged victorious from the largest conflagration the world had ever seen. Brandt and Bahr, in contrast, were the leaders of a rump state, a fractured piece of a defeated nation. Obviously this difference had a profound impact on their goals. Nixon and Kissinger sought (in addition to their own constant desire to achieve personal and partisan success) to enable their nation to gain a lead in the Cold War contest by balancing China against the Soviet Union. Brandt and Bahr, denied the opportunity to act on a national level, instead focused on regional and individual levels.[9]

This becomes apparent with an examination of their main priority, as reflected in their next steps after Moscow: to save what could be saved of Germany, as Bahr would put it.[10] Both knew that they could not end the division of Germany in the foreseeable future, but they hoped to overcome it slowly by increasing contacts across the border and promoting incremental change. They also conceptualized it as part of a regional vision of increased cooperation in the European Community, as Helga Haftendorn has pointed out.[11] No comparable statement can be made about Nixon and Kissinger's attitude to the division of Europe.

Whereas the desire of both "teams" to challenge the status quo through negotiation produced the cooperative component of the détente-Ostpolitik interaction, a discrepancy on the desirability of change in central Europe produced competition. Nixon and Kissinger wanted to restructure the global balance of power and assumed that, if successful, beneficial effects would then flow down to the regional level (particularly in Southeast Asia where, they hoped, it would enable them to achieve "peace with honor" in Vietnam). Under this scheme, what Nixon and Kissinger mostly wanted from European states was to give the administration peace of mind. Key European leaders—and the West Germans in particular—were not to create any distractions in their region while Nixon and Kissinger tried to restructure international relations as a whole. As a result, Nixon and Kissinger did not want alterations to the status quo in Germany in the short term, since it would only add complications to an already complex set of changes. Since the two American leaders did not really want changes in Europe the near future, it follows that they were understandably not prepared to give much for them. This meant, by extension, that they saw little reason for Brandt and Bahr to concede anything (such as official recognition of the German Democratic Republic [GDR]). In contrast, Brandt and Bahr obviously did see reasons to make concessions, to the Americans' dismay.

Nixon and Kissinger by and large managed to restrain themselves from voicing their disapproval of Ostpolitik in public, but complained vociferously to just about anyone in private—including foreign leaders.[12] In December 1970, the president expressed his worries to the visiting British prime minister, Edward Heath. Nixon told Heath that it was "an illusion to suppose that the Soviet Government had any intention of genuinely opening up Eastern Europe." Rather, "their real purpose remained the detachment of Germany from NATO." Nixon said that in the eyes of U.S. officials (presumably meaning himself and Kissinger), "Ostpolitik was a dangerous affair and they would do nothing to encourage it."[13] These comments amazed the British Foreign Office experts charged with assessing them afterwards. As the British ambassador to West Germany pointed out, they "conflict … with numerous public reiterations of support" for Ostpolitik.[14] Nor were these thoughts shared only with the British, with whom the Nixon White House turns out to have worked astonishingly closely. Kissinger had made similar comments to the French one month earlier, saying that the signing of the Moscow Treaty had "considerably deteriorated" the situation of the Western powers.[15] Such talk even made it to the ears of the West Germans; by the end of 1970, Kissinger passed a memo to Nixon noting that rumors were circulating and "Bonn is suspicious that we do in fact oppose Ostpolitik."[16] Years later, Kissinger's memoirs would also display a sense that the West Germans had become too independent.[17] Ostpolitik even achieved a near-impossible feat. For once, it created agreement not only between the president and his national security advisor, but also with the often-ignored secretary of state, William Rogers. All three "considered Ostpolitik a serious error." Kissinger, thinking of the Moscow accord, could not see "what the [West] Germans get except a treaty" with little meaning.[18]

Brandt and Bahr felt differently. Brandt's view was that he was *not* giving anything away. Both he and Bahr were patriots. Although understanding the postwar division of the German nation, they nonetheless regretted it. Rather, Brandt felt that he was simply the first chancellor to *acknowledge* that Germany had already lost its eastern territories. Until better days dawned—and he had no idea how soon this would happen—the best the West Germans could do was to accept reality and try to improve life across the C old War divide. He and Bahr decided that if they did not take action to improve the inhumanities of the division of Germany, no one else was going to. As a result, they would move ahead, and inform, rather than ask advance permission from, the United States and the other occupying powers.

In a particularly clever move, Brandt and Bahr essentially sidestepped large debates about their room to maneuver, or, put another way, the rights and degree of sovereignty inherent in each of the two Germanys. By and large, they bracketed such questions for the future and focused instead on practical matters. Where Nixon and Kissinger repeatedly strove to create the broadest possible globe-spanning linkages between major world events—the opening to China, détente with the Soviet Union, the Vietnam War—Brandt and Bahr, in essence, strove to create small but durable links to the other half of Germany. They did sign treaties with Russia, Poland, and Czechoslovakia, which recognized existing borders, renounced the use of force, and paved the way for various forms of cross-border exchange. They also embedded the whole in the context of their relations with the European Community. However, improving German-German links was their main goal.

Their approach proved to be viable and durable. In the years between 1970 and 1974, Brandt and Bahr successfully concluded detailed accords on almost painfully small matters: agreeing on the nature of wax seals to be used in customs procedures, harmonizing train tracks, fixing toll prices and other road and transit issues, establishing postal service, and investigating the fates of individual political prisoners. They did so via an interlocking network of accords, agreements, and one over-arching document: the German-German Basic Treaty, signed in East Berlin on December 21, 1972. Whereas the postal or transit accords were concerned with practicalities, the Basic Treaty sought to establish more general goals. It committed the two Germanys to acknowledging existing borders and working together peacefully. After tough negotiation, the East Germans even agreed to include a mention of the still-open "national question," meaning the uncertainty about whether a united German nation would ever exist again. This was a tricky issue in the 1970s, since no one knew how long the division would persist; little did the signatories know that a united German nation would in fact reappear less than two decades in the future.

These accords were hardly enormous triumphs. They essentially codified an unhappy Cold War reality in divided Germany. They established a pattern whereby dictators could count on useful regular financial inflows from Bonn. No one involved deceived himself that these treaties were master-pieces of pure idealism in diplomacy. However, by establishing mutually agreed modes of interaction, Bahr's work helped to provide a framework that simultaneously increased East-West interactions, while decreasing the possibility that such interactions could lead to escalatory conflict.[19] And, significantly, the accords lasted. Most of the key components were still in force when the Berlin Wall came down in 1989 and rendered them moot.

Critics of the Ostpolitik treaties accused them of tying down, bit-by-bit, Gulliver-like, a largely undesirable status quo. This criticism came not just from external but also internal sources, in the form of Brandt and Bahr's domestic political opponents in the Christian Democratic Union (CDU). As a result of years of governing and installing civil servants, the CDU was particularly well represented in the West German foreign ministry, which meant that such critics were well-placed to complain to their counterparts in Washington. They found sympathetic listeners there, more so than in their own chancellor's office. One telegram from the West German ambassador in Washington back to the center in Bonn agreed with Washington's anxieties about *his own* government. As Ambassador Rolf Pauls put it, he found himself in sympathy with the American opinion that "an ill-prepared exchange of opinions [with Moscow], in light of current power relations, could easily produce a status quo minus."[20]

Pauls had taken the words right out of Kissinger's mouth, presumably, since Kissinger said almost exactly the same thing to French colleagues.[21] Kissinger could live with the status quo in Germany—he and Nixon had other priorities for change. They wanted to increase U.S. national security through linking and balancing among their various friends and allies world-wide, rather than focusing on small-bore issues. They headed the American government at a time when it was mired in a war in Vietnam and wanted to get out. And, on top of everything else, they had to operate in a new situation of superpower strategic parity. Kissinger emphasized this status when he first talked to Bahr, pointing out that in his opinion such parity neces-sitated a global approach to questions of security.[22]

In view of the cooperative and competitive aspects inherent in the origins of détente and Ostpolitik, how can we understand their interaction in practice? Did the two policies work together, or compete with each other, or both? What does the documentary record tell us? Space constraints do not allow for a detailed reconstruction of day-to-day developments, so a summary with just a few detailed examples is called for. There are five key findings.

First, it is important to note that Ostpolitik commanded consistent attention from Nixon and Kissinger personally. If the two policies failed to mesh, it was not due to lack of attention on the part of Washington. Other small countries might complain about receiving no hearing in the West Wing, but West Germany was not one of them. A measure of this is the enormous number of times Kissinger chose to deal personally with detailed German issues. His office files include a summary chronology of his significant communications concerning the division of Germany. Running from March 1969 to June 1971, there are multiple listings per week and sometimes per day.[23] Why did Kissinger give so much time to German issues? One particularly clear-eyed West German foreign ministry assessment of U.S.-West German relations pointed out that, whatever may be said about shared values or other reasons for a close transatlantic relationship, the roots of Kissinger's interest were clear: "The significance of the Federal Republic of Germany for American politics rests on its unique geographical and political situation in the midst of the European field of powers."[24]

Second, as already hinted above, Kissinger and the West Germans had differing understandings of linkage. Brandt and Bahr understood the connections between their policies and the global contest without needing Kissinger to dictate it to them. Bahr was blunt about what he saw as the connection between his and Brandt's attempt to improve conditions on the ground for East and West Germans, and the headline strategic development: the Sino-Soviet split. As Bahr explained to Kissinger over lunch in April 1970, "the basic Soviet motivation in dealing with the FRG is to get peace and quiet in the West because of the Chinese problem."[25] It even seems that Bahr was more convinced of the importance of China than Kissinger, who expressed doubts about the full extent of Soviet fears of the People's Republic to Nixon in October 1970.[26] But the key point here is that both sides understood the inherent links between disparate issues, even if they disagreed on the extent. This understanding, however, does not mean that the Germans agreed with Kissinger about how to employ the links between the global contest and the local improvements that they were trying to make. With their relentless focus on small-bore issues, the Brandt-Bahr approach was clearly a very different one than Kissinger's big-picture strategy.

Third, it is apparent that Nixon and Kissinger were concerned that West Germany, in its drive for small practical improvements, might make concessions that Washington had hoped to reserve for itself. One of the supporting papers prepared for Kissinger by his advisor Helmut (Hal) Sonnenfeldt argued that an inner-German agreement "will make it exceedingly difficult to obtain Soviet acceptance of ... our proposals for a four power mandate."[27] Sonnenfeldt also pointed out that Bahr might actually be savvy enough to use Kissinger to achieve his own ends, by claiming that his personal backchannel to Kissinger meant that he could ignore U.S. and allied representatives in West Germany, but then doing what none of them wanted in the end.[28]

These second and third findings require a caveat. These competing ideas—about the correct level on which to operate, either locally or globally, and how much to concede—did *not* result in Washington blocking major components of Brandt and Bahr's initiatives (assuming they could have done so, which would have been tricky). In other words, there was a limit to the competition between Washington and Bonn. Neither side wanted to lose the alliance with the other. No available Western documentation shows that, behind closed doors, the West Germans sought daring goals such as full neutrality, and Washington had to cut them off. Since doomsayers often cited such ulterior motives in press denunciations of Ostpolitik at the time, the absence (so far) of such plans is worth noting.

Fourth, it is clear that publicity—or, to be more precise, getting credit in public—was a priority for all involved. Nixon, in particular, worried deeply about Brandt receiving more credit that he did. Given that not only Brandt but also Kissinger went on to win Nobel Prizes for their work at this time, his concern was not unjustified. As Robert Dallek describes it, "Brandt outfoxed and frustrated Nixon and Kissinger. He stole the headlines from them without, in their judgment, advancing toward reliable improvements in East-West relations."[29] As a result, there was little love lost between the two pairs of leaders. Kissinger, privately, would describe Bahr as "reptilian."[30]

An intriguing insight into this strand of Nixon's thinking comes from his reaction to a letter sent to him by an American fiction writer living in Germany. The letter, from Hans Habe, rose to Kissinger's attention via unclear means. He in turn passed it to the president, who marked it up heavily, and approvingly, returning with the following note: "K—a very perceptive and disturbing analysis—I think he is too close to the truth." What argument had so impressed the president? As Habe put it, "It would be asking too much from the average German to realize that your own trip to Moscow means something entirely different than the flirtation between Moscow and Bonn." Nixon was clearly particularly struck by this passage, as he wrote in the margin: "K—one of our greatest mistakes. We must do everything possible to rectify it." The president, in other words, felt a need to establish a public sense that, while his grand strategy of détente and Ostpolitik might be contemporaneous, they were not of equal significance, or merit.[31]

Fifth and finally, for Kissinger the unwanted need to pay attention to European politics at a time when he hoped to focus on Asia and the Soviet Union had an unexpected and startling practical consequence. His desire to maintain the upper hand in shaping European détente forced him to do something he despised. He had to turn to professional bureaucrats for expert knowledge and support; not American bureaucrats, however, but *British* ones.

This assistance took many forms, from silly to significant. On the silly side, Kissinger would often stop in London for consultations while en route to other European capitals. When he did so, he relied on the British Foreign Office to help him exclude Walter Annenberg, the U.S. ambassador in London, from any meaningful interactions. This required elaborate schemes. For example, in-the-know British dinner hosts would distract Annenberg at a prearranged point, allowing Kissinger to slip out for private talks. Such shenanigans prompted a September 1972 communication from D. C. Tebbitt in the British Embassy in Washington to London: "I hope that the remarkable requirements for Dr. Kissinger's visit to London … are not giving too many people too much trouble." He added that "Kissinger greatly enjoys these ruses, particularly if they come off successfully. Our relations with him will therefore prosper the more if we can make our part of the plot work."[32]

On the significant side, the collaboration fed Kissinger's addiction to deception. The paperwork thereby created, abroad from America's rivals, and unaffected by the U.S. Freedom of Information Act of 1967, would presumably be easier to keep secret. "You know how sensitive Kissinger is to recording what he says on his travels," complained Antony Acland, a future British ambassador to the United States, to the then-British ambassador in Paris.[33] And it is clear from what did get recorded that British paperwork went not just to Kissinger's office but also to Nixon's. For example, in May 1973 Kissinger openly discussed a "framework" paper on transatlantic relations from the Foreign Office that had gone to the White House. He also requested input on policy formulation to the European Economic Community (EEC), but explicitly asked that "nothing should be said" to other EEC members about "discussions with the White House."[34]

Clearly, this gave the British unusual influence over West Wing thinking. However, such reliance could have a dark side, as expressed in a letter from British Ambassador Rowley Cromer in Washington back to London on March 7, 1973. Cromer noted that he was, "as always, struck by the astonishing anomaly of the most powerful nation in the world invoking the aid of a foreign government to do its drafting for it, while totally excluding its own

Ministry of Foreign Affairs." He thought that this was "ludicrous, and sooner or later it must change." He concluded that "it is a dangerous and complicated path that we tread and I am always aware of the pitfalls that lurk on either side."[35] The combination of Cromer's worries, plus Watergate, and increasing irritation at Kissinger's practice of inviting guests to meet with him in London as if it were his own capital, caused the Foreign Office to push back. In October 1973, the Foreign Office informed him of its concerns about this practice.[36] Clearly, Kissinger's desire to prevent any domestic competitors from arising in the making of U.S. foreign policy, combined with his need to keep tabs on transatlantic issues, drove him to unusual lengths.

In brief, the documents on this time period show that Ostpolitik received personal and sustained attention from both Kissinger and Nixon. They worried, however, that Brandt and Bahr were giving away too much, in the form of concessions to the Warsaw Pact, for too little, in the form of practical day-to-day improvements. Brandt and Bahr, meanwhile, felt that that was exactly what they could and should achieve.

By setting themselves more achievable goals, the West Germans reached those goals more quickly, and established a more durable policy than Washington did. Sensing this, Nixon and Kissinger worried that Brandt and Bahr might get more public credit than they would, and tried to keep tabs on what was happening in Europe as a result. Keeping up with the details of not only West German but also the corollary European politics of the time caused Kissinger to rely to an inappropriate extent on the British to fulfill his goals.

Consider again the questions raised at the outset. Did détente and Ostpolitik undermine or support each other? And what does their interaction tell us about the ongoing contest between the pursuit of Realpolitik and the pursuit of real improvements in the behavior of dictatorial regimes? Extensive similarities clearly existed between the two policies in both style and substance, and these at times meshed productively. In both Washington and Bonn, two men had concentrated authority over foreign policy largely in their own hands and used it to change the status quo, above the objections of their own bureaucracies. If either side had strongly advocated continuing with business as usual, it would have created greater opportunities for one to undermine the other, but since both wanted change they could not fault the other for desiring the same.

The policies parted company, however, over the level on which they operated. Nixon and Kissinger sought global goals, Brandt and Bahr sought regional ones. At best, Kissinger saw Ostpolitik as an awkwardly fitting subcomponent of his larger plan. As the historian Jussi Hanhimäki has argued, Kissinger tried to find ways to link Ostpolitik to his own central concerns: U.S. relations with the Soviet Union and China.[37] This approach was fundamentally at odds with what Willy Brandt was trying to do. While acknowledging the intrinsic connection between various issues, Brandt instead sought to *unlink* day-to-day German-German relations from the U.S.-USSR contest.

This is not to say that the chancellor wanted to make West Germany neutral. Rather, his goal was something less than that. It was to make specific, low-level advances—as he and Bahr put it, it was a policy of small steps. Brandt was *de facto* attempting to create and then take advantage of the stability offered by Ostpolitik to reduce the daily indignities of human existence in divided Germany. In explaining what he was doing, he would often use a well-known quotation from his distant precursor as chancellor, Otto von Bismarck: politics was the art of making something that seemed impossible possible.[38] For his success in this endeavor, Brandt won extensive domestic support. When he went to the polls to seek approval for his policies in 1972, he won the most immense reelection victory in West German history up to that point.

Kissinger's complaints notwithstanding, it is hard to see how Ostpolitik undermined or restricted his room to maneuver. Take away the independent West German initiative: what would Nixon and Kissinger have done differently? They would still have gone to Beijing. They would still have used the Chinese leverage to create Russian interest in rapprochement. They might personally have received more credit (a not inconsiderable point in their view) for holding a summit with Moscow, since it would have seemed more unique had Brandt not been to Moscow first. But it would not have changed the overall thrust of their policies. Ostpolitik did not significantly undermine détente.

In fact, it is regrettable that Ostpolitik did not undermine détente *more* than it did. Put another way, the successes of Ostpolitik could have informed the shaping of détente. Denied the opportunity to pursue national goals, Brandt and Bahr instead worked on the local and even individual level (for example, by buying the freedom of particular political prisoners). Their focus rested on profound and extensive knowledge of the specific problems involved. Nixon and Kissinger, in contrast, had little use for detailed, expert knowledge on the regions with which they were dealing. As William Burr has pointed out, until he became secretary of state, Kissinger "refused to allow State Department professionals with Chinese or Russian language skills to attend high-level meetings."[39] Put another way, Nixon and Kissinger were making policy involving distant countries on the basis of limited regional expertise. The opposite was true of Brandt and Bahr. They had extensive knowledge of, and a fixation on, improving the daily experience of people in the other half of their own nation, and improving relations with their immediate neighbors. This fixation arose from an intriguing mixture of nationalism and pragmatism.

Brandt and Bahr can be faulted for execution. Critics on the left and right accused them of mistakenly, indeed amorally, prioritizing stable relations with dictators. However, it is hard to disagree with the policy's original goal of improving the experience of daily life in the Cold War. An appreciation for this goal might have undermined, or, to be more precise, helped to counter Nixon and Kissinger's disinterest in such a subject; but it did not. Kissinger remained convinced that such matters were the internal prerogative of the countries involved. Feeling that he had nothing to learn from Brandt or Bahr, Kissinger later found himself forced via the Jackson-Vanik Amendment—which aimed to ease restrictions on Jewish emigration from the Soviet Union to Israel—to look at the domestic as well as the foreign behavior of his negotiating partners.

This is perhaps the most useful finding arising from a comparison of détente and Ostpolitik: grand foreign strategies lacking a hefty dose of understanding for the details of daily life in the regions involved ultimately rest on clay feet. Obviously, it is dangerous to generalize from one comparison; but the outlines of this particular case are clear. Because West Germany had as its primary goal improving life as lived in its target region (at short-term cost but for long-term gain), it succeeded. The United States did not have this goal. How daily life was lived in the Soviet Union or China was not, Nixon and Kissinger thought, a matter with which they should concern themselves.

The comparison of détente and Ostpolitik thus serves as another chapter in the ongoing contest between realism and idealism in the shaping of foreign policy. Obviously no foreign policy will ever be wholly realist or idealist—not even détente and Ostpolitik. But in the struggle to get the right balance between the two, Brandt and Bahr did a better job. While realism may teach that states are like billiard balls—it is not the inside but only the hardness of the external face that matters—historical scholarship in this case suggests otherwise. If a policy is to have more than short-term success, it must be able to become durable and quotidian; in other words, it must yield measurable practical improvements in daily life. For policymakers whose goals are short-term, this is an irrelevant finding; but for those who hope to deal long-term with dictatorial regimes, it matters.

Acknowledgments

I would like to thank the following institutions for research funding: the Alexander von Humboldt Foundation, Bonn; the Mershon Center, Ohio State University; the National Endowment for the Humanities; the Institute for Advanced Study, Princeton; and St. John's College, Cambridge.

Notes

1. Even professional scholars of Nixon and Kissinger downplay it. For example, Ostpolitik receives just a couple of pages of attention in Robert Dallek, *Partners in Power: Nixon and Kissinger* (New York, 2007), 214–217. And it does not even have an index entry in Walter Isaacson, *Kissinger: A Biography* (New York, 1992); Jeffery Kimball, *Nixon's Vietnam War* (Lawrence, Kans., 1998); and Jeremi Suri, *Henry Kissinger and the American Century* (Cambridge, Mass., 2007). Jussi Hanhimäki, *The Flawed Architect: Henry Kissinger and American Foreign Policy* (New York: Oxford University Press, 2004), pays more attention to the topic, mentioning it on ten pages in a 554-page study. For a few comments from Kissinger directly, see Henry Kissinger, *White House Years* (Boston, 1979), 805. One author who looks in detail at the connection between Ostpolitik and détente is Timothy Garton Ash, *In Europe's Name: Germany and the Divided Continent* (New York, 1993). His suggestion of a division of Ostpolitik into three levels, above, is on page 38.
2. Les archives du ministère des affaires étrangères, Paris (hereafter Paris MAE), Europe 1971–76, Sous-Série RFA, 2996, 6.24.1; Entretien entre le chancelier de la republique federal et M. Leo Hamon, Secretaire d'etat aupres du premier ministre a Bonn, 2 juillet 1971, p. 2. The author is grateful to Jennifer Siegel for assistance with French archival materials.
3. Gregor Schöllgen, *Willy Brandt* (Munich, 2003), 62ff.
4. See Hanhimäki, *Flawed Architect*, 85–91.
5. Bahr recalls this in his memoir *Zu meiner Zeit* (Munich: Karl Blessing Verlag, 1996): 122.
6. For a detailed history of the Berlin Wall and attempts to cross it, complete with photos and audio files, see http://www.chronik-der-mauer.de
7. Mary Elise Sarotte, *Dealing with the Devil: East Germany, Détente, and Ostpolitik, 1969–1973* (Chapel Hill, N.C., 2001), 163–164.
8. For more assessments of Brandt, Bahr, and their significance, readers may wish to start with the following: Arnulf Baring, *Machtwechsel: Die Ära Brandt-Scheel* (Stuttgart, 1982); Henry Ashby Turner, Jr., *Germany from Partition to Reunification* (New Haven, 1992); James McAdams, *Germany Divided: From the Wall to Reunification* (Princeton, 1993); Garton Ash, *In Europe's Name*; Stephan Fuchs, *"Dreiecksverhältnisse sind immer*

kompliziert": Kissinger, Bahr, und die Ostpolitik (Hamburg, 1999); Sarotte, *Dealing with the Devil*; Andreas Rödder, *Die Bundesrepublik Deutschland* (Munich, 2004); and Helga Haftendorn, *Coming of Age: German Foreign Policy since 1945* (Lanham, Md., 2006).

9. See the particularly insightful (and concise) discussion of this topic in Rödder, *Bundesrepublik Deutschland*, 35–43.

10. Sarotte, *Dealing with the Devil*, 163.

11. Haftendorn, *Coming of Age*, 163.

12. It is clear from National Security Decision Memorandum (NSDM) 91, November 6, 1970, that Kissinger felt the need to endorse Ostpolitik in public. I am grateful to Irwin Wall for a draft of his paper mentioning the significance of this document. See also Dallek, *Nixon and Kissinger*, 214–215.

13. "Extract from Record of a Meeting between the Prime Minister and President Nixon at the White House on 17/10/70," Foreign and Commonwealth Office file 33/1547 (hereafter FCO), Public Record Office, London (hereafter PRO).

14. R. W. Jackling, "Prime Minister's Conversation with President Nixon on German Question," January 8, 1971, FCO 33/1547, PRO.

15. Télégramme à l'arrivée, Washington, November 27, 1970, No. 7254–7258, Signed Lucet, Amérique 1964–1970, Sous-Série Etats Unis, Politique extérieure, 610, Paris MAE.

16. Henry Kissinger to Richard Nixon, undated but attached to document dated December 18, 1970, HAK Office Files, NSC Files, Country Files, Europe, Box 58, NPMP.

17. This attitude pervades Kissinger's discussion of West Germany in Kissinger, *White House Years*.

18. Dallek, *Nixon and Kissinger*, 214–215.

19. It is worth noting that the official documentary basis for writing the history of Ostpolitik from the internal West German point of view is somewhat uneven. The details of Egon Bahr's negotiations with the GDR have been available in East German collections since the early 1990s (see the bibliography in Sarotte, *Dealing with the Devil*), and the former West German records of the same were published in 2004: Hanns Jürgen Küsters et al., eds., *Dokumente zur Deutschlandpolitik, Die Bahr-Kohl-Gespräche 1970–1973* (Munich, 2004). See also *Akten zur Auswärtigen Politik der Bundesrepublik Deutschland* (Munich, 1995). However, often the most substantive West German files, that is, *Verschlußsachen (VS)*, have special closure rules and are not yet open. For help with German archival matters, the author is grateful to Ernst-Georg Richter, Dr. Hans-Hermann Hertle and Hilde Kroll, Jan Fischer, and Verena Wehling.

20. Politisches Archiv, Auswärtiges Amt, formerly in Bonn, now in Berlin (abbreviated hereafter as *Berlin PA-AA*), B 31–326, vom 01.01.69 bis 31.12.71, telegram 20.01.70, Pauls, pp. 2–3. For more on the sympathies between the CDU and the U.S. government, see Bernd Schaefer,

"Washington as a Place for the German Campaign: The U.S. Government and the CDU/CSU Opposition, 1969–1972," in *American Détente and German Ostpolitik, 1969–1972*, ed. David C. Geyer and Bernd Schaefer (Washington, 2004), 98–108.

21. See note 13, above.

22. Egon Bahr, Vermerk, October 14, 1969, summarizing conversation with Henry Kissinger on October 13, in 439, Egon Bahr Depositorium (EBD), Friedrich-Ebert-Stiftung (FES), Bonn. See also Raymond Garthoff, *Détente and Confrontation: American-Soviet Relations from Nixon to Reagan*, rev. ed. (Washington, D.C., 1994), 19; Keith L. Nelson, *The Making of Détente: Soviet-American Relations in the Shadow of Vietnam* (Baltimore, 1995), 45; and Robin Edmonds, *Soviet Foreign Policy 1962–1973: The Paradox of Super Power* (London, 1975), passim.

23. "Berlin and European Security," HAK Office Files, NSC Files, Country Files, Europe, Box 57, Folder 2, NPMP. Although a chronology for later dates has not yet appeared, there is little reason to doubt that it will be similarly full.

24. The original German phrase translated here as "field of powers" is *Kräftefeld*. See Berlin PA-AA: B31–337, "Aufzeichnung über den gegenwärtigen Stand der deutsch-amerikanischen Beziehungen, Betr.: Aufenthalt des Herrn Bundesministers in New York anlässlich des VN-Vollversammlung vom 26. September bis 5. Oktober 1971," September 6, 1971, 1.

25. Memorandum for the Record, Subject: Luncheon Conversation between Henry Kissinger and Egon Bahr, April 8, 1970, HAK Office Files, NSC Files, Country Files, Europe, Box 57, Folder 1, NPMP.

26. Kissinger to Nixon, October 19, 1970, NSC Files, HAK Office Files, Country Files, Europe, Box 71, NPMP.

27. Sonnenfeldt to Kissinger, March 11, 1971, HAK Office Files, NSC Files, Country Files, Europe, Box 60, Folder 5, NPMP.

28. Ibid.

29. Dallek, *Nixon and Kissinger*, 215–216.

30. Hanhimäki, *Flawed Architect*, 88.

31. Letter from Hans Habe, March 5, 1973, HAK Office Files, NSC Files, Country Files, Europe, Box 61, NPMP. The Habe letter, which appears to have an Italian return address, is accompanied by a cover note, Kissinger to Nixon, March 15, 1973. Kissinger's cover note is curiously worded: "Here is a letter from a very well-known American novelist living in Germany. I think you will find it interesting, even though he has an obvious conservative bias."

32. Letter from D. C. Tebbitt, September 8, 1972, FCO 82/197, PRO.

33. A. A. Acland to Sir Edward Tomkins (British Embassy, Paris), May 11, 1973, FCO 82/307, PRO.

34. See "Record Of Conversation Between the Foreign and Commonwealth Secretary and Dr Henry Kissinger At 3.00 P.M. On Thursday 10 May

[1973] at the Foreign and Commonwealth Office," and "Speaking Notes for Use with Dr. Kissinger, Brief for Sir T. Brimelow [handwritten]," only date on document date of receipt in registry August 8, 1973, but included in paperwork on file of materials for May 1973 meeting with Kissinger, both in FCO 82/307, PRO.

35. Rowley Cromer (British Embassy, Washington, D.C.) to Sir Thomas Brimelow, March 7, 1973, FCO 73/135, PRO.

36. FCO 82/307, PRO, contains various documents expressing concern about the fact that Kissinger seemed to be treating London as his own capital.

37. Hanhimäki, *Flawed Architect*, 86–87.

38. On this general principle, see Carsten Tessmer, "'Thinking the Unthinkable' to 'Make the Impossible Possible': Ostpolitik, Intra-German Policy, and the Moscow Treaty, 1969–1970," in Geyer and Schaefer, *American Détente and German Ostpolitik*, 53–66.

39. William Burr, ed., *The Kissinger Transcripts: The Top Secret Talks with Beijing and Moscow* (New York, 1998), x.

8

The United States and the Making of the Helsinki Final Act

Michael Cotey Morgan

One of the defining moments of Gerald Ford's brief presidency came during his 1976 election campaign against Jimmy Carter. During the second of their debates, panelist Max Frankel of the *New York Times* asked Ford whether the Russians had taken the upper hand in the Cold War. Communism was dangerously popular in France and Italy, the United States had bolstered communist prestige by recognizing East Germany as a legitimate state, and, by signing the Helsinki Final Act, Frankel contended, Ford had effectively accepted Soviet "dominance in Eastern Europe." Ford had prepared for a question along these lines. He insisted that his administration was dealing with Moscow "from a position of strength." Nuclear arms negotiations had benefited the United States and large-scale wheat sales to the USSR were helping American farmers. As for the Final Act, it was hard to make the case that it ratified Soviet control over Eastern Europe because there was no way that the Vatican, one of the thirty-five parties to the agreement, would abandon millions of people to tyranny. This was a solid if longwinded answer, but in his determination to refute Frankel's suggestion, Ford went even further: "There is no Soviet domination of Eastern Europe and there never will be under a Ford administration." Carter pounced on this misstep: "I would like to see Mr. Ford convince the Polish-Americans and the Czech-Americans and the Hungarian-Americans in this country that those countries don't live under the domination and supervision of the Soviet Union behind the Iron Curtain." Worse, Carter said, the Soviets were breaking the promises they had made in Helsinki to allow their people "to migrate, to join their families, to be free, to speak out," and Ford was doing nothing about it.[1]

The exchange encapsulated the heated debate then underway in the United States about the benefits and ethics of détente and highlighted the Helsinki Final Act's place at the center of that debate. Since 1974 at least, a number of American politicians and commentators had been making the case that the Nixon and Ford administrations' efforts to relax superpower tensions had done more harm than good. Through 1975 and 1976, the ranks of these skeptics on both the left and the right—including Carter, Democratic Senator Henry "Scoop" Jackson, and former California governor Ronald Reagan—were growing. Ford was determined to defend himself against their accusations that détente was amoral and required the appeasement of the Soviet Union at the expense of American interests. This objective shaped his reply to Frankel's question and led him, in his enthusiasm, to misspeak. His intention was not to say that Poland and the rest of Eastern Europe were free from Soviet domination, but rather that the United States did not recognize that domination as legitimate. Nevertheless, the mistake reinforced his popular image as a "bumbler" and seemed to substantiate accusations that he lacked both an ethical vision for foreign policy and a firm grasp of the basic issues.[2]

The Helsinki Final Act, one of the highpoints of détente, came in for particular scorn from Ford's opponents. Signed in the Finnish capital in August 1975, it was the product of the Conference on Security and Cooperation in Europe (CSCE), three years of intense and sometimes esoteric negotiations in Geneva involving every country in Europe (except Albania), the United States, and Canada. The agreement consisted of three main sections, known as "baskets." The first, on international security, enumerated ten fundamental principles governing international affairs—including the sovereign equality of states and the inviolability of frontiers—and called for confidence-building measures (CBMs), an attempt to increase military transparency by requiring participants to give advance notification of their troop maneuvers anywhere in Europe and to invite foreign observers to watch the exercises. The second basket promoted international trade, technological exchange, and environmental cooperation. The third basket committed the signatories to the freer international movement of people, ideas, and information, in keeping with a broader promise to uphold citizens' human rights and fundamental freedoms. In practice, this meant the wider circulation of newspapers, the reunification of families divided by the Iron Curtain, and easier emigration from the Eastern bloc. The Final Act was thus a contradictory document. It embodied the tension between the prerogatives of sovereign states and the demands of universal principles, committing its signatories to protect the rights of their citizens but also recognizing the power of governments to determine their own domestic laws and, implicitly, to treat their citizens however they saw fit.

Ford's critics insisted that the Final Act embodied everything that was bad about détente. It did nothing for the United States, they argued, and the first basket's confirmation of the territorial status quo betrayed the hopes of Eastern Europeans for freedom from Soviet tyranny. Reagan said simply, "I think all Americans should be against it."[3] Carter was disappointed that the American government had "ratified the Russian takeover of Eastern Europe."[4] Reaction in the press was similarly negative. In a rare show of unanimity, both the *New York Times* and the *Wall Street Journal* denounced Ford's decision to sign the Final Act. The *Times* argued that the agreement endorsed the continent's "territorial status quo, including the division of Germany and the Soviet Union's huge annexations of East European territory, including all three independent Baltic states plus large chunks of Poland, Czechoslovakia and Rumania."[5] The *Journal* echoed this analysis. The Final Act, it said, accepted "Soviet hegemony in Eastern Europe" and thus amounted to "a formal version of Yalta, without Yalta's redeeming features."[6]

The Nixon and Ford administrations had never been enthusiastic about the Final Act, but neither had they foreseen the storm of controversy that the agreement would provoke. Given that the CSCE's goal was only to produce a declaration, few people in the executive branch believed that the tortuous negotiations were worth the effort, especially compared with the other issues on their agenda. The Vietnam War, nuclear weapons, and the Middle East were more concrete and urgent than an unwieldy multilateral conference of undetermined value. Nixon himself was consistently bored with the CSCE, which merited not even a mention in his memoirs.[7] Kissinger likewise was an early skeptic of the conference's work. In briefing Ford shortly after Nixon's resignation, the secretary of state said the principles under negotiation in Geneva were "meaningless." In his view, airy declarations could not change the underlying realities of the international system.[8] Throughout much of the CSCE's duration, therefore, the White House assigned it a low priority despite the opinion of some career diplomats in the State Department who believed that the negotiations, including those in Basket III, might be useful to the West. Kissinger's chief objective was to keep a low profile at the conference so as to avoid antagonizing either the Soviets, who wanted American collaboration in pushing for a quick end to the conference, or the Western Europeans, who wanted to drag the negotiations out so as to increase the pressure on the Soviets to make concessions on human rights.

By early 1975, however, Kissinger's view of the negotiations began to shift in small but important ways. He endorsed a tougher American position in Geneva and intervened with Soviet leaders to press the Western case. The evolution of his attitude was closely connected to his view of détente. He came to believe that CBMs, by increasing trust and cooperation between the two military blocs, might complement his broader goals for détente, especially a relaxation of the superpower military competition. He recognized that, given Brezhnev's determination to bring the CSCE to a successful conclusion, prolonging the negotiations would moderate Soviet behavior. The conference even offered the prospect of encouraging the Soviet Union's satellites to assert some measure of independence from Moscow. However, few if any of détente's critics saw things this way. As the debate with Carter illustrates, Ford's opponents seized on the agreement as the definitive proof of détente's moral bankruptcy. Ideas of détente strongly influenced the White House's attitude to the CSCE. In particular, they shaped Kissinger's lack of interest in the Final Act's human rights provisions, his belated interest in CBMs, his failure to anticipate the storm of criticism that the agreement would provoke, and, finally, the difficulties he and especially Ford faced in rebutting the accusations leveled by détente's critics.

The Final Act's roots stretch back to a 1954 Soviet proposal for a pan-European security conference. At the time, the idea went nowhere, but the Warsaw Pact's foreign ministers revived it in the late 1960s. In 1969, they declared their desire for a multilateral agreement to renounce the use of force, recognize the immutability of European frontiers, and improve economic, scientific, and cultural relations between East and West.[9] Kissinger told Nixon that the communists' real goal was not to resolve outstanding issues but rather to confirm the territorial status quo so as to increase the legitimacy of the governments in the Soviet bloc. There was also the worry that a conference might create the illusion of progress while leaving fundamental issues unresolved. Kissinger therefore suspected that the communists hoped to encourage a false sense of security on the continent, which in turn might make it possible to abolish both military blocs and squeeze American influence out of Europe. However, he foresaw that the American government might have to participate in the conference in order to forestall a rift with its Western European allies, who were guardedly optimistic about the conference. They believed that the CSCE might benefit NATO, especially by increasing East–West contacts. If the United States were forced to go ahead, Kissinger and the National Security Council (NSC) staff argued, it had to insist that the alliance name a price for its participation and refuse to go any further until the Soviets paid.[10]

Despite the risks, the United States might have been able to reap some benefit from the Soviets' desire for the conference. At the very least, Washington had some bargaining power and an opportunity to coax Moscow into "talk[ing] concretely" about the real problems in East–West relations.[11] Kissinger probed the Soviets to determine their motives. Ambassador Anatoly Dobrynin told him, "We want existing frontiers recognized." Kissinger replied, "No one is challenging the existing frontiers," but said that the United States would agree to participate if certain prerequisites were satisfied.[12] The most important of these conditions, on which NATO was also insisting, were progress toward a four-power agreement on Berlin—a longstanding source of East–West friction—and Soviet agreement to multi-lateral negotiations on conventional force cuts in Europe, officially known as Mutual Balanced Force Reductions (MBFR). Democratic Senate Majority Leader Mike Mansfield was pressing the Nixon administration for sharp cutbacks in the U.S. troop presence in Europe. Nixon and Kissinger hoped that, by convincing the Soviets to participate in MBFR, they could defuse Mansfield's pressure for unilateral force reductions and thus preserve the American military position in Europe. Moscow's ambitions for the CSCE could help the White House address a domestic problem.[13]

Kissinger's conversation with Dobrynin illustrated a crucial disconnect between Soviet and American ideas of détente. International legitimacy was a high priority for Leonid Brezhnev and his colleagues, especially in the wake of the 1968 invasion of Czechoslovakia, which had taken a toll on the USSR's international reputation and its valuable economic ties to the West. Moscow was now looking to recover lost ground, and an international declaration recognizing the permanence of European frontiers, were an important part of this effort. The Soviets also worried about rising tensions with Beijing, and likely hoped that the CSCE would calm the situation in Europe and allow them to concentrate their energies on problems in Asia. For his part, Kissinger could not understand the need to hold a major international conference simply to confirm a postwar status quo that the West had implicitly accepted for nearly thirty years. Instead of wasting time on what he saw as useless phrases, he preferred to focus on concrete issues.[14]

In approaching the negotiations, the Western alliance held firm on its preconditions on MBFR and Berlin. This determination paid off. After a breakthrough in the four-power negotiations over Berlin, the Americans, British,

French, and Soviets reached a deal in September 1971, and the May 1972 Transit Agreement, a product of Willy Brandt's Ostpolitik, helped to normalize relations between East and West Germany. In the meantime, NATO had been painstakingly hammering out a common allied position on the issues it wanted to add to the conference agenda. In the spirit of the 1967 Harmel Report, which established détente as a priority for the alliance, most of the Western Europeans hoped to use the conference simultaneously to promote East–West cooperation and to advance the Western cause in the Cold War. Issues that fit the bill included military confidence-building measures and the freer movement of people, ideas, and information throughout Europe.

A number of State Department officials agreed with the Western Europeans on these points, and were therefore more optimistic than the White House about the CSCE's potential. A State Department-led task force concluded in March 1972 that the United States should to treat the CSCE as an opportunity to make progress "toward lowering the barriers to freer movement" in Eastern Europe and go "beyond modest improvements in the existing pattern of East–West cultural exchanges." Specifically, it recommended that Washington demand looser restrictions on emigration, increased circulation of Western books and newspapers, better working conditions for Western journalists, and an end to the jamming of Radio Free Europe and Radio Liberty. By publicizing the Soviet government's repression of its citizens, the CSCE could increase public support for NATO and energize Eastern European dissidents. Provided that the allies remained united, Moscow's desire to entrench current frontiers offered NATO considerable leverage to achieve these goals.[15] This assessment of the CSCE's potential differed considerably from that of Kissinger and his aides. In the opinion of Helmut Sonnenfeldt, one of his top advisors, the demands for greater freedom of movement were "rather bland" and would do little to advance American interests or the overall project of détente. Maintaining NATO solidarity was the only advisable American objective for the conference. American diplomats had to "try to close it out as soon as possible, with a minimum of damage and commitments."[16]

The State Department's ideas for the CSCE complemented Jackson's arguments for increased pressure on the Soviet Union to meet minimum standards of human rights. At the 1972 Moscow Summit, Nixon agreed to extend most favored nation (MFN) trading status to the Soviet Union, which would reduce American tariffs on imports of Soviet goods. In response, Jackson wanted to make MFN status contingent on the elimination of Soviet restrictions on emigration—especially Jewish emigration—and proposed an amendment to that effect to the legislation implementing Nixon's deal. The Jackson-Vanik Amendment, as it came to be known, irritated the White House but enjoyed considerable public and congressional support because of its forceful expression of American ideals. Nixon and Kissinger, who railed against Jackson's alleged "demagoguery" and political opportunism, saw it as illegitimate interference in Soviet domestic policy and worried that it would antagonize Moscow—and that it did.[17] Kissinger repeatedly complained to his Soviet counterparts about the amendment and, trying to placate them, insisted that it would not change his government's commitment to détente. Achieving the freer movement of people and greater respect for humanitarian principles, whether via the CSCE or congressional pressure, was foreign to his vision of détente. Confronting the Soviets about their domestic policies, Kissinger argued, could never change the way they treated their citizens and would only elicit their ire.[18] He underlined this point at a meeting with State Department officials, asking, "Why is it our business how they govern themselves?"[19] For the time being, however, Jackson was more of an annoyance than a serious threat to détente and the CSCE remained a peripheral issue in U.S. foreign policy.

Progress toward the CSCE began to pick up steam in late 1972. In November, diplomats from thirty-four countries descended on Helsinki for the Multilateral Preparatory Talks (MPT) to establish the conference's rules and agenda. Because Nixon had been concerned that the Soviets would use the CSCE "to break up NATO," he would only accept the slowest possible progress toward the conference.[20] Nevertheless, since the CSCE was, as Kissinger put it, Brezhnev's "major European initiative," Nixon had concluded that the Soviet leader was willing to pay a significant price for success. In Moscow in 1972, Nixon agreed to open the MPT in exchange for MBFR talks, something in which the Soviets had never shown much interest. The force reduction negotiations, useful to Nixon both domestically and internationally, were scheduled to begin within three months of the CSCE's opening session.[21] Given the small stakes at the MPT, and given the opposing imperatives of both NATO solidarity and continued U.S.–Soviet cooperation, the U.S. delegation in Helsinki was instructed not to take a strong position on any issue.[22]

Officials at the State Department, on the other hand, worried that American passivity would antagonize the Western Europeans, whose keen interest in the conference continued to grow. Following this analysis, the United States had to take an active role in the negotiations and join its allies in pressing the Soviets to make concessions. At the MPT, this meant demanding the inclusion of human rights and the freer movement of people and ideas on the CSCE agenda.[23] These arguments held little sway in the White House. Sonnenfeldt argued that the United States had "little to gain ... and something to lose" at the conference. It had to wrap things up as quickly as possible in order to minimize the risks of either an intra-alliance rift or a Soviet propaganda victory. NATO solidarity had to be the government's chief—indeed its only—priority.[24]

As a result, the Americans took a back seat in Helsinki, much to their allies' frustration. In bilateral discussions with the Soviets, American officials in Washington made no particular demands but, in the interest of alliance solidarity, they also rebuffed Soviet offers to strike bilateral bargains about the CSCE.[25] When Soviet Foreign Minister Andrei Gromyko complained about the lack of American involvement in the negotiations, Kissinger denied that he could influence the outcome. "I can't solve all problems," he said. He was walking a diplomatic tightrope, trying to balance the demands of good relations with both the Western Europeans and the Soviets.[26] In such circumstances, this equivocation reflected his own lack of interest in the conference and suited his diplomatic needs. In the wake of his 1973 "Year of Europe" initiative, an attempt to reinvigorate U.S.–European relations that had irritated many of the allies, he hoped to support the Western Europeans without confronting the Soviets. Stonewalling Gromyko in Washington allowed the allies to keep pressing their demands in Helsinki.

Thanks to NATO's common front at the negotiations, by the time the MPT wrapped up in summer 1973, the allies had secured a robust agenda item on human contacts. In a certain sense, the main fight at the CSCE had already been won. The original Warsaw Pact proposals for the conference only aimed to legitimize Moscow's postwar gains in Eastern Europe and had included nothing remotely like these humanitarian questions. Getting them on the conference agenda was a major coup. If the Soviets wanted their conference to succeed, they would have to talk about human rights and make concessions to Western demands on the freer movement of people and circulation of information.

The CSCE itself opened in Geneva in September. Besides human contacts, its agenda included the principles governing relations between states—the main focus of Soviet interest—CBMs, and trade. Gromyko pressed Nixon for some measure of U.S. –Soviet cooperation to ensure that the conference stayed on track and achieved results that would please both superpowers. Without such an arrangement, he warned, the negotiations would drag on endlessly. Nixon seemed to agree: "We must agree where we want to come out ... otherwise it will be a shambles." But, wary as ever of raising Western European suspicions of secret U.S. –Soviet collaboration, he made no promises.[27] The American delegation had arrived in Geneva with no written instructions, and they received no orders to collaborate with the Soviets. On most questions, they had no choice but to avoid the spotlight, using the principle of alliance solidarity as a substitute for official guidance from Washington.[28]

Now secretary of state, Kissinger continued to see the need to humor the Europeans, but still regarded their humanitarian efforts in Geneva as foolish. Though the communists stubbornly refused to give way to NATO demands in Basket III, the Western Europeans kept pushing. Kissinger was unimpressed. Their efforts prolonged the negotiations unnecessarily and annoyed the Soviets. He told Gromyko that the Western allies were simply "crazy on the subject of human contacts." He understood that they believed a robust Basket III might somehow undermine the communist regimes, but, to his mind, the circulation of a few Western newspapers could not threaten the Soviet government's grip on power.[29] Soviet leaders agreed. In Moscow in March 1974, Brezhnev condemned the Western pressure on Basket III, which he saw as illegitimate interference in Soviet domestic policy. "What kind of proposal is it," he asked, "if they want to arrogate to themselves the right to open theaters in the Soviet Union without any control by the Soviet administration? ... It's just wrong to have ideas like that." Reinforcing his host's point, Kissinger observed that the Western Europeans had failed in several wars to change the Soviets' domestic system. Cultural exchanges and diplomacy would not now accomplish what the force of arms had not.[30]

Despite Brezhnev's frustrations, the pace of the negotiations did not increase. The conference seemed to have developed its own momentum, apparently oblivious to external developments. Despite the Yom Kippur War, the expulsion of Nobel literature laureate and dissident Alexander Solzhenitsyn from the Soviet Union, and changes of leadership in the United States, United Kingdom, and France, it continued to grind away. Frustrated at the pace, Kissinger launched his own scheme within NATO to speed things up. Up to this point in the negotiations, the allies had not set firm goals for the CSCE. They agreed on the kinds of things they wanted to push for but had not defined exactly how many Soviet concessions would suffice. In an attempt to change this open-ended approach, Kissinger called for specific targets, hoping to force an end to the negotiations once these goals were met and make it difficult to surprise the Eastern Europeans with new demands. The allies were furious. To them, Kissinger's proposal smacked of a U.S.–Soviet attempt to rig the conference outcome. They insisted that there was no point in limiting what they might wring from the Soviets. The best strategy was simply to keep pushing until it became clear that no more progress was possible.[31]

After this European backlash, Kissinger's opinion of the CSCE began to evolve. By late 1974, a few months after Gerald Ford took office, the conference was occupying increasingly large portions of his meetings with Soviet leaders. His discussions of the CSCE with Gromyko no longer focused, as they had in the past, on U.S.-Soviet collaboration and to accelerate the speed of the negotiations. Although he still joked about his ignorance on some of the more abstruse issues and never suggested that the American delegation in Geneva take a leading role in the proceedings, his attitude toward the Soviets began to harden.[32] Even as he called the CSCE "one of the weirdest negotiations I have ever seen," he pushed the Soviets to make major concessions to Western demands, insisting that "we … need more flexibility from the Soviet side."[33] He went further still on CBMs, demonstrating on a number of occasions his willingness to master the issues and get involved in detailed debate. Here was evidence that Kissinger thought that at least one item on the CSCE's agenda was of value. At the same time, the American delegation in Geneva was toughening its position, moving closer to the Western Europeans and making greater demands of the Soviets. Over the following months, Kissinger's CBM discussions with Gromyko grew increasingly detailed, to the point that they were debating the maximum sizes of units involved and the number of kilometers into Soviet territory over which the measures would apply.[34] Of all the issues on the CSCE's agenda, CBMs were the most concrete, and they complemented Kissinger's realist conception of détente. Though hardly as significant as the SALT negotiations, they could nevertheless increase international stability by publicizing the details of troop exercises and thus reducing the risk that one side might mistake routine training for preparations for an attack.

At the same time as Kissinger's view of the CSCE began to shift, however, domestic attacks on détente began to mount. The critics included both Democrats and Republicans and even prominent members of the Ford administration. In their analysis, the White House had pursued international order with such zeal that it ignored the imperatives of both justice and American power. Jackson, one of détente's earliest critics, argued that the United States was wrong to treat the Soviet Union as a normal great power and ignore the nature of its regime. Nixon, Ford, and Kissinger were too willing, in his opinion, to make unnecessary concessions to the Soviets and were unduly reticent about pressuring Moscow to uphold Western standards of human rights.[35] In December 1974, he brought his eponymous amendment to a vote. It passed easily, delivering a serious rebuke to the White House and leading the Soviets to repudiate their trade agreement with the United States rather than change their emigration policy. One of Jackson's Senate colleagues, Adlai Stevenson III, passed his own amendment requiring Congressional approval of hundreds of millions of dollars of trade credits to Moscow, further infuriating the Soviets.[36] In a *Reader's Digest* article, Nixon's former Secretary of Defense Melvin Laird made the case that the United States had to "shed any lingering illusions we may have that détente means the Russians have abandoned their determination to undermine Western democracy and impose their system on the world ... We must show them that we will no longer tolerate the use of détente as a Russian one-way street." Ford's own Secretary of Defense James Schlesinger insisted that the threat from the USSR was as serious as ever and warned that continued détente risked compromising American security.[37] By early 1975, the White House was beginning to realize that détente was in serious trouble.

Despite all of this criticism, neither Kissinger nor Ford predicted that détente's opponents would set their sights on the CSCE. In mid-1974, Kissinger had dismissed as inconsequential the Final Act's provisions, still in draft form, recognizing the inviolability of international frontiers. The following April, however, he noted that the agreement, even if it did not change the legal status of the Baltic states or European frontiers, had important symbolic value to Moscow. "That is why the Soviet Union wants it," he told Ford.[38] Still, as the end of the negotiations approached, Kissinger gave no indication that that same symbolism would cause domestic political trouble. He did not suggest that the Final Act gave too much away to the Soviets, and he never counseled Ford against signing it.

In mid-1975, as the negotiations in Geneva were moving toward their conclusion, Kissinger launched a major initiative to answer his critics. In Minneapolis on July 15, he gave one of the most significant speeches of his career, the first in a series he called the "heartland speeches." This was an attempt to lay out the rationale behind his foreign policy and build domestic support in the face of widespread skepticism. In the Minneapolis speech, entitled "The Moral Foundations of Foreign Policy," he said that the threat of nuclear destruction required the United States to work with the Soviets to "seek a more productive and stable relationship despite the basic antagonism of our values." In reply to Scoop Jackson's accusations of amorality, Kissinger argued that, although the American government would work to help victims of repression, its power was limited and, besides, survival and coexistence had to take precedence.[39]

Work on the Final Act concluded the following week. The Soviets had accepted Western demands for provisions on the freer movement of information as well as on CBMs. The document, some 23,000 words long, now awaited the signature of the thirty-five participants. Ford had decided that the Final Act's benefits outweighed the drawbacks, but before he left for the CSCE's concluding summit in Helsinki, some of his advisors recognized that the agreement might raise some domestic political difficulties. Shortly before his departure, therefore, he met with the leaders of Eastern European and Baltic émigré groups at the White House. He told them that the United States "has never recognized the Soviet incorporation of Lithuania, Latvia, and Estonia," and, despite the Final Act's Basket I provisions, he was not going to do so in Helsinki. Nevertheless, the public denunciations began even before Ford left for Europe. As mentioned above, the *New York Times* and the *Wall Street Journal* published editorials condemning Ford's decision to support the Final Act. Somewhat more graphically, Solzhenitsyn, now in American exile, declared that at the Helsinki summit "an amicable agreement of diplomatic shovels will bury and pack down corpses still breathing in a common grave."[40] In his speech in Helsinki, Ford tried to reassure those who questioned his motives for signing the Final Act and to underline that he took its guarantees of human rights seriously. "To my country," he said, "they are not clichés or empty phrases. ... It is important that you recognize the deep devotion of the American people and their government to human rights and fundamental freedoms." He concluded, "History will judge this conference not by what we say today, but what we do tomorrow; not by the promises we make but by the promises we keep."[41]

Ford received a standing ovation from the statesmen in Helsinki, but back in the United States his opponents remained implacable. They doubted that the Soviets would keep their promises. Appearing before the American Legion, Ford repeated the speech he had given in Helsinki in an effort to convince the public that he had not abandoned the Eastern Europeans to Soviet domination, though he never went so far as to proclaim their right to self-determination.[42] The criticism ebbed a little toward the end of 1975, but rose again in 1976 as the presidential electoral campaign got underway. The Final Act became one of the linchpins of the opposition to détente, and critics added to it other episodes which, they argued, illustrated the administration's lack of moral compass and its willingness to make unacceptable compromises for the sake of harmony with the Soviets. Campaigning against

Ford for the Republican nomination, Ronald Reagan gave a nationally tele-vised speech in late March. "Wandering without aim," he declared, "describes U.S. foreign policy." He condemned Ford's policy on the civil war in Angola and his refusal to receive Solzhenitsyn at the White House, ostensibly (and actually, as it turned out) for fear of offending the Soviets. He asked why Ford had "traveled halfway around the world to sign the Helsinki Pact, put-ting our stamp of approval on Russia's enslavement of the captive nations."[43] The revelation of the so-called Sonnenfeldt Doctrine—the alleged policy of supporting the Soviet domination of Eastern Europe—offered Reagan and détente's other skeptics further ammunition and appeared to reinforce their accusations about the meaning of the Final Act.

In response, Ford tried to distance himself from détente and take a posi-tion on foreign policy closer to Reagan's, but, in the words of one journalist, this only suggested that he "acted less out of conviction than in response to popular demand."[44] The conservative weekly *National Review* repeatedly condemned Ford's foreign policy and, especially, the Final Act. William F. Buckley derided the government's attempts to defend the agreement, the effect of which was "to sanctify the status quo ... The captive nations will continue under Soviet domination, and never mind that the Soviet empire continues to seek to subvert the governments of other countries and to upset the status quo elsewhere." The magazine also published some verses by the historian and poet Robert Conquest, who warned that "The road to Helsinki is paved with good intentions."[45] Although Ford survived Reagan's challenge for the Republican nomination, he was forced at the party con-vention to accept a policy plank, entitled "Morality in Foreign Policy," which condemned the Final Act.

Jimmy Carter, who defeated Jackson in the Democratic primary contest, attacked Ford's foreign policy in much the same way that Reagan had. He conceded that détente may be an attractive idea, but insisted that "every time we have had a tough negotiation with the Soviet Union we have lost or come in second-best" because the White House was too willing to make con-cessions. Moreover, the secrecy that typically surrounded these negotiations kept the American people in the dark on questions of major importance.[46] Zbigniew Brzezinski, a key member of Carter's foreign policy team, and later his national security adviser, published an article in the journal *Foreign Policy* in which he condemned Ford and Kissinger's foreign policy and argued that "a gap in values and perceptions has opened between America and major parts of the world," and that the United States has been "more generally ori-ented toward preserving the status quo than reforming it."[47] Carter's oppo-sition to the Final Act, which in his view amounted to an abandonment of

Eastern Europe for the sake of preserving the status quo, was based on this same line of analysis.[48] It is hard to say exactly how much Carter's views on foreign policy contributed to his narrow victory at the polls in November 1976, but it is clear that Ford had not adequately responded to the chorus of criticism of the Final Act and of détente. His mistake in his debate against Carter, and the public reaction to the mistake, underscored his vulnerability on foreign policy and his failure to rebut these attacks.

In retrospect, whatever one's judgment of détente in general, Ford was right to sign the Final Act. Thanks especially to the series of follow-up conferences in the late 1970s and 1980s and the efforts of activists in both East and West, the agreement served as a yardstick for measuring the extent to which the Eastern European governments were upholding—or more often failing to uphold—their citizens' basic human rights. As the value of the Final Act became clear, Carter and Reagan both completely reversed their original opposition to it, and came to believe, like Ford, that it had been an important victory for the West. Indeed, after 1991 many commentators made the case that the Final Act had made a major contribution to the collapse of communism and the end of the Cold War.[49] However, it is important to remember that no one at the summit in Helsinki's Finlandia Hall in August 1975 predicted the impact that the CSCE would eventually have. Kissinger opens the chapter on the CSCE in his memoirs by observing that "turning points often pass unrecognized by contemporaries."[50] The Final Act is one of the Cold War's great case studies of unanticipated consequences.

The American attitude to the Final Act grew out of the White House's understanding of détente and illustrates its failure to anticipate the backlash against that strategy. Détente, in Nixon, Ford, and Kissinger's view, aimed to reinforce international stability, and it did so by focusing on concrete issues in U.S.–Soviet and U.S.–Chinese relations. Military questions, whether nuclear arms control, the war in Vietnam, or war in Middle East, were always at the top of the list. By comparison, other issues, including economics and especially human rights, took second place. This is why, for the duration of the CSCE, the White House showed little interest in and had few hopes for Basket III. Kissinger in particular regarded the Western Europeans' demands for Soviet concessions on human rights as an irritant rather than a virtue. He aimed to placate the allies so as to avoid a transatlantic rift, but not to encourage them.

Kissinger does, however, deserve some credit for the creation of the Final Act. His belief in the importance of NATO solidarity allowed the allies to maintain a common front in Geneva and thus to force the Soviet delegation to make concessions, especially on human rights and CBMs. His personal efforts on CBMs further contributed to the West's success. At no point did he share the European's optimism about the Final Act, nor did he believe it would challenge the Cold War's status quo. But at the concluding summit, he admitted to a senior diplomat on the American delegation that his original disdain for the CSCE had been mistaken. The negotiations had proven more valuable than he had expected.[51] This offhand remark may have been an attempt to placate a diplomat who had devoted an enormous amount of time to the conference and took pride in its results. Nevertheless, it does suggest that Kissinger thought differently about the CSCE in 1975 than he had in 1969. He intervened with the Soviets to work out a deal on CBMs because he saw how the measures might reinforce his view of détente. He recognized the leverage that the conference had given the West over the USSR, especially in advancing the MBFR talks. There was even a prospect that the CSCE might help some of the independent-minded Eastern Europeans, notably Tito and Ceausescu, increase their margin of independence from Moscow. This was an interesting reversal of the Soviets' initial plan to use the CSCE to create a rift within NATO.[52]

The same vision of détente that shaped Kissinger's attitude to the CSCE also explains why he and the presidents he served failed to anticipate the hostility that the Final Act, especially Basket I, would encounter in the United States. As Kissinger had put it, Basket I's contents were purely symbolic and had no impact on the material positions of either the Soviet Union or the United States. Moral or ideological criteria did not enter into this calculus. And yet, for large numbers of the American public, and for politicians and journalists on the right and the left, moral considerations were increasingly important in evaluating America's role in the world and its position vis-à-vis the Soviet Union. American society's growing concern for human rights expressed itself in some of the backlash against détente. Détente's critics protested the Final Act because they believed that its endorsement of European frontiers perfectly captured détente's willingness to sacrifice American values for the sake of East–West cooperation. Ford and Kissinger might have blunted some of this criticism by coming out earlier in praise of Basket III, but, because of the ways in which their pursuit of détente obscured their view of humanitarian questions, they were unwilling to put serious human rights pressure on the Soviet Union. For similar reasons, they failed to see the Final Act's virtues before it was too late to set the terms of public debate about the agreement. As a result, through the second half of 1975 and into 1976 they remained on the defensive about the CSCE and about détente more generally.

The Final Act, though a contradictory agreement, was the high point of détente. It exemplified the ways in which East–West cooperation could serve Western ideas of human rights. The Western Europeans' insistence on Basket III illustrated the importance that they attached to these values in foreign policy. But for the United States, the Final Act illuminated, if not the ethical shortcomings of détente, then certainly the low value which the Nixon and Ford administrations attached to the defense of human rights internationally. By contrast with the Western Europeans, the White House never showed much interest in Basket III because, first, it doubted whether standing up for humanitarian principles would serve its foreign policy goals and, second, it accepted the legitimacy of the Soviet regime and refused to question the way it treated its citizens lest such moralizing threaten the prospects for international stability. The debates over the Final Act, both at the negotiations themselves and in American domestic politics, underscore the tension between order and justice in international affairs. Nixon, Ford, and Kissinger's pursuit of order was at the heart of their attitude to the CSCE negotiations, and it both shaped the achievements of their strategy of détente and contributed to that strategy's eventual undoing.

Notes

1. Debate transcript available at PBS's "Debating Our Destiny" web site: http://www.pbs.org/newshour/debatingourdestiny/1976.html
2. Mark J. Rozell, *The Press and the Ford Presidency* (Ann Arbor, Mich., 1992), 147.
3. Quoted in John Robert Greene, *The Presidency of Gerald R. Ford* (Lawrence, Kan., 1995), 153.
4. Quoted in Elizabeth Drew, *American Journal: The Events of 1976* (New York, 1976), 91.
5. *New York Times*, "European 'Security,'" July 21, 1975.
6. *Wall Street Journal*, "Jerry, Don't Go," July 23, 1975.
7. Richard Nixon, *RN: The Memoirs of Richard Nixon* (New York, 1978).
8. Ford–Kissinger memorandum of conversation (memcon), August 28, 1974, National Security Adviser Memoranda of Conversations, 1973–1977, Box 5, August 28, 1974, GRFL.
9. Daniel C. Thomas, *The Helsinki Effect: International Norms, Human Rights, and the Demise of Communism* (Princeton, 2001), 35; and "Public Appeal for a European Security Conference," Budapest, March 17, 1969, Parallel History Project web site: http://www.isn.ethz.ch/php/documents/ collection_3/PCC_meetings/coll_3_PCC_1969.htm

10. Kissinger to Nixon, "Soviet Initiative for a Security Conference", April 4, 1969, NSC Files, USSR Vol. 1, Box 709, NPMP. See also "A Review of United States Policy Toward Europe," January 14,1970, NSC Files, Box 667, Europe—Europe General Jan '69 –May '70 (1 of 2), NPMP.

11. Kissinger to Nixon, "Soviet Initiative for a Security Conference," April 4, 1969, Files, USSR Vol. 1, Box 709, NPMP.

12. Kissinger to Nixon, "Points I Propose to Make to Ambassador Dobrynin at Dinner This Evening," December 22, 1969, NSC Files, Box 711, USSR Vol. VI (Nov. 69—Feb 70) (2 of 3), NPMP; and Kissinger–Dobrynin memcon, December 22, 1969, Henry Kissinger (HAK) Office Files, Box 57, NPMP.

13. For early examples of Kissinger's thinking along these lines, see Kissinger–Dobrynin memcon, July 20, 1970, HAK Office Files, Box 57, NPMP; and Kissinger to Nixon, "European Security Conference," October 19, 1970, HAK Office Files, Box 71, Gromyko 1970, NPMP.

14. John Lewis Gaddis, "Rescuing Choice from Circumstance: The Statecraft of Henry Kissinger," in *The Diplomats, 1939–1979*, eds. Gordon A. Craig and Francis L. Loewenheim (Princeton, 1994), 576.

15. CSCE Interagency Task Force, "Interim Report to the Secretary of State," March 3, 1972, RG 59, Executive Secretariat, Briefing Books 1958–1976, Box 134, Interagency Task Force—Conference on Security and Cooperation in Europe—Interim Report—March 3, 1972, NARA.

16. Sonnenfeldt to Kissinger, March 24, 1972, Nixon Files, NSC Institutional Files, Box H-061, SRG [Senior Review Group] Meeting—European Security Conf.—MBFR 3/29/72 (1 of 2), NPMP.

17. Yanek Mieczkowski, *Gerald Ford and the Challenges of the 1970s* (Lexington, Ky., 2005), 278–279.

18. Kissinger–Gromyko memcon, October 2, 1972, Nixon Files, HAK Office Files, Box 71, Gromyko 1971–1972, NPMP.

19. Quoted in Walter Isaacson, *Kissinger: A Biography* (New York, 1996), 656.

20. Nixon to Rogers, February 3, 1972, *FRUS, 1969–1976*, vol. XIV: 148; editorial note, ibid., 219.

21. Kissinger to Nixon, May 21, 1972, ibid., 971.

22. Jussi Hanhimäki, "'They Can Write It in Swahili': Kissinger, the Soviets, and the Helsinki Accords, 1973–75," *Journal of Transatlantic Studies* 1 (Spring 2003): 41–43.

23. "CSCE Task Force Second Interim Report," n.d. [April 1972], NSC Files, Box 482, MBFR-CSCE Backup Book (Part 3), NPMP; State Department Briefing Book, "Visit of Richard Nixon, President of the United States, to the Union of Soviet Socialist Republics, May 1972," n.d. [May 1972], RG 59, Executive Secretariat, Briefing Books 1958–1976, Box 124, Visit of Richard Nixon to the USSR, May 1972, NARA.

24. Sonnenfeldt to Kissinger, "SRG/VP Meeting—CSCE," September 2, 1972, Nixon Files, NSC Institutional Files, Box H-065, SRG Meeting—CSCE 9/2/72, NPMP.

25. Memorandum for the record, "US–Soviet Views on CSCE Preparatory Negotiations," 19 April 1973, HAK Office Files, Box 77, Moscow Trip— CSCE, NPMP; John J. Maresca, *To Helsinki: The Conference on Security and Cooperation in Europe, 1973–1975* (Durham, N.C., 1985), 3–22.

26. Kissinger–Gromyko memcon, May 6, 1973, Kissinger Transcripts Collection, Digital National Security Archive. Available at: http://nsarchive.chadwyck.com

27. Nixon–Gromyko memcon, September 28, 1973, HAK Office Files, Box 71, Gromyko 1973, NPMP.

28. Maresca, *To Helsinki*, 44–46. See also "Interview with George S. Vest [American Ambassador to the CSCE]," July 6, 1990, Foreign Affairs Oral History Collection of the Association for Diplomatic Studies and Training. Available at http://hdl.loc.gov/loc.mss/mfdip.2004ves01

29. Kissinger–Gromyko memcon, December 22, 1973, HAK Office Files, Box 71, Gromyko 1973, NPMP; Nixon–Gromyko memcon, February 4, 1974, HAK Office Files, Box 71, Gromyko 1974, NPMP.

30. Kissinger–Brezhnev memcon, March 25, 1974, HAK Office Files, Box 76, Secretary Kissinger's Pre-Summit Trip to Moscow March 24–28, 1974: Memcons and reports, NPMP.

31. Arthur Hartman to Sonnenfeldt, July 19, 1974, RG 59, Records of the Office of the Counselor, 1955–77, Box 11, POL 3–1 CSCE—General, NARA.

32. See, for instance, Kissinger–Gromyko memcon, May 7, 1974, HAK Office Files, Box 71 Gromyko 1973, NPMP.

33. Ford–Gromyko memcon, September 20, 1974, National Security Adviser—Presidential Transition File, 1974, Box 1 Letters to and from World Leaders—US–USSR Exchanges, 8/9/74–11/5/74, GRFL.

34. Kissinger–Gromyko memcon, February 16, 1975, RG 59, Records of the Office of the Counselor, 1955–1977, Box 8 Soviet Union Jan–Mar 1975, NARA; Kissinger–Gromyko memcons, May 19 and 20, 1975, RG 59, Records of the Office of the Counselor, 1955–1977, Box 7 Soviet Union April–May 1975, NARA; Kissinger–Gromyko memcon, May 20, 1975, National Security Adviser—Kissinger Reports on USSR, China, and Middle East Discussions, Box 1 May 19–20, 1975—Kissinger/Gromyko Meetings in Vienna (2), GRFL; and Kissinger–Gromyko memcon, July 11, 1975, RG 59, Records of the Office of the Counselor, 1955–1977, Box 7 Soviet Union June–July 1975, NARA.

35. Robert G. Kaufman, *Henry M. Jackson: A Life in Politics* (Seattle, 2000), 242–260.

36. Greene, *Presidency of Gerald R. Ford*, 123.

37. Ibid., 121.

38. Ford–Kissinger memcon, n.d. [April 1975], National Security Adviser Memoranda of Conversations, 1973–1977, Box 10, GRFL.

39. Isaacson, *Kissinger*, 659–660.

40. Quoted in ibid., 658, 661.

41. Quoted in Robert T. Hartmann, *Palace Politics: An Inside Account of the Ford Years* (New York, 1980), 343–344.

42. Ibid., 345; Leo P. Ribuffo, "Is Poland a Soviet Satellite? Gerald Ford, the Sonnenfeldt Doctrine, and the Election of 1976," *Diplomatic History* 14 (July 1990): 391.

43. Greene, *Presidency of Gerald R. Ford*, 166.

44. Joseph Kraft quoted in Rozell, *The Press and the Ford Presidency*, 135.

45. William F. Buckley, "The Helsinki Document," *National Review*, August 29, 1975, 954–955; Robert Conquest, "Proverbs of Détente," *National Review*, January 23, 1976, 31.

46. Quoted in Drew, *American Journal*, 91.

47. Zbigniew Brzezinski, "America in a Hostile World," *Foreign Policy* 23 (Summer 1976): 73.

48. Drew, *American Journal*, 463.

49. Thomas, *Helsinki Effect*, 1–7.

50. Henry Kissinger, *Years of Renewal* (New York, 1999), 635.

51. Author interview with John Maresca, Geneva, December 18, 2005.

52. William G. Hyland, *Mortal Rivals: Superpower Relations from Nixon to Reagan* (New York, 1987), 115.

Part III

Closings

9

Waging War on All Fronts: Nixon, Kissinger, and the Vietnam War, 1969-1972

Lien-Hang T. Nguyen

Although Richard Nixon and Henry Kissinger inherited the Vietnam War when they assumed office in 1969, they made the war their own. Elected on the premise of extricating the United States from Vietnam, Nixon proceeded to spend his first term waging war on all fronts. While fighting the Democratic Republic of Vietnam (DRV) and the National Liberation Front (NLF)—America's enemies since large-scale U.S. intervention in 1965—Nixon and Kissinger also adopted a combative approach toward international allies as well as domestic opponents. The two men were initially confident that they could end the war in short order by neutralizing internal and external threats to their control over Vietnam policy. However, by the end of 1969, when no end to the conflict was in sight, the two men prepared to fight a long war not only in Vietnam but also on the home front. At the start of 1970, they therefore resolved to win the war and the peace gradually in Vietnam by launching attacks against domestic opponents in order to buy time for their strategy in Vietnam and by expanding the war into Cambodia and Laos. Then, in the final stretch of America's Vietnam War, Nixon and Kissinger used the remaining weapons in their arsenal: bringing Sino-Soviet pressure to bear on the North Vietnamese and escalating the war through so-called "madman" tactics. But after four years of waging war on multiple fronts, the contradictions in Nixon and Kissinger's Vietnam strategy became apparent. The Paris Agreement to End the War and Restore the Peace in Vietnam, signed early in 1973, marked official closure for the Americans but only offered temporary respite for the Vietnamese.

During the 1968 campaign, Nixon promised to deliver "peace with honor," meaning the end of American military involvement in Southeast Asia while simultaneously preserving an independent, noncommunist South Vietnam.[1] Differing little from the position of the Democratic nominee, Vice President Hubert H. Humphrey, who also promised withdrawal, Nixon vaguely hinted at possessing a "secret plan" that would bring the troops home without endangering the Saigon regime and thus American credibility. At the Republican National Convention in Miami in August, Nixon unveiled the tentative framework of his strategy.[2] Although far from concrete at that point, the diplomatic centerpiece of this "secret plan" would include negotiations with the Soviet Union. Through the concept of linkage, Nixon intended to compel the Soviets to pressure their North Vietnamese allies to negotiate by using "carrots"—holding out progress on arms control and détente—and later brandishing "sticks"—playing the "China card" and exploiting the Sino-Soviet split.[3] Another important component of Nixon's strategy, one that he revealed fully neither to delegates nor the wider public, was his intention to use "irresistible military pressure" to force Hanoi to accept a settlement on American terms.[4] Since certain aspects of American de-escalation seemed more or less inevitable in the summer of 1968, Nixon spoke at length about reducing the number of American troops and turning more responsibility for the fighting over to the South Vietnamese, a policy of "Vietnamization" formally adopted the following spring.[5]

On November 5, 1968, Nixon narrowly defeated Humphrey, hardly receiving the "mandate to govern" he coveted.[6] During the transition period, he began to plot how best to ensure ultimate control over foreign policymaking in general and Vietnam policy in particular. In his selection of Kissinger as national security advisor, Nixon found a partner in policymaking who was also convinced that America's best chance to "win" included employing great-power diplomacy and exerting major military pressure to force Hanoi's hand at Paris while staving off public disapproval with the war through de-Americanization and Vietnamization. In order to implement their strategy, however, Nixon and Kissinger believed they had to neutralize multiple threats to their authority. On the home front, they held that making and implementing strategy were too important to be left to a cumbersome government bureaucracy, shortsighted Congress, or vagaries of public opinion. To combat these domestic threats they consolidated foreign policymaking in their hands by circumventing the State and Defense departments; went on the offensive against the antiwar segment of Congress and society; and either lied to or kept uninformed the vast majority of the American people.

In addition to internal opponents, Nixon and Kissinger viewed America's ally in South Vietnam as a possible impediment to their designs. Specifically, South Vietnamese President Nguyen Van Thieu might prove obstructionist. Nixon and Kissinger therefore ensured that bilateral, secret talks with Hanoi would take place simultaneously to the four-party public plenum that included the U.S.-Republic of Vietnam (RVN) and DRV-NLF taking place in central Paris. In this way, Washington would secretly maintain strict control of the negotiations.

Confident that he could keep dissenting opinions and the cumbersome bureaucracy in check, and that his hawkish reputation made him the ideal man for the job, Nixon was sure his strategy would end the war within six months.[7] In order to achieve this negotiated end, Nixon and Kissinger concentrated on the secret talks with Hanoi and on getting the Soviets to impress upon the North Vietnamese the need to compromise once at the table. They preferred secret meetings with Hanoi negotiators not only because progress proved impossible in the four-party public forum, but also because closed, bilateral talks would also minimize the role of other government agencies and any potential interference by Saigon. In late March, Nixon approved the first private contact between Henry Cabot Lodge, former ambassador to the RVN and Averell Harriman's replacement as the lead negotiator at Paris, and Xuan Thuy, North Vietnam's negotiator. Although Kissinger was not present at these sessions, he made sure he was the only contact in the second prong of the diplomatic strategy. Kissinger convinced the president to open a direct back channel to Anatoly Dobrynin, the Soviet ambassador to the United States, rather than hold formal talks. Keeping the State Department entirely out of the loop, Kissinger proposed to negotiate on Nixon's behalf to ensure that U.S.-Soviet talks on arms control be linked to an acceptable settlement in Vietnam. As with the U.S.-DRV secret meetings, Nixon wanted the Oval Office to maintain strict control over Soviet negotiations, while Kissinger wanted to make himself indispensable—and Secretary of State William Rogers obsolete—to Nixon.

In order to strengthen their bargaining position vis-à-vis North Vietnam and the Soviet Union, Nixon and Kissinger looked for opportunities to exert major military pressure in Indochina. In late February, Nixon took advantage of improved relations with Cambodian leader, Prince Norodom Sihanouk, to order secret, intensive bombing of Vietnamese communist sanctuaries in Cambodia. Militarily, Nixon reasoned that Operation "Menu," consisting of "Breakfast," "Lunch," "Snack," and "Dessert," limited Hanoi's ability to launch a large-scale offensive in the South. In addition to Menu, Nixon also ordered the resumption of maximum aerial reconnaissance over North Vietnam.[8] The real objective of these military measures, however, was to show Hanoi and Moscow that Nixon was willing to escalate the war in ways Lyndon Johnson was not.

At the same time, Nixon resolved to keep these escalatory measures secret from Congress, the media, the American public, and even his own cabinet members. When Secretary of State Rogers and Secretary of Defense Laird discovered that the president was "contemplating" bombing Cambodia (when in fact he had already made the decision to proceed), they both expressed deep reservations. Laird doubted that the bombings could be kept secret and feared the public backlash if news got out, while Rogers objected to the bombing's potential adverse impact on the Paris negotiations. According to both Nixon's and Kissinger's memoirs, Nixon continued the charade by holding a meeting in the Oval Office on March 16 with Kissinger, Rogers, Laird, and Joint Chief of Staff General Earle Wheeler in which he pretended that the "decision was still open."[9] For his part, Kissinger used the meeting to portray Rogers as an unhelpful recalcitrant.[10] The following day, March 17, the secret bombing of Cambodia began and although the *New York Times* broke the story about "Breakfast," Nixon and Kissinger moved quickly to squash the story and ordered wiretaps on the phones of government employees to discover the leak.

By April, however, Nixon and Kissinger were sorely disappointed that their "madman" tactics had so little impacted the negotiations: neither Moscow nor Hanoi had caved. The Soviets were powerless to pressure Hanoi to settle on Washington's terms and moreover were unimpressed with Kissinger's use of linkage, while in Paris neither Lodge nor Xuan Thuy possessed the necessary clout with their respective governments to negotiate seriously. Nonetheless, on April 14, Kissinger wielded the stick with Dobrynin: unless there was a settlement in Vietnam, "other measures would be invoked which could involve wider risk to U.S.-Soviet relations."[11] These "measures" included mining Haiphong Harbor, possibly halting troop withdrawal, and bombing rail lines up to China.[12] That same night, North Korean fighter jets shot down a U.S. reconnaissance plane. Nixon and Kissinger wanted to respond with force, but at a National Security Council (NSC) meeting on April 16, Rogers, Laird, and Wheeler objected to military retaliation against the North Koreans. Kissinger tried to convince Nixon that a strong U.S. response would show North *Vietnam* that Nixon could be "irrational," but the president, lacking a consensus among his advisors, decided to show restraint. He immediately regretted his decision, took out his frustration elsewhere (Cambodia), and contemplated using nuclear weapons. Kissinger, meanwhile, took advantage of Nixon's regret to consolidate his control over policymaking at the expense of the president's other advisors.

In the spring of 1969, Nixon turned to the "public" face of his strategy to bring "peace with honor." On May 8, the NLF delegation issued its "Ten-Point Overall Solution" that put forward concrete proposals regarding a U.S. troop withdrawal and the formation of a coalition government.[13] Needing to show that he too was committed to progress in Paris, Nixon appeared on television on May 14 to announce his eight-point proposal for peace that included a call for simultaneous withdrawal of American and North Vietnamese troops and acknowledged the NLF's peace proposal by accepting the possibility of a neutral South Vietnam. Although Nixon did not expect Hanoi to respond favorably to his speech, he had hoped for a more positive reception on the home front, including from the press. When it did not materialize, he fell into depression. It did not help his mood that the antiwar movement, which had subsided since the tumultuous days of 1968, now began to stir again.

But if Nixon could not control domestic criticism of his policies, he was sure he could suppress dissent from America's ally in South Vietnam. Following Nixon's televised speech, Kissinger informed the press that the content had been "cleared" by Saigon even though U.S. Ambassador Ellsworth Bunker had only given Thieu the text two days before its delivery. Nor was Thieu pleased by what he read. South Vietnam's ambassador to the United States, Bui Diem, described the administration's proposal as a "shock" and in retrospect saw that the "game of imposition and attempted finesse that would become the Nixon administration's trademark in dealing with its ally had begun with a bang."[14] Exactly one week after Nixon's televised address, Thieu requested a meeting with his superpower patron in Washington or Honolulu. Nixon rejected Thieu's suggestions for potential locales and instead chose the "isolated and desolate" backdrop of Midway Island.[15] During a tense meeting on June 8, Thieu spoke of his desire for the redeployment of American troops and increased aid, while Nixon reiterated America's commitment to troop withdrawal and private negotiations with Hanoi. In exchange for Thieu's compliance, Nixon promised him that Vietnamization would include four years of increased military aid during his first term, followed by four more years of economic support in his second, and that America would insist on mutual troop withdrawal. With little choice in the matter, Thieu had to accept that the United States would pull out 25,000 troops starting in July and that private talks between the

United States and the DRV on the future of South Vietnam would begin soon thereafter.

Although Nixon was able to compel Thieu to acquiesce, North Vietnamese negotiators in Paris were not so easily intimidated. Throughout both the plenary and private bilateral sessions in late May, both sides refused to budge from their positions. Also in late May, Hanoi created the Provisional Revolutionary Government (PRG) to offset the Thieu regime at the Paris talks, while on the U.S. side Lodge expressed his desire to retire as senior negotiator. The Nixon administration needed to convince its head delegate to stay on to counteract Madame Nguyen Thi Binh, the chief delegate for the PRG who represented a powerful element in the communists' commitment to "talking while fighting" [*dam va danh*]. With little progress being made on the negotiating front, Nixon decided to send DRV President Ho Chi Minh a letter that expressed his desire for peace but also issued a threat that if progress toward a settlement did not come by November 1, he would have to resort to "measures of great consequence and force."[16] Following this stern letter, the first secret meeting took place between Kissinger and Xuan Thuy on August 4.

In order to provide cover for Kissinger's secret meeting with the North Vietnamese in Paris, Nixon in mid-1969 embarked on a public relations campaign to shore up support for his policies with constituents at home and with allies abroad. In late July, the president departed on an around-the-world trip during which he revealed to reporters what became known as the Nixon Doctrine. Short of war with a major power, he declared in Guam, the nations of Asia engaged in civil wars would have to fend for themselves. At the end of his tour of Southeast Asia, Nixon took up Thieu's invitation to visit Saigon. By becoming first American president to stay at the Presidential Palace in the Republic of Vietnam, Nixon's visit sent the message to Thieu's allies and adversaries that he still enjoyed U.S. support.[17] Privately, though, Nixon sent mixed messages to Thieu. On the one hand, he declared his intention to escalate the war in order to force Hanoi to settle at Paris; on the other, he let the South Vietnamese president know that additional American troop withdrawals would follow a systematic timetable.

Meanwhile, Kissinger had less success with the North Vietnamese. The first meeting with the DRV negotiators yielded few results, as was evident in the response to Kissinger's opening question: would there be a reply to Nixon's letter to Ho Chi Minh? No, Xuan Thuy answered, and for the rest of the meeting neither side budged from its position. When the reply finally came at the end of August, Nixon felt it underscored the futility of merely making threats. The Vietnam Workers' Party Politburo, on the behalf of a dying Ho Chi Minh, sent what Nixon considered a "cold rebuff."[18] Although Ho Chi Minh's death in early September was a major blow to the communist cause, North Vietnamese strategy at Paris did not change.

Nixon had reached a crossroads. His strategy to end the war within the first year had failed, and his ultimatum to Hanoi having fallen on deaf ears. Moreover, his advisors were split on how to proceed. Kissinger urged ending the war quickly by pushing for a settlement and, if Hanoi remained obstinate, forcing the North Vietnamese into submission through sharp military action. Rogers and Laird, on the other hand, advised caution and feared that escalation would upset Congress and spark major unrest at home. Nixon, exhilarated by Neil Armstrong's walk on the moon in late July and incensed by North Vietnamese defiance, leaned toward toughness and thus Kissinger's plan. The national security advisor, exploiting the president's mood, figured out a way to isolate Nixon from alternate points of view: he asked and received approval for the formation of a Special Vietnam Study Group, which he would chair.[19] Kissinger also ordered trusted members of NSC staff to explore military options that would lead to the crystallization of the contingency plan known as "Duck Hook." Duck Hook constituted a revised version of the military plan formulated in April, before events in North Korea intervened. Kissinger's NSC staff, known as the "September Group," examined the consequences of a four-day attack that would include massive bombing of twenty-nine major targets, mining ports, and harbors, and possibly even using tactical nuclear weapons.[20]

Throughout the rest of September and October, Kissinger moved aggressively to win Nixon's approval for the implementation of Duck Hook. In September, the national security advisor sent a bleak assessment of the situation in South Vietnam, had his staff prepare a presidential speech announcing the military plan, and worked on linkage by sending threats to Moscow via Dobrynin that the president considered the Vietnam War the crucial issue in U.S.-Soviet relations.[21] But when Rogers and Laird found out about Duck Hook and Nixon's November 1 deadline to Hanoi leaders, they increased their opposition to Kissinger's plan.[22] Playing on Nixon's insecurities of mounting domestic criticism of his war effort and pointing out the flaws in Kissinger's military plans, these more moderate presidential advisors won the day: Duck Hook did not go forward. In urging the president to pay more attention to long-range solutions like Vietnamization, Rogers and Laird were supported by the advice offered to Nixon by a counterinsurgency expert,

Sir Robert Thompson, who gave an upbeat yet cautious assessment of the likelihood of American success in South Vietnam.[23]

While preparing for a protracted struggle in Vietnam, Nixon turned his attention to two upcoming antiwar demonstrations, Moratorium and Mobilization Against the War. Although his approval ratings rose with each troop withdrawal announcement (June and September), overall public support for the war continued to drop. As a result, he decided to launch a preemptive attack against opponents at home rather than the ones abroad in order to buy more time for his Vietnam strategy. He appealed for support on Capitol Hill and delivered a television address targeting the "silent majority" of Americans who, he claimed, backed administration policy. The measures worked to increase both congressional and popular backing, but the president was nonetheless haunted by the decision to cancel Duck Hook.

At the start of 1970, Nixon continued to pay more attention and pour more resources into Vietnamization, even though intelligence estimates reported increasing pessimism in Saigon regarding American strategy. Early in the year, Nixon announced that 150,000 troops would be withdrawn from Vietnam by the spring of 1971. Knowing that the United States would still possess 344,000 troops at the end of 1970 and that Vietnamization was in full swing by this point, Nixon was confident that his diplomatic-military offensives would ultimately succeed in garnering an American-dictated peace. On the negotiating front, however, Nixon was less optimistic. In late November, when Lodge officially resigned from his post, Nixon did not appoint a replacement, the better to show his dissatisfaction with the progress of the Paris talks. Kissinger, self-assured in his negotiating abilities, persuaded Nixon to let him reopen secret talks with Hanoi. On February 21, 1970, Kissinger met for the first time with Le Duc Tho, a powerful member of the DRV Politburo. Over the next three years, the two men would be locked in battle over such issues as mutual versus unilateral withdrawal, timetables, the political composition of the post-peace South Vietnamese government, and the nature of the demilitarized zone (DMZ). However, until late in the process the world never knew about these diplomatic battles that decided that fate of thousands of American and millions of Vietnamese lives. Not only did the substance of the secret talks rarely parallel the public plenary sessions, but the Kissinger-Le Duc Tho negotiations were also kept secret from State, Defense, and other government agencies. And although Thieu had consented to these private, bilateral talks in 1969, he never agreed to the agenda that would dominate the negotiations and that would lead to an American-dictated peace.[24]

Le Duc Tho and Kissinger met twice more before events elsewhere in Indochina allowed Nixon to make an attempt at changing the balance of power on the ground. In February 1970, Nixon and Kissinger tried to implement secret bombings of targets in the Plain of Jars in northern Laos, as they had done in Cambodia. Intended to be hidden from the American public, the B-52 raids were reported in the *New York Times*. Many in Congress condemned the raids. At the time, Nixon and Kissinger publicly justified the bombings as a response to North Vietnamese attacks on Souvanna Phouma's neutralist government and argued that it helped Vietnamization and troop withdrawal.[25] In reality, they had been wresting control over Laos policy from the State Department and by 1970 were more or less successful. Although congressional hearings forced Nixon to acknowledge the secret war in Laos in late February, he continued to send allied troops covertly from Thailand in support of Hmong guerillas fighting against the North Vietnamese and their Laotian allies.

Events in neighboring Cambodia eclipsed not only the Laotian bombing but the fighting in Vietnam as well. On March 18, General Lon Nol staged a coup d'état against Prince Sihanouk while the latter was out of the country. The action caught both U.S. and Vietnamese (North and South) officials by surprise. Nixon nevertheless moved quickly to extend diplomatic recognition to the Lon Nol government and sent military and economic assistance to Phnom Penh. South Vietnamese forces, for their part, began conducting operations on Cambodian territory on March 27. Meanwhile, the North Vietnamese reached out to the mercurial prince by issuing a formal statement on March 25 condemning the coup, supporting Sihanouk's cause to reclaim his authority, and withdrawing its diplomats from Phnom Penh.[26]

After much deliberation in Washington, U.S.-ARVN [Army of the Republic of Vietnam] forces launched Operation "Toan Thang" (Total Victory) in late April in order to destroy the military headquarters of the Vietnamese resistance in the South, the so-called Central Office for South Vietnam (COSVN), and to clear out communist sanctuaries in neighboring Cambodia. The U.S.-ARVN invasion of Cambodia failed to destroy the elusive COSVN and did not significantly change the military balance of power, but the invasion held great consequence for Nixon at home. Following swift criticism from Republican and Democratic senators of the first phase of Operation Toan Thang, Nixon delivered a televised address on April 30 explaining how the joint U.S.-ARVN "incursion" saved American lives and facilitated negotiations. Few were persuaded, and the invasion revitalized the antiwar movement. Throughout May, antiwar protests erupted in cities and on college campuses.

At Kent State University in Ohio, four students were shot dead and nine were wounded when the National Guard opened fire on demonstrators and bystanders after four days of intense confrontation that began as a peaceful protest against the Cambodian invasion. After Kent State, millions of students across the country took part in demonstrations not only against the war in Southeast Asia but also against the killings at home.

Nor was the antiwar agitation confined to college campuses. It reached into newsrooms, into Congress, even into the offices of senior advisers. On April 29 Kissinger's top aides, Anthony Lake and Roger Morris, tendered their letters of resignation from the NSC staff, citing increasing alienation from the domestic and foreign policies of the Nixon administration.[27] While Kissinger faced dissension in his ranks, Nixon had to contend with Capitol Hill. A few days into Operation Toan Thang, Senators Sherman Cooper (R-KY) and Frank Church (D-ID) proposed an amendment that would essentially cut off all military funding for operations in Cambodia after June 30. Senators George McGovern (D-SD) and Mark Hatfield (R-OR) took their dissatisfaction with Nixon one step further when they proposed an amendment that would terminate all funding for operations in Indochina by the end of 1970 and require the administration to pull out all troops by the end of 1971. In a symbolic act of defiance, the Senate overwhelmingly voted to repeal the Tonkin Gulf Resolution of 1964 that had given Johnson the authority to use military force in Southeast Asia. Although the various amendments failed to pass, Nixon and Kissinger were on high alert: time was running out at home for their war in Vietnam. Instead of reevaluating his strategy as a result of the domestic crisis, however, Nixon that summer struck back at his domestic enemies. As he assuaged domestic opinion by pulling American troops out of Cambodia by the end of June, he approved what became known as the Huston Plan, named after the White House aide who drafted the 43-page report on proposed security options. In what historian George C. Herring has described as "one of the most blatant attacks on individual freedom and privacy in American history," Nixon expanded his arsenal against the antiwar movement to include opening mail, electronic surveillance, and even burglary.[28]

The Paris negotiations, meanwhile, having halted due to the Cambodian negotiations, resumed in late summer. Yet the deadlock remained. Although the United States refused to comply with the DRV-PRG demand for the removal of the Thieu regime, the South Vietnamese president believed he had much to fear. In preparation for the unveiling of a "major initiative for peace" through a televised address scheduled for October 7, Nixon needed

Ambassador Bunker to gain Thieu's acquiescence. Although Bunker tried to emphasize that Nixon's proposal would not affect the political terms, which were for the South Vietnamese to determine, Thieu feared that Nixon's new initiative that would call for a "ceasefire in place" had replaced Washington's demand for mutual withdrawal. Fortunately for Thieu, the North Vietnamese had already rejected Nixon's offer when informed of it in the secret talks in September; on October 9 they shot it down publicly. Nixon, though, aimed his major new initiative for peace not at the Vietnamese but, rather, at the American public, which was about to go to the polls in a midterm election. Whether this effort to defuse the war issue produced success is hard to say: Republicans gained modestly in the Senate and lost modestly in the House, and few of the races turned on Vietnam.

As 1970 drew to a close, neither Nixon nor Kissinger could see an imminent end to the Vietnam War. Particularly for the national security advisor, negotiations with Hanoi had yielded frustratingly little success, leading him to start considering a "decent interval" solution.[29] In other words, Kissinger looked to end the war with American credibility intact but not to preserve the Saigon regime long term. Nixon, on other hand, had not yet abandoned the prospect of victory, meaning the indefinite survival of an independent, noncommunist South Vietnam. Even though the president did not hold out much hope for Vietnamization, he had not yet implemented two principal elements of his strategy: major military action and superpower diplomacy.[30] With troop withdrawals continuing, 1971 would be the year that South Vietnamese and American forces made "a show of strength"—that is, while there were still enough U.S. combat troops left in Vietnam to prove effective. As in 1970, Nixon decided to launch the 1971 offensive not in South Vietnam but in a neighboring "neutral" country that had been pulled into the struggle long before by both sides in the conflict.

Originally proposed by U.S. Commander Creighton Abrams, Operation "Lam Son 719," named after a famous Vietnamese battle in 1427 against the Chinese, aimed at destroying the capability of the People's Army of Vietnam (PAVN) to mount a major offensive by attacking the remaining communist supply line to the South, the Ho Chi Minh Trail.[31] Since using American troops in another ground operation in Indochina was out of the question politically, South Vietnamese armed forces would carry out the attacks along Route 9 toward the PAVN logistics center, located near the Laotian village of Tchepone. The United States would provide air support. The intent of this major "show of strength" was to prove the success of Vietnamization to the world and to prove to the communists that Nixon was not afraid of expanding the ground war into Laos. If Lam Son 719 failed, however, it would not only undermine South Vietnamese morale and U.S. faith in the ARVN, but would also bolster the communist war effort against the Saigon government.

Nixon and Kissinger believed the gamble was worth taking. Thieu did not, and he may have had the better argument. Because the Cambodian invasion cast a large shadow over planning for the Laotian operation, Lam Son 719 was doomed to fail before a single South Vietnamese soldier crossed over the Laotian border. Resolutions to curtail the expansion of the war and to bring about the end of American troop involvement abounded in Congress as strategy deliberation over Lam Son 719 took place. In the House of Representatives, lawmakers proposed to cut off operations in Cambodia while in the Senate George McGovern and Mark Hatfield reintroduced a revised Disengagement Act.[32] In an attempt to avoid the mistakes of Cambodia, Nixon and Kissinger this time tried to involve Rogers and Laird in the decision making—at least to a point. When State and Defense balked, particularly after Rogers discovered that the enemy had acquired the military plans for Lam Son 719 and were prepared to counter the operation by amassing soldiers in the area, Nixon paid them no heed: he went ahead and ordered the attacks to begin February 7. The South Vietnamese, with American air support, were able to inflict major damage on the numerically superior North Vietnamese army, but in the end, Lam Son 719 went down as a defeat for the RVN. Cameras caught the ARVN's hasty retreat on film and tape, broadcasting images of the operation's failure around the world.[33]

Nixon and Kissinger had taken the gamble on South Vietnam's behalf and lost. They also suffered major setbacks at home in the aftermath of the Laos invasion, as major events on the domestic front in the spring of 1971 contributed to the pressure on the administration to end the war. Earlier in the year the Vietnam Veterans Against the War (VVAW) launched its "Winter Soldier" investigation into U.S. war crimes, with members recounting atrocities they witnessed in Vietnam. In late March, one of those responsible for these crimes was ostensibly brought to justice when Lieutenant William Calley was found guilty for the murder of twenty-two Vietnamese civilians in Son My village on March 16, 1968. However, on April 2, 1971, the president intervened by freeing Calley from jail, placing him under house arrest, and initiating the process for reviewing the verdict. Nixon's intervention in the Calley case, along with his April 7 announcement of additional troop withdrawals, failed to defuse the veterans' anger at the administration's perpetuation of the war. Throughout the spring, the veterans staged effective demonstrations in the nation's capital. The most poignant act occurred on April 23 when seven hundred VVAW members laid down their medals and ribbons on the steps of the Capitol Building.

Nixon's domestic woes did not abate in the late spring and summer. Following the veterans' demonstrations, hundreds of thousands of protesters gathered in Washington to shut down the government. Although Nixon left town during the "May Day" actions, he went on the offensive against the antiwar Left by ordering the arrests of thousands of demonstrators on questionable grounds. Then, on June 13, another bombshell: the *New York Times* began printing the first of a series of articles based on top-secret documents given to the paper by a former Pentagon official and consultant to Kissinger, Daniel Ellsberg. These documents, which became known as the Pentagon Papers, were part of a multi-volume study of U.S. decision making regarding Vietnam from 1945 to 1967 commissioned by former Secretary of Defense Robert S. McNamara. Nixon's policies were not part of the study, and several advisers urged him to refrain from intervening. Nixon had other ideas; with Kissinger's enthusiastic support he took the offensive against his domestic foes. He ordered an injunction against the *New York Times*, obtained an indictment against Ellsberg, and formed a group known as the "Plumbers" to break into the offices of real and potential domestic adversaries. The *Washington Post* and various other newspapers continued to print the Pentagon Papers, and all charges against Ellsberg would eventually be dropped when the Plumbers' illegal activities were exposed in the ensuing Watergate scandal.

Nixon continued to play for time. Positive developments in Soviet-American détente and Sino-American rapprochement in the spring of 1971 convinced him that he could bring Sino-Soviet pressure to bear on the North Vietnamese. Accordingly, Nixon sent Kissinger to Paris with the most sweeping peace proposal to date, the implicit instruction that if Hanoi rejected the U.S. offer, Nixon would escalate the military and diplomatic pressure. On May 31, Kissinger presented Hanoi with a seven-point proposal that essentially amounted to unilateral American withdrawal.[34] The North Vietnamese countered with a nine-point plan that set a withdrawal date for U.S. and allied troops for December 31, 1971, as well as the ousting of Thieu, in return for Hanoi's agreement to American provisions.[35] Before the next secret meeting, scheduled for July 12, Nixon gained an opportunity to use Chinese pressure on the North Vietnamese when Kissinger met with Zhou Enlai in Beijing. In addition to discussing Nixon's visit to China set for early 1972, the national security advisor linked Chinese help to secure an honorable American withdrawal from Vietnam to the Taiwan issue and PRC representation in the United Nations.[36] Believing he had set into motion the diplomatic isolation of Hanoi, Nixon steadfastly rejected North Vietnamese demands for Thieu's ouster throughout the rest of the secret meetings in the summer of 1971. With the South Vietnamese presidential elections in early October, Nixon could not risk losing his staunch ally in Saigon. Sure enough, Thieu prevailed in the election, drawing a suspiciously high 94.3% of the vote.[37] In the weeks thereafter the Paris talks, both public and private, stalled.

Nixon and Kissinger intended 1972 to be the year of reckoning in the Vietnam War. In the previous three years, they had neutralized opponents at home and allies abroad in order to wage war against the communists in the manner they saw fit. Victory had not come, but Nixon intended to use his two major weapons—great-power diplomacy and military escalation—yet again in 1972. Although Kissinger had aimed for the shrewder goal of extricating the United States before the end of the year and preventing the collapse of South Vietnam for a "decent interval" of a few years, Nixon hoped he could force the North and South Vietnamese to accept a settlement dictated by the United States as well as retain the option of reentering the war at a later point when America's sham peace failed.[38]

Yet he harbored doubts and insecurities about Vietnam and how the war would affect his chances for reelection. Accordingly, he opened the year with a strong public relations campaign. In early January, the president scored favorable points with the American public by announcing that he would withdraw 70,000 additional troops by May 1. Then, at the end of the month Nixon and Kissinger sought to place Hanoi on the defensive by making public the secret negotiations and announcing a new peace plan in order to show the American people that Hanoi was to blame for the breakdown of the Paris talks.[39] Finally, in late February Nixon undertook his historic trip to China where he reiterated Kissinger's request for Chinese aid in ending America's war in Vietnam by pressuring their allies in Hanoi to settle. Although the Chinese made no promises and little mention of Vietnam was made in the Shanghai Communiqué, according to Kissinger the Chinese summit succeeded in furthering the diplomatic isolation of Hanoi.[40]

Powerless to stop the Beijing summit, North Vietnamese leaders postponed their upcoming meeting with the Americans from March 20 to April 15, citing U.S. air attacks on North Vietnam in February. The real reason for Hanoi's postponement became clear on March 30, 1972, when an estimated 15,000 PAVN troops, armed with Soviet tanks and weaponry, crossed the DMZ in a large-scale offensive that swept along Route 9.[41] The official Vietnamese statement at the time (and after) claimed that the offensive was launched strictly to alter the military balance of power on the ground. However, the timing of the Spring Offensive reveals that Hanoi also intended to send a powerful message to its allies: the Vietnamese war would not be derailed by big power summits.

Although détente would be put at risk, Nixon ordered the bombing of the Hanoi area and the mining of the North Vietnamese ports in early May as retaliation against the communist offensive. The resultant "Linebacker I" campaign not only sent a message to the North Vietnamese to cease its attacks on South Vietnam but also to the Soviets and Chinese that they needed to place more pressure on the North Vietnamese to return to the negotiating table rather than supply Hanoi with more tanks.[42] Soviet leaders were divided on whether or not to hold the summit, but ultimately Brezhnev chose bettering Soviet-American relations over demonstrating ideological solidarity. In the end, both the Chinese and Soviets issued only diplomatic protests to the bombing of their ships as a result of Linebacker I, and indicated that American attacks should not derail rapprochement or détente.[43] Moreover, Nixon appeared victorious on the domestic front as well. Even without the phony letters of support sent by the Committee for the Reelection of the President (CREEP), public response to Nixon's firm military response was positive. In July, when the Democratic Party selected an outspoken dove, Senator George McGovern, as its presidential nominee, Nixon's second term seemed all but assured. Linebacker I confirmed to Nixon that he could reap great rewards by escalating the war.

Furthermore, Nixon's plan to bring Sino-Soviet pressure to bear on the North Vietnamese also seemed to be working. Soviet President Nikolai Podgorny traveled to Hanoi in order to convince the North Vietnamese to return to the negotiating table, while on July 12 Zhou Enlai engaged Le Duc Tho in a long discussion aimed at persuading Hanoi to drop its insistence on Thieu's ouster.[44] Although Zhou Enlai used flattery to try to soften Hanoi's position, Le Duc Tho rejected the Chinese leader's attempts to make Thieu more palatable as only one of three representatives in a coalition government.[45] As the negotiating record reveals, however, throughout the summer and fall of 1972 Le Duc Tho was willing not only to accept Thieu's participation in a coalition government alongside the PRG and third parties, but also, after Kissinger resisted the idea of a coalition government, a looser body called the Committee of National Reconciliation.

As the Chinese and Soviets pressured the North Vietnamese to do more negotiating and less fighting, Kissinger hoped to convince Nixon to aim for a settlement before the U.S. presidential election. On the eve of the vote, Kissinger, who wanted to secure his place in the administration and in history, flew to Saigon from Paris with a draft in hand in order to seal the deal. But Thieu used the remaining weapon in his arsenal: his refusal to go along with U.S. demands. When Thieu balked, Nixon, feeling threatened by the media attention lavished on his national security advisor, took delight in Kissinger's failure. Refusing to proceed with the agreement without Thieu's approval, Nixon ordered Kissinger to break off talks at Paris.

On November 7, Nixon received the affirmation he had sought for so long: he won re-election by an overwhelming majority of the vote. On Vietnam, the invigorated president turned to bullying his way to peace by threatening the North Vietnamese with "disastrous consequences" if they did not negotiate and warning the South Vietnamese they would strike a unilateral deal with Hanoi if they did not cooperate.[46] Neither Vietnamese party capitulated.[47] Nixon turned up the heat on Hanoi, launching "Linebacker II," also known as the Christmas Bombings, on December 18. During the twelve-day campaign, 3,420 sorties carpet-bombed mainly the Hanoi-Hai Phong area, inflicting severe damage to North Vietnam physically and psychologically. Unlike the public support for Linebacker I, however, Nixon suffered severe domestic criticism for Linebacker II. Nixon's "madman" bombing campaign tested the American public who had voted Nixon into office to end the war in 1968 and voted for him again in 1972 because peace seemed imminent. Internationally, too, many observers were highly critical of the bombing campaign.

On January 8, 1973, talks between Le Duc Tho and Kissinger resumed. Although the Chinese and Soviets issued strong condemnations of the fiercest bombing campaign in the Second Indochina War, both communist powers did Nixon's bidding by exerting pressure on Hanoi to settle.[48] Encouraged by Nixon's bombing, Thieu continued to hold out for PAVN withdrawals and other significant changes to the agreement but, upon the very real threat of immediate cutoff of U.S. aid, the South Vietnamese president finally relented on January 21. On January 23, 1973, Nixon and Kissinger's Vietnam War ended with the signing of the Paris Agreement on Ending the War and Restoring the Peace in Vietnam.

After waging war on multiple fronts not only against communist enemies but also against domestic opponents and foreign allies, Richard Nixon and Henry Kissinger succeeded in negotiating a settlement that contained neither peace nor honor. By consolidating decision making in their hands, the two men effectively muted any dissension to their policies but also silenced voices of reason and restraint. Nevertheless, throughout the period 1969–1973 Nixon and Kissinger struggled with the conflicting forces and contradictory interests at work in their Vietnam policy. To appease public opinion, they made dramatic gestures to push forward de-Americanization and Vietnamization, in effect sending Hanoi the message that it could hold out at Paris and telling Saigon that it could no longer rely on the United States. At the same time, they made good on threats to Hanoi by exerting maximum military pressure that increased public criticism and congressional opposition to their policies. By the war's end, Nixon and Kissinger were forced to rely on their only remaining weapon, triangular diplomacy; and although it succeeded in gaining North Vietnam's acquiescence at Paris, it also alienated the South Vietnamese in the process. After more than four years of battling internal and external foes, Nixon and Kissinger had lost not only the war but also the peace.

Notes

1. George C. Herring, *America's Longest War*, 4th ed. (New York, 2002), 271–276.
2. Larry Berman, *No Peace, No Honor: Nixon, Kissinger, and Betrayal in Vietnam* (New York, 2001), 45.
3. Jeffrey Kimball, *Nixon's Vietnam War* (Lawrence, Kans., 1998), 75.
4. Richard Nixon, *No More Vietnams* (New York, 1985), 103–107.
5. Kimball, *Nixon's Vietnam War*, 73.
6. See Berman, *No Peace, No Honor*, 35.
7. See the diary entry for October 8, 1969 in H. R. Haldeman, *The Haldeman Diaries: Inside the Nixon White House* (New York, 1994), 96.
8. "Memorandum for the Record," Box 136, Viet-nam Country Files, Vietnam, Vol. 1 through 3/19/69, National Security Council Files (NSCF), NPM.
9. Richard Nixon, *RN: The Memoirs of Richard Nixon* (New York, 1978), 381; Henry Kissinger, *White House Years* (Boston, 1979), 246–247.
10. Kimball, *Nixon's Vietnam War*, 135.
11. "Memorandum From the President's Assistant for National Security Affairs (Kissinger) to President Nixon," April 15, 1969, Box 489, President's Trip Files, Dobrynin/HAK, 1969 [part 2], NSC Files, NPM.
12. Kimball, *Nixon's Vietnam War*, 142.
13. See "May 8, 1969 entry," in Bộ Ngoại Giao [Ministry of Foreign Affairs], *Đại sự ký chuyên đề: Đấu tranh ngoại giao và vận động quốc tế trong*

những chiến chông Mỹ cứu nước (hereafter *Đâu tranh ngoại giao*) [Important Account of a Special Subject: The Diplomatic Struggle and International Activities of the Anti-American Resistance and National Salvation] (Hanoi: Internal Foreign Ministry Publication, 1987), 222–223.

14. Bui Diem, *In the Jaws of History* (Bloomington, Ind., 1987), 258.
15. Nguyen Tien Hung and Jerrold Schecter, *The Palace File* (New York, 1986), 37.
16. Quoted in Berman, *No Peace, No Honor*, 39.
17. Nguyen Tien Hung, *Palace File*, 40.
18. See Attachment: August 25, 1969, Ho Chi Minh to Nixon, in "Memorandum From the President's Assistant for National Security Affairs to President Nixon," Box 106, Country Files, Vietnam, "S" Mister, Vol. I., Kissinger Office Files, NSCF, NPM.
19. Kissinger to Nixon, September 5, 1969, Box 139, Vietnam Country Files, Vietnam, Vol. X, September 1969, NSCF, NPM.
20. Kimball, *Nixon's Vietnam War*, 161–163.
21. See *FRUS, 1969–1976*, vol. VI: 410–411.
22. Kimball, *Nixon's Vietnam War*, 164.
23. Thompson, using his experience gained in the British campaign in Malaya, convinced Nixon that it would take two years before Vietnamization would succeed. See Robert Thompson, *Peace is Not at Hand* (London, 1974), 71–72.
24. See Berman, *No Peace, No Honor*, 68.
25. Kimball, *Nixon's Vietnam War*, 194.
26. Lưu Văn Lợi, *Năm mươi năm ngoại giao Việt Nam, 1945–1990, Tập 1: 1945–1975* [Fifty Years of Vietnamese Diplomacy, 1945–1990, Vol. 1: 1945–1975] (Hanoi, 1996), 292.
27. See Berman, *No Peace, No Honor*, 75–76.
28. Herring, *America's Longest War*, 295.
29. Kissinger to Nixon, September 22, 1970, sub: A Longer Look at the New Communist Proposal on Vietnam, Folder: Paris Talks, July–Sept. 1970, Box 3, WH/NSC: POW/MIA, NPM. See also, Kissinger, *White House Years*, 972.
30. For Vietnamization, see Lewis Sorley, *A Better War: The Unexamined Victories and Final Tragedy of America's Last Years in Vietnam* (New York, 1999), 214–215.
31. See Nguyen Tien Hung, *Palace File*, 42.
32. Kimball, *Nixon's Vietnam War*, 243.
33. See Sorley, *A Better War*, 237–263.
34. Kissinger, *White House Years*, 1018.
35. See June 26, 1971 entry in BNG, *Đâu tranh ngoại giao*, 287.
36. See Qiang Zhai, *China and the Vietnam Wars, 1950–1975* (Chapel Hill, N.C., 2000), 196.
37. Bui Diem, *In the Jaws of History*, 292–294. Subsequent investigations revealed that Thieu's subordinates had tampered with South Vietnam's electoral laws.

38. Berman, *No Peace, No Honor*, 255.

39. See Pierre Asselin, *A Bitter Peace: Washington, Hanoi, and the Making of the Paris Agreement* (Chapel Hill, N.C., 2002), 32–33.

40. Kissinger, *White House Years*, 1087.

41. See Bộ Quốc Phòng, Viên Lịch Sử' Quân Sử' Việt Nam [Ministry of Defense, Institute of Military History] (BQPVLSQSVN), *Các chiến dịch trong kháng chiến chống Mỹ, củu nuớc* [The Offensives in the Anti-American Struggle for National Salvation], 1954–1975 (Hanoi, 2003), 274–287.

42. See Kimball, *Nixon's Vietnam War*, 304.

43. To add insult to injury, Beijing compounded Hanoi's logistical problems by refusing to redirect Soviet aid through PRC territory given the dangers of North Vietnamese ports. See Telegramme l'arrivee, diffusion reservee: "Visit de M. Katuchev a Hà Nội," 5/1972, Asie Oceanie, Cambodge-Lao-Vietnam, Nord Vietnam, Carton 69, Archives du ministere des affaires etrangeres, Paris.

44. Ilya Gaiduk, *The Soviet Union and the Vietnam War* (Chicago, 1996), 240–241.

45. See "Buổi tiếp d/c Lê Đú'c Thọ tại Bắc Kinh, 12–07–1972 [Lê Đú'c Thọ's meeting in Beijing, July 12, 1972], Hồ so' biên bản tiếp xúc của phòng LT, Văn phòng Trung u'o'ng Đảng [Minutes of Meetings File in the Archives, Office of the Central Committee of the Party] reprinted in BNG, *Đấu tranh ngoại giao*, 328 and for the translated version, see meeting between Zhou Enlai and Lê Đú'c Thọ on July 12, 1972 in Odd Arne Westad, et al, ed., "77 Conversations Between Chinese and Foreign Leaders on the Wars in Indochina, 1964–1977," Cold War International History Project, Working Paper No. 22, 182–184.

46. Berman, *No Peace, No Honor*, 180–197. On how the PRG also stalled the peace in October 1972, see Robert K. Brigham, *Guerrilla Diplomacy: The NLF's Foreign Relations the Viet Nam War* (Ithaca, 1998), 108–110.

47. For the South Vietnamese side, see Nguyễn Phú Đú'c, *The Viet-Nam Peace Negotiations: Saigon's Side of the Story* (Christiansburg, Va., 2005), 340–366. For the North Vietnamese side, see Lu'u Văn Lò'i and Nguyễn Vũ Anh, *Các thu'o'ng lu'ợng Lê Đú'c Thọ-Kissinger tại Paris* [Le Duc Tho-Kissinger Negotiations in Paris], 2nd ed. (Hanoi, 2002), 543–583.

48. See Zhai, *China and the Vietnam Wars*, 206; Gaiduk, *Soviet Union and the Vietnam War*, 244.

10

The End of the Vietnam War, 1973–1976

Robert D. Schulzinger

In the four years from the signing of the Paris Peace Accords on Vietnam in January 1973 until the end of the administration of President Gerald Ford in January 1977, the Vietnam War ended and reflections on its meaning began. In early 1973, hopes were high that the cease-fire signed at Paris would lead to a genuine peace. Yet fighting among the forces of the government of the Republic of (South) Vietnam (RVN), the Democratic Republic of (North) Vietnam (DRV) and the National Liberation Front (NLF) never stopped. In 1975 the war in Vietnam ended in total defeat for America's ally, South Vietnam.

The proper lessons to be learned from the end of the Vietnam War remained an area of contention for decades after 1975. For Richard Nixon and Henry Kissinger, the defeat of the RVN represented a failure of the United States to honor its commitments and a loss of U.S. credibility with both allies and adversaries. They wrote extensively in the years following 1975 that the end of the war was a "lost victory" for the United States. They claimed that the Paris Peace Accords had created conditions for the RVN to succeed, but that the Democratic-controlled Congress snatched defeat from victory when it denied military aid to the RVN in 1974 and 1975. Nixon's and Kissinger's view that the end in Vietnam was an American betrayal was not widely shared by the public at the time. In 1975 and 1976, Americans believed that the South Vietnamese had lost the war through their own incompetence. Nixon's and Kissinger's critics contended that their personal reputations for having crafted a flawed peace in 1973 were at stake, not the credibility of the United States.[1]

Nixon and Kissinger expected the Paris agreement of January 1973 to give South Vietnam an opportunity for, but not a guarantee, of survival. They assured President Nguyen Van Thieu that the United States would continue military assistance. After Ford became president in August 1974, the tide of battle in Vietnam shifted ever more in favor of the more highly motivated forces of the North and the NLF. Congress rejected Ford's and Kissinger's appeals to provide additional military aid to South Vietnam in 1975, and the revolutionaries defeated the South in April 1975. Kissinger argued that American credibility had been damaged by the defeat of South Vietnam, and the United States tried to isolate North Vietnam, now renamed the Socialist Republic of Vietnam (SRV).

When Nixon's second term began in January 1973, negotiations between the United States and the DRV had borne fruit in a wide-ranging agreement ending the war. In the agreements signed on January 27, 1973, the United States, the DRV, the RVN, and the NLF agreed on a cease-fire in place, the return of prisoners of war, the removal of U.S. military forces from Vietnam, recognition of the government of President Nguyen Van Thieu of the RVN, recognition of the Provisional Revolutionary Government (PRG) of the NLF as a legitimate political organization, and a process of national reconciliation between the government of South Vietnam and the PRG.

The Paris agreements of 1973 produced mixed reactions among the parties fighting in Vietnam. Americans considered the agreements to be the end of a long and costly war, and the public applauded Nixon and Kissinger for their diplomatic skills. For the North Vietnamese and the Communist revolutionaries of the South, the agreements fulfilled their hopes that the United States would remove its military forces from Vietnam and stop fighting. Leaders in Hanoi and the NLF believed that the cease-fire represented a temporary suspension of a political and military campaign to unify Vietnam under communist rule. South Vietnam greeted the accord with trepidation. According to U.S. Ambassador Ellsworth Bunker, President Thieu "appeared resigned" to accepting the agreement. Thieu wrote Nixon that he agreed to sign only because of the American position "that U.S. aid will be cut off if I do not join you."[2] Thieu resented that the agreements permitted more than 200,000 troops of the People's Army of Vietnam to remain in the South, while at the same time required the withdrawal of American forces. Though Thieu welcomed the provisions of the agreement recognizing his legitimate authority, he feared that the South could not defend itself against the North and the NLF if the war resumed.

In retrospect, the Paris Peace Accords have been seen as deeply flawed. Political scientist Larry Berman has characterized the Accord as a "Jabberwocky agreement," a confusing, almost nonsensical document. Berman concluded that the agreement greatly resembled proposals put forth by the NLF in 1969 and that "many tens of thousands died [between 1969 and 1972] for very little."[3] Historian Jeffrey Kimball has written that the Paris Agreement was designed to save face for the United States. It created a "decent ... interval to permit Nixon and Kissinger to claim that they had provided Thieu with a chance to survive."[4]

The cease-fire promised by the Paris agreements barely took hold in 1973 before the war resumed. There were occasional scenes of reconciliation in South Vietnam, and the Army of the Republic of Vietnam (ARVN) allowed NLF fighters to retrieve their dead for a dignified burial. But such events were rare. The cease-fire pertained only to the United States, and the other parties to the conflict continued to fight. A U.S. pacification report in April stated that the "ceasefire appeared to have initiated a new war, more intense and more brutal than the last."[5]

American attention was focused on events elsewhere in the world or on the growing Watergate scandal at home. The public expressed concern only for the return of prisoners of war, promised on March 26, 1973, the deadline stipulated for their repatriation. The vast majority of POWs were held by the RVN and the PRG. Saigon returned 26,880 POWs to the communists; the PRG claimed that an additional 15,000 remained. The communists turned over 5,336 ARVN soldiers to the RVN out of a total of 31,981 listed as missing. Americans paid far greater attention to their own list of 591 POWs, all of whom came back within the sixty-day time frame. American service personnel serving in South Vietnam also left the country, and by the end of March only 159 marines remained to guard the U.S. embassy in Saigon. Across South Vietnam the departure of the Americans left many Vietnamese without work and fearful for their future. The first consequence of the departure of the Americans was a sharp recession. The bars serving soldiers, the markets for cameras, watches, calculators, television sets, and motor scooters had lost their best customers and had to depend on ARVN troops to survive.

The South Vietnamese army numbered over one million men in 1973. Nixon promised Thieu that the United States would supply the most modern American military equipment to the ARVN after the cease-fire, but the South Vietnamese president did not trust the American assurances. He doubted that either Nixon or the American public cared that much about the future of South Vietnam now that the U.S. POWs had returned home from captivity. The ARVN had learned to fight a high-tech war from their American mentors, who were always ready to sacrifice equipment but more careful of the lives of their soldiers. No one knew how the ARVN would perform in battle if they feared for the sources of supply.

Southern anxiety about the government's capacity to survive a resumption of the war increased in the wake of a visit by Kissinger to Hanoi in February. Kissinger wanted to establish what he called a rough "equilibrium" among the parties, in which all sides felt they had a stake in preserving the Paris Accords. Kissinger assured his negotiating partner Le Duc Tho and Prime Minister Pham Van Dong that "one day the DRV could see in the United States a country that was interested in its development." He gave details about the amount of reconstruction aid the North could expect. The West German government promised a modest $30 million to all the countries of Indochina (Vietnam, Laos, and Cambodia) once a "real peace" had been achieved. Kissinger also spoke about an offer from Nixon of $3.25 billion in reconstruction aid for the DRV over the next decade. Pham Van Dong considered this to be "an obligation of the U.S. in view of the destruction caused to the country." Nixon did qualify the offer by noting that Congress actually appropriated money, and Kissinger told the North Vietnamese that there was "enormous domestic opposition" to providing aid to the DRV. "You have to let us manage this opposition," he told the North Vietnamese. Kissinger also told Dong and Tho that it was "totally useless" for them to bring up America's moral obligation to provide the aid, because "until we get the money" from Congress "there is nothing we can do about it." Dong had little sympathy for the Nixon administration's purported difficulties with lawmakers, because, he reminded Kissinger, "when the war was going on, then the appropriation was so easy."[6]

Back home in Washington, there appeared to be some support for aid to the North. Arkansas Senator J. William Fulbright, a Democrat and chair of the Foreign Relations Committee, said that "Vietnam is behind us," so Congress would be likely to fund the aid. Secretary of State William Rogers also noted that "I don't think we are going to have any problems" going forward with "the business of peace and reconstruction" in North Vietnam. But these views proved wildly optimistic after congressional opinion turned sharply against North Vietnam when returning POWs recounted horror stories of mistreatment. The Senate passed a resolution on April 5 requiring congressional approval of economic assistance to the DRV.[7]

For his part, South Vietnam's President Thieu remained deeply suspicious that the United States would make good on Nixon's promise of military assistance to the RVN. He met with Nixon in San Clemente in early April. Although Nixon pledged "the U.S. will meet all contingencies in case the agreement is grossly violated," he was entangled by Watergate and found it hard to focus on Vietnam.[8] Admiral Thomas Moorer, chairman of the Joint Chiefs of Staff, noted that "Watergate was bubbling like mad" when Thieu met with Nixon. Nixon told Thieu that the United States would help the RVN modernize the ARVN "at the one billion dollar level" and he spoke of "economic aid in the $800 million range." But Kissinger thought these numbers were fanciful since congressional support for any aid for South Vietnam "was eroding fast."[9]

When Thieu returned to Saigon, he ignored Nixon's admonition to try harder to make the cease-fire with the PRG work. Instead, he ordered the ARVN and the air force (VNAF) onto the offensive for the remainder of 1973 to weaken the PRG and convince the United States that his military was worth supporting. The North and the PRG responded with their own attacks designed to keep open their supply lines to their forces in the South. The communists had the better of the fight. In mid-October, communist forces captured a South Vietnamese militia outpost between Hue and Da Nang. At the end of October there was intense fighting in the far south to gain control of the "rice road" between the Mekong Delta and Saigon. Thieu ordered his forces to "consider every grain of rice as a bullet."[10] Also in October Kissinger and Tho were awarded the Nobel Peace Prize for negotiating the Paris agreements. Kissinger gratefully acknowledged his share of the prize, and the award proved to be highly popular in the United States. On the other hand, Le Duc Tho refused to accept the prize because "peace has not really been established in South Vietnam."[11]

Public attention in the United States subsequently quickly shifted away from Vietnam. The October War between Israel and Egypt and Syria threatened to involve the United States and the Soviet Union in the fighting. The war also sparked a spike in the price of petroleum which initiated a worldwide economic recession. South Vietnam's economy was especially hard hit by the 338 percent rise in the price of gasoline. Per capita income dropped 25 percent in 1973. With the American military gone, spending by the remaining U.S. contractors shrank from $400 million in 1971 to $100 million in 1973. Unemployment in the RVN rose to 27 percent and inflation hit 65 percent in 1973. ARVN soldiers were especially hard hit, and their month's pay was barely enough to support them and their families for a week. The ARVN could not maintain its authorized strength of 1.1 million. It needed between 200,000 and 240,000 replacements each year, but the draft provided only 100,000 to 150,000. Annual desertion rates mounted to between 15,000 and 20,000 by the end of 1973.[12]

Watergate approached a crescendo in October, when Nixon refused to turn over tape recordings of his conversations about the Watergate cover-up to Archibald Cox, the special prosecutor, and fired him. The House of Representatives commenced impeachment proceedings. Ambassador Graham Martin feared that American preoccupation with the Middle East war and Nixon's Watergate troubles would make Washington neglect Indochina. He desperately cabled Kissinger that "time is crucial here" and that the RVN needed the $1 billion in military assistance.[13]

In early 1974, Nixon asked Congress for $850 million in combined military and economic assistance. Congress, reflecting the public's desire to stay out of fighting in Vietnam, did not act on the request. Kissinger did not press Congress hard for the money, hoping to avoid further antagonizing the DRV. One of Kissinger's aides told Martin that "Henry's attitude is that he wants to maintain a polite tone even when Ducky [Kissinger's nickname for Le Duc Tho] is vituperative."[14] At the same time, however, Kissinger told Congress that the RVN's military was powerful enough that defeating it "was not an easy assignment for Hanoi." Other administration officials were even more upbeat. Secretary of Defense James Schlesinger said that the ARVN was giving a "splendid" account of itself in battles with the PAVN and NLF.[15]

The military situation on the ground in Vietnam was much bleaker for the South than optimists in Washington projected. The PAVN went on the attack against the ARVN, which lost a large amount of ammunition. Casualties were high on both sides, but the North was able to replace men at a faster rate than was the South. The defense attaché in Saigon reported that by September the North had ten divisions numbering about 200,000 men in the South.[16]

Congressional "doves" opposed Nixon's request for $850 million as an effort at throwing good money after bad and prolonging a war that had gone on too long. Senator Hubert Humphrey—who had campaigned against Nixon for the presidency in 1968—said that additional money for South Vietnam "might buy time, but it won't buy peace." Massachusetts Senator Edward Kennedy, one of the most outspoken congressional opponents of Nixon's war policies and a prospective Democratic candidate for president in 1976, said the time had come to put a stop to the United States' "endless support for an endless war."[17]

Frustrated by such opposition, Martin returned home in the summer of 1974 to press Congress to approve a reduced aid package of $750 million to the RVN. He presented a relentlessly optimistic picture of the military, political, and economic prospects of South Vietnam. He said that the recession had hit the South Vietnamese hard, but their economy was not on the verge of collapse. "Politically," he told a congressional committee, "the South Vietnamese government is stronger than ever." If the United States would provide the military aid, then the RVN could resume the offensive. Members of Congress remained highly skeptical about the South Vietnamese government's effectiveness or survivability. When a Defense Department official repeated Martin's glowing assessment, Representative Patricia Schroeder, a Colorado Democrat, mocked him: "I have a feeling you believe in the tooth fairy."[18]

Martin's relentless optimism may not have swayed Congress, but it emboldened South Vietnamese officials not to negotiate with the DRV or the PRG. One member of Congress told the South Vietnamese that "we are cutting you down to $700 million which is enough for you to defend yourself and sit down and work out a political settlement." The South Vietnamese preferred to listen to Martin. One of Thieu's principal aides said that "if the U.S. ambassador in Saigon showed no visible sign of concern the situation could not be hopeless."[19]

In the midst of the congressional debate over aid to Vietnam, the Watergate scandal reached its climax with Nixon's resignation from the presidency on August 9. Thieu was badly shaken by Nixon's departure and retreated to his office where his aide Nguyen Tien Hung recalled him "closing his eyes, biting his lips, and grinding his right fist into the palm of his left hand."[20] Publicly Thieu expressed confidence that "the government and people of the United States of America will continue the policy which has been pursued by five U.S. presidents ... and maintain their cooperation with the government and people of Vietnam.[21] President Ford reassured Thieu that the commitments Nixon had made to aid South Vietnam were "still valid and will be fully honored" by the new administration.[22]

Each side in Vietnam perceived Nixon's resignation through the lens of its own interests. Thieu wanted Ford to continue Nixon's policies. He cabled the American president that South Vietnam had worked to implant the Paris agreements, and the "only obstacle to peace and political solutions in Vietnam resides in the stubborn and bellicose attitude of the North Vietnamese."[23] The Communist side saw Nixon's fall as just retribution visited on a hated adversary. Liberation Radio, the voice of the PRG, claimed that Nixon's downfall was the price he paid for his "perfidious and cruel" policies in Vietnam. The PRG said he had been "unmasked ... as a war criminal in Vietnam and as a deceitful, double dealing, and crafty swindler."[24]

At the end of August, Congress approved $700 million in military and economic aid. That represented a substantial reduction from the $1 billion Martin thought necessary, but it was much more than the $400 million some war opponents thought was all that the U.S. should supply. The *Washington Post* captured congressional ambivalence toward continued assistance to South Vietnam when it editorialized that the aid honored "the principle of American steadfastness" even though the government of South Vietnam "is far from a model regime."[25]

Ford's initial policies toward Vietnam stressed continuity with Nixon and reliance on Kissinger's advice. On September 12, the president and the secretary of state met with the bipartisan congressional leadership to stress the need for an additional $500 million in military and economic aid for South Vietnam in 1975. He told the lawmakers that "we must assure that what we are trying to do in Vietnam is not destroyed through a lack of funding or that our hands are tied in using those funds." Kissinger stressed that what mattered in Vietnam had less to do with conditions in that country than with the ability of the United States to conduct an effective foreign policy elsewhere. "If we bug out of Vietnam, it would affect our whole foreign policy and the reliance that countries can place on us."[26] In October, Ford wrote Thieu that the United States "will continue to make every effort to provide you the assistance you need."[27]

But in the fall of 1974, Ford's standing deteriorated with the public and Congress. He pardoned Richard Nixon of all Watergate-related crimes, which proved to be highly unpopular. Democratic candidates running in the congressional elections opposed the president's request for the $500 million supplemental funds. The Democrats increased their majorities with a gain of 47 seats in the House and two in the Senate. Ford faced an extremely hostile Congress opposed to a renewed American involvement in Vietnam in 1975. His relationship with Henry Kissinger changed as well. Ford and his personal staff increasingly perceived Kissinger as a political liability who advocated deeper involvement in Vietnam to vindicate his diplomacy leading to the Paris Accords.

President Thieu's position also deteriorated at the end of 1974. Prime Minister Tran Thien Khiem explained to visiting Deputy Secretary of Defense William P. Clements Jr. that congressional refusal to provide all the aid Ford requested had wrecked morale. "The people recognize," he complained, "that the government of Vietnam could no longer count on U.S. air support." Anticorruption demonstrations erupted across cities of South Vietnam. Marchers chanted "we want a president who serves the people, not a president who steals from the people!" Thieu responded with a mixture of concessions and repression. He closed antigovernment newspapers and banned demonstrations, but he also dismissed hundreds of ARVN officer accused of incompetence or corruption, including the commanders of three of the four military corps in charge of defending the country.[28]

Thieu's domestic difficulties and the prospect of declining American support emboldened the revolutionaries in both South and North Vietnam in late 1974. The PRG announced that it would no longer negotiate with the government of the RVN "as long as Nguyen Van Thieu and his gang remain in power in Saigon." Commanders of the PAVN expanded their war aims in the South from harassing the ARVN to "liberate the people and hold the land." The PAVN pressed with attacks in the coastal plain south of Da Nang and in the Mekong Delta.[29]

The North began its offensive with a moderate-scale attack across the Cambodian border on December 7. Fighting raged for a month, and at midnight on January 6 the PAVN struck the RVN rangers defending Phuc Binh, the capital of the province of Phuc Long, eighty miles northwest of Saigon. The fighting routed the ARVN, nearly all of whose 5,400 soldiers were killed or captured. Some ARVN forces fought well, but other units threw down their arms and fled. Many ARVN soldiers were killed by bombs dropped from VNAF planes flying at high altitude to avoid communist antiaircraft fire. Crucially, the United States did not send its own air force bombers into action to beat back the communist assault. The communist capture of Phuc Binh was the first loss of a provincial capital by South Vietnam since the short-lived communist takeover of the northern city of Quang Tri during the spring offensive of 1972.[30]

Le Duan, the first secretary of the North's Vietnam Workers (Communist) Party, was jubilant at hearing the news of the victory in Phuoc Long. He proclaimed that "never have we had military and political conditions so perfect or a strategic advantage so great as we have now."[31] On January 9 the military command in Hanoi singed off on a plan for a final offensive in the South, expected to last at least a year, to defeat the Thieu government and install the PRG in power.

Three days after North's success at Phuc Binh, Communist forces commenced a major offensive against ARVN positions and cities on the coastal plain three hundred miles north of Saigon. Saigon officials did not expect the United States to return air or ground forces to the fighting, but they expressed a hope that "the fall of Phuc Binh could prove a blessing in disguise if it could strength President Ford's hand in delaying with a hostile Congress.[32]

In late January, Ford asked Congress to provide an additional $300 million in military assistance to the RVN, but he stressed that the United States was not going to be actively involved in the fighting again. Ford's aides argued that the assistance would bolster U.S. credibility with allies far removed from Southeast Asia. One of Ford's senior political advisers told cabinet secretaries that "if our adversaries see our constancy and determination lacking here, they may be tempted to test our will in other areas of the world."[33] Kissinger told the cabinet members that "We are asking only for enough to make it. We must have enough!" Once more he indicated that the aid request mattered more for American credibility elsewhere in the world than it would determine to outcome in Vietnam. "It will hurt our international negotiating power if we do not stand in Vietnam."[34] He said that the aid would give Saigon a two-to-three-year window to survive and then be able to stand on its own. Given the nearly twenty-year experience of U.S. military assistance to the RVN and its continuing weakness, it is hard to see that its fighting capacity would improve soon. As the historian Jussi Hanhimäki observes, "How could one possibly make the case in early 1975 that if the United States only gave aid for another two-year period, South Vietnam would finally be viable on its own?"[35]

Many members of Congress simply did not believe the future of Vietnam was very important to the United States in 1975, and the war was now the South's, not America's, to win or to lose. Longtime opponents of the U.S. war in Vietnam countered the administration's arguments that the South was unwilling to use its stockpiles of armor and ammunition, significantly larger than those of the North, because it feared that the United States would not make up any losses. California Democratic Representative Robert Leggett believed that "by continuing to shower money on the war making machines we have created in Indochina, we encourage a style of warfare that is expensive, but not very creative." Other members of Congress believed that additional military aid to South Vietnam would reverse what most Americans considered to be the principal achievements of the Paris agreements, namely, the withdrawal of American forces from Vietnam and the return of POWs. Representative Richard Ottinger, a Democrat from New York, said the "commitment the United States made in entering the Paris agreement was that we were going to get out." Wisconsin Democrat Les

Aspin, another prominent congressional dove, feared that the request for military assistance was the prelude for the return of U.S. troops to Vietnam "followed by fighting, casualties, and maybe, worst of all, American POWs. We would be back in the quagmire."[36]

Congress decided against additional military aid, and the North Vietnamese offensive rolled on. On March 14, the PAVN captured the provincial capital of Ban Man Thuot in the central highlands. Thieu reversed a long-standing policy of refusing to withdraw from an inch of South Vietnamese territory. He announced a new policy of "light at the top, heavy on the bottom" in which his army's best troops would retreat to form a line defending Saigon. He acted without planning, forcing his ill-prepared and demoralized troops to execute the difficult military maneuver of withdrawal under fire. Thomas Polgar, the CIA station chief in Saigon, believed that "the South Vietnamese had no strategic concept."[37] By March 20, the government had lost or abandoned without a fight ten of forty-four provinces, and on that day the ARVN evacuated Hue without a fight. The frantic retreat from the North sickened many commanders. One officer told an American reporter, "We were very angry, very ashamed" at the order to withdraw without a fight.[38]

Half a million refugees—including government officials, deserting soldiers, farmers, and businesspeople—jammed the roads from the north to the south and from the highlands to the coasts. Hundreds of thousands of terrified ARVN troops, their families, RVN government officials, and civilians crowded into Da Nang. On March 26, the U.S. announced an airlift of twelve thousand people a day from Da Nang to Saigon. CIA Director William Casey told Ford of "terrible mob scenes" at the airport and port of Da Nang. Only a few civilians had been able to board the evacuation craft because "law and order has broken down completely and it's almost impossible" for the U.S. to remove the weakest refugees.[39]

Ford sent Army Chief of Staff Frederick Weyand on a one-week fact-finding mission to Vietnam. He returned on April 4 with the gloomy assessment that "the Government of Vietnam is on the brink of a total military defeat." Even if Congress approved more military aid the government's chance for survival was "marginal at best."[40] Weyand also opposed a recommendation by General William C. Westmoreland, the former American military commander in Vietnam, for the United States to renew air strikes over the North. He did propose, however, that Ford use troops to help evacuate the remaining six thousand U.S. personnel and approximately ten thousand South Vietnamese who worked with the Americans.[41] Ford requested $300 million in military aid from Congress on April 10, but there was little likelihood of approval. Members of Congress informed the president that as far as they were concerned, the war was over and the South had lost. Representative Robert Michel, an Illinois Republican, told the White House that his constituents believed that the reluctance of the South Vietnamese to fight meant that "we can only provide humanitarian assistance."[42]

Kissinger blamed Congress for betraying an ally. He told Ford that it was "a disgrace" that Congress would not approve additional aid. Ford asked Kissinger what his predecessors would have done in the current crisis. Kissinger believed that "Kennedy would have ratted out. Nixon may have bombed—he was vicious about these things." The only president for whom Kissinger had anything good to say was Lyndon Johnson who, he insisted, "wouldn't have bugged out." Kissinger claimed that "this is the first time that American domestic reactions, principally in the Congress, have impacted seriously on a foreign government.... By not giving aid to South Vietnam and with the Russians and Chinese consistently giving aid to North Vietnam, there developed an imbalance whereby the North Vietnamese Army had much greater force."[43]

Thieu resigned the presidency on April 21 in favor of Vice President Tran Van Huong. Thieu told the nation that he had always opposed the Paris agreement because it legitimized the NLF and allowed the North to keep its forces in the South. He recalled how U.S. aid had been crucial in blunting the North's offensives during Tet in 1968 and in the spring of 1972, but now the United States had abandoned Vietnam. He blamed Kissinger for not making good on Nixon's pledge of military aid and he angrily refused the secretary of state's offer of asylum in the United States.[44]

In the days after Thieu resigned, fissures opened between Ford and Kissinger. The president read the public mood as wanting to put the Vietnam War in the past. Kissinger, furious at seeing his apparent diplomatic triumph at Paris turn to ashes, blamed a weak and unfaithful Congress. At an address he delivered at Tulane University on April 23, Ford said that the United States could regain its pre-Vietnam War pride, "but it cannot be achieved by re-fighting a war that is finished as far as America is concerned." As soon as Ford spoke the words "finished as far as America is concerned," the ten thousand people in the basketball arena erupted into a thunderous standing ovation. When they took their seats, Ford went on: "I ask that we stop re-fighting the battles and the recriminations of the past." On the plane back to Washington, Ford pointedly informed the press that he had included the language about the end of the American war in Vietnam on his own, without having consulted Kissinger.[45]

The war was not completely over, though. An unnatural calm hung over Saigon for a few days. Even though North Vietnamese tanks were on the outskirts of town and near Tan Son Nhat airport, they held back from a final assault. Ford told a meeting of the National Security Council on April 24 that it was "very important for us to stay there as long as we can contribute, in a way that will not promote panic."[46] On April 27, President Huong resigned in favor of General Duong Van Minh, a neutralist. Minh had led the coup against Ngo Dinh Diem in 1963, but he had been ousted in another army uprising in January 1964, because it appeared at the time that Minh wanted to negotiate an end to the fighting with the North and the NLF. Now he had his chance by offering the approaching communists a cease-fire, but they refused.

On April 28 the PAVN and the NLF began their final assault on Saigon with an attack on Tan Son Nhat airport. That evening in Washington, Ford met with his advisers and made the final decision to evacuate Americans from the embassy in Saigon. Secretary of Defense Schlesinger recommended using helicopters in the evacuation rather than deploying airpower to provide cover. He reported that there were 4,000 North Vietnamese sappers in Saigon and "they will attack the embassy if we attack." Kissinger recommended that the United States save the Americans before rescuing the Vietnamese.[47]

On April 29, more than ten thousand frightened South Vietnamese who depended on the Americans rushed to the fence of the U.S. embassy, desperately seeking admission to the supposed safety of the grounds and possible aerial evacuation to ships in the South China Sea. "Can someone tell me what the hell is going on?" Kissinger shouted when he heard that Vietnamese had boarded helicopters. "The orders are that only Americans are to be evacuated." Kissinger also demanded that Ambassador Martin immediately lead the remaining Americans onto helicopters for flights to the American aircraft carriers off the coast.[48] On the morning of April 30 the triumphant fighters of the NLF and the PAVN drove their tanks into the presidential palace and hoisted the flag of the NLF, ending the war with a communist victory.

In the United States, the end of the war was a somber time. Most Americans, including President Ford, preferred not to dwell on the recent past. Officials of both Republican and Democratic administrations had made the decisions which had taken the United States down a disastrous path in Vietnam, so there was little political advantage for either side to blame the other. Kissinger told others to avoid looking for scapegoats for

American mistakes in Vietnam. He told the State Department staff, many of whom had long opposed continued American presence in Vietnam, "we're not going to be vicious. We're not going to accuse anyone of having been wrong." He believed that "people are going to feel badly" after the war is over. Yet he continued to insist that the way the Vietnam War ended had grave consequences for the United States. He explained that he kept asking for congressional approval of aid to South Vietnam even when he knew the request would be denied because "the dignity and self respect of the United States" was at stake. "Above all," he explained, the disgraceful abandonment of South Vietnam would "affect our ability to conduct an effective foreign policy after it is over." He predicted "even the eighty five percent" of the American people who wanted the United States out of the war were likely to have regrets "when it's all over and their government has cooperated in killing the people with whom it fought for ten years."[49]

On April 30, Kissinger told the White House staff gathered in the East Room the United States was going to "pay a price" for the communist victory. He predicted that the Soviet Union would test the United States over the next few months, probing for weakness, and doubting the fortitude of the American public. Eventually, though, he expected the public to regain their courage to confront their adversaries. America's foes who celebrated at its defeat in Vietnam were "doing so prematurely." Kissinger also indirectly but unmistakably criticized Ford for courting public opinion in 1975 by not forcefully reentering the war. Kissinger warned politicians who basked in the warm glow of public approval for having extricated the United States from Vietnam to reflect upon the fate of British Prime Minister Neville Chamberlain after he signed the Munich agreement with Adolf Hitler in September 1938. "He was the most popular man in England in 1938—eighteen months later he was finished."[50]

Official Washington perceived the North's triumph in April 1975 as a humiliation which would have severely negative consequences for United States in the near future. Kissinger told Ford on May 5 that "the public and congress want to be tranquilized about the results of Vietnam. But if you don't speak out about the consequences, in a year we will have real problems."[51] Most notably American allies would feel vulnerable to attack and unsure of American willingness to protect them. Philip Habib, a former negotiator at the Paris peace talks, told Kissinger's staff that long-time allies who had prospered and felt secure under an American shield "now see the shield is full of holes, and they are all concerned that the U.S. shield does not provide them the protection they think is necessary for their own development."[52]

Kissinger's fears that after the Vietnam War emboldened revolutionaries would undermine the stability of America's Asian allies like Thailand, Indonesia, and the Philippines, proved to be erroneous. The war exposed the nearly insurmountable difficulties the United States encountered in creating a nation with a legitimate government in the midst of a civil war. A State Department team concluded that the United States was ill-equipped to comprehend the complexities of societies gripped by insurgencies. "Since our ability to understand the politics of countries such as Vietnam is limited," State observed, "it follows that our attempts *to manipulate political forces*" in other parts of Asia "*may well fail.*"[53]

Kissinger considered the State Department's conclusion to be a direct challenge to his view that American credibility was at stake in Vietnam and ordered a response from the Natonal Security Council (NSC) staff. Although the NSC decried the State Department's analysis as unduly pessimistic about the ability of the United States to shape events to its liking, it did not suggest any particular policies: "The real curse of Vietnam may be that the war had a universal effect but did not provide a universal catechism."[54] The conclusion was vintage Kissinger—a sweeping generalization that provided limited policy guidance.

The United States groped for a policy in the wake of the Vietnam War. It undertook a series of measures to harass and embarrass the victorious government of Vietnam. The Ford administration also imposed a trade embargo on Vietnam. It consistently used its veto in the United Nations Security Council to block its membership in the world body. It also vetoed its membership in the World Bank and the International Monetary Fund.

American officials' anger erupted when more than two hundred thousand refugees, mostly former government officials, members of South Vietnam's armed forces, contract employees of the United States government, and their families began to flee Vietnam, mostly in small, unseaworthy boats beginning in May 1975. This exodus crystallized Washington's animosity toward the new government in Vietnam. The Ford administration requested one hundred million dollars from Congress to resettle sixty thousand Vietnamese refugees in the United States. Congress was skeptical. As Senator Robert Byrd, the Democratic whip, explained, "there is no political support for it in the country."[55]

Despite American bitterness toward Vietnam, some contacts continued between the U.S. and Vietnamese governments. The United States and the SRV conducted desultory negotiations regarding the opening of diplomatic relations in the six months after the war. Hanoi wanted the United States to acknowledge the communists' legitimate control over all of Vietnam. On a more practical level, the SRV hoped that by improving diplomatic relations with Washington, President Ford would make good on Nixon's promise to provide over three billion dollars in reconstruction aid to Vietnam. But the United States had no desire to provide economic aid and little interest in validating Hanoi's claim to sovereignty over all of Vietnam. However, one issue did arouse keen American interest: the fate of the 2,500 Americans listed as missing in action remained unresolved in mid-1975. The Defense Department believed them to be dead, but their remains had not been recovered. The United States wanted an accounting from Vietnam about these MIAs.

Talks between Vietnam and the United States opened in Paris in June 1975 and continued until the end of the year, but the two sides could not reach an agreement. The Ford administration tried to frustrate the new government of the SRV by refusing to end the embargo or offer reconstruction aid. At the beginning of the negotiations, W. R. Smyser of the NSC staff told Kissinger that despite Vietnam's evident desire for American aid and an end to the embargo, "I do not see any hope ... that we could really improve relations unless the Vietnamese drop" their demand for economic aid. Smyser thought that the Vietnamese mistakenly believed American public opinion "favors aid to North Vietnam, or can be persuaded to favor it."[56] Every time the SRV brought up earlier American promises of economic assistance, the Americans took it as extortion. The Vietnamese negotiators hinted that they would provide information regarding the fate of MIAs if the United States came up with the promised aid. Kissinger summarily rejected this approach, telling Ford "Hanoi is obligated under both the Paris Agreement and the Geneva Convention to account for the missing. Linkage [of U.S. aid to information on the MIAs] is unacceptable."[57]

Vietnamese diplomats badly miscalculated the dynamics of American politics in the wake of the Vietnam War. Since opposition to U.S. involvement in the Vietnam War had grown after 1967, the Vietnamese believed that a majority of Americans opposed the tough stance of the Nixon and Ford administrations. While a small fraction of the U.S. antiwar movement did identify with the revolutionaries' cause, the vast majority of the war's opponents simply wanted the United States out of Vietnam and cared little about the future of the country. Negotiations between the United States and Vietnam broke down completely at the end of 1975. As the *Washington*

Post concluded, American public opinion was no longer divided over the war in Vietnam, because most Americans simply wanted to forget about it. "Vietnam would be foolish to expect a nickel's worth of American aid, the *Post* said."[58]

Only the MIA issue aroused public concern. In September 1975, the House of Representatives created a special committee to investigate the fate of American MIAs. Members of the committee disagreed over how generous the United States should be toward the SRV. Some favored lifting the economic embargo to encourage the SRV to account for MIAs. Others took a harder line, demanding that the SRV provide information on MIAs before the United States would consider economic ties. The Ford administration opposed all American inducements to Vietnam and asserted that the Vietnamese had "a clear, unequivocal and unilateral responsibility to account" for MIAs. Only after the SRV was forthcoming on the MIA issue would the United States even consider extending diplomatic relations to Hanoi. Otherwise, Ford said, the United States would "dignify and reward their posture of linking an accounting of our men to our providing them money."[59] National Security Adviser Brent Scowcroft advised Ford that a full Vietnamese accounting for American MIAs and a promise not to export their revolution were prerequisites for ending the embargo and proceeding toward normal diplomatic relations. Scowcroft thought that "we have been badly stung already," and we should "make major gestures toward Vietnam only after we have obtained a complete accounting for all our missing men."[60]

The memory of the Vietnam War was an issue used by several candidates during the presidential campaign of 1976. President Ford faced a strong challenge for the Republican nomination from a conservative, former California Governor Ronald Reagan. Reagan condemned the Ford administration's handling of foreign policy across a broad front. According to Reagan, Kissinger's and Ford's efforts to foster détente with the Soviet Union had weakened American standing in the world. Similarly, Reagan denounced Ford's negotiations with the SRV, however tentative they may have been, as another sign of American weakness. He promised the National League of Families that he would obtain a full account of MIAs the first week he was president. Reagan's challenge forced Ford to state that he had "never said we would open diplomatic relations" with Vietnam under any circumstances. Reagan's close ties to the League made it difficult for him to proceed with normalization. Ford maintained this tough stance after he secured the Republican nomination in the summer. Kissinger told Ford that "the Vietnamese need us" more than we need them. "I would have no objection to their waiting [to enter the UN] for a new administration. That's less trouble for us."[61] In September the United States vetoed the SRV's application for membership in the United Nations.[62]

Jimmy Carter, Ford's Democratic opponent in the fall election, also made Vietnam an issue. He criticized decisions made by a generation of American leaders in Vietnam, and he pledged not to intervene in other nations' internal affairs the way the United States had done in Vietnam's civil war. He praised the good judgment of the American public for having "learned the folly of our trying to inject our power into the internal affairs of other nations. It is time that our government learned that lesson too."[63] He promised to avoid the lies and deceptions that had characterized presidential statements about Vietnam. Carter observed that war had exposed the limits of American power, and he implied that the United States would use its military much more sparingly in his administration. Most of all, Carter promised to put the memory of Vietnam behind the country by healing the deep divisions over military service. He criticized the Ford administration's clemency program for draft offenders for benefiting only the more highly educated and prosperous young men who had the resources to fashion a convincing plea for clemency. He promised a broad pardon to men who had been convicted of draft evasion. Carter narrowly defeated Ford in November 1976. Although discussions of Vietnam played a relatively minor role in the voters' choice, the Democrat gained some support because he seemed untainted by the mistakes of Vietnam.

The end of the Vietnam War also became the lens through which Americans saw military intervention in the late twentieth and early twenty-first century. Those who perceived the last years of the Vietnam War as having been a disgraceful example of the United States having abandoned people who had put their trust in the American assurances, tended either to favor assertive U.S. foreign polices or to favor limiting commitments the United States could not keep. In either case, however, they believed that properly applied military force was an important element of U.S. foreign policy. Others, who believed that the United States had been misguided in becoming involved in Vietnam in the first place and thought the Paris Accords effectively ended American fighting in the war, were highly skeptical about the effectiveness of military intervention.

Notes

1. For a full discussion of the "lost victory" debate see Gary Hess, *Explaining American Failure: The Debate over the Vietnam War* (Malden, Mass., forthcoming 2009), chap. 8; Richard M. Nixon, *No More Vietnams* (New York, 1985), 178, 182–183; Henry Kissinger, *Ending the Vietnam War: A History of America's Involvement in and Extrication from Vietnam* (New York, 2003), 550–551; Jussi Hanhimäki, *The Flawed Architect: Henry Kissinger and American Foreign Policy* (New York, 2004), 389; Larry Berman, *No Peace, No Honor: Nixon Kissinger and Betrayal in Vietnam* (New York, 2001), 246; Jeffrey Kimball, *Nixon's Vietnam War* (Lawrence, Kans., 1998), 78, 101; Robert Dallek, *Nixon and Kissinger: Partners in Power* (New York, 2007), 619; and John Mueller, "Reflections on the Vietnam Antiwar Movement and on the Curious Calm at the War's End," in *Vietnam as History*, ed. Peter Braestrup (Lanham, Md., 1984), 151–157.

2. Ellsworth Bunker to Henry Kissinger, January 21, 1973, and Nguyen Van Thieu to Richard Nixon, January 21, 1973, U.S. Policy in the Vietnam War, 1969–1975, VW 01220, DNSA.

3. Berman, *No Peace, No Honor*, 246.

4. Kimball, *Nixon's Vietnam War*, 370.

5. Robert D. Schulzinger, *A Time for War: The United States and Vietnam, 1941–1975* (New York, 1997), 306.

6. Memcons: Discussions in Hanoi with Le Duc Tho and Pham Van Dong, February 10, 11, 1973, KT 00665, 00666, DNSA.

7. Schulzinger, *A Time for War*, 309–310.

8. Nguyen Tien Hung and Jerrold L. Schecter, *The Palace File* (New York, 1986), 163.

9. Schulzinger, *A Time for War*, 311.

10. Ibid., 312.

11. Ibid., 313.

12. Ibid., 315; James H. Willbanks, *Abandoning Vietnam: How America Left and South Vietnam Lost Its War* (Lawrence, Kans., 2004), 204–206.

13. Schulzinger, *A Time for War*, 314.

14. Ibid., 315.

15. Quoted in Willbanks, *Abandoning Vietnam*, 213.

16. Ibid., 213.

17. Ibid., 216.

18. Schulzinger, *A Time for War*, 315.

19. Ibid., 316.

20. Hung and Schecter, *The Palace File*, 238, 241.

21. Ibid., 241.

22. Ford to Thieu, August 9, 1974, USPVW 1969–1975, VW 01251, DNSA.

23. Thieu to Ford, August 22, 1974, USPVW, VW01253, DNSA.

24. Schulzinger, *A Time for War*, 317.

25. Ibid., 315.

26. Memcon, Ford and Bi-partisan Congressional Leadership, September 12, 1974, USPVNW, 1969–1975, VW 01261, DNSA.

27. John R. Greene, *The Presidency of Gerald R. Ford* (Lawrence, Kans., 1995), 133.
28. Schulzinger, *A Time for War,* 318.
29. Ibid., 319.
30. Ibid.
31. Quoted in Willbanks, *Abandoning Vietnam,* 228.
32. Schulzinger, *A Time for War,* 319.
33. Ibid.
34. Hanhimäki, *Flawed Architect,* 389.
35. Ibid.
36. Schulzinger, *A Time for War,* 320.
37. Ibid., 321.
38. Ibid.
39. Ibid.
40. Ibid.
41. Ibid., 323.
42. Ibid.
43. Hanhimäki, *Flawed Architect,* 394n25.
44. Thieu's resignation speech, April 21, 1975, UPVNW, 1969–75, VW01441, DNSA.
45. Schulzinger, *A Time for War,* 325.
45. Ibid., 326.
47. Ibid.
48. Ibid., 327.
49. Kissinger's staff meeting, April 11, 1975, KT 01568, DNSA.
50. Schulzinger, *A Time for War,* 327.
51. Kissinger's meeting with Ford, May 5, 1975, KT01610, DNSA.
52. Kissinger's staff meeting, May 7, 1975, KT101611, DNSA.
53. "Lessons of Vietnam," May 9, 1975, U.S. Policy in the Vietnam War, 1969–1975, VW O1538, DNSA. Emphasis in original.
54. NSC Response to State Department's "Lessons of Vietnam," May 12, 1975, U.S. Policy in the Vietnam War, 1969–1975, VW O1539, DNSA.
55. Gerald R. Ford, *A Time to Heal: The Memoirs of Gerald R. Ford* (New York, 1979), 257.
56. W. R. Smyser to Kissinger, June 9, 1975, United States Policy in the Vietnam War, 1969–1975, VW 010524, DNSA.
57. Robert D. Schulzinger, *A Time for Peace: The Legacy of the Vietnam War* (New York, 2006), 6.
58. Ibid.
59. Ibid.
60. Scowcroft to Ford, February 1, 1976, U.S. Policy in the Vietnam War, VW 01546, DNSA.
61. Memcon, "Vietnamese Membership in the UN General Assembly and International Financial Institutions," August 17, 1976," KT 02023, DNSA.
62. Schulzinger, *A Time for Peace,* 7.
63. Quoted in Gaddis Smith, *Morality, Reason, and Power: American Diplomacy in the Carter Years* (New York, 1986), 29.

Part IV

Flashpoints, Hotspots, and Allies

11

The Weight of Conquest: Henry Kissinger and the Arab–Israeli Conflict

Salim Yaqub

If a single drive motivated Henry Kissinger's entire approach to the Arab–Israeli conflict, it was to shield Israel from pressure to withdraw from all or most of the territory it had occupied in the 1967 Arab–Israeli War. From 1969 to 1973, when Kissinger served as Richard Nixon's national security advisor, much of that pressure came from the State Department, which promoted a comprehensive settlement involving Israel's withdrawal from nearly all of the occupied territory. Kissinger strongly opposed this policy on the grounds that it would reward America's Cold War adversaries and place intolerable strains on the U.S. –Israeli relationship. Nixon, for his part, officially countenanced the State Department's approach but refused to implement it, a response that had as much to do with domestic American politics as with the effectiveness of Kissinger's internal critique.

Following the 1973 Arab–Israeli War, which broke out shortly after Kissinger became secretary of state, pressure for Israeli withdrawal came primarily from the international community, including America's closest allies. In this phase Kissinger's efforts were far more decisive. In a brilliant performance, Kissinger devised and implemented a diplomatic strategy that dramatically eased the pressure on Israel to conduct a wholesale withdrawal from occupied Arab land. For the price of some modest Israeli concessions on the Sinai Peninsula, and merely a token one on the Golan Heights, he engineered Egypt's effective removal from the Arab–Israeli conflict. This diplomatic coup would, in the years to come, permit Israel to consolidate its occupation of Syrian and Palestinian land, all but precluding a return to the 1967 borders. In the process, Kissinger lured Egypt away from its quasi alliance with the Soviet Union, depriving Moscow of a major asset in the Middle East and weakening its overall position in the Cold War. Yet the very success of Kissinger's diplomacy, insofar as it fortified Israeli occupation, embittered America's relations with much of the Arab world and thus contributed to the emergence of new threats to the United States.

As with most subjects relating to Kissinger, historians are divided over the legacy of his Middle East diplomacy. Some credit Kissinger with establishing a diplomatic foundation that has underlain most subsequent efforts to resolve the Arab–Israeli conflict.[1] Others stress the ephemeral nature of his achievement, noting that a lasting peace, especially between Israel and the Palestinians, remains elusive.[2] Each claim is half right. Kissinger did leave an enduring legacy for Arab–Israeli diplomacy, but it was a legacy of managing the conflict, not of resolving it. Egypt's effective removal from the conflict by the mid-1970s made it extremely unlikely that another full-scale Arab–Israeli war would occur, but it also reduced the prospects for addressing other Arab parties' dissatisfaction with the status quo and thus for achieving ultimate reconciliation. Similarly, the step-by-step process that Kissinger initiated after 1973 did become the standard pattern of U.S. Middle East diplomacy in later administrations. What few historians have grasped, however, is that Kissinger *deliberately* designed the step-by-step approach to be a mechanism for Israel's indefinite occupation of Arab land, a function it continued to serve in later decades, whatever the intentions of his successors.

When the Nixon administration took office in early 1969, it faced a tense and volatile situation in the Middle East. In the June 1967 Arab–Israeli War, Israel had decisively defeated its Arab neighbors, seizing the Sinai Peninsula and Gaza Strip from Egypt, the West Bank from Jordan, and the Golan Heights from Syria. In November 1967, the U.N. Security Council passed Resolution 242, which called for Israel's withdrawal from Arab land in exchange for the Arab states' recognition of Israel's right to live in peace and security. In places, however, the resolution was ambiguous and subject to conflicting interpretation. It did not say explicitly which should come first, the Arab states' recognition of Israel or Israel's withdrawal from Arab territory. Not surprisingly, the Israelis favored the first interpretation while the Arabs insisted on the second. Moreover, because the resolution referred merely to "territories occupied in the recent conflict" rather than to "*the* territories," Israel claimed that it was authorized to retain significant portions of that land. At the time of the resolution's passage, however, U.S. officials privately assured the Jordanian government that the omission of the definite article was meant to facilitate only minor changes in Israel's borders. In a September 1968 speech, President Lyndon Johnson declared that any changes in Israel's borders "cannot and should not reflect the weight of conquest."[3]

By early 1969 Egypt was engaging in artillery and commando attacks against Israeli positions in the Sinai Peninsula; these operations became known as the War of Attrition. Apparently, Egyptian president Gamal Abdel Nasser hoped to prevent the military status quo from solidifying and to force the international community to compel Israel's withdrawal from the Sinai and the other occupied Arab territories. Israel responded to the War of Attrition by staging commando raids and air attacks against Egyptian military bases and facilities on the west side of the canal.[4] To the new Nixon administration, the escalating violence underscored the urgency of attempting to resolve, or at least contain, the Arab–Israeli conflict.

The Nixon administration was sharply divided over Middle East policy. Secretary of State William Rogers, to whom Nixon initially assigned primary responsibility for the Arab–Israeli conflict, wanted to follow a more "even-handed" approach than the Johnson administration had done. Like many other officials in his department, Rogers believed that the Arab–Israeli status quo was deeply damaging to U.S. geopolitical interests. As long as Israel continued to occupy the lands it had seized in 1967, Arab resentment against the United States would grow, and this in turn would facilitate the spread of Soviet influence and radical Arab nationalism in the Middle East. To halt the erosion in America's position, Rogers hoped to pursue a comprehensive settlement whereby the Arab states agreed to make peace with Israel in exchange for Israel's withdrawal from nearly all of the occupied territory. Such a settlement, he wrote Nixon in September 1969, "must be based on a map not very different from the one that existed before the 1967 war."[5]

In 1969 Kissinger had no direct authority over Middle East policy, but he had strong views on the matter and frequently shared them with the president. Kissinger noted that two of the Arab states seeking to recover land from Israel, Egypt and Syria, had close ties to the Soviet Union. Helping either country regain territory, he later wrote in his memoirs, "would give the Soviets a dazzling opportunity to demonstrate their utility to their Arab friends." Kissinger wanted to delay any settlement until after Arab countries had reduced their ties to the Soviet Union and reoriented themselves toward the United States. This would show "that in the Middle East friendship with the United States was the precondition to diplomatic progress."[6]

Cold War strategy aside, Kissinger strongly opposed reinstating the 1967 borders. He apparently accepted Israel's claim that those borders were indefensible.

In August 1974 he told President Gerald Ford, "Israel considers that [the 1967 borders] would be the end of Israel. The country was only 12 kilometers wide in some places" and thus vulnerable to Arab attack. Even if the 1967 borders could be justified in principle, Kissinger knew that Israel would fiercely resist any attempt to impose them, causing acute domestic difficulties for any American administration that joined in the effort. Such a scenario would raise serious moral issues as well. The only way to achieve the 1967 borders, Kissinger wrote in his memoirs, would be to force them on Israel "by the threat of economic pressure and diplomatic isolation, thereby threatening its very existence." Kissinger was unwilling to do this to "an ally so closely linked with my family's fate in the Holocaust."[7] While Kissinger's characterization of America's options is dubious—surely there was a middle ground between supporting Israeli expansionism and threatening Israel's existence—it is hardly surprising that Kissinger, a Jewish refugee from Hitler's Germany, would have viewed Israel's challenges through the prism of the Nazi experience. In any event, such existential considerations were far more evident after the 1973 war, when it became conceivable that the United States might actually force Israel to withdraw to the 1967 borders. From 1969 to 1973 Kissinger opposed Rogers's proposals mainly on Cold War grounds.

Nixon had sympathy for both Rogers's and Kissinger's positions. While the president accepted Rogers's view that resentment over U.S. support for Israel was radicalizing the Arab world and facilitating the spread of Soviet influence, he also shared Kissinger's desire to prevent Moscow from reaping the benefits of any Middle East settlement. "In short," writes William B. Quandt, the Middle East scholar and former Kissinger aide, "Nixon embodied in his own mind the two competing paradigms for how best to tackle the Arab–Israeli conflict." Domestic politics further complicated Nixon's outlook. Because of American Jews' historical attachment to the Democratic Party, Nixon could never hope to receive the support of most Jews. Indeed, Kissinger recalled, "The President was convinced that most leaders of the Jewish community had opposed him throughout his political career"—an attitude Nixon reciprocated by making anti-Semitic comments in private. At the same time, Nixon recognized that Jews were an important political constituency whose opposition should, and could, be blunted. By the early 1970s a host of domestic and international issues—crime, busing, international terrorism, the mistreatment of Soviet Jews—was challenging the traditional liberalism of American Jews, providing the Republican Party with a rare opportunity to expand its share of the Jewish vote.[8] Throughout his first term, with an eye to the 1972 election, Nixon sought to attract Jewish support by distancing himself from, and at times undermining, the initiatives of his own State Department.

In late 1969 Rogers unveiled an ambitious formula for Middle East peace that became known as the Rogers Plan. In exchange for Israel's withdrawal from territories occupied in 1967, the Arab states were to make peace with Israel. In a December 9 speech summarizing the plan, Rogers declined to specify borders for Israel, but he said that "any change in the pre-existing lines ... should be confined to insubstantial alterations" and "should not reflect the weight of conquest"—an exact repetition of Lyndon Johnson's language of a year earlier. The Rogers Plan also called for the demilitarization of the Sinai Peninsula, safe passage of Israeli vessels through the Suez Canal and the Strait of Tiran, a negotiated settlement of Jerusalem's status on the basis of shared Israeli and Jordanian administration, and a resolution of the Palestinian refugee issue through a combination of repatriation and resettlement.[9]

Kissinger strongly opposed the Rogers Plan, for reasons mentioned above: the plan would allow Arab states that had received substantial support from the Soviet Union (most immediately Egypt but eventually Syria as well) to recover territory at the expense of Israel, an ally of the United States. He also doubted that Israel would ever agree to a wholesale withdrawal from Arab land. Nixon, too, had little faith in the plan, but he permitted Rogers to present it anyway. As Nixon later wrote in his memoirs, "I knew that the Rogers Plan could never be implemented, but I believed that it was important to let the Arab world know that the United States did not automatically dismiss its case regarding the occupied territories.... With the Rogers Plan on the record, I thought it would be easier for the Arab leaders to propose reopening relations with the United States" severed at the time of the 1967 war. Yet Nixon also needed to placate Israel's American supporters, who, like the Israeli government itself, angrily accused Rogers of appeasing the Arab states. So Nixon instructed Leonard Garment, his adviser on Jewish affairs, to give private assurances to Israeli Prime Minister Golda Meir and American Jewish leaders that the president had no intention of pursuing the Rogers Plan.[10]

Occasionally, Nixon and Kissinger directly encouraged Jewish and Israeli opposition to Rogers. In October 1969, as Rogers was preparing his plan, Kissinger reported to Nixon, "As you requested, I told Len Garment to organize some Jewish Community protests against the State Department's attitude on the Middle East situation and Len promised to take prompt action." Garment recalls that in January 1970 Kissinger told him, "The president has a little errand for you." Garment was to meet Meir at New York's La

Guardia Airport, where the prime minister was beginning a speaking tour of the United States, and "[t]ell her wherever she goes, in all her speeches and press conferences, we want her to slam the hell out of Rogers and his plan." By this time, both Israel and Egypt had rejected the Rogers Plan.[11]

In early 1970 the War of Attrition sharply escalated. In response to a wave of devastating Israeli bombing raids deep inside Egyptian territory, Nasser convinced the Soviet government to provide Egypt with surface-to-air missiles, known as SAM-3s, that were capable of shooting down Israeli aircraft. The SAM-3s forced an end to Israel's deep penetration raids. In the spring Egypt began moving the missile sites closer to the Suez Canal, in an effort to extend the antiaircraft shield to the east bank and permit an eventual Egyptian crossing of the canal.[12]

In June Nixon authorized Rogers to launch another, more modest initiative that became known as the second Rogers Plan. It called on Egypt and Israel to cease all military hostilities for three months' time and to "refrain from changing the military status quo" on either side of the Suez Canal. Egypt and Israel accepted the agreement, which went into effect in early August. Egypt immediately violated the agreement by installing additional missile sites on the west side of the canal. The Israelis bitterly protested, but the cease-fire held. Rogers, whose personal prestige was invested in the agreement, was slow to acknowledge the Egyptian violations, a fact that infuriated the Israelis and caused him to lose some credibility with Nixon.[13]

Rogers's stock suffered a further decline in September 1970, when fighting erupted between the Jordanian army and the Palestine Liberation Organization (PLO), which, under the leadership of Yasser Arafat, had established a state-within-a-state on Jordanian soil. A column of Syrian tanks crossed into northern Jordan to assist the PLO. Kissinger, who managed the administration's response to the crisis, had little difficulty convincing Nixon that the Syrian incursion was a Soviet-inspired test of American resolve, though other U.S. officials disputed this conclusion.[14] Eager to shore up Jordan's pro-Western King Hussein, Nixon and Kissinger asked Israel if it would be willing to intervene on Hussein's behalf should such an operation become necessary, and Israel agreed to do so. Although Hussein succeeded in repelling the Syrian invasion and defeating the PLO without external assistance, the crisis allowed the Israelis to score points with Nixon. It also appeared to vindicate Kissinger's globalist perspective and to discredit Rogers's even-handed approach.[15]

Rogers was down but not yet out, as evidenced by his response to a surprising Egyptian initiative. In February 1971 Anwar Sadat, who had become president of Egypt following Nasser's death the previous fall, offered to conclude a peace agreement with Israel if it relinquished all of the Arab territory occupied in 1967. It was the first time an Arab leader had publicly contemplated formal peace with Israel. Equally noteworthy was Egypt's willingness for Israel's withdrawal to be accomplished in stages, a departure from the standard Arab demand that Israel withdraw to the 1967 borders immediately. Sadat called for an initial Israeli pullback from the east bank of the Suez Canal that would be linked to a timetable for Israel's withdrawal from the rest of the Sinai Peninsula and the remaining occupied territories.[16]

Encouraged by Sadat's initiative, Rogers lobbied Nixon for authorization to press Israel to respond favorably. "The Egyptians have basically agreed to give [the Israelis] all that they've demanded," Rogers told the president, "and there's no reason for Israel to continue to refuse to settle." Kissinger, however, saw no point in pushing for Israeli withdrawals without first securing Soviet concessions in exchange. The Soviet ambassador "has been on his knees with me for things like this. We might have gotten something from them and this way will get nothing." Kissinger also argued that any attempt to pursue Sadat's offer would provoke a bitter and politically costly confrontation with Israel. The State Department, he warned Nixon, was proposing "a major approach to the Israelis that they have almost no choice but to reject.... You will recall the violent Israeli reaction of January 1970 against the US positions of the previous October and December." (Kissinger neglected to mention the part he and Nixon had played in encouraging that "violent Israeli reaction.") Much to Kissinger's dismay, Nixon authorized Rogers to travel to the Middle East to pursue his initiative. At the same time, Nixon publicly declared that he would not "impose a settlement in the Mideast" and instructed Kissinger to give the Israelis private assurances that the president supported their position of refusing to relinquish the Golan Heights.[17]

Rogers made no headway during his trip. Although Sadat reacted favorably to Rogers's initiative, the Israelis resisted it. Apparently steeled by Nixon's assurances, Golda Meir and her cabinet held fast to their position that in any final settlement Israel must retain the eastern Sinai, the Golan Heights, East Jerusalem, and substantial portions of the West Bank. In July 1971 Nixon authorized Joseph Sisco, the assistant secretary of state for Near Eastern affairs, to go to Israel to see if its government could be more flexible. But the president, William Quandt writes, "pointedly refused ... to promise that he would exert pressure on Israel if Sisco encountered difficulty. In brief, Sisco was on his own." Not surprisingly, the Israelis refused to budge. A frustrated Sadat publicly warned that, if Egypt could not regain its lost territory through diplomacy, it would have to resort to hostilities instead.[18]

As the 1972 election approached, however, Nixon was growing even less inclined to press Israel for concessions, a circumstance that permitted Kissinger's further eclipse of Rogers. During a December 1971 visit to Washington by Meir, Nixon agreed to supply Israel with military aircraft over the next three years and pledged that Israel would no longer be bound to the Rogers Plan. In January 1972, H. R. Haldeman, Nixon's chief of staff, wrote in his diary that the president

> had a directive that Henry wanted sent to Rogers about the planes
> to Israel and the Israel-Egypt negotiations. P[resident] decided that I
> should handle the directive.... He wants Rogers to know ... that we
> can't have the American Jews bitching about the plane deliveries. We
> can't push Israel too hard and have a confrontation.... We must not
> let this issue hurt us politically.[19]

Rogers got the message. On February 2 he wrote Nixon that "[i]n this year of 1972" the State Department would "avoid confrontations with the Israelis on various issues, and avoid putting forward American blueprints to resolve the problem." Grateful for such partiality, the Israeli government all but officially endorsed Nixon for reelection, which he won in a landslide. Nixon received 34 percent of the Jewish vote, up from 17 percent in 1968.[20]

Over the course of 1973, evidence mounted that Egypt was preparing a military offensive in the Sinai and that oil-producing Arab states might curtail oil shipments to the United States in retaliation for its support of Israel. Nixon took both threats seriously, but the Watergate scandal, which became a national preoccupation in the spring of 1973, prevented him from devoting much time or energy to the Arab–Israeli conflict. Kissinger had the ability to focus on the issue but little inclination. In a February 22 telephone conversation with Joe Sisco, he argued that the time was not ripe for diplomatic intervention. "Give it two years and let enough frustration build up," Kissinger said, "and then there is a chance" for a settlement. "The frustration level is at a ... peak right now," Sisco protested. In a May 29 phone conversation, Deputy Secretary of State Kenneth Rush told Kissinger that American oil company executives were worried about the possible use of the oil weapon: "all the heads of these companies say we've got to do something to show—to calm this emotional upsurge in the Middle East." "But they are always wrong Ken," Kissinger said. "Every year they have another pet project to calm it, and they are never right."[21]

On October 6, 1973, Egyptian and Syrian forces launched major assaults against Israeli positions in the Sinai Peninsula and Golan Heights, respectively, taking the Israelis by surprise. Over the next two days, the Egyptians advanced six miles east of the Suez Canal and Syrian forces overran Israeli defenses in the southern Golan. In a panic, the Israelis appealed to Washington for immediate assistance.

Kissinger, not Nixon, dominated American policymaking during the 1973 war. Two weeks earlier, Kissinger had replaced Rogers as secretary of state while retaining his old position as national security advisor. Thus Kissinger controlled not just the machinery of the State Department but the National Security Council staff as well. Moreover, by the fall of 1973 Nixon was almost entirely consumed by Watergate, which would force him from office in less than a year. For these reasons, the new secretary of state enjoyed extraordinary freedom of action on the international stage. Taking charge, Kissinger arranged for a massive American airlift of arms to Israel that, combined with poor coordination between Egypt and Syria, enabled the Israelis to push the attackers back to the 1967 cease-fire lines and even seize additional Egyptian and Syrian territories. In mid-October Israeli forces, which had already crossed to the western bank of the Suez Canal, swung south and east to trap the Egyptian Third Army on the eastern bank. Meanwhile, in retaliation for the U.S. airlift to Israel, several oil-producing Arab states imposed an embargo on oil shipments to the United States and some Western European countries, causing major dislocations in the global economy.[22]

On October 20 Kissinger flew to Moscow, where he and Soviet leaders worked out the terms of an immediate cease-fire, which the U.N. Security Council passed as Resolution 338. But the Israelis pressed on and completed their encirclement of Egypt's Third Army, prompting Leonid Brezhnev, the Soviet leader, to send a message to Nixon threatening unilateral intervention on Egypt's behalf if Israeli military actions continued. Kissinger, now back in Washington, convened a meeting of high-ranking administration officials (excluding the president, who was despondent over Watergate) to craft a response to Moscow's challenge. The group arranged to have a tough letter sent to Brezhnev, over Nixon's name, forcefully rejecting the ultimatum. Kissinger and his colleagues also placed U.S. nuclear forces worldwide on heightened alert. Though not publicly announced, the alert was expected to generate extensive electronic signal traffic that the Soviets would detect, leaving them in no doubt about U.S. resolve. The crisis eased the next day when the Security Council passed Resolution 340, which reaffirmed the cease-fire and authorized the deployment of a U.N. peacekeeping force composed of nonpermanent members of the council, thus ruling out intervention by the great powers. This time, the cease-fire was observed.[23]

As the October War ended, a new phase in Kissinger's Middle East diplomacy began. Whereas Kissinger had previously avoided extensive personal involvement in the Arab–Israeli dispute, he now threw himself into "shuttle diplomacy" between Israel and each of its principal Arab rivals, which refused to deal directly with Israel as long as it continued to occupy their land. Kissinger's challenge was twofold: to achieve a disengagement of forces on the Sinai and Golan fronts, and to eliminate or ameliorate the conditions that had provoked the war in the first place.

Underlying all of Kissinger's diplomatic efforts was a basic dilemma. On the one hand, Kissinger realized that Arab grievances could not be ignored quite as blithely as before. By launching a war that had brought the superpowers to the brink of confrontation, and by imposing an oil embargo that had damaged the global economy, the Arab states had shown they could threaten world stability. Moreover, Western European nations and Japan, which had all been severely affected by the embargo, were now joining the Soviet bloc and Third World nations in calling for a rapid Israeli withdrawal from the territories seized in 1967. Washington faced diplomatic isolation if it continued its unquestioning support of the Israeli position. On the other hand, Kissinger strongly opposed pushing the Israelis back to the 1967 borders. Not only would those borders leave Israel less secure (or so he believed), but getting Israel to accept them would require brutal pressure of a sort that Kissinger, for moral and personal reasons, was unwilling to exert.

To resolve his dilemma, Kissinger needed some mechanism that created the illusion of progress toward the 1967 borders while ensuring that those borders would never actually be restored. It had to appease international demands for Israeli withdrawal even as it neutralized the Arab pressures that generated those demands. Kissinger found that mechanism in "step-by-step" diplomacy: a series of separate, bilateral, and incremental negotiations between Israel and each of its main Arab antagonists. By compartmentalizing the negotiations in this manner, Kissinger could exploit the lack of cohesion among the Arab states. Key here was the attitude of Sadat, who was extremely eager to end his country's conflict with Israel. Egypt had acute economic problems, which could not be addressed as long the country remained on a war footing. Indeed, there were growing indications that Sadat would be willing to conclude a separate agreement with Israel, resulting in the recovery of Sinai territory, without absolute assurances that the remaining Arab claims would be satisfied. With Egypt thus removed from the conflict, the other Arab states would find it extremely difficult to resume major hostilities, and again galvanize world opinion, to compel Israel's withdrawal to the 1967 borders. As Kissinger confided to Israeli leaders in February 1974, "once you have taken Egypt out of confrontation with you altogether, the capability of Syria without Egypt to cause trouble is reduced, I think.... Then you face only Syria."[24]

There was another reason to work closely with Egypt. It was becoming increasingly clear that Sadat wanted to take Egypt out of the Soviet orbit and reorient it toward the United States. Thus an Egyptian-Israeli deal would not only ease international pressure for the 1967 borders but dramatically reduce Soviet influence in the Middle East. At the same time, Kissinger needed to avoid moving too conspicuously in this direction lest Moscow catch wind of his strategy and attempt to disrupt it. To reassure the Soviets that they would not be excluded from Arab–Israeli diplomacy, Kissinger urged that the two superpowers cosponsor an international conference in Geneva at which Israel and its Arab neighbors, with the encouragement and assistance of an anxious world community, could map out the contours of an overall settlement. In reality the Geneva Conference, which was held for a few days in December 1973, was a purely cosmetic affair at which no substantive negotiations occurred. After tendentious public speeches by Israeli, Egyptian, and Jordanian delegates (Syria did not attend because its president, Hafiz al-Asad, already smelled a rat), the conference adjourned and never reconvened. Kissinger returned to the more meaningful task of brokering a bilateral Egyptian-Israeli agreement over the Sinai.[25]

For such a deal to succeed, however, Sadat needed political cover. He could not *appear* to be moving toward a separate peace with Israel, which other Arab actors would strongly oppose. The best way to avoid such an appearance, Kissinger concluded, was to ensure diplomatic movement on the Golan, where some sort of disengagement of Israeli and Syrian forces was necessary in any event. Moreover, showing that Washington could deliver tangible Israeli concessions on the Golan would make it easier for the oil-producing Arab states to end their embargo. So in early 1974, following the conclusion of an initial Egyptian-Israeli disengagement agreement (which separated the contending forces and restored a thin sliver of the Sinai to Egypt), Kissinger threw himself into the task of brokering an agreement on the Golan.[26]

The Israelis, however, had no interest in withdrawing from any part of the Golan, all of which they regarded as vital to their security. The most they would consider was a disengagement of forces that restored the line that had existed on October 6, 1973—the day the war began—leaving Syria with no territorial gains from the conflict. Asad, knowing this, was suspicious of Kissinger's mission, which he saw as a mechanism for extracting Syrian concessions (such as the return of Israeli prisoners of war) without significant Israeli concessions in return. To allay Asad's suspicions, Kissinger pressed the Israelis to vacate the Syrian city of Quneitra, which lay just to the west of the October 6 line. This would give Asad something to show for the negotiation. Meanwhile, Kissinger assured Syrian leaders that further withdrawals were in the offing. "What Syria and Israel agree upon [in the disengagement talks] will not be the final thing," he told Syria's foreign minister in May, "because it will lead to another phase."[27]

Kissinger well knew, however, that the Israelis were determined to hold on to the Golan and that Syria would be lucky just to get back Quneitra. Rather than challenging Israel's annexationist agenda (as he led the Syrians to believe he was doing), Kissinger accepted it as a given. He even advised the Israelis on how best to avoid further withdrawals on the Golan. On February 27 he told Israeli negotiators that as far as he was concerned the October 6 line, with a possible modification for Quneitra,

> will be the final line. I must also say that whether you can hold that position in the face of certain diplomatic pressures that will arise depends on the degrees to which you can keep Syria isolated, other problems solved, and the energy problem taken out of the way. If you can achieve all these things, I can't believe that the world is going to die on the issue of the Golan Heights.[28]

The key, Kissinger insisted, was to achieve a far-reaching agreement with Egypt before the Syrians realized that there would be no further withdrawals on the Golan after Quneitra: "If ... one went the route ... of perhaps not going to the absolute end with Egypt but so close to the end that they'd be in effect politically out of it, then Syria is effectively isolated."[29] Here, Kissinger unveiled the basic strategy he was to pursue for the next year-and-a-half: removing Egypt from the Arab–Israeli conflict in order to ease regional and international pressure on Israel for a return to the 1967 borders.

In the spring and early summer of 1974, Kissinger's diplomatic efforts bore fruit. In mid-March the Arab oil producers, citing progress in the Israeli-Syrian negotiations, announced a suspension of their embargo. In late May, after a grueling month-long shuttle, Kissinger successfully concluded an Israeli-Syrian disengagement agreement. Syria returned the Israeli POWs and ended a low-level war of attrition it had waged in the aftermath of the cease-fire. Israel relinquished the additional Syrian territory it had captured in the October War and vacated Quneitra, though not before demolishing what remained of the city.[30]

The Egyptian and Syrian disengagement agreements were widely hailed as remarkable successes for American diplomacy. Kissinger's international stature now exceeded that of Nixon, who, increasingly crippled by Watergate, could do little more than watch from the sidelines and privately grumble about Israeli and Jewish intransigence.[31] In mid-June Nixon traveled to the Middle East to enjoy some of the acclaim that Kissinger's efforts had generated. Nixon received a warm welcome in the region, especially in Egypt, where huge, jubilant crowds lined his motorcade route. Meeting privately with Asad in Damascus, Nixon intimated that he would do his best to promote Arab interests, despite the baneful influence of "our Jewish-controlled press." With scarcely more credibility, Nixon told Asad not to worry about the Golan: "Let me give you an example. If you want to push a man off a cliff, you say to him take just one step backward, then another and another. If he knew where he was going, he would take no steps."[32]

Kissinger, of course, had no intention of coaxing an unwitting Israel "off the cliff" of the Golan Heights. In early August he told Israel's foreign minister that, while he could envision a full Israeli withdrawal from Sinai, "I do think it is impossible to accept the 1967 frontiers with Syria, and I think it is impossible with Jordan,"[33] a reference to the West Bank. Three weeks later Kissinger lamented to Gerald Ford, who had become president following Nixon's resignation on August 9, that Nixon had promised Asad too much. The question of the Golan "is a very difficult point," Kissinger said. "I have bobbed and weaved all over the place on this. We can't be pinned down.... [But] Nixon didn't like confrontations. Asad really launched on him and Nixon in the heat of the argument promised the 1967 borders."[34] Actually, during that same trip to the Middle East, Kissinger had spoken to the Saudi foreign minister in much the same way that Nixon had spoken to Asad: "We are pushing [the Israelis] back bit by bit, and each bit breaks the back of some of the opposition in Israel.... We push them more every 3–6 months. We know there will be no peace until the '67 borders, but we can't say it" publicly.[35] Whatever the form of Kissinger's reassurances to Arab leaders, the underlying objective was the same: to conceal the extent of U.S. support for Israel's annexationist designs until Egypt's removal from the conflict had rendered those designs secure.

In the summer and fall of 1974, Kissinger briefly advocated an Israeli-Jordanian agreement over the West Bank involving a partial Israeli withdrawal from that territory—or at least conspicuous negotiations in pursuit of that goal. King Hussein was an old friend of the United States who had sat out the 1973 war. It could not appear that Washington was doing less for his country than for Egypt and Syria, which had not only resorted to force but done so with Soviet arms. Yitzhak Rabin, who succeeded Golda Meir as Israel's prime minister in June, was eager to conclude a second agreement over the Sinai that further neutralized Egypt. He had little interest in an Israeli-Jordanian deal. Kissinger noted that the PLO was quickly gaining international recognition and urged Rabin to act while Jordan could still negotiate over the West Bank; better to face Hussein now than Arafat later. Kissinger's warning was prescient. At their summit meeting in Rabat, Morocco, in October 1974, the Arab states designated the PLO "the sole legitimate representative of the Palestinian people," stripping Hussein of authority to negotiate on behalf of West Bank Palestinians. In November the U.N. General Assembly granted the PLO observer status, and Arafat himself came to New York to address that body. The Palestinian issue was now at the forefront of the Arab–Israeli conflict. The Israelis would have nothing to do with the PLO, and Kissinger, citing the organization's "vociferous rejection of Israel's right to exist," endorsed Israel's position. The West Bank initiative was dead.[36]

Actually, the PLO's position was more ambiguous than Kissinger acknowledged. By 1974 Arafat and other pragmatic PLO leaders were inching toward acceptance of a historic compromise: a Palestinian mini-state on the West Bank and Gaza living alongside Israel. Although it would be more than a decade before the PLO as a whole could openly embrace such an outcome, hints of it were detectable in some of the PLO's public declarations at the time. In Cairo in June 1974, the Twelfth Palestine National Council (the PLO parliament in exile) vowed "to establish the people's national, independent, and fighting authority on every part of Palestinian land that is liberated." The qualifier "that is liberated" implied that the PLO might eventually settle for something less than all of Mandate Palestine.[37]

Whether or not Kissinger appreciated these nuances, he was determined to complete Egypt's effective removal from the Arab–Israeli conflict. Ideally, such an operation would have unfolded in tandem with—and thus under the political the cover of—limited agreements on other Arab–Israeli fronts. But with the West Bank off the table, and with Israel still refusing to consider further withdrawals on the Golan, Kissinger decided, in late 1974, to proceed directly to a second Sinai agreement. His challenge was to reconcile the key demands of the parties. Egypt wanted Israel to withdraw to the eastern side of the Mitla and Giddi passes and to relinquish the oil fields at Abu

Rudeis and Ras Sudr, in the western Sinai. Israel wanted Egypt formally to renounce its state of belligerency against Israel and to sign an agreement of long duration.[38]

One of the ironies of Kissinger's Middle East diplomacy is that the harder the secretary worked to fortify the Israeli position, the more difficult his relations with the Israeli government became. Throughout his shuttle diplomacy, Kissinger argued that a few modest Israeli concessions would go a long way toward neutralizing regional and international pressures for a full restoration of the 1967 borders. Israeli leaders grasped the logic of this argument but found it extremely difficult, for domestic political reasons, to deliver those concessions. So Israel often resisted Kissinger's efforts, and never more fiercely than during the Sinai talks in the spring of 1975.

On a trip to the region in March, Kissinger made considerable headway in softening Egypt's position. While balking at formal nonbelligerency, Sadat said he was willing to renounce the use of force against Israel, to cease hostile propaganda in state-controlled media, to ease his country's boycott against Israel, and to allow any new agreement to remain in effect until superseded by another agreement. Sadat also dropped his demand that the agreement be linked to progress on the Syrian and Palestinian fronts and pledged not to assist Syria if it resumed hostilities with Israel. To Kissinger, these concessions effectively satisfied Israel's security requirements. Moreover, Egypt was coming under growing pressure from the Syrians and other Arabs not to conclude another bilateral agreement with Israel, so it was crucial that Sadat's stance be vindicated. "Sadat is conceding more than I ever thought possible," Kissinger reported to Ford on March 18, "but if he goes beyond a certain point he will be destroyed." Kissinger urged Israel to accept Sadat's terms without further haggling.[39]

The Rabin cabinet had other ideas. Its domestic position was precarious, with hawkish critics accusing it of failing to uphold Israeli security. Although the cabinet agreed to relinquish the oil fields, it refused to vacate the passes and continued to demand formal nonbelligerency. Kissinger was outraged. Egypt's concessions were historic, he lectured Israeli leaders on March 22. By fixating on the issue of formal nonbelligerency, the Israelis were missing the larger import of Sadat's moves toward a separate peace. Throughout his shuttle diplomacy, Kissinger said, "[t]here was a conviction that this process, while it was in the United States' interest, was also in Israel's interest—splitting all the Arabs, keeping the Soviets out, keeping the Europeans and Japanese quiescent—and that this in itself was a quid pro quo for Israel, and for this reason we thought an agreement would be reached." But Israeli shortsightedness had wrecked this prospect. "All our strategy which we devoted ourselves to for a year and a half is smashed. Let's not kid ourselves; we've failed." Kissinger returned home the next day.[40]

In the wake of the failed shuttle, the Ford administration embarked on an ostentatious "reassessment" of its Middle East policy. For several weeks the administration commissioned studies, held high-level meetings, and solicited the views of outside experts. On one level the exercise was a genuine review of policy options in light of the failure of Kissinger's March shuttle. On another level it was a piece of political theater designed to frighten the Israelis into adopting more conciliatory positions. The theatrical component itself operated on two levels. Publicly, Ford, Kissinger, and other administration officials insisted that the reassessment was an innocuous exercise in no way directed against Israel. Privately, the administration considered dramatic changes in U.S. policy—including support for a comprehensive settlement arranged at a reconvened Geneva conference—confident that the Israelis would catch wind of these deliberations and draw the proper conclusions. Kissinger's remarks in successive White House meetings in late March tell the story: "I think we need psychological warfare against Israel.... We should keep Geneva dangling.... But the press campaign is that this is just a minor misunderstanding and we can go back to business as usual."[41] It was a diplomatic replay of the nuclear alert of October 1973, when an unannounced elevation of the U.S. defense posture generated extensive signal traffic that Moscow was expected to pick up. This time the resulting "chatter" was intended for Israeli ears.

The Israelis got the message. Instead of capitulating, however, they launched a vigorous campaign in the American press and on Capitol Hill to neutralize the administration's pressure. In late May seventy-six U.S. senators sent a public letter to Ford urging him to support Israel diplomatically and to "be responsive to Israel's urgent military and economic needs." Ford privately scoffed that the letter "could have been written in the Israeli Embassy" and vowed it would have no impact on his decision making, but the episode underscored the domestic political costs of antagonizing the Israelis.[42]

Over the course of the reassessment, three policy options emerged. The first was to resume the search for a Sinai settlement along the lines recently attempted. The second was to encourage Israel to relinquish a larger piece of the Sinai in exchange for deeper political concessions from Egypt. The third option was to go to Geneva and unveil a detailed American plan for a comprehensive settlement, involving an Israeli withdrawal from virtually all of the territory occupied in 1967. No one doubted that Israel would fiercely resist this last course and that Washington would have to apply unrelenting pressure to prevail. Even so, the comprehensive approach was gaining support within the administration and among the U.S. foreign policy establishment generally.[43]

Surprisingly, Kissinger himself advocated a comprehensive settlement. "On balance," he wrote the president on April 21, "the greatest advantage seems to lie with trying for an overall settlement. Trying for another set of interim agreements in the present atmosphere—especially when Syria becomes involved—would generate almost as serious a confrontation with Israel and its supporters as going for an overall agreement." Ford agreed. "I am tilting more and more to a comprehensive settlement," he told Kissinger a week later. "I get the impression there is increased polarization, and to start all over again I don't think it is worth it." On May 8 Ford said to Kissinger, "For us to go back to the step-by-step when Israel is frozen just won't work."[44]

While there is every indication that Ford genuinely favored a comprehensive approach, it appears that Kissinger had grave private misgivings about it. In his memoirs, Kissinger wrote that during the period of reassessment he made

a private pact with myself: if the step-by-step approach had to be abandoned and the United States was driven to state terms for a settlement, I would resign. The disparity between Israel's perception of its margin of survival and ours would become too difficult to bridge. If we prevailed, we would break Israel's back psychologically; if we failed, we would have doomed our role in the Middle East.

Kissinger then went on to make the striking statement quoted earlier in this essay, concerning his unwillingness to force withdrawal on "an ally so closely linked with my family's fate in the Holocaust."[45]

Assuming that Kissinger was honestly reporting his private doubts—which were consistent, after all, with his overall record of shielding Israel from outside pressure—how can they be reconciled with his simultaneous support for an imposed comprehensive settlement? A reasonable hypothesis is that Kissinger was playing a game of diplomatic chicken: in driving U.S. policy toward the brink of a comprehensive settlement (an outcome he dreaded nearly as much as the Israelis did), he gambled that Israel would seek to avert this catastrophe by making the necessary concessions to revive the step-by-step approach.

As it happened, both Egypt and Israel supplied the required concessions, and Kissinger was spared his moment of truth. As early as March 29, Sadat had unexpectedly announced that he would reopen the Suez Canal (which had been closed since the 1967 war) and extend the mandate of the U.N. peace-keeping force stationed on Egyptian soil. In June he proposed that American civilians man observation posts in the Sinai, providing further assurances that Egypt would never resume hostilities there. Sadat's concessions breathed new life into the step-by-step approach, and over the ensuing summer Ford and Kissinger pressed the Israelis to respond favorably, occasionally brandishing the threat of a comprehensive settlement in Geneva. At summer's end the Israelis relented. In the Sinai II Agreement of September 1975, Israel relinquished the Abu Rudeis and Ras Sudr oil fields and withdrew to the east of the Mitla and Giddi passes. Most of the vacated territory became a buffer zone occupied by U.N. forces and American civilian observers. Without granting formal nonbelligerency, Egypt agreed to refrain from the threat or the use of force and to permit nonmilitary cargoes going to and from Israel to pass through the Suez Canal.[46]

Meanwhile, in a series of secret letters to Rabin, Ford pledged to provide Israel with additional military and economic aid and to consult closely with Israel before making any further diplomatic moves on the Arab–Israeli front. The president promised to "give great weight to Israel's position that any peace agreement with Syria must be predicated on Israel remaining on the Golan Heights." He also pledged that the United States would refrain from recognizing or negotiating with the PLO as long as it refused to recognize Israel. This self-imposed restriction would prevent the United States from dealing with the Palestinians' chosen leadership until the late 1980s.[47]

Shortly after Sinai II was concluded, Kissinger called the agreement "the greatest achievement since the opening to China."[48] It was typical of Kissinger that his benchmark for greatness was another accomplishment to which he had been central, but there is no denying that Sinai II was highly consequential. Although it contained no formal nonbelligerency clause, the agreement effectively removed Egypt from the Arab–Israeli conflict, an outcome formalized in the Camp David agreements of 1978–1979, whereby Egypt, in exchange for Israel's withdrawal from the rest of the Sinai, recognized and made peace with the Jewish state. The subtraction of Egyptian power from the Arab–Israeli equation dramatically reduced the likelihood of another full-scale Arab–Israeli war. Indeed, none has occurred since October 1973.

But if Kissinger's diplomacy ruled out another Arab–Israeli war, it also ruled out an equitable settlement of the underlying dispute. Relieved of decisive military pressure from its Arab neighbors, and of diplomatic pressure from the world community that military pressure would have generated, Israel was able to consolidate its hold over the remaining occupied territories through, among other things, the extensive construction of Jewish settlements. Such "facts on the ground" have all but guaranteed that, in any final settlement of the Arab–Israeli conflict, Israel will not return to the 1967 borders. Kissinger's diplomacy, by design, abetted Israeli expansionism.

Now past its fortieth year, the Israeli occupation that Kissinger fortified inspires profound opposition to U.S. policy throughout the Arab world. While by no means the only source of anti-American sentiment in the region, it is at or near the top of almost every bill of indictment. Such opposition has sometimes taken the form of violent attacks against the United States or its allies, and these in turn have provoked escalating U.S. military intervention in the Middle East. Intervention brings more antagonism, and both erode the bonds of global community. The weight of conquest burdens us all.

Notes

1. Kenneth W. Stein, *Heroic Diplomacy: Sadat, Kissinger, Carter, Begin, and the Quest for Arab–Israeli Peace* (New York, 1999), 268; Robert Dallek, *Nixon and Kissinger: Partners in Power* (New York, 2007), 619. Kissinger himself, not surprisingly, belongs to this school. See Henry A. Kissinger, *Years of Renewal* (New York, 1999), 347.
2. Robert D. Schulzinger, *Henry Kissinger: Doctor of Diplomacy* (New York, 1989), 238–240; Steven L. Spiegel, *The Other Arab–Israeli Conflict: Making America's Middle East Policy, from Truman to Reagan* (Chicago, 1985), 312–314.
3. Charles D. Smith, *Palestine and the Arab–Israeli Conflict*, 4th ed. (New York, 2001), 285–290, 305–307; William B. Quandt, *Peace Process: American Diplomacy and the Arab–Israeli Conflict Since 1967*, rev. ed. (Berkeley, 2001), 41–46; Douglas Little, *American Orientalism: The United States and the Middle East Since 1945* (Chapel Hill, N.C., 2002), 282; Lyndon B. Johnson, address to B'nai B'rith meeting, September 10, 1968, *Department of State Bulletin* (hereafter *DSB*), October 7, 1968, 348.
4. Smith, *Arab–Israeli Conflict*, 311–312.
5. Little, *American Orientalism*, 285.
6. Henry Kissinger, *White House Years* (Boston, 1979), 352, 354.
7. Memorandum of conversation (hereafter memcon), Gerald Ford, Kissinger, and Brent Scowcroft, August 12, 1974, National Security Adviser, Memoranda of Conversation, 1973–1977 (hereafter HAK/Memcons), box 4, GRFL; Kissinger, *Years of Renewal*, 428.
8. Quandt, *Peace Process*, 59; Kissinger, *White House Years*, 564; Dallek, *Nixon and Kissinger*, 169–71; Raphael Medoff, *Jewish Americans and Political*

Participation: A Reference Handbook (Santa Barbara, Calif., 2002), 193–196; William Safire, *Before the Fall: An Inside View of the Pre-Watergate White House* (Garden City, N.Y., 1975), 564–575.

9. Quandt, *Peace Process*, 67–68; William Rogers, address to the Galaxy Conference on Adult Education, December 9, 1969, *DSB*, January 5, 1970, 7–11.

10. Richard M. Nixon, *The Memoirs of Richard Nixon* (New York, 1978), 479; Kissinger, *White House Years*, 372, 376.

11. Kissinger to Nixon, October 2, 1969, Henry A. Kissinger Office Files, Country Files, Middle East (hereafter HAK/ME), box 129, folder: "Middle East [Israel, Jordan, Egypt] [Oct 69-May 71] [1 of 2]," NPMP; Leonard Garment, *Crazy Rhythm: My Journey from Brooklyn, Jazz, and Wall Street to Nixon's White House* (Cambridge, Mass., 2001), 192.

12. David Korn, *Stalemate: The War of Attrition and Great Power Diplomacy in the Middle East, 1969–1970* (Boulder, Colo., 1992), 165–204, 225–234.

13. Ibid., 263–268.

14. Talcott Seelye, who led a special State Department task force on the Jordan crisis, later insisted that "Moscow's involvement in fomenting the crisis did not exist to the best of our knowledge. In fact, we had reliable intelligence reports indicating that the Soviets sought to restrain Syria." Quoted in Donald Neff, *Fallen Pillars: U.S. Policy Towards Palestine and Israel Since 1945* (Washington, 1995), 175.

15. Quandt, *Peace Process*, 75–83.

16. Ibid., 88–89.

17. Memcon, Nixon and Rogers, April 22, 1971, HAK/ME, box 129, folder: "Middle East [Israel, Jordan, Egypt] [Oct 69-May 71] [2 of 2]," NPMP; Kissinger to Nixon, March 9, 1971, ibid.; telephone conversation (hereafter telcon), Kissinger and H. R. Haldeman, February 28, 1971, Henry A. Kissinger Telephone Conversations, Chronological File (hereafter HAK/Telcons), box 9, folder: "1971 23–28 Feb.," NPMP; telcon, Nixon and Kissinger, February 28, 1971, ibid.; Kissinger, *White House Years*, 1282; president's news conference, March 4, 1971, *PPP, 1971*, 393.

18. Memcon, Rogers, Golda Meir, et al., May 6, 1971, *Declassified Documents Reference System Online*, document CK3100548322; William B. Quandt, *Decade of Decisions: American Policy Toward the Arab–Israeli Conflict, 1967–1976* (Berkeley, 1977), 143.

19. H. R. Haldeman, *The Haldeman Diaries: Inside the Nixon White House* (New York, 1994), 486–487.

20. Spiegel, *Other Arab–Israeli Conflict*, 211; Quandt, *Peace Process*, 94; Rogers to Nixon, February 2, 1972, HAK/ME, box 134, folder: "Rabin— 1972 Vol 3 [1 of 1]," NPMP; Ira N. Forman, "The Politics of Minority Consciousness: The Historical Voting Behavior of American Jews," in *Jews in American Politics*, ed. L. Sandy Maisel (Lanham, Md., 2001), 153.

21. Telcon, Kissinger and Joseph Sisco, February 22, 1973, HAK/Telcons, box 18, folder: "1973 22–26 Feb," NPMP; telcon, Kissinger and Kenneth Rush, May 29, 1973, HAK/Telcons, box 20, folder: "1973 16–30 May," NPMP.

22. Quandt, *Peace Process*, 105–118.

23. Ibid., 118–124; Kissinger, *Years of Upheaval* (Boston, 1982), 545–599.

24. Memcon, Kissinger, Meir, et al., February 27, 1974, NSC Files, Presidential/HAK Memcons (hereafter NSC/Memcons), box 1028, folder: "Memcons, Jan 1974–28 Feb 1974, HAK & Presidential (1 of 3)," NPMP.

25. Stein, *Heroic Diplomacy*, 117–121, 128–145; Patrick Seale, *Asad of Syria: The Struggle for Middle East Peace* (Berkeley, 1988), 230–234.

26. Spiegel, *Other Arab–Israeli Conflict*, 274.

27. Memcon, Kissinger, 'Abd al-Halim Khaddam, et al., May 18, 1974, NSC/Memcons, box 1029, folder: "Memcons, 8 May 1974–31 May 1974, HAK & Presidential (2 of 3)," NPMP.

28. Memcon, Kissinger, Meir, et al., February 27, 1974, NSC/Memcons, box 1028, folder: "Memcons Jan 1974–28 Feb 1974 HAK & Presidential (1 of 3)," NPMP.

29. Ibid.

30. Spiegel, *Other Arab–Israeli Conflict*, 277–280; Seale, *Asad*, 245–246.

31. Memcon, Nixon, Shirley Temple Black, and Scowcroft, February 28, 1974, NSC/Memcons, box 1028, folder: "Memcons Jan 1974–28 Feb 1974 HAK & Presidential (1 of 3)," NPMP; memcon, Nixon and congressional leadership, April 24, 1974, NSC/memcons, box 1028, folder: "Memcons 1 Mar 1974–8 May 1974 HAK & Presidential (1 of 4)," NPMP.

32. Kissinger, *Years of Upheaval*, 1134; memcon, Nixon, Asad, et al., June 16, 1974, *Digital National Security Archive* (hereafter *DNSA*), document KT01206.

33. Memcon, Kissinger, Yigal Allon, et al., August 1, 1974, *DNSA*, document KT01270.

34. Memcon, Ford, Kissinger, et al., August 23, 1974, HAK/Memcons, box 5, GRFL.

35. Memcon, Kissinger, 'Umar al-Saqqaf, et al., June 15, 1974, HAK/Memcons, box 4, GRFL.

36. Quandt, *Peace Process*, 157–159; Kissinger, *Years of Renewal*, 358–365, 368–370, 382–385.

37. Alain Gresh, *The PLO, the Struggle Within: Towards an Independent Palestinian State* (London, 1985), 168.

38. Quandt, *Peace Process*, 159–162.

39. Ibid., 162; Kissinger to Ford, March 18, 1975, National Security Adviser, Kissinger Reports (hereafter HAK/Reports), box 3, folder: "March 7–22, 1975, Kissinger Trip Vol. II (3)," GRFL.

40. Kissinger, *Years of Renewal*, 405–421; memcon, Kissinger, Rabin, et al., March 22, 1975, HAK/Reports, box 4, folder: "March 7–22, 1975, Kissinger Trip Vol. II (9)," GRFL.

41. Quandt, *Peace Process*, 163–165; memcons, Ford, Kissinger, et al., March 26, 27, & 28, 1975, HAK/Memcons, box 10, GRFL.

42. Spiegel, *Other Arab–Israeli Conflict*, 296–297; memcon, Ford, Harold Wilson, et al., May 30, 1975, HAK/Memcons, box 12, GRFL.

43. Quandt, *Peace Process*, 165.

44. Kissinger to Ford, April 21, 1975, Presidential Country Files, Middle East and South Asia, box 1, folder: "Middle East—General (8)," FL; memcons, Ford and Kissinger, April 28 & May 8, 1975, HAK/Memcons, box 11, GRFL.
45. Kissinger, *Years of Renewal*, 428.
46. Ibid., 428–456; Quandt, *Peace Process*, 165–168.
47. Ibid., 169–170.
48. Memcon, Ford, Kissinger, et al., September 26, 1975, HAK/Memcons, box 15, GRFL.

12

The Danger of Geopolitical Fantasies: Nixon, Kissinger, and the South Asia Crisis of 1971

Robert J. McMahon

It was the most boisterous, near-ecstatic crowd New York's Madison Square Garden had seen in many a year. Nearly 40,000 fans fortunate enough to secure tickets packed the legendary arena for a landmark one-day event: an afternoon and evening concert featuring ex-Beatles George Harrison and Ringo Starr, Bob Dylan, Eric Clapton, Ravi Shankar, and several other luminaries from the ordinarily separate worlds of rock and roll and traditional Indian music. The artists were performing free of charge in order to raise funds for, and call attention to, the desperate plight of millions of East Bengali refugees who had recently fled their East Pakistan homeland to escape a raging, government-initiated civil war.

By any standard, the August 1971 concert was a spectacular success and a major cultural event. Indeed, a quarter-century later the Rock and Roll Hall of Fame in Cleveland marked its anniversary with a special exhibit. A reporter for *Rolling Stone* called it "a brief, incandescent revival of all that was best about the sixties." Shankar, a Bengali who had family members in devastated East Pakistan, had persuaded his friend Harrison to organize a high-profile benefit concert to raise funds for the refugees. He insisted, in interviews, that it was a "totally nonpolitical event." Yet political overtones were ever-present. More than a few performers condemned the American government for not doing more to meet an enormous humanitarian crisis. Between the raga and rock portions of the concert, the house lights dimmed for the screening of a disturbing film that graphically depicted conditions at the refugee camps in India, showing "crows picking at carrion, children bloated with malnutrition, and the dead and dying victims of cholera." The liner notes for the album of the concert that appeared shortly thereafter, moreover, made clear the responsibility for those events. They accused the Pakistani army of unleashing "a deliberate reign of terror" on the people of East Pakistan, precipitating what was "undoubtedly the greatest atrocity since Hitler's extermination of the Jews."[1]

In the Nixon White House, the East Bengali refugee crisis spurred an entirely different response. Nixon's secret, voice-activated taping system recorded numerous meetings during which he and Henry Kissinger privately ruminated about the tragedy unfolding on the Indian subcontinent. Yet hardly a shred of sympathy or concern for a human rights catastrophe of epic proportions was expressed by either man. Nixon and Kissinger focused exclusively on what they saw as the grave geopolitical ramifications of the Pakistani government's bloody crackdown on East Pakistan's autonomy movement and the flood of refugees into neighboring India it had triggered. Since the millions of dispossessed East Bengalis being housed and fed in India were badly straining its resources, they worried that Prime Minister Indira Gandhi's government might use the refugee issue as a pretext to launch a war against Pakistan. The result, Nixon and Kissinger feared, could be the dismemberment of Pakistan, a humiliating defeat for an ally of the United States and China, a severe blow to the developing Sino-American rapprochement, and a geostrategic triumph for India and what they characterized as its Soviet patron.

On July 16, 1971, during a rump meeting of the National Security Council (NSC) at Nixon's San Clemente retreat, the president acknowledged that world opinion favored the Indians. Conceding that "it might be right," he nonetheless described the Indians as "a slippery, treacherous people" who would like nothing better than to use this tragedy to destroy Pakistan. Admitting that he harbored a "bias" against India, Nixon vowed that the country would not receive "a dime of aid" if it intervened in East Pakistan. Kissinger, in trademark fashion, agreed heartily with his chief patron. He called the Indians "insufferably arrogant" and warned that if a war broke out on the subcontinent the Chinese could well intervene militarily–and then "everything we have done [with China] will go down the drain."[2]

On August 11, ten days after the Madison Square Garden extravaganza, Nixon made some equally revealing comments during a rare appearance before a meeting of the Senior Review Group (SRG), in the White House.

"The Pakistanis are straightforward—and sometimes extremely stupid," he remarked. "The Indians are more devious, sometimes so smart that we fall for their line." Although he held "no brief" for recent Pakistani actions, Nixon insisted that the United States could not allow the Indians to use the refugee influx as a pretext for deploying military force to break up Pakistan. In an argument that a psychologist might characterize as a classic instance of projection, the president said he was convinced that the Indians wanted to do exactly that; indeed, "that is what he might want to do if he were in New Delhi." The smart, devious, coldly self-interested Indians, in other words, a people for whom Nixon had just pronounced his loathing, might act just as *he*—the self-styled, unsentimental realist—would were he in their shoes.[3]

This chapter will show how Richard Nixon's strong pro-Pakistani and anti-Indian prejudices, in conjunction with a deeply held set of geopolitical assumptions about the nature of great power relations in the Cold War, exerted a controlling—and highly distorting—influence on U.S. policy toward the watershed South Asia crisis of 1971. As Dwight D. Eisenhower's vice president, he had been a vocal advocate of the alliance with Pakistan from its very conception. Nixon had traveled to South Asia in early December 1953, and had come away highly impressed with the resolution and anticommunist bona fides of Pakistan's leaders. His immediately preceding stop in India, on the other hand, just deepened his personal disdain for what he saw as the arrogance and hauteur of Prime Minister Jawaharlal Nehru and his inner circle. It also reinforced his contempt for the policy of nonalignment that India's ruling elite was determined to continue. "Pakistan is a country I would like to do everything for," he told Eisenhower's NSC. "The people have less complexes than the Indians. The Pakistanis are completely frank, even when it hurts. It will be disastrous if the Pakistan aid does not go through."[4]

Nixon was so closely associated with the Pakistani-American alliance and so widely viewed as a friend of Pakistan that most top military and civilian officials in that country, unsurprisingly, rooted openly for his presidential bid in 1960. His defeat and the Kennedy administration's pronounced tilt toward nonaligned India over the next several years just confirmed their worst fears about the pro-Indian sensibilities of the Democrats. Nixon's favorable view of Pakistan and its leaders was, if anything, reinforced during his years out of office. During his several trips to Pakistan during those years, President Mohammed Ayub Khan and his associates invariably rolled out the red carpet for him. In stark contrast, Indian leaders held Nixon at arm's length during his visits there, their coolness and slights reconfirming the prejudices of a famously insecure individual with a pronounced tendency to personalize all political and diplomatic differences.[5]

Nixon brought that baggage with him to the Oval Office. From the very outset of his presidency, it affected the whole tenor of U.S. policy toward South Asia. "Nixon, to put it mildly," Kissinger recalled in his memoirs, "was less susceptible to Indian claims of moral leadership than some of his predecessors; indeed, he viewed what he considered their alleged obsequiousness toward India as a prime example of liberal softheadedness."[6] The close relationship between Pakistan and China that had proved to be a major sore point for presidents John Kennedy and Lyndon Johnson, moreover, loomed less as an obstacle to Nixon than an opportunity. He was convinced that the continued isolation of China no longer served American interests, and that the Sino-Soviet split presented enticing strategic possibilities for driving a wedge between the two communist rivals. Pakistan's friendly ties with China, cemented by their common disdain for India, provided one promising avenue for establishing indirect Sino-American contacts.

Nixon's first weeks in office coincided with a period of severe internal convulsions within Pakistan. The regime of President Ayub Khan, Pakistan's strongman since 1958—and a Nixon favorite—faced mounting domestic unrest. West Pakistan's Zulfikar Ali Bhutto, head of the populist Pakistan People's Party, and East Pakistan's Sheikh Mujibur Rahman, leader of the autonomy-seeking Awami League, were helping to stoke an ugly series of street protests, demonstrations, riots, and strikes aimed at undermining Ayub's reign. By late January, those grew increasingly confrontational and bloody. Following the opposition's declaration of a massive general strike on January 24, Ayub imposed curfews within the nation's major cities and called out the army to restore order in Dacca, Karachi, Lahore, and other key urban centers. Kissinger alerted Nixon to this budding political crisis in a memorandum of January 27. "In the short run Ayub, backed by the army, should be able to restore order," it predicted, "but these troubles reflect widespread dissatisfaction which could eventually topple his regime." The CIA reported "a steady deterioration of Ayub's political base" and forecast "increasing political instability."[7]

Especially threatening to Pakistan's cohesion and vitality, as the administration's South Asia experts correctly noted, were the longstanding grievances of the East Bengalis. Comprising more than half of the country's total population, the East Bengalis constituted an ethnically, linguistically, and culturally distinct group. Although a numerical majority, they were typically treated as outsiders by the ruling elites of West Pakistan. The Punjabis and Pathans, in particular, who had dominated the nation's military and its civil service since the country's birth, often disparaged the easterners, denied them proportional access to the nation's resources, and clung to political power in the center through jerry-rigged electoral procedures. The charismatic Sheik Mujibur Rahman, or "Mujib" as his followers universally referred to him, insisted upon the establishment of more equitable voting procedures that would ensure fair representation for East Pakistan. Any such reforms, however, would surely erode West Pakistani political dominance, perhaps even opening the door to an autonomous East Pakistani polity. Ayub's chief problem, assayed Thomas L. Hughes, the State Department's chief intelligence officer, derived from "mass urban and East Pakistani hatred of his regime." East Pakistan's secession, given the depth of current resentments, could not be ruled out as one possible outcome. Indeed, Hughes observed that "the country will be fortunate if it emerges from this period of stress as a single entity."[8]

On March 25, a dispirited Ayub resigned from office, handing the reins of power over to General Agha Mohammed Yahya Khan. The clamor in the streets, combined with declining support for the health-plagued Ayub among his own military colleagues, forced the long-serving ruler's hand. "I cannot preside over the destruction of my country," he told his fellow Pakistanis in a somber radio address announcing his decision. In resigning, Ayub proclaimed martial law and abrogated the constitution. Yahya, the affable and well-liked senior army commander, assumed the position of head of a temporary martial law administration.[9]

The Nixon administration was not unduly alarmed by this turn of affairs. In a succinct analysis for Nixon of the recent power shift, Kissinger speculated that the army doubtless believed, as he did, that it could maintain political control through strong-arm tactics. Yet Kissinger also recognized that the larger issue concerned how the people of East Pakistan would respond. "If East Pakistan reacts violently to what it may consider a virtual coup by the West Pakistani establishment which has long dominated the country," he warned, "the situation in the East Wing would be very dangerous."[10] U.S. Ambassador Benjamin Oehlert emphasized that the main reason for the establishment of Yahya's martial law government was to strengthen the central government so as "to prevent East Pakistan from obtaining national political power proportionate to [its share of the] population."[11]

Nixon's first major overseas trip brought him to the Indian subcontinent that summer. The president traveled first to New Delhi, where his meetings with Prime Minister Gandhi were cordial. The one issue that, predictably, triggered the sharpest exchanges concerned the possible resumption of U.S. arms sales to Pakistan. This matter, which had plagued U.S.–Indian relations ever since the U.S.–Pakistani mutual security agreement of 1954, once again proved incendiary. In response to Kissinger's notification that U.S. arms sales policies toward the region were currently under review, Foreign Secretary T. N. Kaul exploded. India, he exclaimed, needed a substantial defense establishment since it faced the Chinese threat. "What is the threat to Pakistan!" he thundered. Kissinger sought to assuage Kaul by explaining matter-of-factly that the United States had no interest in upsetting Indo-Pakistani relations. The Indian diplomat implored him not to aggravate the situation, then, by repeating the "mistake of 1954"—an allusion to the U.S.–Pakistani military pact of that year.

When the American and Indian heads-of-government joined the meeting, the conversation became more general. Nixon emphasized, in broad terms, that the United States would not join any "anti-Chinese condominium," a policy orientation that he disparaged as "disastrous" on any long-range basis. He referred obliquely to his desire for improved relations with China, but offered no specifics. Nixon also stressed, perhaps to counter his reputation as reflexively anti-Indian, that he had voted for every India aid bill since his election to Congress.[12]

Nixon's one-day stop in Pakistan, on August 1, 1969, was marked from the beginning by much greater warmth and mutual understanding. Yahya publicly praised the American leader as "an old friend of Pakistan." Nixon, for his part, promised "to restore a relationship of friendship based on mutual trust." The two leaders spent surprisingly little time discussing Pakistan's monumental political challenges. Plainly, Nixon did not believe that the recent declaration of martial law or the simmering regional autonomy dispute warranted U.S. advice or intervention; he considered them purely internal matters. Nixon, in fact, assured Yahya that his martial law government enjoyed firm U.S. support. The president also promised the Pakistani general that the United States would carefully consider his request to purchase U.S. arms, a matter Yahya characterized as critical to Pakistan's defense needs.

In a private meeting, the essence of which was not shared with any U.S. officials other than Kissinger and a few of his NSC staff members, Nixon informed Yahya that the United States sought to end its isolation of China. He asked the Pakistani president if he would be willing to serve as an intermediary in getting that view across to Chinese Premier Zhou Enlai. Yahya readily assented, doubtless sensing a golden opportunity to strengthen his bargaining leverage with the United States during a time of great political uncertainty. The two men found themselves in full accord on the need for China to be both engaged by and integrated into the wider international community.[13] The next day, White House Chief of Staff H. R. Haldeman recorded in his diary that Yahya "made a strong impression" on Nixon as "a real leader, very intelligent, and with great insight into Russia-China relations."[14]

On August 28, in a follow-up meeting between Kissinger's assistant Harold H. Saunders and Pakistani Ambassador Agha Hilaly, arranged at Kissinger's behest, the two officials discussed the implications of Nixon's request. The NSC staffer stressed that Nixon would appreciate it if Yahya could convey to Zhou, "at some natural and appropriate time," that the president "would welcome accommodation with Communist China." Saunders also requested that any communications between the United States and China, via Yahya's good office, go through Kissinger and Hilaly. Left unstated, but clearly understood by both parties, was that the State Department was not to be privy to any of these secret communications. Hilaly agreed to those terms and, on October 16, informed Kissinger that Yahya wanted to know precisely what message he should convey to the Chinese premier. After receiving instructions from Nixon, Kissinger stated that Yahya should communicate that the United States was interested in normalizing relations with China and was serious about opening a private dialogue toward that end.[15]

Grateful to Yahya for his willingness to undertake and keep secret the important role of unofficial diplomatic intermediary between Washington and Beijing, Nixon urged a relaxation of the current U.S. military equipment embargo as the most appropriate reward. Throughout 1969 and early 1970, the bureaucracy undertook an extensive reassessment of U.S. military supply policy for the subcontinent, in response to Nixon's directive. Yet the results of that effort deviated radically from Nixon's preferences. In fact, after arduous debate and deliberation the State Department took the position that the policy, first announced in April 1967, which banned the direct sale of arms to both India and Pakistan, should be maintained. It forwarded this recommendation to the president on February 10, 1970. Nixon balked. He insisted that the United States should find a way of "doing something for Pakistan." Accordingly, in June 1970, Nixon approved a one-time exception to the military supply policy, allowing a limited quantity of arms sales—a policy change for which Yahya expressed gratitude. The reaction in India, on the other hand, was one of outrage—as the State Department's South Asia experts had predicted.[16]

It bears emphasizing that, throughout 1969 and 1970, South Asia issues absorbed little of Nixon's and Kissinger's energies. The proposed China

opening counted among their highest priorities, to be sure, but after a promising beginning, the Pakistani-Chinese channel had grown cold by mid-1970.
As Kissinger later noted, with characteristic bluntness: "Our policy objective
on the subcontinent was, quite simply, to avoid adding another complication
to our agenda." Yet that objective was to prove elusive in the extreme.[17]

On December 7, 1970, voters across Pakistan participated in a long-
delayed national election, the freest and fairest in the country's young history.
The results constituted a political earthquake. In East Pakistan, Mujib and
his Awami League party, campaigning on a plank of full regional autonomy,
gained an astonishing 160 of the province's allocated 162 seats. Because
Yahya had earlier conceded, under pressure, to accept a one-person–one-
vote electoral system, the separatist-leaning Awami Leaguers now held an
absolute majority in the 300-seat National Assembly—and the fate of the
country's unitary state in their hands. The central government's sluggish,
ineffectual, and seemingly insensitive response to a devastating cyclone and
tidal wave in East Pakistan that killed an estimated 200,000 people earlier
that fall helped turn what would, under any circumstances, have been a big
win for the Awami League into a rout.

On December 9, just two days after the election, the secret Pakistan-China
channel suddenly went from cold to hot. Hilaly delivered a message from
Zhou to Nixon that day, conveyed via Yahya, in which the Chinese premier
stated that a special Nixon-appointed representative would be welcomed
in Beijing. In a reply, agreed upon by Nixon and Kissinger and transmitted
through Yahya's good offices, the American policymakers suggested to Zhou
that such talks encompass all matters connected with the improvement
of relations between the two countries. As Nixon and Kissinger awaited a
Chinese reply—which they did not receive for more than four months—
they were careful not to take any steps that might disrupt Rawalpindi's role
as a conduit for messages to and from Beijing. That factor exerted an important influence, accordingly, on their reaction to events in Pakistan.[18]

Over the next three-and-a-half months, an ominous political impasse
developed. Despite repeated efforts, Yahya, Mujib, and Bhutto—the three
key actors—could not agree upon constitutional arrangements acceptable
to each. The most basic challenge Yahya faced was finding a formula that
could reconcile East Bengali demands for autonomy with his determination to hold intact a unitary Pakistani state. U.S. experts grasped the gravity of the resulting stalemate. By early 1971, State Department, CIA, and
NSC analysts were predicting that either secession or a bloody repression
appeared probable. On March 1, 1971, South Asia hands Harold Saunders

and Samuel Hoskinson informed Kissinger that, given "the constellation of political forces and interests in Pakistan," a mutually agreeable compromise seemed highly unlikely. Anticipating an early East Pakistani bid for independence, they asked a crucial question: "If there is secession how active should the U.S. be in trying to avoid bloodshed?"[19]

On March 6, the SRG met to weigh U.S. policy options. The interdepartmental committee, chaired by Kissinger, saw few palatable choices. "We have no control over the events which will determine the outcome and very little influence," lamented Under Secretary of State U. Alexis Johnson. Johnson offered a grim assessment of likely developments. If Yahya chose to use force, not only would a "blood-bath ensue," but West Pakistan would have no hope of reestablishing control over East Pakistan. "In general, we would like to see unity preserved," Johnson summed up. "If it cannot be, we would like to see the split take place with the least possible bloodshed or disorder." No one disagreed. Kissinger and other participants concurred with the view that "force won't work," but guessed that Yahya might see no other choice but to use it anyway. "To coin a phrase," quipped Director of Central Intelligence Richard M. Helms, "Yahya's attitude is that he did not become President of Pakistan to preside over the dissolution of the Pakistan state." Without any explanation or elaboration, Kissinger introduced another factor into the meeting when he observed that Nixon "will be very reluctant to do anything that Yahya could interpret as a personal affront." Capturing the prevailing sense of the senior officials in attendance, Johnson concluded: "There is a case to be made for massive inaction."[20]

Kissinger made exactly that recommendation to Nixon. "It is undesirable for us to intervene now since we could realistically have little influence on the situation," the national security adviser reasoned, "and anything we might do could be resented by the West Pakistanis as unwarranted interference and jeopardize our future relations." Although he noted that a bloody civil war might be imminent, Kissinger urged inaction, arguing that Yahya was at least doing everything possible to achieve a political settlement.[21]

On March 25, Yahya threw the hammer down. He ordered the Pakistani army to crush the Awami League and arrest its leaders. In a public address, the general labeled them as disloyal traitors and voiced his determination to restore order.[22] The next day, Kissinger notified Nixon that the Pakistani army was using overwhelming force to repress the secession movement in East Pakistan. Again, he counseled strict non-interference—a view with which Nixon was in full accord. Avoiding involvement at this stage had the advantage of ensuring that "we do not prematurely harm our relationship with West Pakistan."[23] Later that day, Kissinger reported the president's decision for noninvolvement to the Washington Special Actions Group (WSAG), another key interdepartmental committee that he chaired. "He doesn't want to do anything," Kissinger explained. "He doesn't want to be in the position where he can be accused of having encouraged the split-up of Pakistan." Accordingly, even though intelligence assessments were now forecasting a civil war leading to an independent East Pakistan, the United States "would not undertake to warn Yahya against a civil war."[24]

Conditions rapidly deteriorated on the ground in East Pakistan, with a substantial loss of life suffered by ill-armed Bengalis seeking to resist the predominantly West Pakistani armed forces. On March 28, Hoskinson informed Kissinger that "the army now appears to have embarked on a reign of terror aimed at eliminating the core of future resistance." The brutality of the military, especially around Dacca, raised a troubling, new issue. "Is the present U.S. posture of simply ignoring the atrocities in East Pakistan still advisable," asked Hoskinson, "or should we now be expressing our shock at least privately to the West Pakistanis?" He added that "the full horror of what is going on will come to light sooner or later."[25]

Plainly, those human rights issues did not trouble either Nixon or Kissinger. On March 29, Nixon asked his national security adviser if there was any important international news to report. "There's nothing of any great consequence Mr. President," Kissinger remarked. "Apparently Yahya has got control of East Pakistan." "Good," Nixon replied, observing that the use of power sometimes pays off. "The use of power against seeming odds pays off," Kissinger responded, finishing the president's sentence. "Cause all the experts were saying that 30,000 people can't get control of 75 million. Well, this may still turn out to be true but as of this moment it seems to be quiet." Nixon offered his own sweeping, if deeply cynical, historical perspective. "Well maybe things have changed," the president ruminated. "But hell, when you look over the history of nations 30,000 well-disciplined people can take 75 million any time. Look what the Spanish did when they came in and took the Incas and all the rest. Look what the British did when they took India.... To name just a few." The next day, Nixon coldly calculated the stakes for the United States in the unfolding crisis. "The main thing to do is to keep cool and not do anything," he instructed. "There's nothing in it for us either way."[26]

On April 9, the State Department received a passionately argued cable offering a different perspective. Signed by Archer Blood, the consul general at Dacca, and all twenty members of his staff, it vehemently objected to the

U.S. policy of strict nonintervention. That policy, Blood stated, "serves neither our moral interests broadly defined nor our national interests narrowly
defined." He blasted his own government for failing "to denounce the sup-
pression of democracy"; for failing "to denounce atrocities"; and for "bending
over backwards to placate the West Pak[istani] dominated government" in
a mistaken effort to minimize the "deservedly negative international public
relations impact" of its recent actions. With unprecedented boldness, Blood
and his colleagues castigated the "moral bankruptcy" of America's policy of
silence in the face of a conflict in which "the overworked term genocide is
applicable."[27]

Rather than shaking the complacency at the upper reaches of the Nixon
administration, the dissent cable just provoked a "kill-the-messengers"
reaction. Shortly after seeing it, Secretary of State William Rogers phoned
Kissinger. "I wanted to talk about that goddam message from our people in
Dacca," an agitated Rogers barked. "It's miserable. They bitched about our
policy and have given it lots of distribution so it will probably leak. It's inex-
cusable." Kissinger, who had not yet seen the offensive telegram, expressed
concern that it would find its way into the hands of Massachusetts Senator
Ted Kennedy, a vocal opponent of the administration's South Asia policy.[28]
The same day that the consulate general at Dacca was imploring official
Washington to recognize the moral imperative at stake in East Pakistan,
Kissinger was rejecting the option of providing food to the people of that
embattled province. "It would be as though, in our civil war," he commented
dismissively, "the British had offered food to Lincoln on the condition that it
be used to feed the people in Alabama."[29]

Although the sentiments expressed in the Dacca cable received a sympathetic hearing among the administration's leading South Asia hands, they
had no impact whatsoever on Nixon's attitudes. Indeed, Blood and most of
his fellow dissidents soon found themselves transferred to other posts. The
overriding priority for Nixon, though still a tightly guarded secret within the
administration, remained the desire not to upset the status quo with Yahya
while he was serving as the chief conduit for communications between
Washington and Beijing. The Pakistan channel trumped any moral, humanitarian, or political reservations about the nonintervention policy.

A chorus of reservations, and condemnations, *were* being issued, particularly by liberal newspapers, prominent columnists, and key members of the
Democratically controlled Congress. "Washington's persistent silence on
recent events in Pakistan is increasingly incomprehensible in light of eye
witness evidence that the Pakistani Army has engaged in indiscriminate

slaughter," declared the *New York Times* on April 7. On May 4, a bipartisan group of nine senators informed Rogers of their growing concern over the administration's inertia on aid to the East Pakistanis. Two days later, by unanimous voice vote, the Senate Foreign Relations Committee passed a resolution calling for an immediate suspension of American military aid and arms sales to Pakistan.[30]

The large number of deaths attributable to the brutality of the Pakistani army proved especially controversial. A *Chicago Tribune* correspondent, one of a small number of reporters allowed back into East Pakistan in early May, described the damage he witnessed upon his return as "reminiscent of World War II" and accused the Pakistani army of engaging in "indiscriminate killing." On July 5, the *Washington Post* blasted both "the army's appalling and indiscriminate slaughter" and the "astonishing and shameful record" of continued U.S. arms supplies by the Nixon administration. "For the shabbiest of political reasons," it commented, "the United States is supplying military equipment to a brutal regime that has killed an estimated 200,000 of its citizens and driven some six million others out of their country." The Nixon administration, added the outspoken Senator Kennedy—at the time viewed as a likely presidential contender in 1972—continues to "whitewash one of the greatest nightmares of modern times."[31]

Nixon's and Kissinger's fixation on the secret opening to China partially explains their equanimity in face of such harsh criticism. That it emanated, for the most part, from liberal bastions that they considered strongholds of their sworn political enemies also made it easier to discount. After all, had not liberals always reflexively supported India and opposed Pakistan? Concrete progress on the China front, facilitated by Yahya, served to strengthen such views. On April 27, Nixon received a long-awaited message from Zhou affirming his government's willingness to receive publicly in Beijing a special envoy of President Nixon. All "modalities, procedure and other details of the high-level meeting and discussion," his message indicated, were to be made through Yahya's good offices. On May 10, Nixon replied, proposing a secret meeting on Chinese soil, "preferably within convenient flying distance from Pakistan," with Kissinger serving as his representative.[32] That same day, Nixon met with a special envoy from Yahya. Calling Pakistan's president "a good friend," Nixon said he could "understand the anguish of the decisions which he had to make" and emphasized that he was not going to interfere with Pakistan's political difficulties.[33]

"The President is eager to avoid a break with Yahya," Kissinger told a May 26 meeting of the WSAG.[34] One week later, Kissinger privately suggested to Nixon that so long as Pakistan served as "the gateway to China" it was important to buoy up Yahya. "Even apart from the Chinese thing," blustered Nixon, "I wouldn't do [anything] to help the Indians, the Indians are no goddamn good." Disregarding the severe problems imposed on India by the massive refugee flux, the president speculated that the Indians "in their usual idiotic way are playing for little stakes, unless they have in the back of their minds that they could turn East Pakistan into a sort of protectorate that they could control from Calcutta."[35]

On July 8, Kissinger feigned a stomach illness during a visit to Pakistan and bowed out of all his scheduled activities, presumably to recover at Nathiagali, a mountain resort. In actuality, with the knowledge of a mere handful of U.S. and Pakistani officials, he surreptitiously flew from Rawalpindi to Beijing for the eagerly anticipated meetings with the Chinese. Yahya's intercession had not only made the visit possible but the Pakistani had ensured that the secrecy so important to Nixon and Kissinger was not breached. Kissinger and Zhou discussed a wide range of issues during their two days of intensive talks, including developments in South Asia. Zhou made clear the depth of Chinese hostility toward India and voiced his apprehension about Indian expansionist tendencies. The veteran Chinese diplomatic and political leader observed that Indo-Pakistani relations were growing more tense, creating the serious prospect of an Indian attack on Pakistan. "The turmoil in East Pakistan in a very great way is due to India," he charged. "We cannot but pay attention to this."[36]

Upon his return, Kissinger could hardly contain his excitement about the evident breakthrough in Sino-American relations. In a memorandum for the president, Kissinger gushed that the state visit that Nixon was now scheduled to make, in February 1972, could "turn a page in history." Yet he also acknowledged a downside: that the Chinese-American rapprochement now underway "will send enormous shock waves around the world" whose impact might prove difficult to manage. One such place was India, where the national security adviser predicted that the administration's new China policy "will increase the already substantial hostility" there toward the United States.[37] Given their strongly negative views toward the Indians, it is hardly surprising that neither Nixon nor Kissinger expressed much concern about that particular consequence of the China opening. In fact, Nixon's upcoming China trip only strengthened their determination not to rock the boat with Pakistan, virtually ensuring increased tension between Washington and New Delhi. Another factor reinforced their pro-Pakistani inclinations: a determination to demonstrate to the Chinese that the United States stood behind their common Pakistani ally and that it would deal firmly with their common Indian adversary. In this critical sense, the smoldering crisis on the subcontinent increasingly stood for Nixon and Kissinger as a test—a test from which they believed the Chinese would draw lessons about the reliability, resolve, and muscularity of the Americans.

On August 9, Prime Minister Indira Gandhi signed a friendship treaty with the Soviet Union. Although less than a formal bilateral alliance, the agreement did pledge that the two nations would consult during crises and that neither would support a third party against the other. Regional specialists viewed the treaty as Gandhi's protective response to what struck many Indians as the sudden emergence of a U.S.–Pakistani-Chinese entente. The Soviet Union, for its part, was vying to counter the incipient Sino-American rapprochement. Nixon and Kissinger exaggerated the treaty's significance, however, erroneously depicting India in its wake as a Soviet client state. The Indo–Soviet pact thus played into the inveterate Nixon–Kissinger penchant for viewing regional events through a superpower prism. "If there is a continued heavy outflow of refugees," Kissinger warned the WSAG, "India will use it as a pretext to go to war. This will blow our China policy." He insisted upon the need to remain firm since "the Indians are playing an absolutely ruthless game."[38] The refugees did continue to flow out of East Pakistan, the failure of Yahya to put forward meaningful political concessions compounding the problems caused by the army crackdown and what was by then a raging, Indian-supported insurgency within the province. By late October, according to a U.S. report, an estimated nine million East Bengalis had moved to India, thirteen percent of the prewar population of East Pakistan.

With a military confrontation looming on the subcontinent, Gandhi arrived in Washington, on November 4, for talks with Nixon, Kissinger, and other top U.S. officials. The Nixon-Gandhi conversations resembled a "dialogue of the deaf," in the apt characterization of one State Department officer. Each side simply reiterated well rehearsed positions while sidestepping the key issues of India's huge refugee burden and the political impasse in Pakistan that was fueling it. In his memoirs, Kissinger writes that the Nixon-Gandhi meetings on November 4 and 5 "were without doubt the two most unfortunate meetings Nixon had with any foreign leader."[39] Yet at the time, Nixon and Kissinger congratulated each other on how well they had handled a foreign leader who each found unusually prickly and condescending. "While she was a bitch, we got what we wanted too," opined Kissinger. "She will not be able to go home and say that the United States didn't give her a warm reception and therefore in despair she's got to go to war." Nixon read-

ily concurred. "We really slobbered over the old witch," he commented."
"You slobbered over her in things that did not matter," his national security
adviser chimed in, "but in things that did matter, you didn't give her an inch."
Oddly, the two policy makers judged the length and quality of the symbolic
red carpet they laid out for a ruler they loathed as the most important aspect
of the visit. Yet each also suspected that little could be done to dissuade
India from soon initiating a military offensive against Pakistan.[40]

To everyone's great surprise, Pakistan made the first military move, launching air attacks from West Pakistan against Indian territory on December 3.
Gandhi immediately ordered an attack in the east, which had originally been
planned for December 4, while authorizing a more limited military action
in the west. The United States, nonetheless, did not hesitate to brand India
the aggressor. Kissinger scoffed at the notion that the Pakistanis could be so
charged, equating that proposition with blaming the Finns for attacking the
Soviet Union. "Pakistan thing makes your heart sick," Nixon lamented to
Kissinger. "For them to be done so by the Indians and after we have warned
the bitch," he muttered glumly.[41]

By December 5, the Indians had easily established their military superiority in the field, prompting a series of frantic telephone conversations and
meetings between Nixon and Kissinger as they sought to salvage something
from what looked like an imminent policy debacle. What most troubled them
were the imagined geopolitical consequences of an Indian victory. "What
we are seeing here is a Soviet-Indian power play to humiliate the Chinese
and also somewhat us," Kissinger proclaimed at one point, eliciting Nixon's
firm agreement. On another occasion, he suggested that Pakistan's defeat
"will be the Suez '56 of our Administration." It would leave the Chinese
"despising us" and the Russians thinking that "they backed us down." All the
global gains made since the China initiative seemed to them on the verge
of evaporating overnight. Personal pique colored their assessments as well,
with both men venting their fury at what they saw as Gandhi's deception.
She "suckered" him in their talks, Nixon complained bitterly. "But let me
tell you she's going to pay," he vowed. "She's going to pay." In that context,
a furious Nixon first proposed the idea that China might be encouraged to
pressure India by moving troops to their shared border. Kissinger found the
option promising. "Damn it. I am convinced if the Chinese start to move the
Indians will be petrified."[42]

Within a few days, the president and his most trusted adviser allowed
that high-risk notion to harden into a serious policy option. At an important
meeting of December 8, Kissinger proposed that, since East Pakistan now

seemed unsalvageable, the administration should at least "scare the Indians off" from a full-scale attack on West Pakistan. A recent bit of intelligence, secured by the CIA from a source close to Gandhi's cabinet, suggested that she was, in fact, planning such an attack. Consequently, Nixon and Kissinger decided to ask the Chinese to move troops to the Indian border to discourage an Indian move to "dismember" West Pakistan. "We can't do this without the Chinese helping us," Nixon stressed. "The Indians have got to get a little scared." In a telephone conversation later that day, Kissinger urged Nixon to further up the ante by sending a U.S. aircraft carrier and other military forces into the area. Doing so, he ventured, could show that Washington was seeking to prevent "a Soviet stooge, supported by Soviet arms, from overrunning an ally"—which would, in turn, uphold American honor and credibility. Nixon liked the idea, though he was not yet ready to make a firm commitment.[43]

In line with the insular decision-making system they preferred, which had become even more exaggerated in this episode because of their certainty that the State Department and intelligence agencies were full of Indophiles, Nixon and Kissinger made virtually all of the key decisions themselves. They had deliberately cut themselves off from the government's leading South Asia experts and thus permitted no alternative voices to be heard at this critical juncture.

The next day, Nixon wavered somewhat, telling Kissinger that they needed to take account of the "realities of the situation." Referring to the partition of Pakistan as a fait accompli and noting that the East Pakistanis had warmly greeted Indian troops as liberators, he asked: "Why then are we going through all of this agony?" Kissinger's instant response reveals the strategic anxieties that fueled his geopolitical vision. "We are going through this agony to prevent the West Pakistan army from being destroyed," he began. "And secondly, to retain our Chinese arm. And thirdly, to prevent a complete collapse of the world's psychological balance of power, which will be produced if a combination of the Soviet Union and the Soviet armed client state can tackle a not insignificant state without anybody doing anything." If the United States would only "put enough chips into the pot," he said, it could persuade the Soviets to call a halt to Indian military activities. "I have to tell you honestly I consider this our Rhineland," he exclaimed, offering a facile analogy to the crisis precipitated by Hitler in 1936. Evidently fortified by Kissinger's argument about the high stakes at play in South Asia, Nixon ordered the U.S.S. *Enterprise* carrier task force to head immediately to the Indian Ocean. On December 10, Kissinger flew to New York to meet with

China's U.N. representative, Huang Hua. In their meeting, Kissinger urged that the Chinese move troops to the Indian border and came away with the impression that the request would meet a favorable response.[44]

On December 12, the crisis reached its apex. Convinced that the Chinese were about to alter the strategic equation dramatically with a sudden redeployment of troops, Nixon and Kissinger congratulated each other for their boldness and resolution. "It's a typical Nixon plan," a fawning Kissinger remarked. "I mean it's bold. You're putting your chips into the pot again." Although the national security adviser admitted the "high possibility" that the ploy would fail, he said reassuringly: "but at least we're coming off like men. And that helps us with the Chinese." Nixon agreed, emphasizing that the Chinese, the Soviets, and the Indians needed to be shown that the "man in the White House" was tough. In the middle of the conversation, General Alexander Haig entered the room with important news. The deputy national security adviser reported that the Chinese had requested a meeting on an urgent basis, which they all agreed meant that the Chinese "are going to move."

The conversation verged on the surreal, with Kissinger noting that a Chinese military move might trigger a countering military move by the Soviets. "If the Soviets move against them and then we don't do anything, we'll be finished," he proclaimed. "So what do we do if the Soviets move against them," asked Nixon. "Start lobbing nuclear weapons in, is that what you mean?" They entertained, momentarily, the idea that perhaps they should now discourage the very Chinese troop movements they had requested. But, Kissinger quickly concluded, it would be too late now to do so. "If we call them off," moreover, "I think our China initiative is pretty well down the drain." Nixon agreed. After talking loosely about how this might represent, in Kissinger's melodramatic phrase, the "final showdown," Nixon admitted to seeing the impending confrontation involving Washington, Moscow, and Beijing in "Armageddon terms." At one point, Kissinger even speculated that the outcome of the crisis—if "Pakistan is swallowed by India, China is destroyed, defeated, humiliated by the Soviet Union—could be "a change in the world balance of power of such magnitude" that the security of the United States could be compromised for at least several decades. Not to be outdone, Nixon offered an even grimmer scenario. "Now we really get into the number games," he observed. "You've got the Soviet Union with 800 million Chinese, 600 million Indians, the balance of Southeast Asia terrorized, the Japanese immobile, the Europeans of course will suck after them, and the United States the only one, we have maybe parts of Latin

America and who knows." He never finished the thought; he did not have to. When Kissinger responded, "This is why, Mr. President, you'll be alone," Nixon bravely retorted: "We've been alone before."[45]

Fortunately for all concerned, the crisis suddenly eased, rendering moot all the posturing and doomsday imaginings that make that December 12 Oval Office meeting one of the eeriest of the entire Nixon presidency—and perhaps of the whole Cold War. That afternoon, Haig found out that the Chinese had no inclination whatsoever to move their troops to the Indian border. Rather, the urgent meeting they requested concerned their decision to support a U.N. resolution calling for a cease-fire in West Pakistan. On December 14, the Pakistani military commander in the east signaled his willingness to surrender. Two days later, the Indian commander accepted his surrender, and that night, Gandhi proposed a cease-fire in West Pakistan. The crisis that Nixon had depicted in "Armageddon terms" just a few days earlier was suddenly over—without a superpower confrontation.

The Nixon–Kissinger policy in South Asia derived partly from a set of deeply held biases against India but largely from a grievous misreading of local circumstances. Here, as elsewhere, they insisted on filtering regional developments through the distorting prism of superpower relations. Purposely isolated from their own leading regional, intelligence, and military experts, Nixon and Kissinger came to believe their own worst-case scenarios: that the Indo-Pakistani confrontation of 1971 endangered the whole struc- ture of great-power relations that they were seeking to reorder; and that it placed in jeopardy Soviet-American detente, Sino-American rapproche- ment, and what stood for them as the all-important issue of U.S. credibility. As a result, they courted massive risks—going so far as to urge a Chinese intervention, even though they recognized that such a move could have trig- gered a Soviet counterintervention. There is perhaps no starker case during this era of the Nixon–Kissinger penchant for ignoring regional realities while simultaneously believing, and acting on, geopolitical fantasies.

Notes

1. *Rolling Stone*, September 2, 1971; *Life*, August 13, 1971, 21–23; *Washington Post*, August 2, 1971; *New Yorker*, August 14, 1971, 28–30; "The Concert for Bangla Desh" (Apple Records, 1971).
2. Memorandum for the record of NSC meeting, July 16, 1971, *FRUS, 1969–1976*, vol. XI: 264–266.

3. Memorandum for the record of an SRG meeting, August 1, 1971, ibid., 323–329.
4. Memoranda of discussion at NSC meetings, December 16 and 23, 1953, NSC Series, Whitman File, Dwight D. Eisenhower Papers, Eisenhower Library, Abilene, Kans.
5. Robert J. McMahon, *Cold War on the Periphery: The United States, India, and Pakistan* (New York, 1994).
6. Henry Kissinger, *White House Years* (Boston, 1979), 848.
7. CIA Intelligence Memorandum, February 6, 1969, *FRUS, 1969–1976*, E-7: document 4.
8. Thomas L. Hughes (Director of the Bureau of Intelligence and Research) to William Rogers, February 20, 1969, ibid., document 9.
9. Richard Sisson and Leo E. Rose, *War and Secession: Pakistan, India, and the Creation of Bangladesh* (Berkeley, 1990).
10. Kissinger to Nixon, March 25, 1969, *FRUS, 1969–1976*, E-7: document 13.
11. Oehlert to the State Department, April 25, 1969, ibid., document 18.
12. Memoranda of conversations, July 31 and August 1, 1969, ibid., document 29.
13. Editorial note, *FRUS, 1969–1976*, vol. XVII: 52; memoranda of conversations, August 1, 1969, *FRUS, 1969–1976*, E-7: documents 31 and 32; Dennis Kux, *The United States and Pakistan, 1947–2000: Disenchanted Allies* (Washington, 2001), 181–182.
14. H. R. Haldeman diary entry, August 2, 1969, in *The Complete Multimedia Edition of the Haldeman Diaries* (Santa Monica, Calif., 1994).
15. Memorandum of conversation between Saunders and Hilaly, August 28, 1969, *FRUS, 1969–1976*, vol. XVII: 74–75; memorandum of conversation between Kissinger and Hilaly, October 16, 1969, ibid., 107–108; Kissinger to Nixon, December 23, 1969, ibid., 153–154.
16. Kissinger to Nixon, April 13, 1970, *FRUS, 1969–1976*, E-7: document 57.
17. Kissinger, *White House Years*, 848–850.
18. Record of discussion between Kissinger and Hilaly, December 16, 1970, *FRUS, 1969–1976*, vol. XVII: 251–252.
19. Saunders and Hoskinson to Kissinger, March 1, 1971, *FRUS, 1969–1976*, vol. XI: 2–5.
20. Minutes of SRG meeting, March 6, 1971, ibid., 8–16.
21. Kissinger to Nixon, March 13, 1971, ibid., 17–20.
22. Sisson and Rose, *War and Secession*.
23. Kissinger to Nixon, March 26, 1971, *FRUS, 1969–1976*, vol. XI: 22.
24. Minutes of WSAG meeting, March 26, 1971, ibid., 26–28.
25. Hoskinson to Kissinger, March 28, 1971, ibid., 33–35.
26. Transcript of telephone conversations between Nixon and Kissinger, March 29 and 30, 1971, ibid., 35–37.
27. Consulate General in Dacca to the State Department, April 6, 1971, ibid., 45–47.
28. Transcript of telephone conversation between Rogers and Kissinger, April 6, 1971, ibid., 47–48.

29. Minutes of SRG meeting, April 9, 1971, ibid., 61.
30. *New York Times*, April 7, 1971; *New York Times*, May 5, 1971; *Washington Post*, May 7, 1971.
31. *Chicago Tribune*, May 13, 1971; *Washington Post*, July 5, 1971; *Washington Post*, July 24, 1971; *New York Times*, July 14, 1971.
32. Zhou to Nixon, April 21, 1971, *FRUS, 1969–1976*, vol. XVII: 300–301; message from the Government of the United States to the Government of the People's Republic of China, May 10, 1971, ibid., 318–319.
33. Memorandum of conversation between Nixon, Ahmad, and Hilaly, *FRUS, 1969–1976*, vol. XI: 112–116.
34. Minutes of WSAG meeting, May 26, 1971, ibid., 155.
35. Editorial note, ibid., 167–168.
36. Memorandum of conversation between Zhou and Kissinger, July 10, 1971, *FRUS, 1969–1976*, vol. XVII: 401–402.
37. Kissinger to Nixon, July 14, 1971, ibid., 453–455.
38. Minutes of WSAG meeting, September 26, 1971, *FRUS, 1969–1976*, vol. XI: 398.
39. Dennis Kux, *India and the United States: Estranged Democracies* (Washington, 1993), 297–302; Kissinger, *White House Years*, 878–879; memorandum for the president's files, November 4, 1971, *FRUS, 1969–1976*, vol. XI: 493–499.
40. Editorial note, *FRUS, 1969–1976*, vol. XI: 499–500.
41. Transcript of telephone conversation between Nixon and Kissinger, December 3, 1971, ibid., 593–594.
42. Telephone conversations between Nixon and Kissinger, December 5, 1971, ibid., 632–647.
43. Editorial notes, ibid., 700–706.
44. Editorial note, ibid., 721–724; memorandum of conversation between Kissinger and Huang, December 10, 1971, ibid., 751–763.
45. Editorial note, ibid., 779–783.

13

History from Below: The United States and Latin America in the Nixon Years

Mark Atwood Lawrence

Latin America ranked at the bottom of Richard Nixon and Henry Kissinger's global priorities. In public, the president and his national security adviser phrased their view diplomatically, suggesting merely that the time had come to scale back U.S. ambitions in the hemisphere. Behind closed doors, the two spoke more bluntly. "Latin America doesn't matter," Nixon exclaimed in 1971. "People don't give one damn about Latin America," he added. "The only thing that matters in the world is Japan, China, Russia, and Europe."[1] Kissinger differed only in the sophistication with which he expressed himself. Latin America, like the rest of the third world, was "not important," Kissinger told the Chilean foreign minister in 1969. "Nothing of importance can come from the South. History has never been produced in the South. The axis of history starts in Moscow, goes to Bonn, crosses over to Washington, and then goes to Tokyo."[2] These were the sorts of places where Kissinger felt comfortable—and where he expected to leave his mark on history. "London, Paris, Rome, and Bonn seemed close," he wrote in his memoirs. "Mexico City seemed far away, Rio de Janeiro or Buenos Aires beyond reach."[3]

Such a distorted sense of geography led Nixon and Kissinger to entertain exceedingly modest ambitions in Latin America. They wished simply to foster sufficient stability to ensure that the region would not interfere with their grand designs elsewhere. Political turmoil in the hemisphere threatened to torpedo those plans in two ways. It might weaken American credibility or prestige by inviting Soviet or Cuban advances in areas of traditional American predominance, or it might constrain the administration's freedom of maneuver internationally by stirring domestic criticism. To prevent such setbacks, Nixon and Kissinger—and, from August 1974, Gerald Ford—used an array of carrots and sticks to keep the hemisphere quiet and even made significant tactical concessions to Latin American governments when circumstances left no choice. What counted was the result—low-key preservation of the status quo—rather than the methods employed to achieve it. Still, one method appealed more than any other and came to be the hallmark of the administration's approach in the hemisphere: reliance on friendly dictators to squelch unrest and protect U.S. interests. There was nothing new in this approach, but Nixon and Kissinger carried it to unprecedented lengths. By the end of 1973, the United States backed military or civilian dictators throughout Central and South America, while just two countries—Venezuela and Costa Rica—practiced free elections.

Viewed narrowly in terms of its ability to prevent major setbacks for the United States in the hemisphere, Nixon and Kissinger's approach succeeded. At a time of mounting restiveness against U.S. dominance in the hemisphere, Washington avoided the extension of Soviet or Cuban power and helped quash leftist challenges, most spectacularly in Chile. For eight years, Latin America impinged minimally on the U.S. foreign policy agenda, leaving Nixon and Kissinger free to make history as they believed it should be made. Viewed more broadly, however, their approach to Latin America was a failure. By helping to suppress demands for political and social change, the Republican administrations exacerbated underlying tensions to the point where explosions became more likely, perhaps even, as historian Walter LaFeber puts it, inevitable.[4] Nixon and Kissinger were out of office by the time Latin America forced its way back toward the top of the U.S. foreign policy agenda in the late 1970s and early 1980s, but their policies helped generate crises that would hound the Carter and Reagan presidencies and bring immense suffering across the region. It turned out that Latin America was quite capable of making history, after all, and by the late 1970s Washington had no choice but to acknowledge it.

Nixon and Kissinger's behavior in Latin America failed in another way too. Reliance on repressive methods contributed to the dramatic reorientation of U.S. domestic politics that doomed the policies that they sought to implement not only inside the hemisphere but around the globe. Alongside the Watergate scandal, stunning revelations about the administration's behavior in Chile fed a growing conviction in Congress and among the American public that the United States had strayed from its moral foundations. This sentiment opened the door to Jimmy Carter's emphasis on human rights and then, much more powerfully, to the moralizing hawkishness of Ronald Reagan. In both presidencies, Kissingerian "realism" languished in deep disrepute. Even in later years, critics of Kissinger and Nixon held up the administration's activities in Latin America as prime evidence of the bankruptcy of their larger approach to foreign affairs.[5] The irony is rich: Nixon and Kissinger's overall record has been deeply tarnished by their performance in the part of the world that mattered to them least.

By the time Richard Nixon took office in January 1969, Washington had long ago abandoned the ambition and enthusiasm that had driven U.S. policy toward Latin America at the start of the decade. Amid great fanfare in 1961, President John F. Kennedy had proclaimed the Alliance for Progress, a massive initiative to promote economic and political development in the hemisphere. But the Alliance was struggling by the end of Kennedy's thousand days and unraveled completely under the stewardship of Lyndon Johnson, who shared little of his predecessor's concern with the region. Mounting expenditures in Vietnam led Congress to cut American aid programs, while fears of Soviet or Cuban advances in the hemisphere caused Washington to back away from Kennedy's antimilitarism. Johnson sent U.S. troops to the Dominican Republic in 1965 and backed military coups in Brazil and Bolivia in 1964 and then in Argentina in 1966. Beset by Vietnam and other problems, Johnson hoped merely to keep Latin America off his agenda by buttressing political stability in the region any way he could.

There was, then, nothing revolutionary about the approach that Nixon and Kissinger brought with them to the White House. The decisive shift in U.S. policy had come in the mid-1960s as the Democrats adjusted to changing circumstances. Only in one respect did the Nixon administration break new ground. Unburdened by the grand ambitions to which Kennedy had staked the Democrats, it was far more willing than its predecessors to acknowledge forthrightly how much times had changed. The Alliance had been "greatly oversold" and had "largely failed to achieve its twin goals of economic development and democratization," asserted a March 1969 National Security Council paper that called for a more "realistic" approach.[6] NSC aide Robert E. Osgood expressed the idea more eloquently a few months later. "The great contribution of the Nixon Administration," wrote Osgood, "should be the deflation of rhetoric, the dismantlement of Grand Designs, and the reestablishment of American policy on the more solid foundation of candor, realism, and a more modest conception of what the United States can achieve."[7]

The administration's approach rested in part on an optimistic assessment of Soviet and Cuban intentions in the hemisphere. As Nixon settled into office, Moscow—just a few years removed from its spectacular nuclear gamble in Cuba—seemed content to focus on peaceful development of relations with Latin American governments. Meanwhile, Havana, stymied by Soviet conservatism, effective countersubversion efforts throughout Latin America, and declining enthusiasm for the Cuban revolutionary model, showed little desire to challenge the United States in the hemisphere.[8] Indeed, Fidel Castro increasingly looked to Africa as a far more promising field for his revolutionary ambition.[9]

But the Nixon-Kissinger approach also reflected deep pessimism about underlying social and political trends in the region and the ability of the United States to alter the situation. Just like the architects of the Alliance for Progress a few years earlier, Nixon administration officials believed that ordinary Latin Americans were becoming dangerously frustrated by the slow pace of political and economic change. New York Governor Nelson Rockefeller, commissioned by Nixon to undertake a fact-finding mission to Latin America, developed the idea in a gloomy report he submitted to the president in August 1969. There was a "restless yearning" across Latin America for a better way of life, Rockefeller wrote. Yet a range of interlocking problems—poverty, population growth, urbanization, unemployment, illiteracy, and corruption—was blocking progress, fueling widespread desperation. "The seeds of nihilism and anarchy are spreading throughout the hemisphere," the report stated. Most alarming of all, Rockefeller predicted that unrest would have increasingly anti-U.S. overtones since so many Latin Americans saw the United States as a bulwark of the oppressive status quo.[10] Radical upheavals threatened to tarnish U.S. credibility and, in the worst case, to create new opportunities for Soviet or Cuban meddling.

To lessen the risk of instability, officials concluded that Washington must continue, within tighter constraints, to demonstrate a commitment to economic development. In sharp contrast to the Alliance era, however, the administration insisted that the United States had little capacity to improve conditions, no matter how much money it pumped into the region. "We no more than King Canute can command the tides," asserted one NSC study, which predicted an "authority crisis" for the United States in the years ahead as its influence inevitably waned. "Despite our preponderance in wealth and power," the NSC reported, "our ability to directly control and channel developments in Latin America will be increasingly inhibited by rising anti-American nationalism, self assertiveness, and growing social and political complexity in the area."[11]

These two alarming trends—mounting social instability and the declining ability of the United States to do anything about it—led the Nixon administration to conclude that the best hope for checking radicalism in the hemisphere lay in backing the indigenous forces that shared the same objective: the political right and often the military. In the Alliance era, Kennedy and, to a lesser extent, Johnson had anguished about whether to recognize military regimes that stomped on democratic principles even as they strongly backed U.S. policies. The Nixon administration showed no such qualms. Reliance on military regimes seemed the best way to accomplish Washington's objectives at a time of growing pessimism about U.S. capabilities to shape foreign societies. It also meshed well with the president's longstanding convictions about the suitability of Third World societies for democracy. At least since Venezuelan protesters had stoned his vice-presidential motorcade during his visit in Caracas in 1958, Nixon had taken a dim view of Latin Americans.[12] As president, he speculated that they, like other people in the third world, were best suited to authoritarianism. "People in the world are at different stages of development," he told an aide in 1971. "And each needs a system that's his own."[13]

Nixon's determination to support reliable governments also sprang from his eagerness to lessen U.S. military obligations around the world. Anxious about a widening gap between commitments and resources as the Vietnam War dragged on, the president declared that the United States would be more cautious about committing its own forces abroad. Instead, under a policy dubbed the "Nixon Doctrine," Washington would protect its interests by providing military aid to help key allies willing to act on the U.S. behalf. In Latin America, such an approach promised not only to lower costs but also to minimize the danger of provoking populations already seething with anti-Americanism.

All of these ideas culminated in a major presidential speech on Halloween 1969. Nixon hoped the address, delivered before a hemisphere-wide television audience, would be "the most meaningful one that [Latin Americans] had heard in years."[14] In contrast to his predecessors, he boasted, he would offer no "platitudes" and would close the "rhetoric gap" that had he believed had harmed hemispheric relations.[15] Indeed, Nixon opened the speech by lowering expectations. "For years, we in the United States have pursued the illusion that we alone could re-make continents," he stated. "We have sometimes imagined that we knew what was best for everyone else and that we could and should make it happen. Well," he admitted, "experience has taught us better." His administration would aim for "a more mature partnership" that accorded Latin Americans a more equal role and more realistically took account of what could be accomplished. Nixon declared that he would offer "no grandiose promises and no panaceas." Instead he promised "action."[16]

Observers had little difficulty recognizing the speech as a blueprint for inaction. Nixon's one concrete economic proposal—to permit Latin American nations to spend U.S. aid money elsewhere in the hemisphere as well as in the United States—fell short of Latin American governments' insistence that they be allowed to use the funds anywhere in the world. Beyond that, the president offered only vague promises to reform U.S. trade practices, to create a new multilateral mechanism for distributing U.S. aid, and to give the region special importance in Washington by upgrading the assistant secretary of state for inter-American affairs to the undersecretary level. All in all, complained a New York Times editorial, Nixon's proposals were "considerably more modest than many had expected."[17] The Washington Post went further, charging that Nixon's agenda was "so unambitious as to be embarrassing." The speech, added the Post, was a "signal of retreat" that seemed to rest on cynical confidence that the region, "left to its own devices, won't get seriously out of hand."[18] A Post cartoon depicted President Nixon pushing Latin America out to sea in a rickety sailboat powered only by the wind of his own speech.

Fixated on the death of the Alliance for Progress, the U.S. media offered little comment on the brief section of the speech that would prove most significant in years to come. Near the end of the address, Nixon stated that the United States had a "preference" for democracy in other nations. Nevertheless, he added, the United States recognized that "enormous, sometimes explosive forces of change" were operating in Latin America, producing instability and frequent changes of government. Henceforth Washington would no longer anguish over whether to extend diplomatic recognition to nondemocratic regimes. "On the diplomatic level," Nixon averred, "we must deal realistically with governments in the inter-American system as they are."[19] The president himself was responsible for this relatively gentle phrasing, having repeatedly edited drafts of the speech to avoid giving the impression that the United States preferred dealing with dictators. In moments of candor, however, Nixon was more honest. The day before the speech, he confided to Kissinger that, regardless of what he was about to tell the world, he did in fact "favor dictatorships."[20]

The administration's determination to preserve stability in the hemisphere in a low-profile manner became abundantly clear between 1970 and 1973, when Nixon and Kissinger coped with their only two Latin American crises. In their origins, the two crises had little in common. One of them began suddenly when U.S. officials discovered what they believed to be evidence of Soviet efforts to use Cuban territory to enhance its strategic military power—a power play apparently aimed at tilting the balance of superpower relations. The other, a protracted confrontation with the Chilean Left following Salvador Allende's presidential victory in 1970, followed years of U.S. anxiety about Chilean politics and seemed to conform closely to the pattern of popular radicalization that the Nixon administration dreaded throughout the hemisphere. Yet it responded to the two challenges in similar fashion—by working boldly to block challenges to the status quo but doing so in ways calculated to avoid drawing attention to the region. In both cases too, the Nixon administration achieved its immediate goals.

Neither the Johnson administration nor, in its first months, the Nixon administration expected a direct challenge from the Soviet Union in the Western hemisphere. U.S. officials believed that the missile crisis had left Soviet leaders unwilling to take serious risks in Latin America, while driving a wedge between Moscow and Havana that made collaboration unlikely. It was therefore jarring when U.S. intelligence reports during the summer of 1970 hinted that the Soviets were building a submarine base at Cienfuegos, on Cuba's southern coast. The problem, as U.S. officials saw it, was not that a base would make an appreciable difference in Soviet military capabilities. Although it promised to enable the Soviet navy to increase the number of submarines patrolling the Western hemisphere, analysts acknowledged that it would only "marginally" increase the number of nuclear weapons that could hit the United States.[21]

What concerned the Nixon administration were the geopolitical implications of Soviet behavior. U.S. studies repeatedly speculated that Moscow hoped to demonstrate that its attainment of nuclear parity with the United States meant that it could begin to chip away at Nikita Khrushchev's 1962 promise to limit Soviet military deployments in Cuba. "For Khrushchev's successors, a successful return to Cuba with a military presence will symbolize the end of a period of Soviet weakness," declared the State Department.[22] Upon close examination of the 1962 deal, officials acknowledged there never had been a formal agreement ruling out the reintroduction of missiles, much less missiles based on submarines. But the administration, already anxious about declining U.S. influence in the hemisphere, insisted that the exchange of letters ending the missile crisis had established an implicit agreement under which Moscow guaranteed never to install offensive weapons in Cuba. The danger lay in the possibility that other governments would see establishment of a submarine base as a failure to enforce that bargain and therefore as evidence of U.S. weakness. "If they succeed in establishing themselves [in Cuba]," wrote one NSC aide, "they will have demonstrated to much of the world that the balance of forces has shifted significantly since their defeat in Cuba eight years ago."[23] The base seemed to be, as Kissinger wrote later, "part of a process of testing under way in different parts of the world."[24]

Through careful press leaks, the administration made clear its alarm about Soviet activities. For a moment in early August, it appeared that Moscow had received the message and would back down. The Soviet chargé d'affaires in Washington delivered a note reaffirming the 1962 understandings. Within six weeks, however, new photo reconnaissance indicated that the Soviets were still working on the base. This development presented the administration with a dilemma—whether to confront the Soviets and risk transforming the issue into a major crisis or to continue to seek a quiet resolution. Kissinger was willing to risk a public confrontation, but Nixon insisted on the latter course. In part, that strategy reflected a belief that Moscow was merely testing U.S. resolve and would back down without a struggle if the United States continued to dwell on the issue. In part, too, it stemmed from fear that a big crisis over Cuba would stir up the media, public opinion, and conservatives in Congress, who, as CIA Director Richard Helms complained, were the "jumpiest people in the world about Cuba."[25] Nixon, who understood Cuba's radioactive potential in American domestic politics, dreaded that some "clown senator" would demand a blockade and distract attention from the administration's priorities.[26] At a moment when the White House wanted maximum publicity for a presidential trip through Europe, the administration had no interest in a major diplomatic clash.

The climactic moment came on September 25, when Kissinger privately confronted Soviet Ambassador Dobrynin. Kissinger accused the Soviets of practicing "maximum deception" and insisted that Washington would view further construction with "utmost gravity."[27] But he also left the door open for the Soviets to back down before the issue became any more public. This approach paid dividends on October 6, when Dobrynin handed Kissinger a note from the Soviet government denying any intent to violate the 1962 understanding. Over the next few days, the two men exchanged additional documents clarifying what kinds of naval activities would be accepted at Cuban ports. Although the Soviets refused to guarantee that no nuclear-capable Soviet vessels would ever visit Cuba, the United States clearly had won a diplomatic victory. Within days, a submarine tender and other Soviet ships left Cienfuegos, and Soviet media reported that Moscow had no intention of building a base in Cuba. Confident that the crisis had passed, Nixon consistently downplayed the whole matter over the following months.

The administration's success in coping with Cuba may have stiffened its resolve in its other Latin American crisis, which emerged just as the Cienfuegos affair was heating up. On September 4, 1970, Salvador Allende Gossens, a socialist who maintained close ties with both Moscow and Havana, won a slender plurality in the Chilean presidential election. Washington had worried for years about Allende and had helped defeat his most recent presidential bid in 1964. In 1970, however, conditions in Chile favored Allende as never before. Accelerating social stratification bolstered the Left, while Allende's opponents divided their votes between a right-wing and a centrist candidate.[28] Efforts by the CIA and U.S. corporations operating in Chile to weaken Allende came to naught, confronting Washington with a trouble prospect: the inauguration of an avowed Marxist as the democratically elected leader of a Latin American nation.

U.S. anxiety stemmed partly from fear about the impact of Allende's election within the hemisphere. Despite quipping in 1969 that Chile was no more than a "dagger pointed at the heart of Antarctica," Kissinger concluded that the consolidation of the Allende government would pose "some very serious threats," not least the danger that Chile might become a "support base and entry point" for Soviet and Cuban activities in the hemisphere.[29] Nixon feared that Allende's example would embolden the Left by giving "courage to others who are sitting on the fence in Latin America." As in the Cuban crisis, both men also feared worldwide fallout. If Allende took power, Nixon fretted at an NSC meeting on November 7, "the picture projected to the world will be his success"—and, inevitably, U.S. failure. "All over the world it's too much the fashion to kick us around," the president asserted.[30] Kissinger feared that the example of an elected Marxist government might have "precedent value" for other parts of the world. "The imitative spread of similar phenomena elsewhere would in turn significantly affect the world balance and our own position in it," Kissinger wrote to the president.[31]

Beset by all of these worries and frustrated that the CIA had not been able to prevent Allende's election in the first place, the Nixon administration began the secret scheming that resulted three years later in the coup that brought General Augusto Pinochet to power. "I don't see why we have to let a country go Marxist just because its people are irresponsible," averred Kissinger with the administration's characteristic disdain for democracy.[32] The administration's high-level group for intelligence operations, the Forty Committee, adopted a two-track policy to get rid of Allende. Track I involved the use of pressure and $250,000 in bribes to persuade the Chilean parliament to refuse ratification of Allende's electoral victory. When that ploy showed little promise, Track II—the effort to encourage a military coup—moved to the center of U.S. planning. Nixon promised at least $10 million for the operation and demanded the "best men we have" for the job. The key method of undermining Allende, he instructed Kissinger and CIA Director Helms, would be to "make the economy scream."[33] But U.S. agents also began to approach Chilean military officers.

Washington soon recognized, however, that its efforts were unlikely to bring success in the short term. The first bold move by Chilean conspirators—an attempt to kidnap Chief of Staff Rene Schneider, an outspoken defender of the country's constitution and therefore a major obstacle to a coup—turned to disaster on October 22, when Schneider was killed rather than abducted. Two days later, the Chilean parliament confirmed Allende as president. Impressed by the return of stability in Chile, the Nixon administration settled in for a long siege. In early November, Nixon established the policy that would guide U.S. behavior from that point forward. Washington would maintain a "correct but cool" posture toward Chile but would "seek to maximize pressures on the Allende government to prevent its consolidation and limit its ability to implement policies contrary to U.S. and hemispheric interests." More specifically, the administration would use every available economic lever to punish Chile while seeking cooperation with other Latin American nations, especially Brazil and Argentina, to isolate Allende.[34] In short, as Kissinger wrote, the aim was to "keep pressure on every Allende weak spot in sight."[35]

Allende's government fell in 1973 partly under the weight of its own tactical blunders.[36] But the Nixon administration bears primary responsibility for fomenting the coup that brought Pinochet to power and led to Allende's death, probably by his own hand, on September 11. Between 1970 and 1973, U.S. authorities helped cripple the Chilean economy, cultivated close relations with key military officers, backed opposition movements, and collected information on the Chilean Left to be handed over to a new government in the event of a sudden shift to the right.[37] Following the coup, Nixon expressed relief that the United States had escaped direct implication. "Our hand doesn't show on this one," he told Kissinger, who was even less willing to take credit. "We didn't do it," Kissinger asserted, although he acknowledged that the United States had "helped" produce the coup by creating conditions "as great as possible" for the Chilean military to act.[38] Such nervousness about taking credit, the result of heightened sensitivity about political attacks as the Watergate scandal unfolded, obscured the genuine sense of accomplishment that the two men felt about Chile. A "pro-Communist" government had been eliminated from the hemisphere, boasted Nixon. If it were the Eisenhower period, added Kissinger, "we would be heroes."[39]

The administration's successes in Cuba and Chile were mere stop-gap achievements. Washington prevented major setbacks but did little to address the underlying regional problems that the administration had seen back in 1969. As the National Security Council looked back over the first Nixon term, in fact, it glumly concluded that the situation had only gotten worse. "The level of polemics and confrontation has ... risen," the NSC reported in a May 1973 study. "We have not been as successful in limiting the damage to our interests as we had anticipated or in preserving as large a measure of our influence in the Hemisphere as we had hoped," the study lamented. In part, the NSC blamed Washington's failure to deliver on Nixon's 1969 pledge to implement special trade concessions for Latin America. Virtually nothing had come of that promise, while U.S. aid continued to decline. But the paper also blamed the Latin Americans for not adequately appreciating the constraints under which the administration was operating at a time of massive distractions in other parts of the world and budgetary restrictions imposed by Congress. Latin American expectations of U.S. assistance were so high that probably no amount of U.S. largesse would have satisfied them, the NSC asserted.[40]

In an effort to improve relations, Kissinger in late 1973 launched a diplomatic offensive known as the "New Dialogue." Technically, the goal was to reinvigorate hemispheric cooperation by creating new mechanisms for discussion of divisive issues including trade policy, energy, and foreign investment. Above all, though, its aim was political—to demonstrate that the United States still wished to have a "special relationship" with Latin America. In fact, behind the scenes, that proposition was a matter of debate within the administration. Officials broadly agreed that U.S. dependency on oil produced in Third World states, as well as the general emergence of the third world in international forums such as the United Nations, necessitated reappraisal of the way Washington interacted with those parts of the globe. One group, led by Treasury Secretary Paul Volcker, opposed awarding special privileges for particular regional groupings. Kissinger acknowledged the drawbacks of such an approach but nonetheless advocated revitalization of the traditional special relationship with Latin America. Since other parts of the world were busily forming blocs, he contended, the United States would risk isolation by refusing to stick with past practice.[41]

The New Dialogue yielded few results, however, and new problems quickly overtook the momentary good will that it generated. For one thing, the region started to feel the effects of the global oil crisis stemming from the 1973 war in the Middle East. In many countries, soaring fuel prices exacerbated economic problems brought on by growing defense expenditures and massive debts incurred during the Alliance for Progress period. Nations found themselves unable to pay for U.S. food and other goods, dramatically worsening trade deficits and lowering already-dismal standards of living across the hemisphere. In Guatemala, for example, a $12 million trade deficit in 1972 mushroomed to $112 million three years later. El Salvador's $12 million surplus turned into a $104 million deficit over the same period.[42] Meanwhile, as the corresponding recession deepened in the United States, Congress offended many Latin American governments by passing new trade restrictions, notably the Trade Act of 1974, which punished all members of OPEC—whether or not they had participated in the oil boycott—by excluding them from the general U.S. system of trade preferences. OPEC members Venezuela and Ecuador responded with predictable fury, but the rest of the hemisphere also viewed the act as stark evidence of U.S. insensitivity. The extent of the damage was reflected in a 20–0 vote within the Organization of American States (with the United States abstaining) to condemn the legislation as "discriminatory and coercive" and contrary to OAS principles.[43]

Just as controversy over the Trade Act was peaking, U.S-Latin American relations were further jolted by media revelations about clandestine CIA activities around the world—the first of the spectacular exposés on U.S. intelligence operations that would culminate in the Church Committee investigations. Although the early reports focused on other parts of the world, some Latin American leaders—even close U.S. allies—read the revelations as evidence that similar kinds of activities were taking place in their own nations. Suspicions focused not just on government agencies but also on U.S. corporations. "Because many Latin Americans ... perceive the activities of U.S. corporations as representing a generalized threat of intervention in their domestic affairs, there is a growing tendency to consider joint CIA–corporate intervention as a general problem—and occasionally as a convenient scapegoat for domestic difficulties," asserted one State Department study.[44]

Declining U.S. influence in the hemisphere became especially clear in connection with OAS policy toward Cuba. In 1964, the organization had unanimously imposed a trade embargo on the island. But by the early 1970s a significant majority of Latin American governments, no longer inclined to see Castro's regime as a threat, were chafing under those restrictions and demanding that nations be free to set their own policies. In fact, by 1975 Argentina, Mexico, Venezuela, Peru, Panama, and several Caribbean nations had already rendered the OAS restrictions practically meaningless by establishing bilateral diplomatic and trade relations with Cuba. The Ford administration insisted on the need for continued sanctions to isolate Castro and to force Moscow to spend valuable resources keeping the island's economy afloat. U.S officials increasingly recognized, however, that many Latin American nations viewed the sanctions not only as an undue economic burden but also as an expression of unwelcome U.S. dominance in the hemisphere. Starting in 1973, officials expected that these countries would soon be able to muster the votes to abolish the sanctions.

In order to ease tensions over the issue and to avoid the embarrassing spectacle of Latin American nations simply flouting U.S. preferences, the administration decided to make a virtue of necessity by cooperating with the majority to put an end to the sanctions.[45] To be sure, Washington made clear its intention to maintain a bilateral embargo against Cuba. But, expecting the worst for the OAS sanctions, it agreed to a special meeting in November 1974 to vote on the issue. To Washington's surprise, the proposal to abolish the embargo narrowly failed to achieve the required two-thirds majority. Recognizing that the issue would continue to poison hemispheric relations, however, the Ford administration backed a proposal to alter OAS decision-making procedures to allow for ending sanctions by a simple majority— another concession aimed at dampening anti-Americanism by demonstrating flexibility. At their May 1975 meeting, OAS governments approved this plan.[46] Finally, to the administration's immense relief, the issue dropped off the OAS agenda.

For a time during 1974 and 1975, the White House secretly considered an even bolder way to close the gap between the United States and Latin America: ending bilateral sanctions and seeking an accommodation with Castro. Since taking office in 1969, the Republicans had resisted the idea of rapprochement with Cuba and persistently downplayed the possibility when it emerged publicly. Conventional wisdom held that sanctions played a positive role by punishing Castro for his efforts to subvert other governments and by burdening the Soviet Union with the costs of maintaining Cuba's economy. As it became clear that the OAS sanctions would be lifted, however, some U.S. officials concluded that the United States risked losing its authority in the region if it failed to keep up with changing attitudes. "Initiation of contacts with the Cubans could keep us from being the last to do so and maintain some initiative and leadership in our own hand," NSC aide Stephen Low advised Kissinger in a remarkable statement of declining U.S. clout in the hemisphere.[47] With key members of Congress expressing support for an opening to Cuba, U.S.–Cuban discussions intensified dramatically in mid-1975. In the end, the opening came to naught, defeated by Havana's resistance to Washington's sweeping demands for Cuban concessions and by Cuba's massive military intervention in Angola, the culmination of mounting Cuban support for revolutionary movements in Africa.[48] The result may be less significant, however, than the fact that Nixon and Ford, long adamant in their hostility to Cuba, were willing to entertain the effort. Changing circumstances in the hemisphere led them to pursue their central objective—preservation of U.S. leadership and the stability that that implied—through a bold tactical adjustment.

With respect to only one country—Panama—did Nixon and Ford fully implement a concessionary policy. Lyndon Johnson had committed the United States to this path in 1964, when he declared his willingness to negotiate a new treaty giving Panama much greater control over the Panama Canal. Quasi-colonial U.S. domination of the waterway had long embittered relations not just with Panama but with all of Latin America. U.S.–Panamanian talks produced a draft treaty in 1967, but the effort collapsed amid shifting political climates in both countries. Following the 1972 election, Nixon and Kissinger decided to resume the talks, reasoning, like their Democratic predecessors, that a new treaty would remove a major irritant in U.S.-Latin American relations and give the United States a more secure, albeit diminished, role in managing and defending the canal. The extent of global support for Panama became clear in March 1973, when only a U.S. veto blocked a United Nations Security Council resolution demanding speedy negotiations. Kissinger foresaw inevitable crisis if Washington refused to bend. "Demonstrations, pressure, terrorism, even guerrilla warfare would, over time, rally all of Latin America against us, and isolate us in every international forum," Kissinger wrote in his memoirs.[49] U.S. officials also feared that the Panamanian leader, General Omar Torrijos, would turn to the Soviet Union if Washington failed to pursue a new treaty.[50]

Dramatic progress came at last in 1974, when Kissinger and Panamanian Foreign Minister Juan Antonia Tack agreed on an eight-point formula that pointed the way toward an agreement. The United States promised to return the canal to Panamanian sovereignty and assured Panama an equitable share of toll revenues, while Panama agreed that the United States would have the right to defend the canal. By the time this agreement was reached, the Ford administration judged that the 1976 election was too close to risk the political damage that might come from such a treaty. The effort therefore lay in abeyance until February 1977, when the Carter administration resumed talks. The treaty that was signed on September 7, 1977, owed a great deal, however, to progress achieved under Kissinger's guidance.[51]

The concessions that the Republican administrations contemplated in Cuba and enacted in Panama were not, however, illustrative of any general shift in the U.S. approach to the hemisphere. In both cases, Washington saw a concession as a tactical adjustment in order to pursue old objectives—political stability and U.S. leadership—in a time of declining American clout. In most of the hemisphere, U.S. policy underwent no such reconsideration. Indeed, at precisely the moment when Washington was most seriously pondering bold leaps in Cuba and Panama, elsewhere in Latin America it was going further than ever before in practicing the policy it had quietly embraced in 1969—partnerships with reliable authoritarian regimes. While maintaining its close relations with Central American regimes, the administration consolidated and expanded its network of allies further south. In Argentina, the Ford administration immediately recognized the military junta that came to power in March 1976. In Chile, meanwhile, Kissinger left no doubt that the Ford Administration, despite sniping in the U.S. Congress about human rights abuses, embraced the new strongman, Augusto Pinochet, and had little desire to see the restoration of democracy. During his trip to Santiago for an OAS meeting in June 1976, Kissinger said as much directly to Pinochet. The administration, he told the Chilean leader, had to respect concern in Congress about human rights abuses but did not share it. "We are sympathetic with what you are trying to do here," Kissinger affirmed. "We wish your government well."[52]

At the same time, the Ford administration showed toleration—and occasionally outright support—for efforts by the growing roster of South American military governments to cooperate with one another to eliminate their political opponents, ranging from Marxist guerrillas to mere advocates of democracy. Starting in November 1975, intelligence services in Chile, Argentina, Paraguay, Bolivia, and Uruguay (later joined by Brazil) initiated Operation Condor, a coordinated campaign of kidnap, murder, and torture that led to an unknowable number of deaths. These activities occurred mainly within South America but sometimes spilled over to Europe and North America, as when former Chilean Foreign Minister Orlando Letelier was assassinated in Washington, D.C., in September 1976. All in all, as investigative journalist John Dinges asserted in a 2004 study, "Condor elevated human rights crimes to the highest level of state policy, under the direct control and manipulation of the heads of state and ministers of government."[53] U.S. authorities had no apparent role in launching the program but were clearly aware of it and offered their support. Washington made available a radio network headquartered in the Panama Canal Zone, provided a telex system to facilitate communication between governments, and supplied information to Operation Condor's central data bank in Santiago. At the same time, Kissinger and other U.S. officials consistently made clear to participating regimes that Ford administration had no interest in stopping their activities. Although Washington occasionally admonished South American governments for human rights violations, as during Kissinger's 1976 trip to Santiago, Washington demonstrated that it sympathized with their goals and would not interfere in their repressive activities.[54] Condor, after all, aligned directly with the goal that Nixon, Ford, and Kissinger had been pursuing since 1969. Latin American governments, although dependent on U.S. arms supplies, were effectively policing their own societies, stamping out political unrest and the unpredictability that came with the practice of democracy.

As the 1976 presidential election approached, senior administration officials expressed confidence that the relationship with Latin America, after a rocky few years, had improved dramatically and that the future was bright. "The tone of US-Latin American relations is better than at any time in the recent past," Kissinger declared following his trip to Santiago in June.[55] Undersecretary of State for Economic Affairs William D. Rogers, who had just completed a two-year stint as the undersecretary for Latin America, was even more bullish about the significance of the recently completed OAS meeting. "Historians may some day come to mark it as the end of one critical era and the beginning of another," Rogers wrote.[56] He was right—but in precisely the opposite way from what he suggested.

By persistently propping up the status quo over eight years, the Republican administrations had created a powerful illusion of success. By 1976, reliable authoritarian regimes governed almost all of Latin America. Panama had largely been neutralized as a source of unrest, and Cuba showed few aspirations to play a disruptive role within the hemisphere. In crucial ways, however, the Nixon-Ford achievements masked enormous problems. Most obviously, Cuba, far from defeated in its bid to spread revolution, merely diverted its attention to Africa, where 20,000 Cuban troops dealt the United States enormous setbacks in Angola.[57] More fundamentally, the U.S. approach to Latin America fostered conditions that would produce chaos in the region—and the jettisoning of their entire U.S. approach to the hemisphere—in the few years that followed Ford's departure from the White House.

Throughout the hemisphere, political repression combined with persistent economic crisis to intensify the sense of social grievance against the prevailing order. In Central America in particular, discontent drove a power-ful shift within the Catholic church, which became a significant force for resistance and change even as authoritarian governments held onto power in the mid-1970s. Still, a small surge of violence involving state security forces and rebellious *campesinos* was already visible in these years in El Salvador, Nicaragua, and Guatemala. Even within the U.S. bureaucracy, some forward-looking officials saw harbingers of trouble ahead. NSC aide Stephen Low worried in April 1975, for example, that the United States was becoming too close to the regime of Nicaraguan dictator Anastasio Somoza Debayle and needed to appoint representatives in Managua who would preserve a "proper distance" from the regime's excesses. Low noted that Somoza's standing in his country had "markedly suffered" in recent times and that there was "a growing question about how long he can maintain himself in power."[58] Few in Washington took note of this kind of advice.

By far the most significant problem for the Ford administration was the backlash that administration policies produced within Washington, especially within Congress. The problem emerged as early as 1973, when the Senate published a report on efforts by the International Telephone and Telegraph Company to prevent Allende from taking office in 1970. In 1974, amid the culmination of the Watergate scandal, the trickle of congressional investiga-tion into U.S. activities in Latin America grew into a flood. Senate reports chronicled more than a decade of U.S. meddling in Chilean politics leading up to the coup and provided details on U.S. complicity in the assassination of General Schneider. Congressional complaints forced the Ford administration to hold back some military aid for Santiago and to admonish some of its Latin American partners about the need for gentler treatment of political oppo-nents. But anxieties about human rights did not seriously impede the admin-istration's conduct of policy toward Latin America as long as it remained in office. Only with the election of Jimmy Carter in 1976 did mounting public concern about the immorality of U.S. foreign policy produce a decisive shift away from the Nixon–Kissinger approach to the hemisphere. Promising a for-eign policy firmly rooted in dedication to human rights and democracy, the Carter administration distanced itself from military regimes and, at one time or another, cut off aid to Argentina, Nicaragua, Chile, and Guatemala.

More than any other event, the overthrow of Anastasio Somoza in 1979 marked the failure of Nixon-Kissinger approach to Latin America. For eight years, Republican administrations had attempted to keep political unrest from challenging the status quo in Latin America. The fact that the Carter administration had helped encourage that outcome by explicitly repudiating the Nixon–Kissinger policy in Latin America only made the defeat clearer. Both abroad and at home, the policy proved to be unsustainable by generating resistance among both Latin Americans and U.S. citizens. Only one indignity remained for Nixon and Kissinger. Latin America, the part of the world that they consistently regarded as least important to U.S. interests, would mar their reputations at least as much as any other region or issue. Since the early 1970s, the two men have come under sharp attack for the cynicism and deception they practiced in Chile. Only in recent years has it become clear that Chile was only the most egregious example of an approach practiced across the hemisphere. With new scrutiny of U.S. policymaking beyond Chile, not least in connection with Operation Condor, Nixon and Kissinger's reputations are likely to sink further still.

Notes

1. Recording of Nixon's meeting with Donald Rumsfeld, March 8, 1971, Nixon tapes, conversation 463–6, http://www.whitehousetapes.org/pages/listen_tapes_rmn.htm

2. Quoted in Seymour M. Hersh, *The Price of Power: Kissinger in the Nixon White House* (New York, 1983), 263.

3. Henry Kissinger, *Years of Renewal* (New York, 1999), 706.

4. Walter LaFeber, *Inevitable Revolutions: The United States in Central America*, 2nd ed. (New York, 1993).

5. See esp. Hersh, *Price of Power;* and Christopher Hitchens, *The Trial of Henry Kissinger* (New York, 2002).

6. NSC report, "A Study of U.S. Policy toward Latin America," March 1969, NSC Institutional Files, Box H-134, NPMP.

7. Osgood to Kissinger, Oct. 14, 1969, NSC Institutional Files, Box H-134, NPMP.

8. National Security Council report, "A Study of U.S. Policy toward Latin America," March 1969, NSC Institutional Files, Box H-134, NPMP.

9. Piero Gleijeses, *Conflicting Missions: Havana, Washington, and Africa, 1959–1976* (Chapel Hill, N.C., 2002), 28–29.

10. Report by Nelson A. Rockefeller, "Quality of Life in the Americas," Aug. 30, 1969, NSC Institutional Files, Box H-024, NPMP.

11. National Security Council report, "A Study of U.S. Policy toward Latin America," March 1969, NSC Institutional Files, Box H-134, NPMP.

12. Alan McPherson, *Yankee No! Anti-Americanism in U.S.-Latin American Relations* (Cambridge, Mass., 2003), chap. 1.

13. Recording of Nixon's meeting with Douglas MacArthur II, April 8, 1971, Nixon tapes, conversation 475–22, http://www.whitehousetapes.org/pages/listen_tapes_rmn.htm

14. Telephone transcript, Nixon and Kissinger, Oct. 24, 1969, Kissinger Telcons, Box 2, NPMP.
15. Nixon's talking points for NSC meeting, Oct. 15, 1969, NSC Institutional Files, Box H-024, NPMP.
16. Nixon speech, Oct. 31, 1969, White House Central File, Subject Categories: speeches, Box 113, NPMP.
17. *New York Times*, "Modest Steps for the Americas," Nov. 2, 1969.
18. *Washington Post*, "Action for Progress in the Americas," Nov. 2, 1969. For an overview of Latin American skepticism about the speech, see *New York Times*, "Latin Reaction to Nixon Speech Mixed," Nov. 2, 1969.
19. Nixon speech, Oct. 31, 1969, White House Central File, Subject Categories: speeches, Box 113, NPMP.
20. Telephone transcript, Nixon and Kissinger, Oct. 30, 1969, Kissinger Telcons, Box 2, NPMP.
21. State Department Intelligence Brief, "The Soviets at Cienfuegos," Sept. 21, 1970, National Security File, Kissinger Papers, Country File, Box 128, NPMP.
22. Ibid.
23. Richard T. Kennedy to Kissinger, Sept. 24, 1970, National Security File, Kissinger Papers, Country File, Box 128, NPMP.
24. Quoted in Hersh, *Price of Power*, 251.
25. Minutes of Senior Review Group Meeting, Sept. 19, 1970, National Security File, Kissinger Papers, Country File, Box 128, NPMP.
26. Quoted in Hersh, *Price of Power*, 252.
27. Alexander Haig to Kissinger, briefing paper for Kissinger's meeting with congressional leaders, November 5, 1970, National Security File, Kissinger Papers, Country File, Box 128, NPMP.
28. See Jonathan Haslam, *The Nixon Administration and the Death of Allende's Chile* (New York, 2005), chapters 1 and 2.
29. Quoted in ibid., 56.
30. Memorandum of conversation, "NSC Meeting—Chile," Nov. 6, 1970, in Peter Kornbluh, ed., *The Pinochet File: A Declassified Dossier on Atrocity and Accountability* (New York, 2003), 119–120.
31. Quoted in Haslam, *Nixon Administration and the Death of Allende's Chile*, 56.
32. Jussi Hanhimäki, *The Flawed Architect: Henry Kissinger and American Foreign Policy* (New York, 2004), 102.
33. Note by Helms, "Meeting with the President on Chile at 1525," Sept. 15, 1970, in Kornbluh, *Pinochet File*, 36.
34. National Security Decision Memorandum 93, "Policy Towards Chile," November 9, 1970, NSC Institutional Files, Box H-220, NPMP.
35. Quoted in Hanhimäki, *Flawed Architect*, 103.
36. Haslam, *Nixon Administration and the Death of Allende's Chile*, especially chapters 5–conclusion.
37. See Nathaniel Davis, *The Last Two Years of Salvador Allende* (Ithaca, 1985); Haslam, *Nixon Administration and the Death of Allende's Chile*; Hersh, *Price of Power*, chaps. 21–22; and Kornbluh, *Pinochet File*.

38. Telephone transcript, Nixon and Kissinger, Kissinger Telcons, Box 22, NPMP.
39. Ibid.
40. NSC report, "U.S. Policy toward Latin America," May 1973, NSC Institutional Files, Box H-197, NPMP.
41. Kissinger, *Years of Renewal*, 723–724.
42. LaFeber, *Inevitable Revolutions*, 206.
43. Kissinger, *Years of Renewal*, 729–730.
44. State Department study, "Issues in U.S.-Latin American Relations," Dec. 16, 1974, National Security Adviser file, Presidential Country Files for Latin America (PCFLA), GRFL.
45. Briefing paper for Brent Scowcroft, "Cuba Policy," Aug. 15, 1974, National Security Adviser file, PCFLA, GRFL.
46. Kissinger, *Years of Renewal*, 728.
47. Low to Kissinger, Sept. 27, 1974, Box 3, National Security Adviser file, PCFLA, GRFL.
48. For the fullest account of these contacts, see Kissinger, *Years of Renewal*, chapter 25.
49. Ibid., 712.
50. NSC report, "Review of U.S. Policy toward Latin America," March 1971, NSC Institutional Files, Box H-177, NPMP.
51. Michael L. Conniff, *Panama and the United States: The Forced Alliance* (Athens, Ga., 1992).
52. Memorandum of conversation, June 8, 1976, National Security Adviser file, PCFLA, GRFL.
53. John Dinges, *The Condor Years: How Pinochet and His Allies Brought Terrorism to Three Continents* (New York, 2004), 18.
54. Ibid., especially 120–125, 156–162.
55. Scowcroft to Ford, July 19, 1976, Box 3, National Security Adviser file, PCFLA, GRFL.
56. Rogers to Kissinger, June 30, 1976, Box 3, National Security Adviser file, PCFLA, GRFL.
57. Gleijeses, *Conflicting Missions*, chapters 12–16.
58. Low to Scowcroft, April 8, 1975, Box 5, National Security Adviser file, PCFLA, GRFL.

14

Nixon Shocks Japan, Inc.

Thomas W. Zeiler

"The present U.S. balance-of-payments position is very precarious," began the report of a task force tapped by President-elect Richard Nixon to provide guidance on foreign economic problems.[1] By the time he took office, the multilateral, market-oriented regime that permitted the United States to spend expansively at home and abroad had reached a crisis point marked by the payments deficit, or the net loss suffered by America from its trade, investment, and monetary exchanges with the rest of the world. Nixon accepted that U.S. power had entered a new era of constraints. No longer did the "American Century" promise outright hegemony. This was a normal course of events; thriving trade partners had arisen from the ashes of World War II. Yet the new president understood that the relative shift in global economic power placed on trial the very liberal, free-trade principles and practices that had girded U.S. dominance over the past quarter century. Nixon determined to address untenable policies, correcting worsening economic imbalances that weakened U.S. leadership and prestige among its anti-communist allies.

Critics have called his response a form of crude mercantilism, a government policy designed to intervene in the global market in ways that maintained the American empire by compelling trade partners to pay more for U.S. security services. Some argue that domestic politics lay at the heart of his approach. They accuse him of using a tough trade and finance agenda to pump up the economy and garner reelection votes from labor and business.[2]

They are all correct. Nixon thought of international trade and finance in terms of bolstering U.S. power. Moreover, he operated foremost as a gut-instinct politician in foreign economic policy, contextualizing trade and monetary affairs in terms of influencing Congress, elections, and public opinion. Whereas the first two decades of the postwar era witnessed the separation of economics from political diplomacy, the 1970s joined the two. To comprehend the linkage, one need only look to the mandate behind the Council on International Economic Policy, established in January 1971 to integrate trade with domestic concerns and strategic foreign policy.[3] General principles of open and fair liberal economics alone would no longer steer America's transactions with the world.

Yet the politicization of foreign economic policy should not be inflated beyond its immediate effects. That is, protests over Nixon's jarring approach to economic relations expressed in the second "Nixon shock" of August 15, 1971, belies his prescient thinking about the transformations facing the country and the capitalist world economy. Style disguised substance, exaggerating the effects of Nixon's policies. *How* he sought to redress America's sliding economic fortunes on the backs of the closest partners, and particularly Japan, has overwhelmed *why* he did so. White House foreign economics czar Peter G. Peterson explained that while trade and finance might be low diplomatic policies, they related directly to U.S. power in the world.[4] The United States could no longer afford unilateral support payments to free-riding allies, especially as the trade balance fell into deficit, gold reserves dropped to dangerously low levels, and uncertainties in the Middle East threatened the flow of cheap oil. Nixon prodded the international economic system into a new era of competition, and he did so without unduly injuring America's trade partners over the long haul.

Actually, he did more than prod: he pushed other nations into a new monetary era. Hence the moniker "Nixon shocks," an appellation reflective of Nixon's willingness to undertake major policy changes without giving prior notice to his allies, especially Japan. The approach played to his sense of the dramatic and it also scored points among nationalist and parochial domestic observers. But the Nixon shocks also attempted to reshape long-standing strategic and economic relationships between the United States, its allies, and its enemies. The most famous shock—the first one—dealt with grand strategy when the president announced in July 1971 plans to visit the People's Republic of China the following February. This bold maneuver would, he hoped, reap diplomatic rewards for the United States by further driving apart the Chinese and Soviets, persuading Beijing to press Hanoi for acceptable peace terms so that America could end its war in Vietnam, and convincing Moscow that its interests lay in easing of tensions with Washington. The first shock also stunned Japan, whose entire postwar foreign policy—at the behest of the United States—had been predicated on separation from China.

The second shock addressed the world economy and U.S. economic troubles. It took as a basic assumption that the Bretton Woods monetary system that had governed monetary relations of capitalist nations since 1944 was moribund and, above all, hurtful to the interests of the United States. Just as he would jolt his enemies into a new strategic posture, so too would Nixon impel the world economy into a new regime of international trade and payments. Specifically, he aimed to wrest the dollar from its grounding in gold—the basis of Bretton Woods—thereby letting exchange rates "float" (appreciate or decline) against other currencies. This would adjust over- or undervalued currencies to the world market, bringing the prices of goods (and, hence, trade and American accounts) into better balance. Both shocks, he hoped, would maintain U.S. power and hegemony, ease American economic woes, and render him unbeatable in his reelection bid in 1972.[5]

The new president reacted to the changed economic landscape of the late 1960s and early 1970s. To be sure, trade and payments problems were not uppermost in his mind, but they related to a host of weaknesses that plagued the economy when Nixon took over, such as inflation, fear of recession, high interest rates, a declining stock market, a squeeze on credit, and a falling dollar. Inflation was the main bogey. The expense of the Vietnam War and President Lyndon Johnson's massive domestic safety net, the Great Society, had driven up consumer prices 5 percent annually by the 1968 election. Liberals hoped to block the upward spiral of prices that so hurt American consumers and workers by growing the economy; seeking to balance the budget, conservatives sought to restore market initiatives by controlling the money supply and reducing the size of the welfare state. Nixon sided with the latter upon coming into office, yet he embraced the political benefits of avoiding austerity measures. He considered wage and price stability, but he also understood that inflation could not be tamed solely at home. America's international accounts proved harmful to the domestic economy, too.

Under the rules of the Bretton Woods monetary system, the U.S. dollar could not be devalued to correct a payments deficit. During the early Cold War, this was welcome. The overvalued dollar made the goods of its allies cheaper. Thus, along with their trade restrictions on U.S. exports, the high greenback aided their recovery. Yet America's overseas trade and payments imbalance steadily deteriorated as time went on. When Europeans (under the powerful six-nation Common Market) and the Japanese were back on their feet as effective trade competitors and protectionists—clearly the case by the Nixon years—the burden on the U.S. economy intensified.[6] With the Bretton Woods dysfunctional, the new president could not longer stand by. A fix, perhaps extraordinary, was in order.

The Nixon shock had little bearing on the prosperity of America's allies. Japan is a case in point, and will serve here as the basis for explaining the Nixon administration's troubled foray into world economic affairs. Japan became a scapegoat for U.S. concerns, a more pliant target than the European Common Market. No doubt, Nixon's harsh policies, intemperate views of allies, and oftentimes hastily conceived remedies were undiplomatic, but as U.S.-Japan economic accounts showed, they were not unwarranted. Rather, Nixon used trade and financial policies as a tactic to achieve his grander strategy of fitting America into the emerging relationship of equals in the Western alliance. A shock—however erratic—served his purposes, both internationally and domestically.

Why train his sights on Japan in order to attack the Bretton Woods system of monetary policy and decades of freer trade doctrine? Because he could. Japan was the weakest diplomatic player in the Western alliance. Unlike an assault on the Europeans or Canadians, a punishing blow to Tokyo would not provoke a major political or economic conflict. Furthermore, Japan could be viewed as the free-rider most benefiting from American largesse; it had become a force in international trade and finance with its security paid for by the United States. Japan's recovery from World War II was complete by 1969. The country had enjoyed a growth rate twice that of the other industrialized nations in the 1960s, emerging as one of the five largest members of the International Monetary Fund (IMF). Low inflation rates and export prices, along with improved design and quality, had quadrupled its sales abroad during the decade. Such growth spoke to the success of American tutelage. It became a worry for the Nixon administration, however, for the U.S. trade surplus rapidly dwindled as Japan's skyrocketed. By the 1970s, Japan accounted for over 15 percent of U.S. imports as exports so far outpaced its imports that its overall trade surplus doubled to $8 billion in just one year, 1970–1971. Japanese market penetration, along with barriers to American products, yielded the United States a $1 billion dollar bilateral trade deficit by Nixon's tenure. Remarkably, just one year into the new decade, that imbalance tripled, and rose above $4 billion in 1972.[7]

Nixon's economic problems with Japan stemmed from the Bretton Woods system, and they drew the attention of U.S. merchants plying their wares overseas and his security team, which warned of dire consequences should the payments trends with Japan (and Canada and Europe) persist.

Under the two institutions of the Bretton Woods agreement, the IMF and World Bank, the monetary system attempted to stabilize exchange rates and balance international payments, as well as finance reconstruction and development. It rested on the foundation of "fixed" exchange rates, in which the U.S. dollar was permanently valued, or "pegged," to $35 worth of gold. All other national currencies derived their value from this peg. When foreigners earned enough dollars from trade, credits, investments, tourism, and the like, they could cash them in for U.S. gold. America's obligation to exchange gold for dollars held in reserve by other nations ate away the advantage of the greenback's rule over the monetary system, particularly because U.S. trade partners began hording dollars and buying gold thanks to their favorable payments balances with America. This situation had reached crisis levels ever since currency convertibility had become the norm in the late Eisenhower years; constant pressure on the dollar prompted periodic runs on Fort Knox gold reserves in the 1960s. The anachronistically undervalued yen, along with European demands on the overvalued dollar, drained gold coffers and worsened the balance-of-payments deficit. The implications were scary. Into international accounts went U.S. funding for overseas troops, bases, and armaments. Should the deficit worsen, support for the dollar would wane as gold supplies shrank, thereby undermining the entire capitalist trade and financial edifice, perhaps undercutting the Western alliance's resistance to communism, and definitely weakening America's dominance (through the dollar) over its allies.[8]

Adding to his woes, domestic political conflict went hand in hand with these tribulations as the American Century soured. In Congress, legislators from both parties, including the traditionally low-tariff Democrats, protested the Cold War liberal-trade consensus. Their constituents suffered from the effects of the downturn, blamed partly (and erroneously) on a traditional scapegoat: imports. Shut out from Japanese markets and facing a tidal wave of competitive imports, the American business community took aim on the seeming juggernaut of private-public sector collusion they called "Japan, Inc."[9] Tokyo had reaped large dividends from the recent round of trade negotiations under the General Agreement on Tariffs and Trade (GATT). While receiving considerable tariff concessions for its exports to the United States, Japan had not opened its market to a commensurate extent. Worse, protectionists charged that such politically charged goods as textiles were flooding the U.S. market, and their outcries intensified as Japanese competition became more potent, the economy struggled, and payments accounts remained in the red. In part, shoddy U.S. craftsmanship, high costs, and a lack of an industrial policy explained the trade troubles. Yet politicians deemed that Japan would pay for its transgressions, perceived or otherwise.

The Nixon administration issued its initial salvo against textile imports, motivated by the desire to quell protectionism. That a president might embrace side deals to preserve the overall trend of liberal trade was not new, nor was a fracas over textiles a novelty: agreements on export restraints had existed since the mid-1950s. What was a break from the past was the pitiless nature of the Nixon approach. The president strong-armed the Japanese into a deal for the sake of domestic observers. Japan took notice, for nearly a third of its exports went to the United States.[10] Merciless and even dismissive behavior on the administration's part, however, should be taken at face value.

It is important to note that officials endorsed the continuation of free-trade policies. Indeed, Nixon endorsed a confidential report of a transition task force, chaired by economic consultant Alan Greenspan, urging him to announce that the country's liberal trade approach would not change, regardless of difficulties. Indeed, removing barriers to trade remained America's cardinal objective. The report warned that should trade restrictions on a specific product such as oil, steel, or textiles be deemed necessary, they should be temporary and negotiated with trade partners. "Protectionism is bad for our image abroad, bad for our economy at home and capable of vitiating our world leadership stance for which we have spent billions of dollars annually—militarily, economically, and in the space program," summed up a Treasury official in March 1969.[11]

That Nixon prioritized a liberal trade agenda was evident from a myriad of documents issued by the normally national-minded constituent agencies as well as the typical internationalist bureaucracies. Indeed, Secretary of State William Rogers wrote that America must "cast off the pall of protectionism that is enveloping international economic relations," push against quota bills at home, and refresh momentum for liberalism by new trade legislation.[12] But even his counterpart in the Commerce Department, Maurice Stans, sought to alleviate irritants in trade. Top on his list were menacing textile problems that might discourage Japan from emerging from trade isolationism and changing policies that varied "markedly from that of the U.S. and even from the principles of such international organizations as the GATT and [the Organization for Economic Cooperation and Development] to which both countries belong."[13] In other words, the health of the free-trade regime hinged, in part, on paying special attention to this reliant ally.

Because the transformation in the U.S.-Japanese trade balance and in Japan's ascendancy was so meteoric, politics intruded on the textile issue.

Prime Minister Eisaku Sato could not deliver on his pledge to his textile industry to open U.S. markets, but Nixon fixated on a show of force against Japanese exports anyway. The president sought limits on man-made and wool textile imports from Asia, a campaign promise from 1968. Thus, officials recognized that "the only viable position that we have with regard to textiles is that it is basically a political problem. Unless an international solution can be found, the Congress will enact restrictive legislation."[14]

So politicized, the ensuing "textile wrangle" absorbed two summit conferences, two ministerial meetings, and nine major negotiations over the next three years.[15] Both nations engaged in such "gross mismanagement" of the conflict, wrote Undersecretary of State and former ambassador to Japan U. Alexis Johnson, that they let textile imports blossom into a political crisis in which policymakers became "pliant tools" of domestic industry.[16] Critics reproach Nixon more than Sato. The latter bungled matters at home; the president bullied a vulnerable ally. In the spring of 1969, Stans thought he could convince the Japanese to limit their shipments voluntarily. By October, Henry Kissinger lamented that trade partners believed that "textiles is only the beginning of our restraint efforts and that other products will follow." He urged the president to dispel such thinking in his message presenting his trade bill to Congress.[17] Yet Nixon was "extraordinarily insensitive" when it came to textiles, claimed National Security Council (NSC) staffer Richard Cooper. He exacerbated Sato's domestic difficulties and unnecessarily elevated bilateral tensions.[18]

Nixon backed quotas on textile imports. This was no bluff. He tried to coax Sato at a summit meeting in November 1969, and again over the next year, to limit exports or face quotas. Nixon believed that he got a promise on export restraints from the prime minister, who said at the meeting that "apart from textiles [the two nations] should move broadly toward freer trade."[19] When Sato did not come through, Nixon accused him of welching. His frustration was clear, especially because he believed that Japan could be "added 'as a fifth finger' to the four existing areas of great power, the United States, Western Europe, the Soviet Union, and China." Instead, Nixon thought Sato was, metaphorically, giving him the finger.[20] Kissinger shared that view, reacting with disdain as he contemptuously referred to the Japanese as "little Sony salesmen" focused on trade advantages and nothing more.[21] Sato retorted that the problem was essentially political and that the request for protection was "contrary to free trade principles." He was right, but such statements did not hold American protectionists at bay.[22]

Nixon could not resist the intensifying pressure in Congress, which had stepped into the matter to the extent that House Ways and Means Committee Chairman Wilbur Mills even bargained with the Japanese himself. By 1971, Mills competed with the president as industry's go-to guy for a quota bill in the event that Nixon and Sato could not make a deal. In addition, he could turn Congress against the president's big trade legislation. Nixon certainly understood the congressman's leverage. In order to preempt Mills, he backed the quota bill, issued his Nixon shocks (the first being the opening to China, which Japan resented, followed by the second of economic measures), and, remarkably, threatened to clamp down on textile imports under the Trading with the Enemy Act of 1917. This unprecedentedly belligerent move, taken not only in peacetime but directed toward a friendly nation, initiated the most miserable period in bilateral relations since the end of the American occupation of Japan. Nixon slapped aside years of Cold War cooperation for narrow domestic concerns.[23]

In the end, moderates failed on both sides. Nixon imposed a "forced settle-ment" of comprehensive textiles quotas, which Japanese producers looked on as Sato's surrender to U.S. coercion. They could hardly be faulted for this complaint. Broad strategic concerns fell by the wayside as domestic politi-cal considerations rushed to the fore. Nixon had been blunt, warning the Japanese that without quotas, Congress might launch a trade war that could threaten important diplomatic interests, such as the reversion of Okinawa to Japan's control. The case of textiles showed that no longer would the United States necessarily subsume particular economic problems under the Cold War umbrella. The textile wrangle put free-riding friends on notice that Nixon meant to shore up American economic power.[24]

As the textile conflict approached its denouement, Nixon precipitated the end of the Bretton Woods monetary system to adjust the world to new realities with the second Nixon shock. His evening television announce-ment on August 15, 1971, described a stunningly unilateral plan to con-tend with the economic problems facing by the United States. When he slammed shut the gold window, preventing allies from exchanging accu-mulations of dollars for bullion, and then imposed a 10 percent surcharge on imports, he advocated the most strident nationalism in American eco-nomic policy since the Great Depression. Like Lenin's program of the 1920s, Nixon's New Economic Policy, as he labeled the second shock, was a dramatic turnabout. The effect on the global monetary system of ending the dollar peg to gold reverberates to this day because it ushered in the era of floating exchange rates. Like the textile tussle, the August 15 actions were a tactic to promote abrupt change, to thrust the world into a new financial regime.

Tokyo entered into Nixon's financial reform picture, for its undervalued yen made its products cheaper in the United States and thus worsened the trade imbalance. However, the United States really had Europe in mind when it set about to remedy its financial difficulties. Focus on the mark, franc, and pound was a natural outgrowth of the status of these major currencies and recognition of the burden of American commitments in Europe. Nixon tried not to alter the price of gold, and to this end, he established the "Volcker Group", named after Undersecretary of the Treasury for Monetary Affairs Paul Volcker, to recommend alternative courses. In March 1969, these advisors counseled either evolutionary changes in the monetary regime or the suspension of gold convertibility as the first step toward junking Bretton Woods entirely. Volcker preferred the former, the course of moderation.[25]

The second option involved a unilateral move to close the gold window, although inter-allied discussions about this possibility occurred for a few years. The Volcker Group warned that the "extent of the shock" would depend on the circumstances; if Nixon took the drastic measure after another substantial loss of gold, then the international reaction "might be less nervous" over time. This calculation proved accurate, although objections preceded reform. As the advisors predicted, countries continued to peg gold to the dollar but they appreciated their exchange rates, as in the case of Japan, or reduced their dollar holdings, like the Europeans. All agreed to some degree of floating exchange rates. However Bretton Woods changed, clearly the Nixon administration struck out on a path of national autonomy in financial decision making. Placing U.S. interests above the monetary system's stability was not a first, for Lyndon Johnson had done the same. That Nixon actually implemented policies that sacrificed currency convertibility on the altar of domestic and security priorities was the striking difference.[26]

The issue must be placed in a context of two-and-a-half years of discussions with European partners, who understood that Nixon would act, though not out of the blue. After all, the U.S. payments deficit fell into arrears by $2.1 billion in just the first two weeks of May 1969, when it had never dropped below $4 billion in an entire year. Improvement was evident in the spring of 1970 after Canada floated its dollar upward. Foreign exchange markets remained relatively quiet over the next year; nations consulted on limited exchange rate flexibility. But even an uptick in the trade balance did not assure a happy future, particularly because all nations sought trade surpluses with the United States. A piecemeal approach begged for a more permanent remedy to remove currency speculation from politics and, most significantly, correct payments imbalances. This was especially true of Japan, with its growing trade surplus and seeming complacency regarding its closed markets that placed America at a distinct disadvantage. The issue came down to whether nations should follow a "low-key" approach to limited rate flexibility, so as not to spark resentment toward the United States, or an "aggressive" plan of prompt manipulation of rates that damned the political fallout.[27]

Thus, when the second Nixon shock came, a revolutionary change was not unexpected. The administration opted for starting anew because the U.S. balance-of-payments deficit of 1971 was running so far above the previous year's level. In anticipation of major currency appreciation against the greenback, the inflow of dollars to Europe and Japan had skyrocketed. These nations could now cash out for ever increasing amounts of gold. Throughout the summer of 1971, the Department of the Treasury pushed for more flexibility in adjusting exchange rates, as well as burden-sharing of foreign aid and defense costs among its allies. The cause of gradualism seemed lost, however. With the forceful politico John Connally at the helm, the Treasury Department counseled an end to the reformist Volcker's "low-key" approach. The Treasury secretary declared the time ripe for monetary aggression.[28]

Connally spoke the language of economic realpolitik that appealed to Nixon. He did not seek isolationism, but he worried that the present course would undermine confidence in the dollar, stability in the monetary system, and sound management in the event of a crisis. Nixon, he argued, had to "realize there is a strong element of thinking within Europe that would take advantage of weakness or clumsiness on our part to promote the Common Market not as a partner but as a rival economic bloc, competing vigorously with the dollar and reducing or shutting out, as best it can, U.S. economic influence from a considerable portion of the world."[29] Connally advised a bold move, namely, exchange rate flexibility and tough controls on capital and trade. In essence, he shared Nixon's paranoid world view in which rival action wielded economic policies designed to hatchet America from its place of leadership in the global trade and financial regimes. As he claimed, "foreigners are out to screw us. Our job is to screw them first."[30]

Connally had plenty of critics. His chief antagonist, Federal Reserve Chairman Arthur Burns, thought such thinking ran contrary to U.S. interests. There was no reason to rush events, Burns countered. A rash devaluation might cause stocks to tumble and nations to retaliate with trade restrictions. "*Pravda* would write that this was a sign of the collapse of capitalism,"

Burns warned.[31] The foreign policy bureaucracy concurred. The NSC, for one, believed that drastic change to the current system of tinkering with rates would cause angry allies to make a run on Fort Knox, thereby compelling Nixon to close the gold window and float the dollar. Such a result "would clearly spill over into our political relations," wrote an NSC staffer to Kissinger.[32]

A two-month calm followed May's distressed exchange markets, but in August 1971 turmoil set in once again and compelled the president to convene his advisors at Camp David. In the historic decision to impose the second shock and slam the gold window, float the dollar, and impose a tariff surcharge—as well as set wage and price controls and reinstitute the investment tax credit at home—Nixon took a comprehensive position to the troubled economy. He preferred Connally's audacity after first leaning toward using only the domestic program to strengthen the dollar. As aide H. R. Haldeman noted, Nixon realized he had no good options. He faced either a continued gold drain or speculation against the dollar. The time had come for change. Once Connally had persuaded him to link the domestic and international agendas, Nixon went for the "big, bold" program, convinced that, like the "China thing," it would hit the newsstands at an unforeseen time for maximum effect abroad.[33]

It did, as foreign leaders protested the Camp David terms. Actually, untying the dollar from gold was not a problem for them. What was startling was the import surcharge, from which some nations (such as America's top trade partner, Canada) wanted exemptions. In the week after the announcement, most foreign exchange markets closed, but a battle already had broken out between France, which refused to revalue the franc, and Germany, which pushed for the float. Key trade partners, including Italy and Germany, were suffering recessions and thus took countermeasures of restricting trade and money. This was the sort of reaction that worried foreign policymakers and Nixon. Thus, he decided to terminate the 10 percent surcharge, a "wasting asset" that unnecessarily irked friends abroad, by the end of the year.[34]

Nixon could not deny the uncomfortable truth, as his critics pointed out, that his broad-brush approach stirred up the sort of economic nationalism that might spill into diplomatic affairs. He used world monetary policy to address domestic and security priorities. To his credit, Nixon preferred an overhaul to a patch in addressing the U.S. payments problem, thereby setting up the floating exchange system that stimulated globalization. But he also mocked a quarter century of multilateralism. Indeed, assessing the controls years later, he admitted that they had been politically expedient but wrong in principle. Priming the domestic economy boosted growth in 1972 and scored Nixon votes in his successful reelection bid that year. Still, his temporary fix had stuck it to the global monetary regime as well as trade partners. "The piper must always be paid," he lamented, "and there was an unquestionably high price for tampering with the orthodox economic mechanisms."[35]

Second thoughts and embellishments of his image as a statesman aside, Nixon need not have worried about the deleterious impact on Japan. In Tokyo, his announcement—along with the issues of China and textiles—raised bilateral diplomatic tensions. This, even though the Japanese were among the key perpetrators of Bretton Woods' demise because of their large dollar holdings earned from large trade surpluses. In fact, up to Camp David, only Japan of the major industrialized nations had avoided exchange rate adjustments and dragged its feet on trade liberalization. Thus, Tokyo realized the import of the second Nixon shock. Although Ministry of Finance officials bitterly protested, the government decided to appreciate the yen within two weeks of Nixon's second shock announcement. The float was settled in the Smithsonian Agreement of December 1971, where Bretton Woods was, for the most part, buried.[36]

The second Nixon shock was crass, but its context and results must be considered, too. The revaluation from 360 to 308 yen against the dollar (a 16.88% adjustment) was not damaging to Japan, particularly as businessmen absorbed the appreciation and, over the next two decades, boosted their export surplus to the United States to astronomical levels. Even Nixon protested too much, for yen revaluation was quite modest in light of Japan's advantaged position and unwillingness to trade in a way commensurate with its big-power status. Japan's "Eight-Point Program to Avoid Yen Revaluation" hinged on enhanced commercial liberalization, investments, and foreign aid, but Stans, Rogers, and Nixon himself correctly deemed the agenda insufficient to expand American exports appreciably and rectify the U.S. payments imbalance.[37]

Due to Tokyo's rather outlandish position in trade and monetary affairs, it could be argued that Nixon placed Japan at the receiving end of his New Economic Policy. In the four months after Camp David, the Japanese stock market lost 10 percent of its value. Tokyo complained bitterly as the administration pounded away on its themes of trade liberalization, aid-sharing, and yen appreciation. The pressure paid off, as Finance Minister Mikio Mizuta announced an end to his country's twenty-two-year support for the 360 yen/dollar rate of exchange. He did not give up easily, though. First, he tried to purchase all the dollars he could. Then, he endured the strong-arm tactics of "Typhoon" Connally, who blew into Tokyo in November 1971 just before the Smithsonian meeting to demand revaluation and more market access. If not, the Treasury warned, then Washington would consider protectionism, a stance backed even by administration free traders back home. Connally insisted that Japan realign the yen in preparation for his talks with the Europeans; the Japanese correctly surmised that he wanted their commitment as leverage to coax Britain, France, Germany, and others to revaluate their currencies.[38]

Nonetheless, Japan believed the Nixon administration was coercive. Its currency appreciation of nearly 17 percent was the highest percentage gain against the dollar of any of the Group of Ten economic powers, Switzerland being next at less than 14 percent. When Japan continued to resist demands for trade liberalization, U.S. Special Trade Representative William Eberle informed Tokyo that its import and export programs were inseparable from monetary policies. Once the Smithsonian accords set exchange rates, however, the Japanese retreated again. They suspended trade talks and resisted any further yen inflation. To grant more market access, new Prime Minister Kakuei Tanaka agreed at a September 1972 summit with Nixon in Hawaii to buy more Lockheed jets. He would not assent to the U.S. Treasury's request to revalue the yen another 10 percent, however, which might stymie his expansionist domestic policies. Tanaka need not have worried. Japan eventually floated the yen, which rose against the dollar, and also continued to enjoy a huge trade surplus with the United States.

Unleashing Connally to browbeat the Japanese made official Washingtonians somewhat uncomfortable, but they fretted too much. Like others, Kissinger disliked the "frontal assault" on trade partners. To be sure, the Connally-Nixon offensive on exchange rates was brusque, but the results did not really alter either the multilateral system or America's relative decline in it. The dollar remained the global currency, yet the international payments imbalance still suffered. Ominously, in 1971, for the first time in the twentieth century, the country ran into its first of a long string of trade deficits. How long the economy could survive under those conditions depended on circumstances, and the oil shock of 1973–1974 immediately put it to the test. Soon overshadowing the second Nixon shock, this latter development resulted in an eventual five-fold skyrocketing of oil prices which, as Kissinger and others noted, created billions of new dollars that added to the turmoil in global exchanges of money. Precipitated by Arab lobbying within the Organization of Petroleum Exporting Countries (OPEC) to embargo shipments of oil to supporters of Israel and to raise the price of world oil, the third "shock" of the Nixon years demonstrated once again that the United States was no longer immune from international economic pressures.[39] In fact, its very hegemony was called into question by OPEC and the payments imbalance prompted by Western competition. The 1970s became a long decade of woeful economic news.

Along with textiles and the dollar, the conflict over market access for American products became the third bête noire of Nixon's trio of assaults on Japan. Critics view his pressure for access for autos and farm goods as severe and off the mark. Like U.S. Ambassador Armin Meyer, some believed Japan's only fault lay in its industriousness, efficiency, and wisdom in promoting exports. Liberalization of its own markets was proceeding apace with Sato's Eight-Point Program. Self-criticism was in order, for many American goods were unappealing. Furthermore, swiping at Japan's import policies overlooked structural differences between the two countries, namely, the highly regulated nature of the Japanese economy. To regain competitiveness, the United States must engage in careful negotiations to lever-open Japan's markets. Yet even Meyer recognized that Nixon's move did not necessarily single out Japan. Instead, the administration aimed to jolt awake Japanese trading companies and the government to the notion of a world trade system in crisis.[40]

Nixon might cudgel Japan, but he also recognized certain realities, chief among them America's struggles with its deteriorating trade balance and Japan's rise to power. Simply, the United States was no longer invincible. Furthermore, as a group of businessmen told him in mid-1971, Japan bought mainly raw materials from the U.S. and sold more expensive finished goods, thereby treating America as a Third World country. Worse, Japan still thought of itself as a weakling, as one industrialist put it, "like the golfer who is shooting in the 80s with the same 25 handicap he used when he was shooting in the 100s."[41]

Thus, the reasoning behind the import surcharge of the second Nixon shock was to warn Japan (and Canada, another surplus exporter) that times had changed. Indeed, many experts believe that Nixon coddled the Japanese too much when accounting for the pain inflicted on such industries as autos, electronics, textiles, as well as the enormous and mounting Japanese trade surplus with the United States. After all, more could be done to alleviate America's $29 billion payments deficit by 1972, of which Japan accounted for $3.2 billion. Some of the Japan, Inc., perspective had a distinctly conspiratorial tone in claiming that Japanese lobbyists eased into the halls of

Congress to assure a U.S. liberal trade agenda. Yet such trade historians as Alfred Eckes make a good case that Nixon, like all postwar presidents, sacrificed some domestic producers and labor to foreign goods. This was done in the name of the Cold War: preserving Asian stability, prosperity, and strength by encouraging Japanese exports and permitting protectionism.[42]

Nixon's style might have been jarring but Japan's glacial response justified his intentions. Its mercantilist network of overt and covert import restrictions threatened the cooperative liberalism of the GATT trade regime, as well as U.S. interests. The administration would remedy a situation that had long festered. "Santa Claus is dead," announced Office of Management and Budget Director George Shultz in November 1971, as Connally sought "a New Deal, a Fair Deal for America in the world." Nixon agreed, lashing out that for "twenty-five years the United States has not bargained hard for a better position in world trade, the goddam [sic] State Department hasn't done its job. We're changing the rules of the game."[43] Beginning with bitter talks with Japanese ministers in Honolulu in December, and lasting into the five-year Tokyo Round of GATT convening in 1974, he determined to open Japan's markets. No doubt the United States restrained imports and exports, too, but Trade Representative Eberle demanded a horse trade. If Japan shaved off at least $1 billion from its bilateral surplus by removing trade restrictions on U.S. computers and agricultural commodities, the Nixon administration would lift the import surcharge.[44]

This brinkmanship persisted, and failed, as the Smithsonian Agreement that revalued the yen proved only a temporary respite to the tensions over market access. On February 9, 1972, as Congress debated tougher dollar legislation, Eberle announced that Japan had agreed to relax import barriers on cars, computers, aircraft, livestock, oranges, and soybeans. This was window dressing of the sort that had occurred during the "grapefruit war" of late 1971, when Japan removed quotas only to impose a seasonal tariff of 40 percent from December through March. In this case, as well as in 1972, Tokyo had agreed to the deal well before administration pressure bore down. And Nixon had returned to coddling, as he really desired Japanese endorsement of a new GATT trade round. He succeeded in that aim; Japan agreed to speed up the start of the Tokyo Round by nine months.[45]

"Typhoon" Eberle got concessions on market openings, called "emergency measures" by the Japanese to sell them at home. Yet Tokyo also stood its ground, resisting significant cuts in agricultural barriers due to the weight of its domestic farmers. Unlike Connally's typhoon, Eberle's just blew out. A July 1972 meeting with Tanaka heard Eberle's complaints about Japanese farm quotas and the "serious distortion of the total market" caused by the over $3 billion bilateral trade deficit. The prime minister's promises to dedicate his "best efforts" to addressing these issues were just platitudes, made in the midst of efforts to launch the Tokyo Round and the distractions of Nixon's reelection campaign.[46] Japan's export surplus with the United States approached $4 billion by 1973.

Empty pledges from Tanaka, peppered with a handful of secret deals removed from the observant eyes of Japanese businessmen to eliminate some import and investment controls, were all that followed until Congress took matters into its own hands. One purpose of the Trade Reform Act of 1974 and the Tokyo Round of GATT was to persuade the Europeans to open their markets to Japanese goods. Pursued since World War II, this campaign came to naught. The administration portrayed its approach to Japan on trade matters as very tough in order to stave off congressional retaliatory action. In general, Congress seemed satisfied, but Senator Russell Long and his Finance Committee added provisions to the Trade Reform Act that imposed restrictions on nations refusing to grant reciprocal concessions at negotiations. The Treasury Department enforced more aggressive antidumping actions, although this trend petered out in the face of Watergate. Congress, not the president, eventually became the enforcer of more protective measures.[47]

Detractors of Japan's foreign economic policies called the situation a trade war, expressing their fears in all sorts of unseemly ways, while the anti-Nixon crowd concurred with Japanese businessmen that the president's foreign economic policy was barbaric. Both sides polarized bilateral economic relations. Enmeshed in domestic politics and foreign policy predicaments, Nixon used trade and financial problems to protect U.S. hegemony overseas and garnish his image at home. His "big play" of August 15, 1971, as well as the textile fracas, were bargaining chips that he might have cast aside for quieter approaches. Still, history cannot be ignored. Japan proceeded to post huge trade gains at America's expense, and the two nations arrived at financial agreements that did not punish the yen or the Japanese economy.[48]

Richard Nixon recognized that the international economic arena had transformed into a competitive battleground in which the United States was losing its footing. This was due not only to its inabilities to produce desirable goods but also because of predatory commercial behavior and fixed, regulatory policies on the part of Japan. In short, Japan did not acknowledge that times had changed since the 1950s. By the late 1960s, its trade surplus became entrenched but its markets stayed closed and its contributions to offsetting the U.S. payments imbalance remained too meager. Soon, Japan's

$4 billion trade surplus of 1973 with America appeared miniscule next to the $87 billion figure registered fifteen years later. Incredibly, that 1988 surplus doubled by 1993.[49] By the latter date, the bubble had burst on Japanese prosperity but in trade, Tokyo pushed onward to new heights.

Nixon understood the future trend of the world economy, or at least the place of the United States in it. His did not so much abandon trade liberalism for nationalistic policies as he took a tougher line toward partners, thereby reflecting the new circumstances of America's relative decline in the global economy. He played politics with his foreign economic policy, as electoral gain was never far from his mind, but he was not blind to change. He treated Japan harshly but only because that nation had assumed a new status as a commercial rival.[50] Although his shocking policy prescriptions were not the most diplomatic ways for the United States to adjust to challenges, his policies provided the touchstones for the open-market trade and floating exchange systems that have been the hallmarks of globalization ever since. Japan's emergence as the world's second-largest economy testified, ironically, to the ultimate futility of Nixonian strong-arm tactics.

Notes

1. Summary of the Report of the Task Force on U.S. Balance of Payments Policies, *FRUS, 1969–1976*, vol. III: 1.
2. For example, see David P. Calleo, "Since 1961: American Power in a New World Economy" in *Economics and World Power: An Assessment of American Diplomacy Since 1789*, ed. William H. Becker and Samuel F. Wells, Jr. (New York, 1984), 430; Allen J. Matusow, *Nixon's Economy: Booms, Busts, Dollars, and Votes* (Lawrence, Kans., 1998), 6, 87; and Francis J. Gavin, *Gold, Dollars, and Power: The Politics of International Monetary Relations, 1958–1971* (Chapel Hill, N.C., 2004), 187.
3. For the CIEP, see Memorandum by President Nixon, January 18, 1971, *FRUS, 1969–1976*, vol. II: 811–812.
4. Matusow, *Nixon's Economy*, 133, 136.
5. Michael Schaller, *Altered States: The United States and Japan Since the Occupation* (New York, 1997), 210; Matusow, *Nixon's Economy*, 141, 167–168.
6. Calleo, "Since 1961," 416–419; Herbert Stein, *Presidential Economics: The Making of Economic Policy From Roosevelt to Reagan and Beyond* (New York, 1986), 134–151; Matusow, *Nixon's Economy*, 4–5.
7. Table Ee533–660, "Exports by country of destination: 1790–2001," and Table Ee551–568, "Imports by country of origin: 1790–2001," in Susan B. Carter, et al., *Historical Statistics of the United States: Earliest Times to the Present*, Millennial Edition Online (New York, 2006).

8. Robert Solomon, *The International Monetary System, 1945–1981*, 2nd ed. (New York, 1982), 5–77.

9. Schaller, *Altered States*, 215.

10. Schaller, *Altered States*, 231.

11. Victor A. Mack, "U.S. Trade Problems and Policies," March 11, 1969, Declassification Record #28668, NSA. See also Report of the Task Force on Foreign Trade Policy, *FRUS, 1969–1976*, vol. IV: 463, 467, 469–470.

12. Rogers to Nixon, March 24, 1969, *FRUS, 1969–1976*, vol. IV: 481.

13. U.S. Embassy (Tokyo), "U.S. and Japanese Trade Politics and the Role of Japanese Non-Tariff Barriers," and attached airgram, April 18, 1969, #74833, NSA. See also Stans to Nixon, March 20, 1969, *FRUS, 1969–1976*, vol. IV: 480.

14. John Petty, Briefing Memorandum, May 5, 1969, *FRUS, 1969–1976*, vol. IV: 525.

15. I. M. Destler, Haruhiro Fukui, and Hideo Sato, *The Textile Wrangle: Conflict in Japanese-American Relations, 1969–1971* (Ithaca, 1979).

16. U. Alexis Johnson, with Jef Olivarius McAllister, *The Right Hand of Power* (Englewood Cliffs, N.J., 1984), 548–549.

17. Kissinger to Harlow, October 23, 1969, *FRUS, 1969–1976*, vol. IV: 563.

18. Richard N. Cooper, "Trade Policy is Foreign Policy," *Foreign Policy* 9 (Winter 1972–73): 31.

19. Summary of conversation, November 20, 1969, *FRUS, 1969–1976*, vol. III: 79. See also memorandum from Peter Flanigan, August 5, 1970, Box 48, White House Special Files: Paul W. McCracken Files, NPMP.

20. Summary of conversation, November 20, 1969, *FRUS, 1969–1976*, vol. III: 79.

21. Quoted in Marvin and Bernard Kalb, *Kissinger* (Boston, 1974), 255–256.

22. Notes of conversation at luncheon, River Club, October 19, 1970, Box 11, White House Special Files: Peter Flanigan Files, NPMP.

23. Timmons and Dent to Nixon, June 4, 1970, *FRUS, 1969–1976*, vol. IV: 602; Robert Solomon to Chairman Burns, June 16, 1970, Box C15, Arthur F. Burns Papers, GRFL; meeting with the President regarding Mills, March 9, 1971, #71711, NSA; Walter LaFeber, *The Clash: U.S.-Japanese Relations Throughout History* (New York, 1997), 351–352; Schaller, *Altered States*, 224–225.

24. Destler, et al., *Textile Wrangle*, 310–313, 320.

25. Talking paper prepared in the Department of the Treasury, February 18, 1969, *FRUS, 1969–1976*, vol. III: 303–304.

26. Volcker Group Paper, March 17, 1969, ibid., 310; Kissinger to Nixon, May 7, 1969, ibid., 329; Joanne Gowa, *Closing the Gold Window: Domestic Politics and the End of Bretton Woods* (Ithaca, 1983), 30–31.

27. Memorandum of conversation at Camp David, U.S. and France, May 3–5, 1970, *FRUS, 1969–1976*, vol. III: 393–395. See also memorandum from Paul McCracken, June 6, 1969, ibid., 337; Volcker Group Paper, September 10, 1970, ibid., 410–413.

28. Paper prepared in the Department of the Treasury, May 8, 1971, ibid., 424–425.
29. Connally to Nixon, June 8, 1971, ibid., 441.
30. Quoted in Diane B. Kunz, *Butter and Guns: America's Cold War Economic Diplomacy* (New York, 1997), 218.
31. Quoted in Richard Nixon, *RN: The Memoirs of Richard Nixon* (New York, 1990), 519.
32. Ernest Johnston to Kissinger, June 23, 1971, *FRUS, 1969–1976*, vol. III: 444. See also H. R. Haldeman, *The Haldeman Diaries: Inside the Nixon White House* (New York, 1994), 342.
33. Editorial notes, *FRUS, 1969–1976*, vol. III: 454–460, 466–467. See also Haldeman, *Haldeman Diaries*, 340.
34. Hormats to Kissinger, November 1, 1971, *FRUS, 1969–1976*, vol. III: 526. See also editorial note, ibid., 484–485; Hormats to Kissinger, September 6, 1971, ibid., 488–489.
35. Nixon, *RN*, 521. For critics, see Fred L. Block, *The Origins of International Economic Disorder* (Berkeley, 1977); David P. Calleo, *The Imperious Economy* (Cambridge, Mass., 1982); C. Fred Bergsten, "The New Economics and U.S. Foreign Policy," *Foreign Affairs* 50 (1972): 199–222; Robert Solomon, *The International Monetary System, 1945–1981* (New York, 1982); and Kunz, *Butter and Guns*, 219–222.
36. For Japanese reactions and decisions, see Robert C. Angel, *Explaining Economic Policy Failure: Japan in the 1969–1971 International Monetary Crisis* (New York, 1991).
37. Ibid., 268; CIA, Directorate of Intelligence memorandum, "Japan's Eight Point Economic Program: Progress and Prospects," September 1971, #73718, NSA.
38. Emery to Irvine, August 19, 1971, and Bryant to Burns, August 20, 1971, Box B65, Burns Papers, GRFL; paper agreed by President Nixon and President Pompidou, December 15, 1971, *FRUS, 1969–1976*, vol. III: 597–598. For Connally, see James Reston, Jr., *The Lone State: The Life of John Connally* (New York, 1989), 403–410; and Matusow, *Nixon's Economy*, 137.
39. Henry Kissinger, *White House Years* (Boston, 1979), 951–958. See also Stephen E. Ambrose, *Nixon: The Triumph of a Politician, 1962–1972* (New York, 1989), 456–458; and Wyatt C. Wells, *Economist in an Uncertain World: Arthur F. Burns and the Federal Reserve, 1970–78* (New York, 1994), 85–89.
40. Armin Meyer, *Assignment Tokyo: An Ambassador's Journal* (Indianapolis, 1974), 173, 240; I. M. Destler, *American Trade Politics*, 2nd ed. (Washington, D.C., 1992).
41. Quoted in LaFeber, *The Clash*, 353.
42. Alfred E. Eckes, Jr., *Opening America's Market: U.S. Foreign Trade Policy Since 1776* (Chapel Hill, N.C., 1995). See also Clyde Prestowitz, *Trading Places: How We Allowed Japan to Take the Lead* (New York, 1988); and Pat

Choate, *Agents of Influence* (New York, 1990). The trade figures are from Schaller, *Altered States*, 231.

43. Patrick Buchanan, memorandum for the president's file, "Leadership Meeting," November 16, 1971, #71698, NSA.

44. Eberle to Volcker, and memorandum, Japanese Trade Measures, December 7, 1971, #74120, NSA.

45. Letter from Eberle to Japanese Ambassador Ushiba, February 9, 1972, *FRUS, 1969–1976*, vol. IV: 686–687; White House memorandum of conversation, January 3, 1972, MR NLN 93–18/15, NSA; Meyer, *Assignment*, 225.

46. Memorandum of conversation, Tokyo, July 29, 1972, *FRUS, 1969–1976*, vol. IV: 699, 701.

47. Eckes, *Opening*, 244–245, 269–270.

48. Michael Barnhart, "From Hershey Bars to Motor Cars: America's Economic Policy Toward Japan, 1945–76" in *Partnership: The United States and Japan, 1951–2001*, ed. Akira Iriye and Robert A. Wampler (Tokyo, 2001), 217, 219. See also Schaller, *Altered States*, 232–241.

49. Thomas W. Zeiler, "Business is War in U.S.-Japanese Economic Relations, 1977–2001" in Iriye and Wampler, *Partnership*, 234. For the arguments surrounding U.S.-Japan trade, see Stephen D. Cohen, *An Ocean Apart: Explaining Three Decades of U.S.-Japanese Trade Frictions* (Westport, Conn., 1998).

50. Tadashi Aruga, "Japan and the United States: A Half-Century of Partnership" in *Japan and the United States: Fifty Years of Partnership*, ed. Chihiro Hosoya (Tokyo, 2001), 29.

15

Thanks for the Fish: Nixon, Kissinger, and Canada

Robert Bothwell

One of the more difficult tasks for Henry Kissinger's assistants while he was secretary of state was extracting time for a visit from the Canadian ambassador. It was a duty Secretary Kissinger accepted with a sinking heart. Watching the ambassador heave into his office followed by a minion loaded down with binders, the secretary tried some heavy humor: "I hope you haven't come to talk to me about the sex life of the salmon."[1] But that, as he knew very well, was the topic, for as long as politeness and a busy schedule would allow.

"I didn't ask for a meeting on Canada," he once told a gathering of the State Department's few Canadianists. "I would not feel unfulfilled tonight if it was my destiny that we didn't have a meeting on Canada. But," he added, "*if* we have a meeting on Canada, or any other subject, the question I would like to have an answer to is, what I am trying to accomplish?"[2]

Canada occupies a peculiar place in American foreign relations—strategically crucial in terms of its geography, economically important as the United States' principal trading partner for most of the twentieth century and on into the twenty-first, and politically underappreciated. There was a disconnect between Canada's economic standing as the world's sixth-largest economy and its political impact in Washington. (By the early 1970s Canada accounted for about a quarter of U.S. imports, considerably more than any other country.) Canada, according to an American diplomat who served there in the early 1980s, really was "a minor Power, [and] it usually [did]n't matter what policy positions Canada [took] because it [could] do nothing about most of them."[3] John Foster Dulles once told the Senate Foreign

Relations Committee that Canada's main importance was as real estate—he was thinking strategically. Lawrence Eagleburger, casting back in 2002 over forty years in and around the U.S. Foreign Service, concluded that in his time Canada had only been important economically. He made an exception for individual Canadians who were useful or impressive in terms of their intelligence or expertise, but as a general rule "Canada" was only to be taken seriously in terms of its economic weight, or economic potential.[4]

It helped considerably that there were in the early 1970s no natural enemies of Canada in the United States. Family ties and immigration patterns played a part in this, for there were many Canadian-born living, mostly invisibly, in the United States. The Canadian-born were actually among the larger groups of immigrants—820,771 in 1970, fewer than residents from Germany or Italy, but more than from Great Britain or Mexico, or any third-world country.[5]

Thanks to the Autopact of 1965, which for the most part abolished tariffs on automobiles and automobile parts manufactured in the two countries, the economies of the Great Lakes region especially were more and more highly integrated. Between 1969 and 1975, Canadian trade to and from the United States more than doubled in value. It did more: in 1970 Canada's perennial trade deficit with the United States in the automotive sector was reversed, a phenomenon that seemed like the inversion of a natural law of Canadian-American relations.[6] The Autopact had even included special safeguards for the Canadian automobile industry, which, it had been assumed, would be at a natural disadvantage in conditions of free trade; accordingly, there were incentives for manufacturers to make cars and trucks in Canada. The trade reversal was noted in Washington, and linked to the safeguards in the official mind, at least in the Treasury. It was not something that stuck in the current consciousness of either Henry Kissinger (then national security adviser) or William Rogers (then secretary of state)—in 1970–1971, they had other preoccupations.

For Henry Kissinger, this combination of factors—economic importance and political unimportance—was enough to place Canada in the second rank of countries, to be dealt with by the State Department, and thus, eventually, Rogers. It did not help that Canada was important economically—for Kissinger, economics was a secondary consideration, and the subject itself, as far as he was concerned, was "the paradise of the second-rate."[7] So Rogers got the Canadian file and managed relations with the assistance of a small staff on the State Department's Canadian desk, and through institutionalized joint ministerial meetings. For content, he could rely on the usual clichés about "our neighbors to the north" who dwelt along "the world's longest undefended border." In the opinion of American diplomats with knowledge of Canadian issues, Rogers managed the subject badly, since neither he nor his cabinet colleagues had the time or the inclination to study their briefs when negotiating with the Canadians. The Canadians counted on this characteristic American obliviousness about small countries and small issues, and sometimes did quite well in negotiations with their American counterparts as a result. Partly as a result of pressure from below, the American side eventually killed regular transborder ministerial meetings.[8] Canadian concerns sometimes erupted across the border—there was Québec terrorism in 1969–1971, and the continuing problem of Quebec separatism thereafter. But Québec was always cast as a potential rather than an immediate problem, and during Kissinger's time in office that was where it stayed.[9]

There were potentially other issues, however. In the Nixon–Ford epoch, Canada was not sound on Vietnam, was indeed a refuge for thousands of draft dodgers fleeing conscription in their homeland. Draft dodgers could not be extradited to the United States. Since there was no conscription in Canada, refusing to obey a draft notice was not a crime in the eyes of Canadian courts. The dodgers' passage across the frontier was generally easy, requiring little more than a neat appearance, a deferential attitude and a judicious silence on the subject of the Vietnam War—or any war.[10] (Canadian immigration officers were by and large veterans of the Second World War, and took a dim view of draft avoidance.) Larry Martin, a draft dodger who stayed in Canada, told an interviewer that it helped that "Draft dodgers came to Canada from middle-class backgrounds. They had information about dodging the draft … [They were] people from college who had some work experience."[11] Martin contrasted the dodgers' experience with that of deserters, usually from working-class backgrounds; and as everyone knew, desertion was a crime in Canada too, and so extraditable. Unlike the dodgers, it was very much in the deserters' interest to live below the public radar, and disappear.

There were probably fewer draft dodgers than usually imagined—some 26,000 males, according to John Hagan's estimate. But if the category is broadened to "war resisters," thus including females, the number is roughly double.[12] Given their education and background, they were well equipped to fit into Canada. In the military sense, Canada was "a different world" from the United States, as the novelist Tim O'Brien put it, but the line dividing the two worlds was frequently invisible, and what lay on the other side was frequently indistinguishable from the country left behind.[13]

It followed that the draft dodgers were invisible immigrants to Canada. Years later they could be found in universities, in journalism, and even occasionally in politics. Occasionally they would emerge into public view on the twentieth or twenty-fifth or thirtieth anniversary of some event in the Vietnam War, but otherwise they were lost among their peers from the Canadian baby boom. Canadians generally thought their country had gained from this American immigration, and in this they were undoubtedly correct. Draft evasion was not, however, a subject that the U.S. government cared to engage with, believing, doubtless correctly, that confronting Canada on draft dodgers would stir up political trouble at home in the United States. It would stir up trouble in Canada too, for the Vietnam War was as unpopular north of the border as it was at home. The draft dodgers were, like Canada, a problem of lesser magnitude.

Finally, there was the economy. This was guaranteed to get Canadian attention, and large parts of the Canadian government were devoted to the formulation and management of transborder trade and investment. That was just as well, because Canadian-American economic relations came under harsh scrutiny from John Connally when he served as Nixon's treasury secretary. Relations between Connally and the Canadians were, if possible, worse than with any of his other negotiating partners. The problem was compounded, from the Canadian point of view, by the fact that Nixon did not much like Trudeau and could not be counted on to contradict Connally's growing animus toward the northern neighbor.

In a larger sense, none of this mattered very much to Kissinger. Security was what came first in his priorities and with Canada, security was not an issue. "We have no way of dissociating from them in the security field," Kissinger later reminded his staff, after he had become secretary of state.[14] Fortunately, there were no great security issues that commanded his attention where Canada was concerned—no probable external threats to North America, on air, sea or land. As a result, the United States no longer devoted significant resources to the problem. And if the United States did not, why should Canada?

There was no need for grand diplomacy when it came to Canada. Kissinger dismissed attempts by his staff to draw attention to Canada's obvious strategic dependence. In a general sense, to be sure, Canada relied on American power to defend its shores, but as a practical matter technology and détente had removed the need for an active defense of the continent. "What is the conclusion from that?" he asked. "Since we are no longer engaged in air defense, we have what hold over them?" And why threaten them with the withdrawal of the American umbrella when everyone knew that was geographically absurd?

Finally, what had the Canadians done to require American pressure? There was no sign that they wanted to move away from their alliance with the United States, and thus, Kissinger argued, it could be said that "the Canadians are not yet moving in an antagonistic direction. And therefore we don't face the problem of leverage."[15] Kissinger had no need to link strategic concerns with other, lesser issues, in order to whip the Canadians into line; that he did not do so gratified Canadian diplomats who avoided linkage like the plague as their first rule in dealing with the United States. In their view, and that of most Canadian observers, Canadian relations with the U.S. government were politically and militarily weak but economically strong. They were, as it happened, quite right, but in a way that in 1969 they could never have predicted, or even suspected.

The assumed strength of Canadian-American economic contacts relied on another, apparently eternal, advantage—the amiable disposition of the American public, when it came to Canada. "The majority of Americans combine a poverty of knowledge with great affection for the country and its people," two academics wrote in 1979. "Ninety-three per cent of the masses and 98 per cent of the elite have been found to express positive sentiments towards Canada, a greater degree of warmth than is expressed towards any other country," according to surveys in the early 1970s.[16]

Not everybody was happy, to be sure. The Vietnam War disturbed Canadians, as it disturbed Americans. One prominent Canadian academic—who fulminated regularly over Vietnam in the op-ed columns of the liberal *Toronto Star*—told an audience at Columbia University that "the identity of basic aims" between the two countries had disappeared, thanks to what he called "a new generation of American imperialists."[17] The Columbia audience doubtless agreed with him. There was, however, no practical consequence to be feared.

Kissinger had heard it all before, at Harvard in the sixties and from assorted academics since his arrival in Washington. In Kissinger's world, words did not count as much as raw strength, power. "Frankly," he told a Canadian opposition politician, Joe Clark, "the great disparity in strength between our two countries and Canada's dependence on the US leads me to believe that any Canadian leader would have to be crazy to invite confrontation with the United States. Consequently," he added, "I am somewhat relaxed about the basic relationship." Kissinger knew that some Canadians were anti-American, and he took for granted that some Canadian words and actions would be "irritating to Americans."[18] That did not matter; it was essentially a reaction to American power. "We are so powerful," he argued in 1974, that "whatever identity they have, they get in opposition to us."[19] As he once put it while shooing the members of State's Canadian desk out of his office: "These are small things. Solve them."[20] In Kissinger's time in government, the irritations never reached the point where they called forth an American response.

A later administration would identify the Canadian prime minister, Pierre Elliott Trudeau, as a major irritant. Trudeau lasted a long time as Canada's head of government—the better part of sixteen years. "We thought he'd never leave," breathed a member of Ronald Reagan's National Security Council (NSC) staff, gratefully, after Trudeau's departure. That impression has been read back into the 1970s, where it seems out of place. Some Americans detected Trudeau's indifference (sometimes misinterpreted as hostility) toward their country, and they were not entirely wrong. "The only American media he bothered following was American movies," according to his campaign manager.[21] And American movie stars, for Trudeau dated the glamorous Barbra Streisand, a fact which Nixon may well have observed and quite possibly resented, according to a highly placed White House official.[22] Certainly Nixon did not spare Trudeau in his off-the-cuff comments, but the president was well known for spraying his expletives in all directions, and Trudeau was hardly unique. Many American observers, and many Canadians too, thought Trudeau anti-American, if not worse—an appeaser of the Soviet Union, or a willing dupe of the communists.[23]

That was not Kissinger's impression. For one thing, Trudeau shared his sense of power relationships. Canada was, obviously, in the American sphere of influence, as Poland was in the Soviet Union's. There was no point in making a fuss about something so fundamental, so axiomatic. Nor did Kissinger see Trudeau as antagonistic. He shrewdly assessed the prime minister as "intelligent, foppish and a momma's boy," a judgment borne out in a recent biography.[24] In his memoirs, Kissinger praised Trudeau's aristocratic demeanor, and lauded Canada's "somewhat aloof position combined with the high quality of its leadership," which gave it "an influence out of proportion to its military contribution."[25]

Most of the time Trudeau behaved himself where the Americans were concerned. (An exception was Ronald Reagan, for whom he had little respect, and showed it.) In his first official visit to Washington, the prime minister compared the Canadian-American relationship to "sleeping with an elephant. No matter how friendly and even-tempered is the beast, one is affected by every twitch and grunt."[26] He did once remark on the "over-whelming presence" in Canada of the United States. This was not exactly a controversial remark, but one mostly notable because of the place where it was uttered—the Soviet Union. Canadians on the right thought it was more than just a philosophical observation. "I am … certain that it was a psycho-logical lapse, since it reflected a deep-seated distrust of the United States and a friendly feeling toward the Soviet Union on the part of the prime minis-ter," the right-tilting Canadian ambassador in Moscow later commented.[27] Trudeau, a veteran of the U.S. embassy in Ottawa claimed, was "brilliant, and we recognized the man's brilliance, and his experience, but we were impa-tient with his advice at times, [his] sermonizing, and his needles."[28] He had no quarrel with Nixon, and if Nixon had a quarrel with him, it was better not to know about it. Nixon in fact had little interest in Canada, though he knew the country somewhat from business affairs in the 1960s.[29]

Trudeau seems to have behaved himself when it came to Nixon, a pru-dent move, though it did not necessarily pay off in terms of Nixon's personal reaction. The Canadian embassy advised, for his first visit to meet Nixon, in March 1969, that Nixon was "a pretty realistic person" who would approach Canada and Trudeau "in a practical and unemotional manner." Ambassador Ed Ritchie advised structuring the discussion in such a way as to balance potential disagreements against "the important interests which the USA shares with Canada."[30] Trudeau appears to have taken Ritchie's advice. He "treated Nixon without any hint of condescension when they were together," Kissinger observed, while Nixon "accorded Trudeau both respect and atten-tion."[31] It was a significant choice of phrase, suggesting on the one hand that Nixon was or could be considered to be Trudeau's social and perhaps intel-lectual inferior, while on the other that Nixon would listen to Trudeau with-out obvious impatience, despite the fact that he was representing Canada. Had the issue ever come up, Kissinger would undoubtedly have agreed with Nixon that time spent on Canadian matters was time wasted. As with other subjects, he presumably listened appreciatively to Nixon's rants about Trudeau and other Canadians. The presidential tapes reveal that Nixon con-sidered Trudeau an "asshole," not a unique distinction in Nixon's world. (The full phrasing was, "That asshole Trudeau was something else.")[32]

The prime minister understood that Nixon was busy and preoccupied with other issues, and accepted that on the highest level of political rela-tions with the Americans they would pass through the hands of a facilitator, Kissinger.[33] But that entailed problems, deriving from Kissinger's lack of inter-est in Canada as well as his boredom with complicated economic subjects.[34]

A very disillusioned William Porter, the U.S. ambassador to Ottawa in the mid-1970s, later claimed that Kissinger "imitated Nixon's attitude toward Canada," and neglected the northern neighbor—to which we can now say, up to a point.[35]

Below that point, on all routine matters, meaning most of the time, Kissinger delegated Canadian affairs to his assistant on the National Security Council, Helmut Sonnenfeldt who in turn passed them on to his assistant, Denis Clift. Sonnenfeldt did his best to keep relations on an even keel, and to maintain the proprieties. It was Sonnenfeldt who fended off the Canadian ambassador, Marcel Cadieux, and prevented him from offering advice on large matters to Kissinger. "Cadieux has been anxious to have an opportunity to see you for some time," Sonnenfeldt once wrote to his superior, "and this occasion presents him with a peg. He is quite pro-US and has been deeply disturbed about adverse trends in US-Canadian relations and what he feels may be some misunderstanding here of Trudeau personally."[36] No dice, and no time: Canada and Cadieux were small matters. Sonnenfeldt had other things to do, and Canada was a minor part of his brief. That left Clift. Clift did not mind. He had a slight connection to Canada, had Canadian relatives, and had "hazy, rosy, positive impressions." Experience, he later wrote, "would sharpen [his feelings] and be calibrated," but he never lost his initial liking for the place.[37]

Because Canada did not engage the attention of anyone senior in the American governmental hierarchy, it sometimes flew comfortably under the political radar. A case in point was the Canadian decision in 1969 to reduce its NATO contribution. Trudeau discussed the possibility with Nixon at their first meeting—the only allied government to be consulted or even informed prior to the announcement of the force reduction. Had Nixon objected, it is possible that the Canadian decision might have been postponed, or altered; but he did not object. Some parts of the administration, especially Defense Secretary Melvin Laird, were not pleased, and said so. Sonnenfeldt counseled moderation, and Kissinger agreed. "If we escalate our language and force a confrontation *now* we will probably magnify the consequences of the Canadian decision out of all proportion," Sonnenfeldt wrote. "There is still room for negotiation, as hinted by Cadieux. We should not slam the door."[38] The key phrase was "out of all proportion"—"these are small things," one can hear Kissinger murmuring. They could be solved, and if they could not, it did not matter very much.

Kissinger and Nixon were soon in the process of removing another long-standing cause of neuralgia in Canadian-American relations through Nixon's eventual trip to China. In the 1950s and 1960s Canadian governments drew back from recognizing Communist China for fear of American displeasure—a well-founded fear, at the time. Trudeau reversed this policy, and in 1970 Canada and China exchanged ambassadors.[39] The Canadians followed up recognition with a major trade fair in 1972 in Beijing, which External Affairs Minister Mitchell Sharp attended; but by 1972, with Nixon's trip to China, Canada was no longer a particularly important item in Chinese diplomacy.[40] What the Chinese most wanted, security, was not something that Canada could provide.[41]

There was no foreshadowing or foreknowledge of what Nixon proposed to do, and no linkage between the Canadian action and Kissinger's secret diplomacy, beyond the obvious fact that Canada's agreement with Beijing showed that recognition could be achieved, if desired.[42] Indeed, the initial American official reaction to Canadian recognition was predictably unfavorable, which doubtless confirmed the Trudeau government and its public in the belief that they had accomplished a notable feat in the teeth of American displeasure. There is no better example to illustrate Kissinger's axiom that "whatever identity they have, they get in opposition to us."

From 1969 to 1973, Kissinger was only occasionally engaged on the Canadian file. It was Rogers who took an interest in Canada's brief terrorist crisis in the fall of 1970, expressing sympathy for the Trudeau government's antiterrorist actions, and apparently meaning it. Kissinger had Vietnam on his plate and on the Vietnamese issue it was sufficient to know that the Canadian government was prepared to assist by joining a truce supervisory commission when and if Kissinger was able to negotiate a truce. Canada was a member of the moribund International Commission for Supervision and Control (ICSC, or more usually ICC) in Vietnam, and had been since 1954. It had been a painful experience, producing neither security nor control for Vietnam or anyone else. But it did mean that Canada had experience in the region, and that apparently qualified Canada to do it again. The early contacts with the Canadians on this subject were handled by Rogers, a clear sign of their relative importance.[43] When peace broke out, early in 1973, Canada obliged, sending a diplomatic and military team to participate in the short-lived International Commission for Supervision and Control. Earlier experience suggested that the most that could be hoped of such a body was supervision of the repatriation of prisoners of war—in the interests of both sides. After that, the truce would break down, as it did; and when it did, the Canadians pulled out. Kissinger remonstrated, but managed only to get a brief postponement of the Canadian action.[44]

Ironically, the main Canadian–American contretemps that occurred during Kissinger's watch was economic, and as such it was something in which neither he nor Rogers was initially much involved. The Nixon administration, like its Democratic predecessors, worried about the American balance of payments. Until 1971 Canada had been mostly exempt from such concerns, because of the perennially negative Canadian trade balance with the United States, and because of the large amount of American direct investment north of the border. As a result, Canada in the 1950s and 1960s received especially favorable treatment on a variety of economic issues—petroleum imports, for example, under Eisenhower, or exemption from Kennedy's interest equalization program. It seemed obvious enough on both sides of the border that erecting new American trade barriers against Canadian goods would impair Canada's ability to buy in the United States, and in addition would likely penalize the Canadian subsidiary of some large American corporation. At the same time, the Canadians relied on occasional American help to avert or counteract their own exchange rate problems, because in their view, shared until 1968 by the U.S. Treasury, a wobbly Canadian currency was not in the United States' own economic interest. The situation seemed so obvious that the Canadian government and its servants gave no thought as to whether this understanding was universally shared. It was not—not by Nixon, and not by his Treasury secretary, John Connally of Texas. Connally focused early on the Autopact, as the most visible sign of unfair Canadian trade practices.[45]

Connally does not seem to have paid a great deal of attention when, in June 1970, Canada floated its dollar, abandoning the peg to the U.S. dollar at 92-and-a-half cents that it had maintained since 1962. The Canadian dollar thereafter floated upward—as high as $1.07 (U.S.) in the mid-1970s. Strangely, this situation did not connect with the Treasury's analysis of American trade and balance-of-payment problems, which were associated, in the Treasury's view, with undervalued foreign currencies. Connally and his officials did, however, raise the problem of Canadian trade surpluses in the automobile trade in discussions with the Canadians during the early summer of 1971; as a result the Canadians were beginning to debate among themselves whether concessions to the Americans might be desirable.[46]

Connally was happy to adopt the position that American trade problems were caused by unfair foreign trade practices. On this point, Connally and Nixon were on the same wavelength. When Nixon told his staff in 1971 that on economic matters, "We have too long acted as Uncle Sugar and now we've got to be Uncle Sam,"[47] he could count on Connally's full agreement.

"My basic approach," the Secretary argued, "is that the foreigners are out to screw us. Our job is to screw them first."[48]

The steady drain on American gold reserves and the imbalance in the country's trade imperiled the United States' ability to manage the international monetary system embodied in the Bretton Woods Agreement of 1944. By 1971, it was plainly only a matter of time until something gave way. Connally and Nixon consulted narrowly, and in consulting did not give positive consideration to Canada—or to any other country. A transcript of the discussion among the small group involved—including Treasury Under-Secretary Paul Volcker and Federal Reserve chairman Arthur Burns—catches the flavor:

> Connally: So the other countries don't like it. So what?
> Volcker: But don't let's close the window and sit—let's get other governments to negotiate new rates.
> Connally: Why do we have to be reasonable? Canada wasn't.
> Burns: They can retaliate.
> Connally: Let 'em. What can they do?
> Burns: They're powerful. They're proud, just as we are ...[49]

In a general sense, Burns was prophetic, though the specific weapon the Canadians would use against Connally was not retaliation, but obstruction.

In August 1971, Connally and Nixon decided it was time to act. The objective was to force an adjustment in terms of trade, essentially by forcing other countries to adjust their exchange rates upward in relation to the American dollar. To ensure that this was done, temporary surcharges were introduced on existing tariffs, bargaining chips to be traded for exchange rate concessions. These measures would apply to all. Even so, it is remarkable, as one history of the Nixon-Kissinger era put it, "how few of the key decisions had been thought through."[50]

But even a sudden announcement takes time, and in pre-internet days that meant an elaborate, if top secret, program of duplication for the thousand and one press releases that had to be composed. To cope with the flow, emergency personnel were drafted in, including, fortuitously, Emerson Brown, the commercial counselor at the U.S. embassy in Ottawa, who was passing through Washington. Leafing through the stacks of paper, he found that Connally was proposing to cancel the Autopact. Unilateral cancellation of an international agreement did not seem the best way of demonstrating that the United States was a reliable international partner. In this case, 32 percent of Canadian exports to the United States would be affected, which would certainly get the Canadians' attention, but in a way that would convince them that the United States was both unreliable and untrustworthy as a trading partner—or perhaps any other kind of partner. Hastily, Brown called Secretary of State Rogers, who in turn called Nixon. The relevant pages were removed from the pile of mimeograph paper, and shredded.[51]

Nixon announced his new economic program in a televised speech on the evening of August 15, 1971. Canadian reaction was initially blasé, until the realization sank in that Canada, too, was identified as a problem for the United States (it was, after all, the United States' largest trade partner) and so was included in Connally's package of import surcharges—in effect, a tariff on tariffs.[52]

Hysteria followed in Canada. Canadian trade with the United States was in danger—70 percent of Canada's exports were in peril. Newspapers pronounced themselves shocked and appalled. Other Canadians were at the very least uncertain as to what it all might mean. A special task force was set up in Ottawa to confront this crisis. Delegations travelled to Washington to meet with Connally. The effect was somewhat spoiled when Connally started off with the Canadians by using the briefing notes intended for the Japanese; observing the puzzled looks from the Canadian delegation, Volcker hastily handed the secretary the correct speaking points, and the meeting began again. The atmosphere was strained if not confrontational; from the American perspective there were no positive results. Meeting followed meeting. At some point, the Canadians seem to have calmed down, and dug in for the duration. They were assisted by the dawning realization that most Canadian exports to the United States entered that country duty-free. The American surtax was just that—a tax on a tax. If the existing tax was zero, well, the resulting surtax would also be zero. It was useful arithmetic.

Connally nevertheless bulled ahead. If the surtax failed to impress, there was always the Autopact. What about that? What about the Canadian safeguards? The Canadians demurred. Connally was asking too much, they murmured. There were politics in Canada as well. The Canadian government would not wish to appear to have "knuckled under" to American pressures, especially with a general election virtually certain in 1972.[53] There were politics in other countries too, that did not respond to Connally's magical formula, "Screw 'em." Yet Connally persisted. The Europeans were proving difficult to crack; to impress or isolate them, progress with the Canadians and Japanese was essential. The Europeans made the point quite forcibly. If the United States could not make progress with the Canadians, the principal trading partner, how could it expect the Europeans to revalue their currencies?[54] Waves of foreign unhappiness began to lap at Kissinger's desk, forcing him to take notice. "I have never understood Connally," Kissinger later said. "Connally was attempting to use Canada as a key element in breaking up European policy."[55] That was ominous, for as Kissinger also later observed, "For Connally, a victory was meaningless unless his victim knew he had been defeated."[56] But first, the victim had to acknowledge defeat.

To avert that fate, Trudeau's foreign policy adviser, Ivan Head, contacted Kissinger, his opposite number, and asked for a meeting between Nixon and Trudeau. The meeting was hastily arranged, and Trudeau arrived for a one-day visit on December 6, 1971. The visit was divided into two. The president and prime minister and their two advisers, Kissinger and Head, met in one room, while senior officials met elsewhere, continuing the series of fruitless Canadian-American encounters that had begun in August. Trudeau and Head later remembered the encounter extremely positively. The prime minister put the Canadian case to Nixon simply and effectively, and Nixon responded positively. The United States, he told Trudeau, would stop trying to force the Canadians to revalue the Canadian dollar, and at the same time the surcharge on Canadian imports would be lifted.[57] Meanwhile the bureaucrats in the other meeting had failed, one more time, to reach agreement. That was because they were pursuing a solution to Connally's obsession, the Autopact.

Nixon's reaction to people, and especially to Trudeau, was never exactly as advertised. To his chief of staff, he said, "That Trudeau, he's a clever son of a bitch." To Kissinger, he asked, "What in the Christ is he talking about?" Trudeau was "a pompous egghead." On this occasion, or later, Nixon ordered up a negative story about Trudeau, to be planted, he hoped, with the columnist Jack Anderson.[58]

Nixon's meeting with Trudeau occurred just before a meeting of the finance ministers of the Group of Ten at the Smithsonian Institution. (The G-10, an association of countries making funds available to the International Monetary Fund, already existed before the 1971 events; both the United States and Canada were members.) The participants agreed to float their currencies, as Canada had already been doing; if the currencies floated freely, and their values were set by the market, then there would be no need in the future for demands for the revaluation of currencies.

The Autopact took another five months to settle, and the meetings went on. The Treasury continued to push for Canadian concessions; and the Canadians resisted. As late as April 12, 1972, the Treasury still favored "unilateral" action to coerce Canada; but by then other U.S. agencies had begun to take another view.[59] Their attitude is described by Harold A. Scott, assistant secretary of commerce, to Kissinger that same day:

With the exception of the White House meeting on December 6, 1971, the mood throughout was conciliatory, courteous and characterized by the Canadians' desire to be helpful without abandoning their traditionally tough negotiating stance and their acute awareness of their domestic political climate.

In my opinion, having been present at all of the meetings, had the United States ever made a firm proposal the Canadians would have gone further than the point where conversations had terminated. Not knowing, however, what were the United States objectives they were cautious on commenting on individual points until the dimensions of the entire package were clearly visible to them.[60]

Surely it was time to bring the whole charade to an end.

The end came unexpectedly because of two unrelated events. First, and widely known, was the fact that Nixon would make his first (and only) official visit to Ottawa in April 1972. More importantly, and also in April, Connally resigned as secretary of the Treasury. Connally's departure had to do with the internal balance of the Nixon administration, and not Canada; nevertheless, its timing was fortuitous, if not coincidental, with the administrative slate-cleaning that usually accompanies ceremonial state visits. Nixon needed a happy and uncontroversial atmosphere for his arrival and departure, and he got it.[61]

Nixon's visit was mainly notable for a well crafted speech to the Canadian Parliament, proclaiming an end to the "special relationship," with its connotations of dependence. At a meeting between Minister of External Affairs Mitchell Sharp and Secretary Rogers, the Canadians remarked "how harmonious our bilateral relations were. Even our recent trade problems related more to details than to fundamentals." When Nixon and Trudeau joined the meeting, the president reminded the Canadians of American foreign exchange difficulties—harking back to Connally's position, but like Sharp he agreed that "in the long term" there was "hardly an iota of disagreement between the two countries."[62] As Sharp later commented, "substantially, the relationship did not change," no matter what rhetorical clouds drifted above.[63]

Sharp was right, over the longer term, but it took one more policy diversion—equally ill-considered—to prove it. This time, however, the policy initiative was Canadian and, more specifically, Sharp's. Shaken by the events of 1971, the Canadian government considered how it could reduce the country's growing economic dependence on the United States. The result was a policy paper that narrowed Canada's international economic policy choices to three options—the status quo, accelerated economic integration with the United States, or a balance between relations with the United States and the rest of the world, meaning Western Europe and Japan. The choice was obvious, under the circumstances, and the policy became known as the Third Option.

The Third Option was published in October 1972, and it absorbed a certain amount of Canada's diplomatic effort over the next few years. Meanwhile, trade with the United States continued to increase, and it became obvious that only a fundamental reorientation of the Canadian economy could alter the trend. The Third Option, Sharp ruefully admitted, "was probably far too difficult an undertaking for any federal government of Canada."[64] The consequences of the failure of the Third Option would not become apparent for some years, indeed, not until the 1980s. When they did, they would stimulate a different policy direction, toward free trade with the United States, and toward the eventual Free Trade Agreement of 1989.

In fact, Canadian-American relations had already improved somewhat through the 1970s. The departure of Richard Nixon helped with the atmospherics, for Nixon's successor Gerald Ford got on much better with Pierre Trudeau. Trudeau's relations with Kissinger needed no improvement, and he was presumably pleased that Kissinger stayed on as secretary of state; for his part, he considered briefings from Kissinger, in Ottawa or Washington, to be one of the perks of office. It was one way of persuading the prime minister to come to Washington, which warmed the atmosphere somewhat and meant that on a personal level Canadian-American relations remained equable.[65] Canada's internal situation, meaning the endless national unity crisis with Québec, did not boil over: the United States government never had to take a position on that thorny problem, or deal with the consequences of Canada's break-up.

The end of the Vietnam War was more practically significant, because with the end of the war there was an end to the endless riots and demonstrations on and off Canadian campuses, and thus an end to the pressure on Canadian politicians to say something, anything, on that issue of the day. OPEC and the oil boycott also encouraged a sense in Ottawa that Canada and the United States were in the same corner on energy. Canada was, at any rate, closer to the American point of view than were the Europeans, which may have encouraged Kissinger to override French objections and invite Canada to join the embryonic economic summit in 1976, thus completing what was for the time being the Group of Seven. In thanking Ford,

Trudeau even suggested that the United States and Canada should mimic the Europeans and discuss their positions in advance of the summit.[66]

For the Canadians, even Trudeau, as Kissinger knew, were predictable and reliable—predictable in their desire to participate in discussions on the shape of the world, but reliable in their attention to the details of their relations with the United States. The topic of fish and all the other bilateral trade issues that Kissinger so dreaded were in the end a control on Canadian activities, and a guarantee that the Canadians, when they had to, would consider their relations with the United States first.

Notes

1. Kissinger quoted by his assistant secretary for economics, Willis C. Armstrong in an conversation—actually several conversations—with the author (hereafter Armstrong interview). It was one of his favorite anecdotes, but regrettably I never noted and dated when he said it.
2. Secretary's Analytic Staff Meeting, March 8, 1974, Kissinger Transcripts, KT01062, DNSA. Emphasis in original.
3. Dwight Mason, political counselor, U.S. embassy, Ottawa, 1980–1983, 1993 interview for the Foreign Affairs Oral History Program.
4. Author interview with Lawrence Eagleburger, Arlington, Virginia, April 2002.
5. By comparison, Mexico was 759,711, Germany 832,000: Campbell Gibson and Kay Jung, "Historical Census Statistics on the Foreign-Born Population of the United States: 1850–2000," U. S. Census Bureau, Population Division, Working Paper no. 81, February 2006, http://www.census.gov/population/www/documentation/twps0081/twps0081.html#trends
6. Dimitry Anastakis, *Auto Pact: Creating a Borderless North American Auto Industry, 1960–1971* (Toronto, 2005), 198, Table C3. Canada had a surplus in the automotive trade from 1970 to 1972, inclusive, and again after 1982.
7. Armstrong interview.
8. Minute by J.R. McKinney, "Re: Proposals for Joint Meetings of Canada/USA Cabinets," December 7, 1978, File 20–1-2-USA, Records of the Department of External Affairs, National Archives of Canada, Ottawa (hereafter DEA). McKinney wrote that "my recollection is that it was an extremely unsatisfactory meeting which left hard feelings on both sides that that this is really what killed the Committee."
9. U.S. consuls in Québec City and Montréal kept an eye on the Québec file, and the U.S. embassy in Paris also occasionally reported on Franco-Québécois contacts.

10. The obfuscation necessarily practiced by draft dodgers at the border means that estimates of draft dodgers and their supporters in Canada were and remain imprecise.

11. Larry Martin, interviewed in Kim Willenson and the correspondents of *Newsweek*, in *The Bad War: An Oral History of the Vietnam War* (New York, 1987), 261–262.

12. John Hagan, *Northern Passage: American Vietnam War Resisters in Canada* (Cambridge, Mass., 2001), 241, Table B5.

13. Tim O'Brien, *The Things They Carried* (New York, 1998), 55.

14. Analytic Staff Meeting, March 8, 1974, Kissinger Transcripts, DNSA.

15. Ibid.

16. Peyton Lyon and Brian Tomlin, *Canada as an International Actor* (Toronto, 1979), 112.

17. James Eayrs, a political scientist from the University of Toronto, quoted in J. L. Granatstein, *Yankee Go Home? Canadians and Anti-Americanism* (Toronto, 1996), 190.

18. Memorandum of conversation, Kissinger and Joe Clark, June 15, 1976, Kissinger Transcripts, DNSA.

19. Memorandum of conversation, President Gerald Ford, Henry Kissinger, Brent Scowcroft, 3 December 1974, Gerald Ford Library, National Security Adviser, Memoranda and Conversations, box 7.

20. Armstrong interview.

21. Quoted in J. L. Granatstein and Robert Bothwell, *Pirouette* (Toronto, 1990), 96.

22. Confidential interview with the author. The same official speculated that sexual jealousy may have played a role in Nixon's attitude to Trudeau. Nixon, after all, did not get to date Barbra Streisand. Curiously, and from an entirely different source, the same speculation showed up in discussions of Trudeau's indirect relations with French president Valéry Giscard d'Estaing.

23. Reagan was said to have read Lubor J. Zink, "The Unpenetrated Problem of Pierre Trudeau," *National Review*, June 25, 1982, 751–756. In the 1960s, Zink had been a columnist for the conservative and by 1982 defunct Toronto *Telegram*.

24. See note 8 above; and John English, *Citizen of the World* (Toronto, 2006), 209ff.

25. Henry Kissinger, *White House Years* (Boston, 1979), 383.

26. Ivan Head and Pierre Trudeau, *The Canadian Way: Shaping Canada's Foreign Policy, 1968–1984* (Toronto, 1995), 179.

27. Robert Ford, *Our Man in Moscow: A Diplomat's Reflections on the Soviet Union* (Toronto, 1989), 119.

28. Mason interview, Foreign Affairs Oral History Program.

29. He had, however, gone to Canada—Victoria, British Columbia—on his honeymoon.

30. Ed Ritchie (Ambassador to United States) to Undersecretary Marcel Cadieux, "Prime Minister's Meeting with President Nixon," March 4,

1969, File 20–10A-9-Trudeau, DEA. The subjects where disagreement was anticipated were NATO, the Chinese seat at the United Nations, fishing problems and territorial disputes, and American immigration quotas on Canadians.

31. Kissinger, *White House Years*, 383.

32. Alexandra Gill, "Nixon's 'Bushy-Haired Bastard' Bites Back," *Globe and Mail* (Toronto), March 23, 2002. See also Lawrence Martin, *The Presidents and the Prime Ministers—Washington and Ottawa Face to Face: The Myth of Bilateral Bliss, 1867–1982* (Toronto, 1982), 256–257. The term came to light during the Watergate hearings of 1973.

33. Head and Trudeau, *Canadian Way*, 180.

34. Kissinger complained about his "boredom" with textile negotiations with Japan and commented that "economic leaders were usually 'political idiots.'" Editorial note, *FRUS, 1969–1976*, vol. III: document 71.

35. Porter letter to the *Washington Post*, February 9, 1978. Kissinger in fact repudiated Porter when the latter, probably following instructions, ventilated some of Washington's grievances to a group of Canadian reporters. See Kissinger's sarcastic comments about Porter to Canadian external affairs minister Allan MacEachen, in memorandum of conversation, December 17, 1975, Kissinger Transcripts, DNSA.

36. Sonnenfeldt to Kissinger, October 26, 1971, NSC files, Box 671, File Canada vol. III, NPMP. Cadieux wished to report to Kissinger Canadian impressions of a visit to Ottawa by the Soviet premier, Alexei Kosygin.

37. A. Denis Clift, *With Presidents to the Summit* (Fairfax, Va., 1993), 200.

38. Sonnenfeldt to Kissinger, May 28, 1969, NSC files, Box 670, Country Files, Canada I.

39. Head and Trudeau describe the government of Taiwan as "dictatorial and brutal" but refrain from characterizing the Maoist regime in Beijing. Head and Trudeau, *Canadian Way*, 223. Canadian recognition is described in Margaret MacMillan, *Nixon in China: The Week that Changed the World* (Toronto, 2006), 214–217.

40. Granatstein and Bothwell, *Pirouette*, 187ff.

41. Nixon described his visit to China to Trudeau when he visited Ottawa in April 1972. Out of the "interminable conversations" with Mao Zedong and Zhou Enlai, Nixon said, it was clear that the Chinese saw the United States "as the only nation in the world which could buffer the most immediate threat to them, which [was] the USSR." Ivan Head to Ed Ritchie, undersecretary for external affairs, April 26, 1972.

42. The Chinese ambassador to Canada was the very senior Huang Hua, selected obviously with an eye to Ottawa's proximity to the United Nations, where he eventually became Chinese ambassador, and to Washington. See Granatstein and Bothwell, *Pirouette*, 186.

43. Memorandum of conversation, March 24, 1969, Box 1949, File POL CAN-US XL POL 27 VIETS, RG 59, NARA. Rogers told Sharp that for peacekeeping in Vietnam, "we always thought of Canada first." The

minutes added: "The Minister thought it would be useful for the Secretary to say that on Canadian television, since the government was being accused of not being neutral in the conflict by supplying arms to the US and not emphasizing a peacekeeping role for Canada."

44. Mitchell Sharp, *Which Reminds Me ... A Memoir* (Toronto, 1994), 216.

45. So had his earlier political patron, Lyndon B. Johnson. At a lunch for the departing Canadian and German ambassadors, Johnson told the surprised Canadian that Canadians thought they were "clever" because "you screwed us on the Autopact." Charles Ritchie interview with the author.

46. Anastakis, *Auto Pact*, 163.

47. Quoted in Robert Bothwell, *Canada and the United States: The Politics of Partnership* (Toronto, 1992), 106.

48. Quoted in Walter LaFeber, *The American Age: United States Policy at Home and Abroad since 1750* (New York, 1989), 612.

49. Quoted in John S. Odell, *U.S. International Monetary Policy: Markets, Power and Ideas as Sources of Change* (Princeton, 1982), 260.

50. William P. Bundy, *A Tangled Web: The Making of Foreign Policy in the Nixon Presidency* (New York, 1998), 268.

51. Emerson Brown interview with the author, January 1988. There is an alternate version in Anastakis, *Auto Pact*, 165. This gives the credit to Julius Katz, a senior State Department official. Quite possibly credit is due to both Brown and Katz.

52. There is, however, one tantalizing suggestion that the Canadians were not entirely irrational in expecting that they might be exempted from the surcharge. Reference was made to the possibility that the Japanese ambassador might mention to Nixon at the end of August "that the administration was considering exempting Canada from the surcharge." Editorial note, *FRUS, 1969–1976*, vol. III: document 71.

53. Mitchell Sharp quoted in Peter Dobell, *Canada in World Affairs*, vol. XVII, *1971 to 1973* (Toronto, 1985), 41.

54. The Dutch argued this vigorously to American diplomats in the Netherlands, saying that Canada, given its "weight in US imports," was in a position to set the example in revaluing its currency after which other countries "would have to push their revaluation." U.S. Embassy (The Hague) to State Department, December 6, 1971, *FRUS, 1969–1976*, vol. III: 587.

55. Memorandum of conversation, July 25, 1972, ibid., 641.

56. Quoted in Bruce J. Schulman, *The Seventies: The Great Shift in American Culture, Society, and Politics* (New York, 2001), 42.

57. Head and Trudeau, *Canadian Way*, 188–189.

58. "Prime Ministers and presidents," http://www.cbc.ca/news/background/canada_us/pms-presidents.html

59. Theodore Eliot to Peter Flanigan, April 12, 1972, *FRUS, 1969–1976*, vol. III: document 89.

60. Harold A. Scott to Kissinger, April 12, 1972, NSC files, Box 671, Canada vol. III, NPMP.

61. The Ottawa visit is mostly remembered for the appearance of an American would-be assassin in the crowd on Parliament Hill; disappointed in his target, the assassin returned to the United States and shot George Wallace instead.

62. "Record of Canada-United States Conversations held in the Cabinet Room ... of the Centre Block of the Parliament Buildings," April 14, 1972, file 20-USA-9 NIXON, vol. 4, DEA.

63. Sharp, *Which Reminds Me*, 180.

64. Ibid., 186.

65. Ivan Head interview with the author, Toronto, 1988.

66. Memorandum of conversation, June 16, 1976, NSC Memoranda of Conversation, Box 19, GRFL.

Index